THROUGH THE DARK CONTINENT
OR
THE SOURCES OF THE NILE AROUND THE GREAT LAKES OF EQUATORIAL AFRICA AND DOWN THE LIVINGSTONE RIVER TO THE ATLANTIC OCEAN

VOL. I.

HENRY M. STANLEY

Table of Contents

ORIGINAL PREFACE.

Before these volumes pass irrevocably out of the Author's hands, I take this, the last, opportunity of addressing my readers. In the first place, I have to express my most humble thanks to Divine Providence for the gracious protection vouchsafed to myself and my surviving followers during our late perilous labours in Africa.

In the second place, I have to convey to many friends my thanks for their welcome services and graceful congratulations, notably to Messrs. Motta Viega and J. W. Harrison, the gentlemen of Boma who, by their timely supplies of food, electrified the Expedition into new life; to the sympathizing society of Loanda, who did their best to spoil us with flattering kindness; to the kindly community of the Cape of Good Hope, who so royally entertained the homeward-bound strangers; to the directorates of the B. I. S. N. and the P. and O. Companies, and especially to Mr. W. Mackinnon of the former, and Mr. H. Bayley and Captain Thomas H. Black of the latter, for their generous assistance both on my setting out and on my returning; to the British Admiralty, and, personally, to Captain Purvis, senior officer on the West Coast Station, for placing at my disposal H.M.S. Industry, and to Commodore Sullivan, for continuing the great favour from the Cape to Zanzibar; to the officers and sailors of H.M.S. Industry, for the great patience and kindness which they showed to the wearied Africans; and to my friends at Zanzibar, especially to Mr. A. Sparhawk, for their kindly welcome and cordial help.

In the next place, to the illustrious individuals and Societies who have intimated to me their appreciation of the services I have been enabled to render to Science, I have to convey the very respectful expression of my sense of the honours thus conferred upon me — to his Majesty King Humbert of Italy, for the portrait of himself, enriched with the splendid compliment of his personal approbation of my services, which with the gold medal received from his royal father, King Victor Emanuel, will forever be treasured with pride — to H.R.H. the Prince of Wales, for the distinguished honour shown me by his personal recognition of my work — to H.H. the Khedive of Egypt, for the high distinction of the Grand Commandership of the Order of the Medjidie, with the Star and Collar — to the Royal Geographical Society of London for its hearty public reception of me on my return, and for the highly valued diploma of an Honorary Corresponding Member subsequently received — to the Geographical Societies and Chambers of Commerce of Paris, Italy, and Marseilles, for the great honour of the Medals awarded to me — to the Geographical Societies of Antwerp, Berlin, Bordeaux, Bremen, Hamburg, Lyons, Marseilles, Montpellier, and Vienna, and to the Society of Arts of London, for the privilege of Honorary Membership to which I have been admitted — to the very numerous distinguished gentlemen who have lent the influence of their authority in the worlds of Science, Letters, and Society to the public favour so liberally extended to me — to all these do I wish to convey my keen appreciation of the honours and favours of which I have been the recipient. And for yet another honour I have to express my thanks — one which I may be pardoned for regarding as more precious, perhaps, than even all the rest. The Government of the United States has crowned my success with its official approval, and the unanimous vote of thanks passed in both Houses of the Legislature has made me proud for life of the Expedition and its achievements.

Alas! that to share this pride and these honours there are left to me none of those gallant young Englishmen who started from this country to cross the Dark Continent, and who endeared themselves to me by their fidelity and affection: alas! that to enjoy the exceeding pleasure of rest among friends, after months of fighting for dear life among cannibals and cataracts, there are left so few of those brave Africans to whom, as the willing hands and the loyal hearts of the Expedition, so much of its success was due.

That the rule of my conduct in Africa has not been understood by all, I know to my bitter cost; but with my conscience at ease, and the simple record of my daily actions, which I now publish, to speak for me, this misunderstanding on the part of a few presents itself to me only as one more harsh experience of life. And those who read my book will know that I have indeed had "a sharp apprehension and keen intelligence" of many such experiences.

In conclusion, I have to thank Mr. Phil. Robinson, the author of 'In my Indian Garden,' for assisting me in the revision of my work. My acknowledgments are also due to Lieut. S. Schofield Sugden, R.N., for the perseverance and enthusiasm with which he recalculated all my observations, making even the irksome compilations of maps a pleasant task. William Clowes and Sons, for the care and despatch with which these volumes have been prepared for the public.

H. M. S.

London, Nov. 15, 1879.

PEEFACE TO THE EDITION OF 1899.

'Through the Dark Continent' was first published in June, 1878, and now that, after an interval of twenty years, another edition is to be issued, it has been thought desirable by the publishers that I should employ the opportunity of reviewing a few of the amazing changes that have taken place in the regions described in the book.

Public speakers, I observe, when they have occasion to refer to the remarkable progress made of late years in Equatorial Africa, vaguely date it as having begun some twenty-five or thirty years ago. In reality, however, the first glimmerings of the dawn only appeared in the latter part of 1875, which was soon after the publication of my appeal for missionaries to Uganda. Although the appeal was almost immediately responded to by the Church Missionary Society, and a sum of £24,000 was collected, the missionaries did not leave England until April, 1876, and it was the 30th June, 1877, before two of the band landed in Uganda.

These two pioneer missionaries, and a third, who had been left behind at the south end of Lake Victoria, were, with myself, the sole Europeans in all Equatorial Africa on that date. I happened to be then about two hundred miles from the west coast, laboriously working my way down the cataracts of the Congo, to put the finishing touch to my exploration of the course of that river, while over two thousand miles eastward of me my two fellow-countrymen were preparing for the great work of converting Uganda to Christianity.

But, after all, the arrival of the missionaries, though an important event, and one that has had large consequences, was but a sign of the dawn. Scepticism as to any good resulting from the bold missionary venture was very general in England, and the publications of the C. M. Society prove that, for some years afterwards, no great hope of success was entertained, and, as if to add to the public disbelief in the efficacy of missionary effort among negro pagans, there came, almost simultaneously with my return from Africa early in the following year, the sad news that two out of the three missionaries had been massacred. Thus, at the beginning of that year, 1878, the surviving missionary in Uganda was the sole white man in all the regions bordering the African equator.

The publication of this book in the following June excited unusual, indeed, I may truly say extraordinary, interest throughout Europe. It was translated into many languages, and the aggregate sales were prodigious. In this country, in France, Germany, Belgium, and Italy, it was discussed from every point of view. It led to much controversy, personal and general, but the British public did not take kindly to the suggestions for immediate action in Africa contained in it. England lost the opportunity of selecting unquestioned her field for enterprise, and so long was she indifferent to the Continent, and the splendid possibilities that awaited her, that Equatorial Africa was well-nigh closed to her altogether.

It happened that there was one person, on the Continent who manifested much more than an abstract interest in Africa, and had, indeed, solicited my services for the development of the Dark Continent — within a few minutes of my return to Europe — but had generously admitted that the people in whose interest I had made my explorations should have the first claim on them. This person was King Leopold II., whose wonderful character and extraordinary ability were then unknown to the world. No Englishman living, not even the geographical expert, paid such close attention to my letters in the Daily Telegraph, my book and speeches on African subjects, as did the King, and no man shared my zeal and hopes for Africa as did His Majesty. I waited from January to November, 1878, to see if on this side of the Channel any serious notice was likely to be taken of my suggestions; but finding public feeling impossible to be aroused here, I then crossed the Channel, and accepted the post of chief agent to the Comite des Etudes du Haut Congo, of which King Leopold was President.

As an illustration of the general indifference in this country to what had been written and spoken about Africa during 1878, I quote what took place between two members of the Royal Geographical Council and myself on a certain date of June of that year.

These two gentlemen called at my rooms, and, seeing my original map of the Congo hanging up, one of them, after a perusal of some of the notes written along the course, turned to me and asked —

"How long do you think it will be before a white man revisits Stanley Falls?"

"Two or three years, I suppose," I replied.

"Two or three years!" he exclaimed. "I expected you were going to say fifty years."

"Fifty years! " I cried. "Why, I will venture to wager that, before twenty years are over, there will not be a hundred square mile tract left to be explored in the entire Continent."

"Oh, come," said the other gentleman, "that is too sanguine a view altogether. I will take your bet — shall we say £10? — and book it."

We booked it there and then. The twenty years have lately expired, but though I cannot claim to have won the wager, it must be admitted that my hasty prediction has closely approached fact.

About the same time. Sir Rutherford Alcock, then President of the Royal Geographical Society, remarked, in his Annual Address, that I had told him that, with money enough, Africa could not only be explored, but civilised and converted into orderly states. It did not seem to me that there was anything surprising in that, but to Sir Rutherford it appeared worthy of public notice. It is of value here only as an indication of the general ignorance that then prevailed in all circles as regards Africa.

Seven years later, after seeing the establishment of one of the African states that promised to be civilised some day, I was introduced by a Canon of Westminster Abbey to a well-known Bishop as one who had "done good work on the Congo."

"Oh, indeed!" said his Lordship, smilingly, "how very interesting; but," he added, hesitatingly, "I am really not sure that I know where the Congo is."

As may be imagined, I was a picture of wide-eyed surprise. For every newspaper in the country had been for months daily publishing something or other about the Congo Conference, and I thought that surely one of the princes of the Church must have caught sight of the name; but such had been the Bishop's culpable inattention to great events in Africa, that the name even had not attracted his notice.

Resuming my proper subject, I became chief agent on the Congo. Every now and then during the six years that I occupied that position, directing the advance into the Congo basin, reports of our doings frequently reached England in one form or another, and still the trend of events seemed unperceived there, though there was considerable stir in Germany, France, Portugal, and Belgium.

Neither, apparently, were the actions of the Germans on the borders of Cape Colony in 1883-84 of a character to excite alarm, suspicion, or even intelligent alertness in the British mind. Lord Derby was not in the least disturbed by the curious inquisitive tone of Bismarck's despatches relating to South Africa, and Lord Granville failed to comprehend the drift of Bismarck's anxiety about the German settlement at Angra Pequena, or that the presence of a German warship in South African waters signified anything.

When it was too late, however, to prevent the seizure of a large territory neighbouring Cape Colony, the British rubbed their eyes, and found that a European Power, which might make itself unpleasant some day to our South African colonists, had wilfully planted itself in close proximity to the Boer states, with which we had already more than once grave misunderstandings. It was then inferred that a similar move, a little further inland, by either the Boers or Germans, would perpetually confine British South Africa to within the narrow limits of Cape Colony, and a suspicious manoeuvre of a German ship of war in Eastern South Africa confirmed the British Government that longer delay would be disastrous to British interests, and the Warren Expedition, which secured to us Bechuanaland, and an open way to the Zambesi, was the result. But before the Berlin Conference of 1884-5 was held, Germany had become the owner of important possessions at various places in Occidental Africa, and was projecting other surprises of a similar kind.

During the sittings of the Conference, which had met to decide the future of the Congo, the words and acts of the assembled Plenipotentiaries received due attention from every journal of importance in the United Kingdom, but they did not appear to impress the public mind as closely affecting British interests. Yet much was happening that, had the warning which was sounded occasionally by experts been taken properly to heart, the significance of the Conference would have been easily recognised.

On the Continent, however, the diplomatic discussions had a most stimulating effect. The people of every state now studied their African maps with a different purpose from the acquisition of mere geographical knowledge. Societies, miscalled "commercial, geographical, or scientific," sprang into existence like mushrooms throughout France, Germany, Italy, Belgium, and Sweden, and in a short time numerous expeditions, disguised by innocent titles, were prepared for Africa.

Within two days after the signing of the General Act of the Conference, the German Emperor proclaimed a protectorate in East Africa over countries whose names were even unknown until the appearance of this book. Our Foreign Secretary was in such dread of Prince Bismarck that he not only acquiesced in this bold act, but obsequiously hastened to instruct our representative at Zanzibar to use his undeniable influence in promoting German interests, and lessen his zeal for our own.

To-day, living as we do under a powerful Unionist Government, which has just triumphed over the Mahdi's successor, and recovered nearly all that the Government of that period had lost, these events may appear incredible, but 1884-85 was a singularly disastrous period for British prestige. The aged statesman who then presided over England's affairs was fast declining in power and ability; but as his influence still continued supreme, the nation was powerless to avert the blunders and misfortunes that so repeatedly shocked us. However, not to dwell upon this painful subject, let me say that when Lord Granville signified to Prince Bismarck that England would oppose no obstacles to German designs in Africa, it naturally followed that the Prince would interpret this as meaning that England would surrender all claims to territory that the Germans might think desirable, and accordingly the East African Protectorate expanded in a marvellously brief time from the coast to the Tanganika, and threatened to absorb the whole of East Africa from Mozambique to the Gulf of Aden. Though priority of discovery and exploration may not under all circumstances constitute a full title to territory, it is certainly aggrieving to find another nation rudely thrusting itself into the field and forcibly seizing upon it.

Fortunately, however, a Company had been formed in 1885 to take over a small concession obtained by Mr. H. H. Johnston at Taveta in East Africa, and as the Germans encroached upon it. Lord Rosebery, who had become Foreign Secretary, took the opportunity of making a firm protest against it, which served to arrest the wholesale absorption that had been meditated, and gave the necessary time for a fuller development of the British project. A delimitation of territory was determined upon to define that which was claimed by Great Britain, Germany, and Zanzibar, and meanwhile the operations of the British Company were suspended to avoid a clashing of interests, and through Lord Rosebery's protest the Germans likewise agreed to prevent their agents from making any new acquisitions in the debatable zone.

In November, 1886, an understanding was arrived at which recognised the sovereignty of Zanzibar as existing over Zanzibar and Pemba, and the smaller islands, within a radius of twelve sea miles of them, as also over those of Lamu and Mafia, and a strip of the mainland ten sea miles in depth.

East Africa was delimited into two spheres of influence, divided by the mouth of the Umbe River, the northern base of Kilimanjaro Mountain, and thence by a line stretching to the eastern shore of the Victoria Nyanza at the 1st degree of south latitude.

On the 25th May, 1887, the Sultan of Zanzibar signed a fifty years' concession of all his rights remaining to him, after the lease he had given to Germany on the 4th December previous, to the British East African Association. In April of the following year the Association, having through its agents concluded treaties with the native tribes to a distance of two hundred miles inland, became the Imperial British East African Company with the nominal capital of £2,000,000, for the purpose of administering the Zanzibar Concession, acquiring territory, and to undertake trading operations.

Meantime, early in 1887, four months previous to the formation of the British East African Association, I had started on my fourth expedition into the Dark Continent, with the object of carrying relief to Emin Pasha, to whom had been entrusted the government of the Egyptian provinces near the Equator, by the late General Gordon. Few persons at the time knew that Emin Pasha was only another name for a Dr. Edouard Schnitzer, and that he was a German Israelite by birth. The fund for the relief was contributed to equally by the Egyptian Government and Sir William Mackinnon's personal friends.

The story of the march to Emin's relief and his arrival at the Zanzibar coast with my expedition, has been related in detail in 'Darkest Africa,' and there is no necessity to give even a summary of it here.

During the journey through the Aruwimi Forest and thence to Zanzibar, we were able to add considerably to our knowledge of the Equatorial regions. That of the great forest itself, with its pigmies and cannibals, was no mean addition, but our march eastward led to the discovery of the snowy range called Ruwenzori, the interesting Semliki Valley and its river, which by following upward brought us in view of the Albert Edward Nyanza, and enabled me to identify it as the lake I had first seen in January, 1876. The topography of the intra-lake region became also much better known; and a little later the outline of the Victoria Nyanza received enlargement by the finding of an unknown south-western bay of important dimensions.

These discoveries were, however, unimportant compared to the effects following our return home and the publication of our experiences. The Brussels Conference of 1890 was preparing to sit, and it was not difficult to impress the Plenipotentiaries with the immediate necessities of the Dark Continent, such as railways, prohibition of importing fire-arms, the suppression of slave-raiding, etc., etc. On the Congo State authorities our revelations had a still more marked effect. Preparations were then commenced to deal with the slave-raiders of the Congo, and the despatch of Vankherkhovin's Expedition to the Upper Welle, that of Captain Stairs to Katanga, and for the definite construction of the railway to Stanley Pool. The spirit of annexation was once more roused, and there was what might be called a race for the possession of the undelimited region west of Lake Victoria. The British East African Company's troops were pushed into Uganda, and the expeditions under Mr. Jackson, Captain Lugard, Major Eric Smith, and Mr. Piggott, performed excellent service in their various explorations.

One of the most important effects of this renewed furore was the conclusion in July of a Treaty between Great Britain and Germany, which nullified the efforts of Emin Pasha and of Dr. Peters to seize upon Uganda and the lake regions west of it. The German Government agreed to surrender all the territory it occupied or claimed north of the British sphere, and the protectorate of Witu and the coast up to Kismayu was transferred to England. This Treaty not only extended the British possessions to the Abyssinian frontier, thus excluding any European competitor for influence on the Upper Nile, but established a British Protectorate over the Sultanate of Zanzibar. In return for the claims surrendered by Germany, England ceded Heligoland, and for the sum of £200,000 Germany received the sovereignty and revenue of the African coast between the Rovuma and the Umbe Rivers.

From the following list of African explorers who have crossed Africa since this book was issued, it will be recognised at a glance how rapid has been the increase of geographical knowledge: —

1. Serpa Pinto from Benguella to Durban 1877-1879.

2. Herman von Wissman from Mossamedes to Quilimane 1881-1882.

3. Arnot the Missionary from Durban to Benguella 1881-1884.

4. Capello and Ivens from Mossamedes to Quilimane 1884-1885.

5. Gleerup from Banana Pt. to Bagamoyo 1883-1886.

6. Dr. Lenz from Banana Pt. to Quilimane 1885-1887.

7. Herman von Wissman from Banana Pt. to Quilimane (2nd journey) 1886-1887.

8. Mons. Trivier. from Loango to Quilimane 1888-1889.

9. Stanley's second journey from Banana Pt. to Bagamoyo 1887-1889.

10. Dr. Johnston from Benguella to Zambezi Mouth 1891-1892.

11. Count von Gotzen from Pangani to Banana Pt. 1893-1894.

12. M. Moray from Bagamoyo to Banana Pt. 1892-1895.

13. E. I. Glave from Zambezi Mouth to Lower Congo 1893-1895.

14. Mons. Miot from Zambezi Mouth to Lower Congo 1893-1896.

15. Mons. Versepuy from Bagamoyo to Kabinda 1895-1896.

16. M Doscamps et Chargois from Zambezi Mouth to Kabinda 1893-1896.

17. M. Foa from Zambezi Mouth to Banana 1896-1898.

18. Mr. Lloyd from Mombasa to Banana 1897-1898.

While previous to the book, since the beginning of the century, there had only been three trans-African explorations: —

1. Livingstone from St. Paul da Loanda to Quilimane 1854-1856.

2. Lieut. Cameron, R.N. from Bagamoyo to Beiiguella 1873-1875.

3. Stanley's first journey from Bagamoyo to Mouth of the Congo 1874-1877.

With regard to the numerous other expeditions which took place since 1878, there is no space for mention, but Joseph Thomson's travels, via Nyassa, to the Tanganika, and his brilliant journey through Masai Land; Count Teleki and Von Hohnel's travels in Eastern Africa, which resulted in the discovery of Lakes Rudolf and Stephanie; Captain Bottego's journey through Somali Land, and Dr. Donaldson Smith's exploration of Somali and Galla Lands were of the first importance. It has, however, required the services of some hundreds of travellers since 1878 to fill up the sum of our present knowledge of the Continent.

In 1878 there was not one European-built boat in all Equatorial Africa. By 1881 there were five, but by December 31st, 1898, there were seventy-two steamers and one hundred and sixty-four steel boats or barges, while there is a very large addition to the African flotillas either on its way, or in process of construction. It may be imagined how much these vessels have expedited exploration when I say that out of the seventeen trans-African explorers no less than thirteen of them were transported with their followers and effects some hundreds of miles on their way.

Even as late as 1890 the construction of railways in Equatorial Africa had not been begun, though years of zealous efforts had been made by myself and others to induce capitalists to undertake them, knowing as we did that they were the best instruments that civilisation could employ for the moral, material, and social elevation of the dark peoples. But just as it took years upon years of publications and speeches to dissipate the unreasoning terror of Africa in the European mind, it required years of preaching and encouraging to induce railway constructors to try Africa as the theatre of their operations. Soon after the conclusion of the Emin Expedition the Congo Railway was commenced, and to-day it is fully employed in traffic, and the 500-franc shares are worth 1700 francs per share, which may be taken as a proof that the shareholders' faith has been munificently rewarded. By the latest news from East Africa we learn that two hundred and forty miles of the Mombasa and Nyanza Railway have been laid, and it is predicted that by May next the locomotive will reach the half-way point to Lake Victoria. In German East Africa thirty miles of railway have been in operation for some time, but there are serious railway projects under consideration, and, it may be, an attempt will shortly be made at construction on an important scale. Meantime, however, the coloured troops are being employed in making a road suitable for wheeled traffic between the port of Dar-es-Salaam and Ujiji, via Kilossa and Tabora, and thus far mules have been used with great success.

But though there are not yet five hundred miles of railway open for train c in Equatorial Africa, considerable extensions are under construction, or being meditated. The British East Africa Railway will, of course, be continued as far as Lake Victoria, as Parliament has provided the necessary money. The Congo State having successfully completed the railway connecting the lower with the upper river, is carrying out surveys for other railways on the Upper Congo. The Zambezi will also in a short time be connected by rail with Lake Nyassa, and we learn that the Bulawayo Railway is to be extended to the Tanganika Lake. My predictions in regard to Africa have so singularly approached realisation thus far that I am tempted on a safer prophecy, which is, that by 1918, there will be five thousand miles of iron roads where there are now not five hundred.

When my letters, calling attention to the spiritual and material needs of Africa, used to appear in the columns of the Daily Telegraph in 1874-77, there was neither mission, school, church, nor any legitimate trade started in the regions near the African Equator. But since 1877 wonderful changes in this respect have taken place. The statistics we have received from the Uganda Protectorate alone tell a remarkable tale of progress. According to these there have been 372 churches and missions established, at which there are 97,575 Christian converts. About 100 Europeans are living in the Protectorate, and the first official report (for 1897) announced that trade to the value of £30,000 had been begun. It will be remembered, perhaps, that it was for long a debatable question whether we should retain Uganda or abandon it.

The country of which the first few chapters of this book treat is now mainly German East Africa. What a change has come over it! No one could have foreseen or dreamed at the time of my march through it that Germany could ever have become the controller of its destiny. I dreamed visions of the future often in the wilds, such as that described in Chapter X., but I saw no Teuton in my dreams. However, it may be all for the best that Germany has annexed it, and England owes too much to Germany for waking her out of her somnolence to begrudge what Bismarck obtained so boldly. The white population of this colony at the end of last year numbered 922, of whom 678 are Germans, and the trade amounted in value to £600,000. It will, no doubt, be a long time before the Arab coast towns undergo any external change, but within their character and scenes are altogether altered. German militarism, which as we know is of the strictest kind, bears no resemblance to Arab supineness and neglect or to Arab customs. The small boys have taken kindly to the dominant spirit, and practise the forms in vogue among the military. There are custom-houses at every port, and permits for travel and sport inland can only be obtained through the goodwill of the Governor. The drastic measures of Von Wissman have long ago suppressed the slave-trade, and the slave-market is now only a memory.

The coast towns are connected by telegraph with each other, and there is cable communication, via Zanzibar, with Europe. Ujiji, the port on Lake Tanganika where I met Livingstone in 1871, possesses now quite a civilised appearance. Its Government buildings are of stone and two-storied, and a long wide street, shaded by mangoes and other fruit trees, runs through the centre of the town. German capital, to the value of £697,000, has been invested in tobacco, coffee, cocoa, tea, cardamom, and vanilla plantations; and I am glad to learn that the Game Laws are strict and effective.

The change in Equatorial Africa is nowhere more conspicuous than in that part described in Chapters XXL-XXXIV. It may be imagined from the fact that a Brussels statistician has collected the titles of 3800 printed works which have been published since 1878 and refer to this part, and in this chronological table he records forty-eight separate explorations of the region.

The progress of trade in the Congo basin can be best represented by the following brief table of imports and exports: —

Year: 1893. Import value: 367,004. Export value: 300,592. Total value: 667,596.

Year: 1894. Import value: 447,789. Export value: 441,268. Total value: 889,057.

Year: 1895. Import value: 427,434. Export value: 485,426. Total value: 912,860.

Year: 1896. Import value: 609,111. Export value: 603,645. Total value: 1,212,756.

Year: 1897. Import value: 887,258. Export value: 698,284. Total value: 1,585,542.

The average value of the annual exports during each of the five preceding years (1888-92) amounted to only £207,921.

From the inception of the Congo State in 1879 to the year 1890 the King of the Belgians personally defrayed all the expenditure; but on July 3rd, 1890, the Belgian Government came to His Majesty's assistance with a lump sum of £200,000, and an annual subsidy, to last ten years, of £80,000 per annum. This amount, with the King's personal subsidy, was for some years later the main support of the State; but in 1898 the revenue from all sources is estimated to amount to £590,608, while the expenditure is £99,477 in excess.

This excess of expenditure some unkindly critics in this country attribute to extravagance, ambition, and what not; but the King justifies his policy by comparing himself to one who had come to a great but wholly undeveloped estate, which was bound to remain unproductive unless a liberal expenditure was incurred for such improvements as would expose its resources and make all parts of it accessible. Now what the Congo State was in 1879 can best be seen by Chapters XXIV.-XXIX. To the ordinary white man it was what may well be termed impenetrable, except at constant peril of his life. It was ravaged by cannibals, fierce warlike tribes, and slave-raiders, and destructive influences of every kind tended to maintain its humanity in an eternal struggle for life and liberty. There were no roads, or means by which the country could be explored. Every tribe barred the ingress of the traveller; and its frontiers on all sides lay exposed to any white stranger who took the trouble to plant a flag; and finally it was made incumbent on every Power owning African possessions to make its occupation effective. Such primary necessities of the State involved large and endless expenses, and few men other than King Leopold would have so long sustained the great undertaking from his private purse. From 1879 to 1890 His Majesty spent about £900,000, and since then the total expenditure of the State has been nearly £3,000,000. To meet this His Majesty's subsidies, amounting to £360,000, the aid from Belgium, £200,000, the Belgian annual subsidies, £720,000, customs duties and taxes, £1,900,000, make a total revenue of £3,180,000, and prove a deficit of £720,000.

As an offset against the deficit, the State possesses nineteen steamers and forty steel barges of the value of £100,000; Government establishments, which we may estimate at £500,000; arms, ammunition, goods, coal, and lumber, at £100,000; investments in the. railway, telegraph, and commercial societies, and plantations, to the value of about £400,000 — the whole of which aggregate £1,100,000. To these, which may be rightly taken as assets of the State, should be added the increment of the land which at present in some places sells at £80 the hectare, for factories and commercial purposes at £4 the hectare, and for agriculture at 8s. the hectare. If the State were offered for sale the value of the land made accessible to market by railway and steam communication would have to be considered. Beyond what has been specified as the State assets, consideration must be given to the now assured growth of the revenue. To-day, exclusive of the subsidies, it amounts to £470,602. When the State reaps the results of its generous aid to the planters of coffee, tea, cocoa, etc., to the railway, now completed, and to the commercial companies, who are now not restricted in their transport of goods and produce, there must necessarily be a material increase each year in the revenue. From all of which summary it does not appear to me that the position of the State is financially unsound; indeed, I am inclined to think it to be otherwise.

His Majesty's policy has been to start the State on lines that must end in prosperity, without regard to personal labour or personal cost, and by his munificent pecuniary advances to the railway, commercial societies, planters, timber merchants, and agriculturists, the result has been that capital to the amount of several millions sterling has gravitated to the Congo. Personally, he may never recover a penny of the £900,000 he devoted to the creation of the State, but to that he is indifferent. Whatever surplus the revenue may furnish will certainly be devoted to assist new enterprises, new railways, increase of shipping, telegraph lines — to anything, in short, that promises expansion of the resources of the State, and enhances the value of the legacy he proposes to bequeath to the people of whom he is King and loyal servant.

An honourable friend of mine has lately delivered a lecture before the Statistical Society with a view to prove that the Congo State was financially a failure.

The Uganda Protectorate, having been established but lately, would naturally present a still more unsatisfactory balance sheet than any of the four territories above mentioned, but it is not derogatory to either British or German Africa that their deficits are so large, for the Congo, during the state of undevelopment, had absolutely no receipts at all, except King Leopold's subsidy, to meet the expenditure.

There is no necessity to labour this matter, but I think it is sufficiently proved that my honourable friend has been mistaken in his views about the financial condition of the Congo State.

Remarkable as has been the progress of the above territories hitherto, my most sincere wish is that there may be still greater acceleration of it during the next twenty years.

HENRY M. STANLEY.

January 1st, 1899.

EXPLANATION.

Part I.

My new mission — The Daily Telegraph — "Yes; Bennett"' — The Lady Alice — My European staff — Disappointed applicants and thoughtful friends — My departure for Africa.

Part II.

The sources of the Nile — Herodotus on the Nile — Burton on the Nile basin — Lake Tanganika — Lake Victoria — Speke, Grant, and Cameron — The Livingstone River — The work before me.

While returning to England in April 1874 from the Ashantee War, the news readied me that Livingstone was dead — that his body was on its way to England!

Livingstone had then fallen! He was dead! He had died by the shores of Lake Bemba, on the threshold of the dark region he had wished to explore! The work he had promised me to perform was only begun when death overtook him!

The effect which this news had upon me, after the first shock had passed away, was to fire me with a resolution to complete his work, to be, if God willed it, the next martyr to geographical science, or, if my life was to be spared, to clear up not only the secrets of the Great River throughout its course, but also all that remained still problematic and incomplete of the discoveries of Burton and Speke, and Speke and Grant.

The solemn day of the burial of the body of my great friend arrived. I was one of the pall-bearers in Westminster Abbey, and when I had seen the coffin lowered into the grave, and had heard the first handful of earth thrown over it, I walked away sorrowing over the fate of David Livingstone.

I laboured night and day over my book, 'Coomassie and Magdala,' for I was in a fever to begin that to which I now had vowed to devote myself. Within three weeks the literary work was over, and I was free.

Soon after this I was passing by an old book-shop, and observed a volume bearing the singular title of 'How to Observe.' Upon opening it, I perceived it contained tolerably clear instructions of 'How and what to observe.' It was very interesting, and it whetted my desire to know more; it led me to purchase quite an extensive library of books upon Africa, its geography, geology, botany, and ethnology. I thus became possessed of over one hundred and thirty books upon Africa, which I studied with the zeal of one who had a living interest in the subject, and with the understanding of one who had been already four times on the continent. I knew what had been accomplished by African Explorers, and I knew how much of the dark interior was still unknown to the world. Until late hours I sat up, inventing and planning, sketching out routes, laying out lengthy lines of possible exploration, noting many suggestions which the continued study of my project created. I also drew up lists of instruments and other paraphernalia that would be required to map, lay out, and describe the new regions to be traversed.

I had strolled over one day to the office of the Daily Telegraph, full of the subject. While I was discussing journalistic enterprise in general with one of the staff, the Editor entered. We spoke of Livingstone and the unfinished task remaining behind him. In reply to an eager remark which I made, he asked: —

"Could you, and would you, complete the work? And what is there to do?"

I answered:

"The outlet of Lake Tanganika is undiscovered. We know nothing scarcely — except what Speke has sketched out — of Lake Victoria; we do not even know whether it consists of one or many lakes, and therefore the sources of the Nile are still unknown. Moreover, the western half of the African continent is still a white blank."

"Do you think you can settle all this, if we commission you?"

"While I live, there will be something done. If I survive the time required to perform all the work, all shall be done."

The matter was for the moment suspended, because Mr. James Gordon Bennett, of the New York Herald, had prior claims on my services.

A telegram was despatched to New York to him:

"Would he join the Daily Telegraph in sending Stanley out to Africa, to complete the discoveries of Speke, Burton, and Livingstone?" and, within twenty-four hours, my "new mission" to Africa was determined on as a joint expedition, by the laconic answer which the cable flashed under the Atlantic: "Yes; Bennett."

A few days before I departed for Africa, the Daily Telegraph announced in a leading article that its proprietors had united with Mr. James Gordon Bennett in organizing an expedition of African discovery, under the command of Mr. Henry M. Stanley. "The purpose of the enterprise," it said, "is to complete the work left unfinished by the lamented death of Dr. Livingstone; to solve, if possible, the remaining problems of the geography of Central Africa; and to investigate and report upon the haunts of the slave-traders." * * * * "He will represent the two nations whose common interest in the regeneration of Africa was so well illustrated when the lost English explorer was rediscovered by the energetic American correspondent. In that memorable journey, Mr. Stanley displayed the best qualities of an African traveller; and with no inconsiderable resources at his disposal to reinforce his own complete acquaintance with the conditions of African travel, it may be hoped that very important results will accrue from this undertaking to the advantage of science, humanity, and civilisation."

Two weeks were allowed me for purchasing boats — a yawl, a gig, and a barge — for giving orders for pontoons, and purchasing equipment, guns, ammunition, rope, saddles, medical stores, and provisions; for making investments in gifts for native chiefs; for obtaining scientific instruments, stationery, &c., &c. The barge was an invention of my own.

It was to be 40 feet long, 6 feet beam, and 30 inches deep, of Spanish cedar 3/8 inch thick. When finished, it was to be separated into five sections, each of which should be 8 feet long. If the sections should be over-weight, they were to be again divided into halves for greater facility of carriage. The construction of this novel boat was undertaken by Mr. James Messenger, boat-builder, of Teddington, near London. The pontoons were made by Cording, but though the workmanship was beautiful, they were not a success, because the superior efficiency of the boat for all purposes rendered them unnecessary. However, they were not wasted. Necessity compelled us, while in Africa, to employ them for far different purposes from those for which they had originally been designed.

There lived a clerk at the Langham Hotel, of the name of Frederick Barker, who, smitten with a desire to go to Africa, was not to be dissuaded by reports of its unhealthy climate, its dangerous fevers, or the uncompromising views of exploring life given to him. "He would go, he was determined to go," he said. To meet the earnest entreaties of this young man, I requested him to wait until I should return from the United States.

Mr. Edwin Arnold, of the Daily Telegraph, also suggested that I should be accompanied by one or more young English boatmen of good character, on the ground that their river knowledge would be extremely useful to me. He mentioned his wish to a most worthy fisherman, named Henry Pocock, of Lower Upnor, Kent, who had kept his yacht for him, and who had fine stalwart sons, who bore the reputation of being honest and trustworthy. Two of these young men volunteered at once. Both Mr. Arnold and myself warned the Pocock family repeatedly that Africa had a cruel character, that the sudden change from the daily comforts of English life to the rigorous one of an explorer would try the most perfect constitution; would most likely be fatal to the uninitiated and unacclimatized. But I permitted myself to be overborne by the eager courage and devotion of these adventurous lads, and Francis John Pocock and Edward Pocock, two very likely-looking young men, were accordingly engaged as my assistants.

I crossed over to America, the guest of Mr. Ismay, of the 'White Star' line, to bid farewell to my friends, and after a five days' stay returned in a steamer belonging to the same Company.

Meantime, soon after the announcement of the "New Mission," applications by the score poured into the offices of the Daily Telegraph and New York Herald for employment. Before I sailed from England, over 1200 letters were received from "generals," "colonels," "captains," "lieutenants," "midshipmen," "engineers," "commissioners of hotels," mechanics, waiters, cooks, servants, somebodies and no-bodies, spiritual mediums and magnetizers, &c. &c. They all knew Africa, were perfectly acclimatized, were quite sure they would please me, would do important services, save me from any number of troubles by their ingenuity and resources, take me up in balloons or by flying carriages, make us all invisible by their magic arts, or by the "science of magnetism" would cause all savages to fall asleep while we might pass anywhere without trouble. Indeed I feel sure that, had enough money been at my disposal at that time, I might have led 5000 Englishmen, 5000 Americans, 2000 Frenchmen, 2000 Germans, 500 Italians, 250 Swiss, 200 Belgians, 50 Spaniards and 5 Greeks, or 15,005 Europeans, to Africa. But the time had not arrived to depopulate Europe, and colonize Africa on such a scale, and I was compelled to respectfully decline accepting the valuable services of the applicants, and to content myself with Francis John and Edward Pocock, and Frederick Barker — whose entreaties had been seconded by his mother, on my return from America.

I was agreeably surprised also, before departure, at the great number of friends I possessed in England, who testified their friendship substantially by presenting me with useful "tokens of their regard" in the shape of canteens, watches, water-bottles, pipes, pistols, knives, pocket companions, manifold writers, cigars, packages of medicine, Bibles, prayer-books, English tracts for the dissemination of religious knowledge among the black pagans, poems, tiny silk banners, gold rings, &c. &c. A lady for whom I have a reverent respect presented me also with a magnificent prize mastiff named 'Castor,' an English officer presented me with another, and at the Dogs' Home at Battersea I purchased a retriever, a bull-dog, and a bull-terrier, called respectively by the Pococks, 'Nero,' 'Bull,' and 'Jack.'

There were two little farewell dinners only which I accepted before my departure from England. One was at the house of the Editor of the Daily Telegraph, where I met Captain Fred. Burnaby and a few other kind friends. Captain Burnaby half promised to meet me at the sources of the Nile. The other was a dinner given by the representative of the New York Herald, at which were present Mr. George Augustus Sala, Mr. AV. C. Stillman, Mr. George W. Smalley, and three or four other journalists of note. It was a kindly quiet good-bye, and that was my last of London.

On the 15th of August, 1874, having shipped the Europeans, boats, and dogs, and general property of the expedition — which, through the kindness of Mr. Henry Bayley, of the Peninsular and Oriental Company, and Mr. William Mackinnon, of the British India Steam Navigation Company, were to be taken to Zanzibar at half-fares — I left England for the east coast of Africa to begin my explorations.

EXPLANATION.
Part II.
The Sources of the Nile.

In the fifth century, before the Christian era began, Herodotus, the first great African traveller, wrote about the Nile and its sources as follows: —

"Respecting the nature of this river, the Nile, I was unable to gain any information, either from the priests or any one else. I was very desirous, however, of learning from them why the Nile, beginning at the summer solstice, fills and overflows for a hundred days; and when it has nearly completed this number of days, falls short in its stream, and retires; so that it continues low all the winter, until the return of the summer solstice. Of these particulars I could get no information from the Egyptians, though I inquired whether this river has any peculiar quality that makes it differ in nature from other rivers. Being anxious, then, of knowing what was said about this matter, I made inquiries, and also how it comes to pass that this is the only one of all rivers that does not send forth breezes from its surface. Nevertheless, some of the Greeks, wishing to be distinguished for their wisdom, have attempted to account for these inundations in three different ways; two of these ways are scarcely worth mentioning, except that I wish to show what they are. One of them says that the Etesian winds are the cause of the swelling of the river, by preventing the Nile from discharging itself into the sea. But frequently the Etesian winds have not blown, yet the Nile produces the same effects; besides, if the Etesian winds were the cause, all other rivers that flow opposite to the same winds must of necessity be equally affected and in the same manner as the Nile; and even so much the more, as they are less and have weaker currents; yet there are many rivers in Syria, and many in Libya, which are not all affected as the Nile is. The second opinion shows still more ignorance than the former, but, if I may so say, is more marvellous. It says that the Nile, flowing from the ocean, produces this effect; and that the ocean flows all round the earth. The third way of resolving this difficulty is by far the most precious, but most untrue. For by saying that the Nile flows from melted snow, it says nothing, for this river flows from Libya through the middle of Ethiopia and discharges itself in Egypt; how therefore, since it runs from a very hot to a colder region, can it flow from snow? Many reasons will readily occur to men of good understanding, to show the improbability of its flowing from snow. The first and chief proof is derived from the winds, which blow hot from those regions; the second is, that the country, destitute of rain, is always free from ice; but after snow has fallen, it must of necessity rain within five days; so that if snow fell, it would also rain in these regions. In the third place, the inhabitants become black from the excessive heat:

kites and swallows continue there all the year; and the cranes, to avoid the cold of Scythia, migrate to these parts as winter quarters: if then ever so little snow fell in this country through which the Nile flows, and from which it derives its source, none of these things would happen, as necessity proves. But the person who speaks about the ocean, since he has referred his account to some obscure fable, produces no conviction at all, for I do not know any river called the Ocean, but suppose that Homer, or some other ancient poet, having invented the name, introduced it into poetry."

Captain Burton the learned traveller has some excellent paragraphs in his 'Nile Basin,' and remarks on this topic in connection with Ptolemy: —

"That early geographer places his lake Nilus a little to the south of the Equator (about ten degrees), and 5° E. long, from Alexandria — that is, in 34° or 35° E. long, by our mode of reckoning. He was led into an error in placing these portions of the interior, bearing, as he conceived, from certain points in the east. Thus he places Cape Aromatum (Cape Asser or Cape Guardafui) in 6° N. lat., which we know to be in 11° 48' 50", being thus, say, 6° out of its true place. He places the lake, the source of the western branch of the river, 1° more to the north and 8° more to the west than the one for the eastern branch; subsequent inquiries may show us that these great features of Africa may yet turn out to be substantially correct.

"We cannot here enter into any disquisition regarding the discrepancies that appear amongst the very ancient authors regarding these parts of Africa. We notice only those that are consistent and most valuable, and as bearing upon the priority of discovery and geographical knowledge. The earliest period we hear of Ethiopia is in the capture of the capital thereof by Moses 1400 years before our era, and 90 or 100 years before the departure of the Israelites from Egypt. Josephus calls it Saba, and states that it was very strong, situated on the River Astosabos, and that the name was changed to Meroe, by Cambyses, in honour of his sister Meroe. There were known to ancient writers three great tributaries to the Nile in Ethiopia, namely, the Astaboras (Tatazze), the Astosabos (Blue River), and the Astapus (White River). Herodotus says the source of the Nile, Astosabos, was twenty days' journey to the south of Meroe, which will bring it to Lake Dembea or Tzana. According to Ptolemy, the position of Meroe was in 16° 25' N. lat., but the ancient astronomer Hipparchus has placed it in 16° 51', which may be taken as the most correct. Caillaud found the vast ruins in 16° 56'. Under Psammeticus, the first Egyptian king that reigned after the final expulsion of the Ethiopian kings from Egypt, 240,000 emigrants from Egypt settled in an island south of the island of Meroe, that is beyond Khartoum, between the Blue and the White Rivers, and at eight days' journey east of the Nubse, or Nubatse. Subsequently the Roman arms extended to those parts. Petronius, the Roman general under Augustus, thirty years before our era, took and destroyed Napata, the ancient capital of Tirhaka, situated on the great northern bend of the Nile at Mount Barkhall, where vast ruins are still found. Meroe certainly, the capital of Queen Candace, mentioned in the New Testament (Acts viii. 27), also fell under the Roman yoke. Nero, early in his reign, sent a remarkable exploring party, under two centurions, with military force, to explore the source of the Nile and the countries to the west of the Astapus or White River, at that early day considered to be the true Nile. Assisted by an Ethiopian sovereign (Candace, no doubt), they went through the district now known as Upper Nubia, to a distance of 890 Roman miles from Meroe. In the last part of their journey they came to immense marshes, the end of which no one seemed to know, amongst which the channels were so narrow that the light boat or canoe in use was barely sufficient to carry one man across them. Still they continued their course south till they saw the river tumbling down or issuing out between the rocks, when they turned back, carrying with them a map of the regions through which they had passed: for Nero's guidance and information. This, it may be remarked, is exactly the case still. The Dutch ladies told us last year that they found the channels amongst these marshes so thick that the lightest canoe, made of bulrushes, scarcely fit to carry one man, could not find room to pass on them or across them. After this Pliny, Strabo, and other Roman authors took notice of this position of Africa, but without giving us anything important or new."

I quote from Captain Burton once more certain passages. "Edrisi, who was born in Nubia, but who wrote in Egypt about A.D. 1400, says, in that part of Ethiopia south and south-west of Nubia is first seen the separation of the two Niles. The one flows from south to north into Egypt, and the other part of the Nile flows from east to west; and upon that branch of the Nile lie all, or at least the most celebrated kingdoms of the Negroes. 'From the Mountains of the Moon,' says Scheadeddin, 'the Egyptian Nile takes its rise. It cuts horizontally the equator in its course north. Many rivers come from this mountain, and unite in a great lake. From this lake comes the Nile, the greatest and most beautiful of the rivers of all the earth. Many rivers derived from this great river water Nubia,' &c.

"From the Arabs we may fairly descend to our own times. The early Portuguese discoverers obtained a great deal of geographical information regarding the interior of Africa, and especially regarding two lakes near the Equator, from one of which, the most northern, the Egyptian Nile was stated to flow. This information was largely used by the French geographer (D'Anville), and the Dutch geographers of that time. Subsequently Bruce and others told us about the great disparity in magnitude between the Blue and the White Rivers; the latter, they asserted, rose far to the south, near to the Equator, and amongst mountains covered with eternal snow. Twenty-five years ago, Mohammed Ali, the clear-sighted and energetic ruler of Egypt, sent an expedition, consisting of several barques well provided with everything necessary, and under able naval officers, to explore the White Nile to its source, if possible. They did their work so far well, but were forced to turn back on the 26th of January, 1840, in lat. 30° 22' N., for want of sufficient depth of water for their vessels. At lat. 3° 30' they found the river 1370 feet broad and say six feet deep. In every day's work on the voyage they gave the width of the river, the depth of the river, the force of its current, its temperature, and the miles (geographical) made good daily."

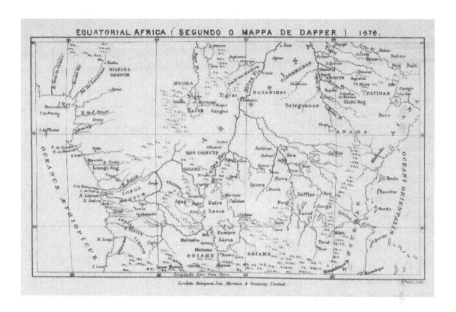

These quotations bring us down to our own times. A few of the principal characters, through whose agency the problem of the Sources of the Nile has been solved, still live. The old African Association became merged in 1831 into the Royal Geographical Society. The change of title seems to have evoked greater energies, and the publications of the new society, the position of its President, his influence, learning, and tact, soon attracted general public attention. In the midst of this, Messrs. Krapf and Rebmann and Erhardt, missionaries located at Mombasa, on the east coast of Africa, announced that Arab traders and natives acquainted with the interior informed them that far inland there was a very large lake, or several lakes, which some spoke of under one collective title. The information thus obtained was illustrated by a sketch map by Mr. Erhardt, and was published in the 'Proceedings of the Royal Geographical Society' in 1856, "the most striking feature of which was a vast lake of a curious shape, extending through 12° of latitude."

Lake Tanganika,

The Royal Geographical Society was induced to despatch an expedition to East Africa for the exploration of this interesting inland region, the command of which it entrusted to Lieutenant Richard Francis Burton, and Lieutenant John Manning Speke, officers of the East Indian Army.

Lieutenant Burton was already distinguished as an enterprising traveller by his book, 'Pilgrimage to Mekka and Medina.' Speke had, until this time, only a local reputation, but bore the character of being a very promising officer, and an amiable gentleman with a fondness for natural history and botanical studies, besides being an ardent sportsman and an indefatigable pedestrian.

Burton and Speke's expedition landed at Zanzibar on the 20th of December, 1856. On the 13th of February, 1858, after a journey of 950 miles, and at a distance of 540 lineal geographical miles from the point of departure on the Indian Ocean, they first sighted and discovered Lake Tanganika. How much they explored of the lake is best illustrated by their map, which is appended to this present volume. Speke first crossed Lake Tanganika to the western side to Kasenge, an island, then returned by the same route to Kawele, the district or quarter occupied at that time by the Arabs, in a large straggling village on the shores of the lake, in the country of Ujiji.

On the second exploration of the lake, Lieutenant Burton accompanied Lieutenant Speke to a cove in Uvira, which is about thirteen miles from the north end of the lake. Unable to reach the extremity of the lake, they both returned to Ujiji. Lieutenant Speke was most anxious to proceed on a third tour of exploration of the lake, but was overruled by his chief, Lieutenant Burton. On the 26th of May, 1858, the expedition turned homewards, arriving in Unyanyembe on the 20th of June.

Lake Victoria

While Lieutenant Burton preferred to rest in Unyanyembe to collect the copious information about the Lake Regions from the Arabs and natives, which we see set forth in a masterly manner in his book. Lieutenant Speke, of a more active disposition, mustered a small force of men, and, with his superior's permission, set out northward on July 9, 1858, on an exploring tour, and on the 30th of the same month arrived at the south end of a lake called by the Wanyamwezi who were with him the N'yanza, or the Lake, and by the Arabs, Ukerewe.

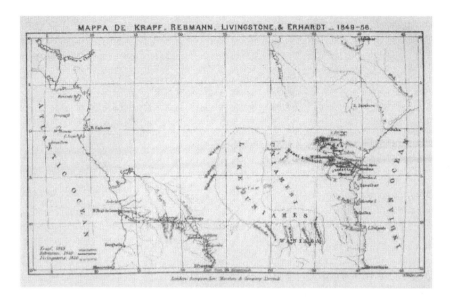

At Muanza, in Usukuma, he took a survey of the body of the water such as might be embraced in a view taken from an altitude of 200 feet above the lake.

In his reflections on the magnitude of the water expanse before him, Speke wrote: "I no longer felt any doubt that the lake at my feet gave birth to that interesting river, the source of which has been the subject of so much speculation, and the object of so many explorers."

And again: "This is a far more extensive lake than the Tanganika; so broad you could not see across it, and so long that nobody knew its length." To this magnificent lake Lieutenant Speke, its discoverer, gave the name of Victoria N'yanza.

From this short view of the Victoria Lake, Speke returned to Unyanyembe, and announced to Lieutenant Burton that he had discovered the source of the White Nile. Lieutenant Burton did not acquiesce in his companion's views of the importance of the discovery, and in his 'Lake Regions' and 'Nile Basins,' in lectures, speeches, and essays in magazines, and conversations with friends, always vigorously combated the theory.

On the 30th of February, 1859, Burton and Spoke's task of exploration, which had occupied twenty-five months, terminated with the arrival of the expedition at the little maritime village of Konduchi, on the Indian Ocean.

On opening John Hanning Speke's book, 'Journal of the Discovery of the Source of the Nile,' we are informed on the very first page that his second important expedition into Africa, "which was avowedly for the purpose of establishing the truth of the assertion that the Victoria N'yanza (which he discovered on the 30th of July, 1858) would eventually prove to be the source of the Nile, may be said to have commenced on the 9th of May, 1859, the first day of his return to England from his last expedition, when, at the invitation of Sir Roderick Impey Murchison, he called at his house to show him his map, for the information of the Royal Geographical Society."

Mr. Speke who was now known as Captain Speke, was intrusted with the command of the succeeding expedition which the Royal Geographical Society determined to send out for the purpose of verifying the theories above stated. He was accompanied this time by an old brother officer in India, Captain James Augustus Grant.

The expedition under Speke and Grant set out from Zanzibar on the 25th of September, 1860. On the 23rd of January, 1861, it arrived at the house occupied by Burton and Speke's expedition, in Tabora, Unyanyembe, having traversed nearly the entire distance along the same route that had been adopted formerly. In the middle of May the journey to Karagwe began. After a stay full of interest with Rumanika, king of Karagwe, they followed a route which did not permit them even a view of Lake Victoria, until they caught sight of the great lake near Meruka, on the 31st of January, 1862. From this point, the expedition, up to its arrival at the court of Mtesa, emperor of Uganda, must have caught several distant views of the lake, though not travelling near its shores. During a little excursion from the Emperor's capital, they also discovered a long broad inlet, which is henceforth known as Murchison Bay, on its northern coast.

On the 7th of July, 1862, the two travellers started in a north-easterly direction, away from the lake, and Speke states that he arrived at Urondogani on the 21st. From this point he marched up the river along the left bank, and reached the Ripon Falls at the outlet of Lake Victoria on the 20th of July. He thus sums up the result and net value of the explorations of himself and companion in the years 1860-62:

—

"The Expedition had now performed its functions. I saw that old Father Nile without any doubt rises in the Victoria N'yanza, and as I had foretold, that Lake is the great source of the holy river which cradled the first expounder of our religious belief. . . . The most remote waters, or top-head of the Nile, is the southern end of the lake, situated close on the 3° lat., which gives to the Nile the surprising length in direct measurement, rolling over 34 degrees of latitude, of above 2300 miles, or more than one-eleventh of the circumference of our globe. Now, from the southern point round by the west, to where the great Nile stream rises, there is only one feeder of any importance, and that is the Kitangule River; while from the southern-most point round by the east, to the strait, there are no rivers of any importance."

...

He christened the falling effluent, where it drops from the level of the lake and escapes northerly into the Victoria Nile, "Ripon Falls," in honour of the Earl of Ripon, who was President of the Royal Geographical Society when the expedition was organised, and the arm of the lake from which the Victoria Nile issued,

Napoleon Channel, as a token of respect to the Paris Geographical Society, who had honoured him with a gold medal for the discovery of Lake Victoria.

Following this paragraph, Captain Speke makes an important statement, to which I beg attention: "One thing seemed at first perplexing, the volume of water in the Kitangule (Alexandra Nile) looked as large as the Nile (Victoria), but then the one was a slow river, and the other swift, and on this account I could form no adequate judgment of their relative values."

On the 4th of June, Captain Speke and Grant embarked at Alexandria, Egypt, for England, where they arrived after an absence of 1146 days.

Though one might suppose that the explorers had sufficient grounds for supposing that Lake Victoria covered an enormous area, quite as large, or, approaching to the 29,000 square miles' extent Captain Speke boldly sketched it, there were not wanting many talented men to dispute each point in the assertions he made. One of the boldest who took opposing views to Speke was his quondam companion, Captain R. F. Burton, and he was supported by very many others, for very plausible reasons, which cannot, however, be touched upon here.

Doctor David Livingstone, while on his last expedition, obtained much oral information in the interior of Africa from Arab traders, which dissected Speke's Grand Lake into five; and it really seemed as if, from the constant assaults made upon it by geographers and cartographers, it would in time be erased from the chart altogether, or become a mere "rush drain," like one of those which Speke and Grant found so numerous in that region. It was evident, therefore, that a thorough exploration of Lake Victoria was absolutely necessary to set at rest, once and for ever, one of the great problems that was such a source of trouble and dissatisfaction to the geographers of Europe and America.

Lake Tanganika Again.

The next European to arrive at the shores of Lake Tanganika, after Burton and Speke, was Dr. David Livingstone. He first saw it as he stood on the verge of the plateau which rises steeply from the surface of the Tanganika at its south-west corner, on the 2nd of April, 1867; and on the 14th of March, 1869, and after traversing nearly the whole of the western shore from the extreme south end of the lake to Kassenge, the island which Speke visited in 1858, he crossed over to the east side and reached Ujiji.

On the 15th of July, 1869, after camping at Kassenge, when on his way to Manyema, he writes in his journal the following opinion of Lake Tanganika; "Tanganika narrows at Uvira or Vira, and goes out of sight among the mountains; then it appears as a waterfall into the Lake of Quando, seen by Banyamwezi."

In his letters home Dr. Livingstone constantly made mention of two lakes, called Upper Tanganika, which Burton discovered, and Lower Tanganika, which Sir Samuel Baker discovered, and which formed, as he said, the second line of drainage trending to and discharging its waters into the Nile.

He makes record in his Journals of the causes which induced him to verify his opinions by a personal investigation of the north end of Lake Tanganika on the 16th of November, 1871, a few days after my arrival, at Ujiji, I being the fourth European who had arrived on the shores of the Lake, in this manner: —

"16th November, 1871. — As Tanganika Explorations are said by Mr. Stanley to be an object of interest to Sir Roderick, we go at his expense and by his men to the north end of the lake."

"24th November. — To Point Kisuka in Mukamba's country. A Mgwaua came to us from King Mukamba, and asserted most positively that all the water of Tanganika flowed into the River Lusize, and then on to Ukerewe of Mteza; nothing could be more clear than his statements."

"25th November. — Our friend of yesterday now declared as positively as before, that the water of Lusize flowed into Tanganika, and not the way he said yesterday! Tanganika closes in except at one point N. and by W. of us."

"26th November. — The end of Tanganika seen clearly, is rounded off about 4' broad from east to west."

On the 29th of November, Livingstone and I, in a canoe manned by several strong rowers, entered into Lusize, or Eusizi, and discovered that it flowed into Lake Tanganika by three mouths with an impetuous current.

The explorations of Livingstone and myself in November 1871 to the north end of Lake Tanganika resolved that portion of the problem, but described only about thirteen miles of coast unvisited by Burton and Speke. On our way back, however, by a southern route to Unyanyembe, we added to the knowledge of the Tanganika coastline, on the eastern side from Kabogo Point as far as Urimba, about twenty miles farther than Speke had seen.

In August 1872, about live months after I had departed from him homewards, he recommenced his last journey. On the 8th of October of the same year he saw the Tanganika again about sixty miles south of the point where he and I bade farewell to the lake, eight months previously. Clinging to the lake, he travelled along the eastern shore, until he reached the southernmost end of it.

From this it will appear evident that the only portion of Lake Tanganika remaining unvisited was that part of the west-end shore, between Kasenge Island and the northern most point of what Burton and Speke called Ubwari Island, and what Livingstone and I called Muzimu Island. Doubtless there were many portions of Livingstone's route overland which rendered the coast line somewhat obscure, and in his hurried journey to Ujiji in 1869, by canoe from Mompara's to Kasenge, a portion of the Uguha coast was left unexplored. But it is Livingstone who was the first to map out and give a tolerably correct configuration to that part of Lake Tanganika extending from Urimba round to the south end and up along the eastern shore to Kasenge Island, as it was Burton and Speke who were the first to map out that portion of the Tanganika extending from Ujiji to a point nearly opposite Ubwari and the north-west, from Ubwari's north end as far as Uvira.

In February 1874 Lieutenant Verney Lovett Cameron, R.N., arrived at the same village of Ujiji, which had been seen by Burton and Speke in 1858, and which was known as the place where I discovered Livingstone in 1872. He had traversed a route rendered familiar to thousands of the readers of the 'Lake Regions of Central Africa,' 'the Journal of the Discovery of the Nile,' and 'How I found Livingstone,' through a country carefully mapped, surveyed and described. But the land that lay before him westerly had only been begun by Livingstone, and there were great and important fields of exploration beyond the farthest point he had reached.

Lieutenant Cameron procured two canoes, turned south, and coasted along the eastern shore of the Tanganika, and when near the southern end of the Lake, crossed it, turned up north along the western shore, and discovered a narrow channel, between two spits of pure white sand. Entering this channel, the Lukuga creek, he traced it until farther progress was stopped by an immovable and impenetrable barrier of papyrus. This channel. Lieutenant Cameron wrote, was the outlet of Lake Tanganika. Satisfied with his discovery, he withdrew from the channel, pursued his course along the west coast as far as Kasenge Island, the camping-place of both Speke and Livingstone, and returned direct to Ujiji without making further effort.

Lake Tanganika, as will be seen, upon Lieutenant Cameron's departure, had its entire coast-line described, except the extreme south end, the mouth of the Lufuvu and that portion of coast lying between Kasenge Island and the northern point of Ubwari, about 140 miles in extent.

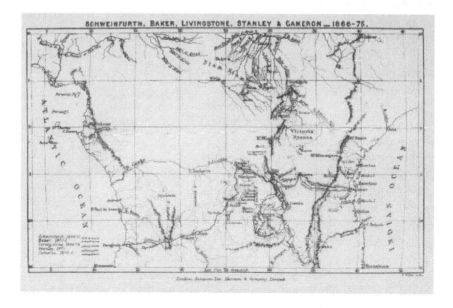

SCHWEINFURTH, BAKER, LIVINGSTONE, STANLEY & CAMERON—1868-75.

Livingstone's Great River.

What we knew distinctly of this great river began with Livingstone's last journey, when he wrote from Ujiji in 1869, repeating what he had already written in 1867, at the town of Cazembe, in a despatch to Lord Clarendon.

Briefly, this last journey began, let us say, at Zanzibar, the date of his arrival being the 28th of January, 1866. On the 19th of March he sailed in H.M.S. Penguin for the mouth of the Rovuma river, after invoking the blessing of the Most High upon his meditated intercourse with the heathen. Effecting a landing at Mikindini Bay, he directed his course in a south-westerly direction, arriving within view of Lake Nyassa on the 13th of September, 1866.

On the 16th of January, 1867, he reached the most southerly streams emptying into the Chambezi, after crossing the mountains which separate the streams flowing east to the Loangwa. He describes the northern slope which gives birth to the affluents of the new river thus: "It is needless to repeat that it is all forest on the northern slopes of the mountains — open glade and miles of forest; ground at present all sloppy, oozes full and overflowing, feet constantly wet. Rivulets rush with clear water; though they are in flood we can guess which are perennial and which are torrents that dry up; they flow northwards and westwards to the Chambezi."

Eight days later, in S. lat. 10° 34', he reached the main river — the Chambezi — a stream "flooded with clear water-banks not more than 40 yards apart, showing abundant animal life in its waters and on its banks as it flowed westwards." Just at the point Livingstone first saw the Chambezi, numerous streams are gathered from all points — northerly, easterly, and southerly, from the westerly slope of the uplands of Mambwe into the main river, which presently becomes a formidable river, and which subsequent explorations proved to enter Lake Bemba on its eastern side.

On the 8th of November, 1867, the traveller makes a very comprehensive statement. It is the evening of his arrival at Lake Mweru or Moero. "Lake Moero seems of goodly size, and is flanked by ranges of mountains on the east and west. Its banks are of coarse sand, and slope gradually down to the water; outside of these banks stands a thick belt of tropical vegetation in which fishermen build their huts. The country called Rua lies on the west, and is seen as a lofty range of dark mountains; another range of less height, but more broken, stands along the eastern shore."

"The northern shore has a fine sweep, like an unbent bow, and round the western end flows the water that makes the River Lualaba, which, before it enters Mweru, is the Luapula, and that again (if the most intelligent report speak true) is the Chambezi before it enters Lake Bemba or Bangweolo."

On page 261, vol i., of 'Livingstone's Last Journals,' he sums up very succinctly what knowledge he has gained of the country which was the scene of his explorations, 1866-67.

"First of all the Chambezi runs in the country of Mambwe, N.E. of Molemba. It then flows S.W. and W. till it reaches 11° S. lat. and long. 29° E., where it forms Lake Bemba or Bangweolo. Emerging thence, it assumes the new name Luapula, and comes down here to fall into Mweru. On going out of this lake it is known by the name Lualaba as it flows N.W. in Rua to form another lake with many islands called Ulenge or Urenge. Beyond this, information is not positive as to whether it enters Tanganika, or another lake beyond that."

On the 18th of July, 1868, the discovery of Lake Bemba or Bangweolo was made by Dr. Livingstone.

On page 59, vol. ii., 'Last Journals,' we think we have an explanation of the causes which led him to form those hypotheses and theories which he subsequently made public by his letters, or elaborated in his journals, on the subject of the Nile Sources.

"Bambarre, 25th August, 1870. — One of my waking dreams is that the legendary tales about Moses coming up into Lower Ethiopia, with Merr his foster mother, and founding a city which he called in her honour 'Meroe,' may have a substratum of fact."

"I dream of discovering some monumental relics of Meroe, and if anything confirmatory of sacred history does remain, I pray to be guided thereunto. If the sacred chronology would thereby be confirmed, I would not grudge the toil and hardship, hunger and pain I have endured — the irritable ulcers would only be discipline."

The old explorer, a grand spectacle and a specimen of most noble manhood in these latter days of his life, travels on and on, but never reaches nearer the solution of the problem which puzzles his soul than the Arab depot Nyangwe, which is situate a few miles south of 4° S. lat. and a little east of 26° E. long, where he leaves the great river still flowing north.

Livingstone never returned to this point, but retracing his steps to Ujiji, thence to the north end of Lake Tanganika and back again to Ujiji and Unyanyembe, directed his course to the southern shore of Lake Bemba, where he died of dysentery in the beginning of May 1873.

In the month of August 1874, Lieutenant Cameron, whom we left at Ujiji after the delineation of that part of Lake Tanganika south of Ujiji, after traversing Livingstone's route to Kasongo's Manyema, and travelling by canoe about thirty-five miles, reaches Nyangwe, his predecessor's farthest point. Though he does not attempt to resolve this problem, or penetrate the region north of Nyangwe, Lieutenant Cameron ventures upon the following hypothesis: "This great stream must be one of the head-waters of the Kongo, for where else could that giant amongst rivers, second only to the Amazon in its volume, obtain 2,000,000 cubic feet of water which it unceasingly pours each second into the Atlantic? The large affluents from the north would explain the comparatively small rise of the Kongo at the coast; for since its enormous basin extends to both sides of the equator, some portion of it is always under the zone of rains, and therefore the supply to the main stream is nearly the same at all times, instead of varying as is the case with tropical rivers, whose basins lie completely on one side of the equator." Lieutenant Cameron illustrates his hypothesis by causing Livingstone's great river to flow soon after leaving Nyangwe straight westward, the highest part of which is only 3° 30' S. lat.

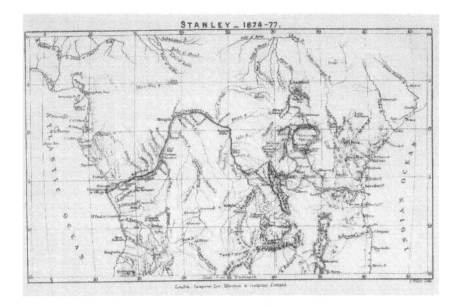

At Nyangwe, Lieutenant Cameron crossed the river, proceeded south with some Arab traders a few days' journey, then, accompanied by guides, travelled still south to Juma Merikani's, or Kasongo's, thence, after a stay of nearly nine months, accompanied by Portuguese traders, he proceeded to Benguella, a small port belonging to the Portuguese Government on the Atlantic Ocean, having crossed Africa from east to west south of S. lat. 4°.

The above is a brief sketch which with the aid of the small maps attached to this volume explains and illustrates the several geographical problems left by my predecessors. I now propose to describe how these problems were solved, and the incomplete discoveries of Burton and Speke, Speke and Grant, and Doctor Livingstone were finished, and how we sighted the lake Muta N'zige, by its broad arm, which I have called Beatrice Gulf, by a comprehensive exploration, lasting, from sea to sea, two years eight months and twenty days; the results of which are to be found embodied in these two volumes, entitled: 'Through the Dark Continent; the Sources of the Nile, around the Great Lakes of Africa, and down the "Livingstone" to the Atlantic Ocean.'

CHAPTER I.

Arrival at Zanzibar Island — Life at Zanzibar — The town of Zanzibar, its roadstead and buildings — The One Cocoa-nut tree and the red cliffs — Selection and purchase of goods for the journey — Residence of Prince Barghash — Busy mornings — Pleasant rides and quiet evenings.

Sept. 21. — Twenty-eight months had elapsed between my departure from Zanzibar after the discovery of Livingstone and my re-arrival on that island, September 21, 1874.

The well-remembered undulating ridges, and the gentle slopes clad with palms and mango trees bathed in warm vapour, seemed in that tranquil drowsy state which at all times any portion of tropical Africa presents at first appearance. A pale-blue sky covered the hazy land and sleeping sea as we steamed through the strait that separates Zanzibar from the continent. Every stranger, at first view of the shores, proclaims his pleasure. The gorgeous verdure, the distant purple ridges, the calm sea, the light gauzy atmosphere, the semi-mysterious silence which pervades all nature, evoke his admiration. For it is probable that he has sailed through the stifling Arabian Sea, with the grim, frowning mountains of Nubia on the one hand, and on the other the drear, ochreous-coloured ridges of the Arab Peninsula; and perhaps the aspect of the thirsty volcanic rocks of Aden and the dry brown bluffs of Guardafui is still fresh in his memory.

But a great change has taken place. As he passes close to the deeply verdant shores of Zanzibar Island, he views nature robed in the greenest verdure, with a delightful freshness of leaf, exhaling fragrance to the incoming wanderer. He is wearied with the natural deep-blue of the ocean, and eager for any change. He remembers the unconquerable aridity and the dry bleached heights he last saw, and lo! what a change! Responding to his half formed wish, the earth rises before him verdant, prolific, bursting with fatness. Palms raise their feathery heads and mangoes their great globes of dark green foliage; banana plantations with impenetrable shade, groves of orange, fragrant cinnamon, and spreading bushy clove, diversify and enrich the landscape. Jack-fruit trees loom up with great massive crowns of leaf and branch, while between the trees and in every open space succulent grasses and plants cover the soil with a thick garment of verdure. There is nothing grand or sublime in the view before him, and his gaze is not attracted to any special feature, because all is toned down to a uniform softness by the exhalation rising from the warm heaving bosom of the island. His imagination is therefore caught and exercised, his mind loses its restless activity, and reposes under the influence of the eternal summer atmosphere.

Presently on the horizon there rises the thin upright shadows of ships' masts, and to the left begins to glimmer a pale white mass which, we are told, is the capital of the island of Zanzibar. Still steaming southward, we come within rifle-shot of the low green shores, and now begin to be able to define the capital. It consists of a number of square massive structures, with little variety of height and all whitewashed, standing on a point of low land, separated by a broad margin of sand beach from the sea, with a bay curving gently from the point, inwards to the left towards us.

Within two hours from the time we first caught sight of the town, we have dropped anchor about 700 yards from the beach. The arrival of the British India Company's steamer causes a sensation. It is the monthly "mail" from Aden and Europe! A number of boats break away from the beach and come towards the vessel. Europeans sit at the stern, the rowers are white-shirted Wangwana with red caps. The former are anxious to hear the news, to get newspapers and letters, and to receive the small parcels sent by friendly hands "per favour of captain."

The stranger, of course, is intensely interested in this life existing near the African Equator, now first revealed to him, and all that he sees and hears of figures and faces and sounds is being freshly impressed on his memory. Figures and faces are picturesque enough. Happy, pleased-looking men of black, yellow, or tawny colour, with long white cotton shirts, move about with quick, active motion, and cry out, regardless of order, to their friends or mates in the Swahili or Arabic language, and their friends or mates respond with equally loud voice and lively gesture, until, with fresh arrivals, there appears to be a Babel created, wherein English, French, Swahili, and Arabic accents mix with Hindi, and, perhaps, Persian.

In the midst of such a scene I stepped into a boat to be rowed to the house of my old friend, Mr. Augustus Sparhawk, of the Bertram Agency. At this low-built, massive-looking house near Shangani Point, I was welcomed with all the friendliness and hospitality of my first visit, when, three years and a half previously, I arrived at Zanzibar to set out for the discovery of Livingstone.

With Mr. Sparhawk's aid I soon succeeded in housing comfortably my three young Englishmen, Francis John and Edward Pocock and Frederick Barker, and my five dogs, and in stowing safely on shore the yawl Wave, bought for me at Yarmouth by Mr. Edwin Arnold, the gig, and the tons of goods, provisions, and stores I had brought.

Life at Zanzibar is a busy one to the intending explorer. Time flies rapidly, and each moment of daylight must be employed in the selection and purchase of the various kinds of cloth, beads, and wire, in demand by the different tribes of the mainland through whose countries he purposes journeying. Strong, half-naked porters come in with great bales of unbleached cottons, striped and coloured fabrics, handkerchiefs and red caps, bags of blue, green, red, white and amber-coloured beads, small and large, round and oval, and coils upon coils of thick brass wire. These have to be inspected, assorted, arranged, and numbered separately, have to be packed in portable bales, sacks, or packages, or boxed according to their character and value. The house-floors are littered with cast-off wrappings and covers, box-lids, and a medley of rejected paper, cloth, zinc covers and broken boards, sawdust and other debris. Porters and servants and masters, employes and employers, pass backwards and forwards, to and fro, amid all this litter, roll bales over, or tumble about boxes; and a rending of cloth or paper, clattering of hammers, demands for the marking-pots, or the number of bale and box, with quick, hurried breathing and shouting, are heard from early morning until night.

Towards evening, after such a glaring day of glaring heat and busy toil, comes weariness: the arm-chair is sought, and the pipe or cigar with a cup of tea rounds off the eventful hours. Or, as sometimes the case would be, we would strike work early, and after a wholesome dinner at 4.30 P.M. would saddle our horses and ride out into the interior of the island, returning during the short twilight. Or we would take the well-known path to Mnazi-Moya — the One Cocoa-nut Tree, where it stands weird and sentinel-like over humble tombs on the crest of an ancient beach behind Shangani Point. Or, as the last and only resource left to a contemplative and studious mind, we would take our easy-chairs on the flat roof, where the cowhides of the merchant are poisoned and dried, and, with our feet elevated above our heads, watch the night coming.

If we take our ride, in a few minutes we may note, at the pleasantest hour, those local features which, with the thermometer at 95° Fahr., might have been a dangerous pleasure, or, at any rate, disagreeable. Through a narrow, crooked, plastered lane, our horses' feet clattering noisily as we go, we ride by the tall, white-washed, massive houses, which rise to two and three stories above our heads. The residences of the European merchants and the officials here stand side by side, and at the tall doorway of each sits the porter — as comfortable as his circumstances will permit. As we pass on, we get short views of the bay, and then plunge again into the lane until we come in view of the worm-eaten old fort, crumbling fast into disuse and demolition. Years ago, behind it, I saw a market where some slaves were being sold. Happily there is no such market now.

We presently catch sight, on our right, of the entrance to the fort at which sit on guard a few lazy Baluchis and dingy-looking Arabs. On our left is the saluting battery, which does frequent service for the ignition of much powder, an antique mode of exchanging compliments with ships of war, and of paying respect to Government officials. The customs sheds are close by, and directly in front of us rises the lofty house and harem of Prince Barghash. It is a respectable-looking building of the Arab architecture which finds favour at Muscat, three stories high and whitewashed — as all houses here appear to be. It is connected by a covered gangway, about 30 feet above our heads, with a large house on the opposite side of the lane, and possesses an ambitious doorway raised 3 feet above the street, and reached by four or five broad and circular-steps. Within the lower hall are some soldiers of the same pattern as those at the fort, armed with the Henry-Martini rifle, or matchlock, sword, and targe. A very short time takes us into a still narrower lane, where the whitewash is not so white as at Shangani, the European quarter. We are in the neighbourhood of Melindi now, where the European who has not been able to locate himself at Shangani is obliged to put up with neighbours of East Indian race or Arabs. Past and beyond Melindi is a medley of tall white houses and low sheds, where wealth and squalor jostle side by side, and then we find ourselves at the bridge over the inlet of Malagash, which extends from the bay up to Mnazi-Moya, or the One Cocoa-nut, behind Shangani. The banks on either side are in view as we pass over the bridge, and we note a dense mass of sheds and poor buildings, amid hills of garbage and heaps of refuse, and numbers of half-naked negroes, or people in white clothes, giving the whole an appearance somewhat resembling the more sordid village of Boulak, near Cairo.

Having crossed the bridge from Melindi, we are in what is very appropriately termed Ngambu, or "t'other side." The street is wide, but the quarter is more squalid. It is here we find the Wangwana, or Freedmen of Zanzibar, whose services the explorer will require as escort on the continent. Here they live very happily with the well-to-do Coastman, or Mswahili, poor Banyans, Hindis, Persians, Arabs, and Baluchis, respectable slave artisans, and tradesmen. When the people have donned their holiday attire, Ngambu becomes picturesque, even gay, and yields itself up to wild, frolicsome abandon of mirth. On working days, though the colours are still varied, and give relief to the clay walls and withered palm-frond roofs, this poor man's district has a dingy hue, which black faces and semi-naked bodies seems to deepen. However, the quarter is only a mile and a half long, and quickening our paces, we soon have before us detached houses and huts, clusters of cocoa-nut palms and ancient mango trees crowned with enormous dark green domes of foliage. For about three miles one can enjoy a gallop along an ochreous-coloured road of respectable width, bordered with hedges. Behind the hedges grow the sugar-cane, banana, palm, orange, clove cinnamon, and jack-fruit trees, cassava, castor-oil, diversified with patches of millet, Indian corn, sweet-potatoes, and egg-plant, and almost every vegetable of tropic growth. The fields, gently undulating, display the variety of their vegetation, on which the lights and shadows play, deepening or paling as the setting sun clouds or reveals the charms of the verdure.

Finally arriving upon the crest of Wirezu hill, we have a most beautiful view of the roadstead and town of Zanzibar, and, as we turn to regard it, are struck with the landscape lying at our feet. Sloping away gradually towards the town, the tropical trees already mentioned seem, in the bird's-eye view, to mass themselves into a thin forest, out of which, however, we can pick out clearly the details of tree and hut. Whatever of beauty may be in the scene, it is Nature's own, for man has done little; he has but planted a root, or a seed, or a tender sapling carelessly. Nature has nourished the root and the seed and the sapling, until they became sturdy giants, rising one above another in hillocks of dark green verdure, and has given to the whole that wonderful depth and variety of colour which she only exhibits in the Tropics.

The walk to Mnazi-Moya will compel the traveller to moralize, and meditate pensively. Decay speaks to him, and from the moment he leaves the house to the moment he returns, his mind is constantly dwelling upon mortality. For, after lounging through two or three lanes, he comes to a populous graveyard, over which the wild grass has obtained supreme control, and through the stalks of which show white the fading and moss touched headstones. Across the extensive acreage allotted to the victims of the sad cholera years, the Prince of Zanzibar has ruthlessly cut his way to form a garden, which he has surrounded with a high wall. Here a grinning skull and there a bleached thigh bone or sunken grave exposing its ghastly contents attract one's attention. From time immemorial this old beach has been the depository of the dead, and unless the Prince prosecutes his good work for. the reclamation of this golgotha (and the European officials urge it on him), the custom may be continued for a long period yet.

Beyond this cemetery is to be seen the muddy head of Malagash inlet, between which and the sea south of Shangani there lies only this antique sand bar, about two hundred yards in breadth. On the crest of the sand bar stands the One Cocoa-nut Palm which has given its name to this locality. Sometimes this spot is also known as the "fiddler's" grave. It is the breathing place of the hard-worked and jaded European, and here, seated on one of the plastered tombs near the base of the One Cocoa-nut Palm, with only a furtive look now and then at the "sleep and a forgetting" which those humble white structures represent, he may take his fill of ocean and watch the sun go down to his daily rest.

Beyond Mnazi-Moya is Mbwenni, the Universities Mission, and close behind are some peculiar red cliff's, which are worth seeing.

From the roof of the house, if we take the "last resource" already mentioned, we have a view of the roadstead and bay of Zanzibar. Generally there ride at anchor two or three British ships of war just in from a hunt after contumacious Arabs, who persist, against the orders of their prince, in transporting slaves on the high seas. There is a vessel moored closer to Frenchman's Island, its "broken back" a memento of the Prince's fleet shattered by the hurricane of 1872. Nearer in-shore float a number of Arab dhows, boats, lighters, steam launches, and two steamers, one of which is the famous Deerhound. One day I counted as a mere matter of curiosity, the great and small vessels in roadstead and harbour, and found that there were 135.

From our easy-chairs on the roof we can see the massive building occupied formerly by the Universities Mission, and now the residence of Captain Prideaux, Acting British Consul and Political Resident, whose acquaintance I first made soon after his release from Magdala in 1868. This building stands upon the extremity of Shangani Point, and the first line of houses which fronts the beach extends northerly in a gentle sweep, almost up to Livingstone's old residence on the other side of Malagash inlet.

During the day the beach throughout its length is alive with the moving figures of hamals, bearing clove and cinnamon bags, ivory, copal and other gums, and hides, to be shipped in the lighters waiting along the water's edge, with sailors from the shipping, and black boatmen discharging the various imports on the sand. In the evening the beach is crowded with the naked forms of workmen and boys from the "go-downs," preparing to bathe and wash the dust of copal and hides off their bodies in the surf. Some of the Arab merchants have ordered chairs on the piers, or bunders, to chat sociably until the sun sets, and prayer time has come. Boats hurry by with their masters and sailors returning to their respective vessels. Dhows move sluggishly past, hoisting as they go the creaking yards of their lateen sails, bound for the mainland ports. Zanzibar canoes and "matepes" are arriving with wood and produce, and others of the same native form and make are squaring their mat sails, outward bound. Sunset approaches, and after sunset silence follows soon. For as there are no wheeled carriages with the eternal rumble of their traffic in Zanzibar, with the early evening comes early peace and rest.

The intending explorer, however, bound for that dark edge of the continent which he can just see lying low along the west as he looks from Zanzibar, has thoughts at this hour which the resident cannot share. As little as his eyes can pierce and define the details in that gloomy streak on the horizon, so little can he tell whether weal or woe lies before him. The whole is buried in mystery, over which he ponders, certain of nothing but the uncertainty of life. Yet will he learn to sketch out a comparison between what he sees at sunset and his own future. Dark, indeed, is the gloom of the fast-coming night over the continent, but does he not see that there are still bright flushes of colour, and rosy bars, and crimson tints, amidst what otherwise would be universal blackness? And may he not therefore say — "As those colours now brighten the darkening west, so my hopes brighten my dark future"?

CHAPTER II.

Seyyid Barghash — His prohibition of slavery, character and reforms — Treaty with British Government by Sir Bartle Frere — Tramways the need of Africa — Arabs in the interior — Arabs in Zanzibar — Mtuma or Mgwana? — The Wangwana, their vices and virtues — A Mgwana's highest ambition — The Wanyamwezi "the coming race."

Oct. 1874. — The foot-note at the bottom of this page will explain all that need be known by the general reader in connection with the geography of the Island of Zanzibar. Any student who wishes to make the island a special study will find books dealing most minutely with the subject at all great libraries. Without venturing, therefore, into more details than I have already given in 'How I found Livingstone,' I shall devote this chapter to the Sultan of Zanzibar — Barghash bin Sayid — the Arabs, the Wangwana, and the Wanyamwezi, with whose aid the objects of the Anglo-American Expedition were attained.

It is impossible not to feel a kindly interest in Prince Barghash, and to wish him complete success in the reforms he is now striving to bring about in his country. Here we see an Arab prince, educated in the strictest school of Islam, and accustomed to regard the black natives of Africa as the lawful prey of conquest or lust, and fair objects of barter, suddenly turning round at the request of European philanthropists and becoming one of the most active opponents of the slave-trade — and the spectacle must necessarily create for him many well-wishers and friends.

Though Prince Barghash has attributed to myself the visit of those ships of war under Admiral Cumming, all who remember that period, and are able, therefore, to trace events, will not fail to perceive that the first decided steps taken by the British Government for the suppression of the slave-trade on the east coast of Africa were due to the influence of Livingstone's constant appeals. Some of his letters, they will remember, were carried by me to England, and the sensation caused by them was such as to compel the British Government to send Sir Bartle Frere in the Enchantress, as a special envoy to Zanzibar, to conclude a treaty with Prince Barghash. When the Prince's reluctance to sign became known, the fleet under Admiral Gumming made its appearance before Zanzibar, and by a process of gentle coercion, or rather quiet demonstration, the signature of the Prince was at last obtained. One thing more, however, still remained to be done before the treaty could be carried into full effect, and that was to eradicate any feeling of discontent or sullenness from his mind which might have been created by the exhibition of force, and this I was happy to see, was effected by the hospitable reception he enjoyed in England in 1875. There was a difference in the manner and tone of the

Sultan of 1874 and of 1877, that I can only attribute to the greater knowledge he had gained of the grandeur of the power which he had so nearly provoked. We must look upon him now as a friendly and, I believe, sincere ally, and as a man willing to do his utmost for the suppression of the slave-trade.

The philanthropist having at last obtained such signal success with the Prince, it is time the merchant should attempt something with him. The Prince must be considered as an independent sovereign. His territories include, besides the Zanzibar, Pemba, and Mafia islands, nearly 1000 miles of coast, and extend probably over an area of 20,000 square miles, with a population of half a million. The products of Zanzibar have enriched many Europeans who traded in them. Cloves, cinnamon, tortoise-shell, pepper, copal gum, ivory, orchilla weed, indiarubber, and hides have been exported for years; but this catalogue does not indicate a tithe of what might be produced by the judicious investment of capital. Those intending to engage in commercial enterprise would do well to study works on Mauritius, Natal, and the Portuguese territories, if they wish to understand what these fine, fertile lands are capable of. The cocoa-nut palm flourishes at Zanzibar and on the mainland, the oil palm thrives luxuriantly in Pemba, and sugar-cane will grow everywhere. Caoutchouc remains undeveloped in the maritime belts of woodland, and the acacia forests, with their wealth of gums, are nearly untouched. Rice is sown on the Rufiji banks, and yields abundantly; cotton would thrive in any of the rich river bottoms; and then there are, besides, the grains, millet, Indian corn, and many others, the cultivation of which, though only in a languid way, the natives understand. The cattle, coffee, and goats of the interior await also the energetic man of capital and the commercial genius.

First, however, the capitalist must find means of carriage, otherwise he will never conquer African difficulties. Cutting roads through jungles, and employing waggons, are mere temporary conveniences, requiring great outlay, patience, and constant reinforcement of work and energies. Almost as fast as the land is cleared, it is covered again — so prolific is the soil — -with tall wild grasses of the thickness of cane, and one season is sufficient to undo the work of months of the pioneer. Cattle die, tormented out of life by the flies or poisoned by the rank grasses; natives perish from want of proper nourishment, and, while suffering from fatigue and debility, are subject to many fatal diseases.

A tramway is one thing that is needed for Africa. All other benefits that can be conferred by contact with civilisation will follow in the wake of the tramway, which will be an iron bond, never to be again broken, between Africa and the more favoured continents.

However energetic the small merchant may be, he can effect nothing permanent for the good of a country that has neither roads nor navigable rivers, whose climate is alike fatal to the starved hamal as it is to the beast of burthen. The maritime belt must first be crossed by an iron road, and another must tap the very centre of the rice-fields of the Rufiji valley, in order to insure cheap, nutritious food in abundance. To a company, however, which can raise the sum required to construct a tramway. East Africa holds out special advantages. The Sultan himself offers a handsome sum, five lakhs of dollars or, roughly, £100,000, and there are rich Hindis at Zanzibar who, no doubt, would invest large sums, and thus the company would become the principal merchants along the line. The Sultan has also poor subjects enough who would be only too glad of the opportunities thus afforded to work for reasonable pay, so that very little fear need be entertained of lack of labour. Besides, there are natives of the interior who, after two or three bold examples, would soon be induced to apply for employment along the line.

Those whom we call the Arabs of Zanzibar are either natives of Muscat who have immigrated thither to seek their fortunes, or descendants of the conquerors of the Portuguese. As the present Sultan calls himself Barghash the son of Sayid, the son of Sultan, the son of Hamid, so all Arabs, from the highest to the lowest of his subjects, are known by their proper names — Ahmed, or Khamis, or Abdullah, as being the sons of Mussoud, of Mustapha, or of Mohammed. Some of them boast of unusually long pedigrees, and one or two I am acquainted with proclaimed themselves of purer and more aristocratic descent than even the Sultan.

The Arab conquerors who accompanied Seyyid Sultan, the grandfather of the present Seyyid Barghash, took unto themselves, after the custom of polygamists, wives of their own race according to their means, and almost all of them purchased negro concubines, the result of which we trace to-day in the various complexions of those who call themselves Arabs. By this process of miscegenation the Arabs of the latest migration are already rapidly losing their rich colour and fine complexions, while the descendants of the Arabs of the first migration are now deteriorated so much that on the coast they can scarcely be distinguished from the Aborigines. While many of the descendants of the old settlers who came in with Seyyid Sultan, still cling to their homesteads, farms, and plantations, and acquire sufficient competence by the cultivation of cloves, cinnamon, oranges, cocoa-nut palms, sugar-cane, and other produce, a great number have emigrated into the interior to form new colonies. Hamed Ibrahim has been eighteen years in Karagwe, Muini Kheri has been thirty years in Ujiji, Sultan bin Ali has been twenty-five years in Unyanyembe, Muini Dugumbi has been eight years in Nyangwe, Juma Merikani has been seven years in Rua, and a number of other prominent Arabs may be cited to prove that, though they themselves firmly believe that they will return to the coast some day, there are too many reasons for believing that they never will.

None of the Arabs in the interior with whom I am acquainted ever proceeded thither with the definite intention of colonisation. Some were driven thither, by false hopes of acquiring rapid fortunes by the purchase of slaves and ivory, and, perceiving that there were worse places on earth than Africa, preferred to remain there, to facing the odium of failure. Others borrowed large sums on trust from credulous Hindis and Banyans, and having failed in the venture now prefer to endure the exclusion to which they have subjected themselves, to returning and being arrested by their enraged creditors. Others again are not merely bankrupts, but persons who have fled the vengeance of the law for political offences, as well as ordinary crimes. There are many who are in better circumstances in the interior than they would be on their own island of Zanzibar. Some of them have hundreds of slaves, and he would be a very poor Arab indeed who possessed only ten. These slaves, under their masters' direction have constructed roomy, comfortable, flat-roofed houses, or lofty cool huts, which, in the dangerous and hostile districts, are surrounded by strong stockades. Thus, at Unyanyembe there are sixty or seventy large stockades enclosing the owner's house and storerooms, as well as the numerous huts of his slaves. Ujiji, again, may be described as a long straggling village, formed by the large tembes of the Arabs; and Nyangwe is another settlement similar to Ujiji. Many of the Arabs settled in the pastoral districts possess large herds of cattle and extensive fields where rice, wheat, Indian corn, and millet are cultivated, besides sugar-cane and onions, and the fruit trees of Zanzibar — the orange, lemon, papaw, mango, and pomegranate — are now being gradually introduced.

The Arabs of Zanzibar, whether from more frequent intercourse with Europeans or from other causes, are undoubtedly the best of their race. More easily amenable to reason than those of Egypt, or the shy, reserved, and bigoted fanatics of Arabia, they offer no obstacles to the European traveller, but are sociable, frank, good-natured, and hospitable. In business they are keen traders, and of course will exact the highest percentage of profit out of the unsuspecting European if they are permitted. They are staunch friends and desperate haters. Blood is seldom satisfied without blood, unless extraordinary sacrifices are made.

The conduct of an Arab gentleman is perfect. Indelicate matters are never broached before strangers; impertinence is hushed instantly by the elders, and rudeness is never permitted. Naturally, they have the vices of their education, blood, and race, but these moral blemishes are by their traditional excellence of breeding seldom obtruded upon the observation of the stranger.

After the Arabs let us regard the Wangwana, just as in Europe, after studying the condition and character of the middle classes, we might turn to reflect upon that of the labouring population.

Of the Wangwana there will be much written in the following pages, the outcome of careful study and a long experience of them. Few explorers have recorded anything greatly to their credit. One of them lately said that the negro knows neither love nor affection; another that he is simply the "link" between the simian and the European. Another says, "The wretches take a trouble and display an ingenuity in opposition and disobedience, in perversity, annoyance, and villainy, which rightly directed would make them invaluable." Almost all have been severe in their strictures on the negro of Zanzibar.

The origin of the Mgwana or Freeman may be briefly told. When the Arabs conquered Zanzibar, they found the black subjects of the Portuguese to be of two classes, Watuma (slaves) and Wangwana (freemen). The Freemen were very probably black people who had either purchased their freedom by the savings of their industry or were made free upon the death of their masters; these begat children who, being born out of bondage, were likewise free. Arab rulers, in classifying their subjects, perceived no great difference in physique or general appearance between those who were slaves and those who were free, both classes belonging originally to the same negro tribes of the interior. Thus, when any of these were brought before the authorities convicted of offences, the question naturally asked was, "Are you a Mtuma, a slave, or a Mgwana, a freeman?" A repetition of these questions through a long course of years established the custom of identifying the two classes of Zanzibar negroes as Watuma — slaves — and Wangwana — freemen. Later, however, came a new distinction, and the word Watuma, except in special and local cases, was dropped, for, with the advent of the free native traders direct from the mainland, and the increase of traffic between Zanzibar and the continent, as well as out of courtesy to their own slaves, the Arabs began to ask the black stranger, "Are you Mgwana, a freeman, or Mshensi, a pagan?" In disputes among themselves the question is still asked, "Are you a slave or a freeman?" but when strangers are involved, it is always, "Are you Mgwana, a freeman or a native of Zanzibar, or a Mshensi, a pagan or an uncircumcised native of the mainland?"

It will be thus seen that the word "Wangwana" is now a generic, widely used, and well understood for the coloured natives of Zanzibar. When, therefore, the term is employed in this book, it includes alike both the slaves and the freemen of Zanzibar.

After nearly seven years' acquaintance with the Wangwana, I have come to perceive that they represent in their character much of the disposition of a large portion of the negro tribes of the continent. I find them capable of great love and affection, and possessed of gratitude and other noble traits of human nature; I know too, that they can be made good, obedient servants, that many are clever, honest, industrious, docile, enterprising, brave and moral; that they are, in short, equal to any other race or colour on the face of the globe, in all the attributes of manhood. But to be able to perceive their worth, the traveller must bring an unprejudiced judgment, a clear, fresh, and patient observation, and must forget that lofty standard of excellence upon which he and his race pride themselves, before he can fairly appreciate the capabilities of the Zanzibar negro. The traveller should not forget the origin of his own race, the condition of the Briton before St. Augustine visited his country, but should rather recall to mind the first state of the "wild Caledonian," and the original circumstances and surroundings of Primitive Man.

Louis Figuier says: "However much our pride may suffer by the idea, we must confess that, at the earliest period of his existence, man could have been but little distinguished from the brute. His pillow was a stone, his roof was the shadow of a wide-spreading tree, or some dark cavern, which also served as a refuge against wild beasts."

And again, in his chapter on the 'Iron Epoch,' he notes how "From the day when iron was first placed at man's disposal, civilisation began to make its longest strides, and as the working of this metal improved, so the dominion of man — his faculties and his intellect — real activity — likewise enlarged in the same proportion." And at the end of a most admirable book, he counsels the traveller, "Look to it, less thy pride cause thee to forget thy own origin."

Being, I hope, free from prejudices of cast, colour, race, or nationality, and endeavouring to pass what I believe to be a just judgment upon the negroes of Zanzibar, I find that they are a people just emerged into the Iron Epoch, and now thrust forcibly under the notice of nations who have left them behind by the improvements of over 4000 years. They possess beyond doubt all the vices of a people still fixed deeply in barbarism, but they understand to the full what and how low such a state is; it is, therefore, a duty imposed upon us by the religion we profess, and by the sacred command of the Son of God, to help them out of the deplorable state they are now in. At any rate, before we begin to hope for the improvement of races so long benighted, let us leave off this impotent bewailing of their vices, and endeavour to discover some of the virtues they possess as men, for it must be by the aid of their virtues, and not by their vices, that the missionary of civilisation can ever hope to assist them. While, therefore, recording my experiences through Africa, I shall have frequent occasion to dilate upon both the vices and the virtues of the Wangwana as well as of the natives of the interior, but it will not be with a view to foster, on the one hand, the self-deception of the civilised, or the absurd prejudices created by centuries of superior advantages, nor, on the other hand, to lead men astray by taking a too bright view of things. I shall write solely and simply with a strong desire to enable all interested in the negro to understand his mental and moral powers rightly.

The Mgwana or native of Zanzibar, who dwells at Ngambu, is a happy, jovial soul. He is fond of company, therefore sociable. His vanity causes him to be ambitious of possessing several white shirts and bright red caps, and since he has observed that his superiors use walking-sticks, he is almost certain, if he is rich enough to own a white shirt and a red cap, to be seen sporting a light cane. The very poorest of his class hire themselves, or are hired out by their masters, to carry bales, boxes, and goods, from the custom-house to the boat, or store-room, or vice versa, and as a general beast of burden, for camels are few, and of wheeled vehicles there are none. Those who prefer light work and have good characters may obtain positions as doorkeepers or house-servants, or for washing copal and drying hides for the European merchants. Others, trained as mechanics, obtain a livelihood by repairing muskets, manufacturing knives, belts, and accoutrements, or by carpentering and ship-building. There is a class of Wangwana living at Ngambu, in the small gardens of the interior of the island, and along the coast of the mainland, who prefer the wandering life offered to them by Arab traders and scientific expeditions to being subject to the caprice, tyranny, and meanness of small estate proprietors. They complain that the Arabs are haughty, grasping, and exacting; that they abuse them and pay them badly; that, if they seek justice at the hands of the Cadis, judgment, somehow, always goes against them. They say, on the other hand, that, when accompanying trading or other expeditions, they are well paid, have abundance to eat, and comparatively but little work.

But the highest ambition of a Mgwana is to have a house and shamba or garden of his own. The shamba may only be large enough to possess a dozen cocoa-nut-trees, a dozen rows, thirty yards long, of cassava shrubs, half-a-dozen banana plants, half-a-dozen rows planted with sweet-potatoes, and two or three rows of ground-nuts; nevertheless, this would be his garden or estate, and therefore of priceless estimation. At one corner of this tiny but most complete estate, he would erect his house, with an exclusive courtyard, which he would stock with half-a-dozen chickens and one goat, which last he would be sure to spoil with kindness. Three hundred dollars would probably be the total value of house, garden, chickens, goat, domestic utensils, tools, and all, and yet, with this property, he would be twice married, the father of four or five children, and even the owner of a domestic slave or two. If such be his condition, he will snap his fingers at the cruel world, and will imagine himself as prosperous, well-to-do, and comfortable as any Arab in Zanzibar. But he is seldom spoiled by this great prosperity. He is a sociable, kindly-disposed man, and his frank, hearty nature has won for him hosts of friends. Beer made of fermented mtama or Indian corn, wine of the palm or cocoa-nut milk, or the stronger eau de vie sold by the Goanese in the town at twenty -five cents the bottle, serve to diffuse and cement these friendships.

It is to the Wangwana that Livingstone, Burton, Speke and Grant owe, in great part, the accomplishment of their objects, and while in the employ of these explorers, this race rendered great services to geography. From a considerable distance north of the Equator down to the Zambezi and across Africa to Benguella and the mouth of the Livingstone, they have made their names familiar to tribes who, but for the Wangwana, would have remained ignorant to this day of all things outside their own settlements. They possess with many weaknesses, many fine qualities. While very superstitious, easily inclined to despair, and readily giving ear to vague, unreasonable fears, they may also, by judicious management, be induced to laugh at their own credulity and roused to a courageous attitude; to endure like Stoics, and fight like heroes. It will depend altogether upon the leader of a body of such men whether their worst or best qualities shall prevail.

There is another class coming into notice from the interior of Africa, who, though of a sterner nature, will, I am convinced, as they are better known, become greater favourites than the Wangwana. I refer to the Wanyamwezi, or the natives of Unyamwezi, and the Wasukuma, or the people of Usukuma. Naturally, being a grade less advanced towards civilization than the Wangwana, they are not so amenable to discipline as the latter. While explorers would in the present state of acquaintance prefer the Wangwana as escort, the Wanyamwezi are far superior as porters. Their greater freedom from diseases, their great strength and endurance, the pride they take in their profession of porters, prove them born travellers of incalculable use and benefit to Africa. If kindly treated, I do not know more docile and good-natured creatures. But the discipline must not be strict, until they have had opportunities of understanding their employer's nature and habits, and of comprehending that discipline does not mean abuse. Their courage they have repeatedly proved under their Napoleonic leader Mirambo, in many a well-fought field against the Arabs and Wangwana. Their skill in war, tenacity of purpose, and determination to defend the rights of their elected chief against foreigners, have furnished themes for song to the bards of Central Africa. Tippu-Tib has led 500 of these men through distant Bisa and the plains of Rua: Juma Merikani has been escorted by them into the heart of the regions beyond the Tanganika: Khamis bin Adallah commanded a large force of them in his search for ivory in the intra-lake countries. The English discoverer of Lake Tanganika and, finally, I myself have been equally indebted to them, both on my first and last expeditious.

From their numbers, and their many excellent qualities, I am led to think that the day will come when they will be regarded as something better than the "best of pagazis;" that they will be esteemed as the good subjects of some enlightened power, who will train them up as the nucleus of a great African nation, as powerful for the good of the Dark Continent, as they threaten, under the present condition of things, to be for its evil.

CHAPTER III.

Organisation of the Expedition — The shauri — "Poli, poli" — Msenna's
successful imposture — Black sheep in the flock — The Lady Alice
remodelled — Sewing a British flag — Tarya Topan, the millionaire —
Signing the covenants — "On the word of a white man" — Saying good-bye
— Loading the dhows — Vale! — Towards the Dark Continent.

Nov. 1874. — It is a most sobering employment, the organizing of an African
expedition. You are constantly engaged, mind and body; now in casting up
accounts, and now travelling to and fro hurriedly to receive messengers, inspecting
purchases, bargaining with keen-eyed, relentless Hindi merchants, writing
memoranda, haggling over extortionate prices, packing up a multitude of small
utilities, pondering upon your lists of articles, wanted, purchased, and
unpurchased, groping about in the recesses of a highly exercised imagination for
what you ought to purchase, and cannot do without, superintending, arranging,
assorting, and packing. And this under a temperature of 95° Fahr.

In the midst of all this terrific, high-pressure exercise arrives the first batch of
applicants for employment. For it has long ago been bruited abroad that I am ready
to enlist all able-bodied human beings willing to carry a load, be they Wangwana
or Wanyamwezi, Wagalla, Somali, Wasagara, Wayow, Wajindo, Wagogo, or
Wazaramo. Ever since I arrived at Zanzibar, since which date I have been absent
exploring the Rufiji river, I have had a very good reputation among Arabs and
Wangwana. They have not forgotten that it was I who found the "old white man"
— Livingstone — in Ujiji, nor that liberality and kindness to my men were my
special characteristics. They have also, with the true Oriental spirit of
exaggeration, proclaimed that I was but a few months absent; and that, after this
brief excursion, they returned to their homes to enjoy the liberal pay awarded
them, feeling rather the better for the trip than otherwise. This unsought-for
reputation brought on me the laborious task of selecting proper men out of an
extra-ordinary number of applicants. Almost all the cripples, the palsied, the
consumptive, and the superannuated that Zanzibar could furnish applied to be
enrolled on the muster list, but these, subjected to a searching examination, were
refused. Hard upon their heels came all the roughs, rowdies, and ruffians of the
island, and these, schooled by their fellows, were not so easily detected. Slaves
were also refused, as being too much under the influence and instruction of their
masters, and yet many were engaged of whose character I had not the least
conception until, months afterwards, I learned from their quarrels in the camp how
I had been misled by the clever rogues.

All those who bore good characters on the Search Expedition, and had been despatched to the assistance of Livingstone, in 1872, were employed without delay. Out of these the chiefs were selected: these were, Manwa Sera, Chowpereh, Wadi Rehani, Kacheche, Zaidi, Chakanja, Farjalla, Wadi Safeni, Bukhet, Mabruki Manyapara, Mabruki Unyanyembe, Muini Pembe, Ferahan, Bwana Muri, Khamseen, Mabruki Speke, Simba, Gardner, Hamoidah, Zaidi Mganda, and Ulimengo.

But before real business could be entered into, the customary present had to be distributed to each.

Ulimengo, or the World, the incorrigible joker and hunter-in-chief of the Search and Livingstone's expeditions, received a gold ring to encircle one of his thick black fingers, and a silver chain to suspend round his neck, which caused his mouth to expand gratefully. Rojab, who was soon reminded of the unlucky accident with Livingstone's Journal in the muddy waters of the Mukondokwa, was endowed with a munificent gift which won him over to my service beyond fear of bribery. Manwa Sera, the redoubtable ambassador of Speke and Grant to Manwa Sera — the royal fugitive distressed by the hot pursuit of the Arabs — the leader of my second caravan in 1871, the chief of the party sent to Unyamyembe to the assistance of Livingstone in 1872, and now appointed Chief Captain of the Anglo-American Expedition, was rendered temporarily speechless with gratitude because I had suspended a splendid jet necklace from his neck, and ringed one of his fingers with a heavy seal ring. The historical Mabruki Speke, called by one of my predecessors "Mabruki the Bull-headed," who has each time in the employ of European explorers conducted himself with matchless fidelity, and is distinguished for his hawk-eyed guardianship of their property and interests, exhibited extravagant rapture at the testimonial for past services bestowed on him; while the valiant, faithful, sturdy Chowpereh, the man of manifold virtues, was rewarded for his former worth with a silver dagger, gilt bracelet, and earrings. His wife was also made happy with a suitable gift, and the heir of the Chowpereh estate, a child of two years, was, at his father's urgent request, rendered safe by vaccine from any attack of the small-pox during our absence in Africa.

All great enterprises require a preliminary deliberative palaver, or, as the Wangwana call it, "Shauri." In East Africa particularly shauris are much in vogue. Precipitate, energetic action is dreaded. "Poli, poli!" or "Gently!" is the warning word of caution given.

The chiefs arranged themselves in a semi-circle on the day of the shauri, and I sat a la Turque fronting them. "What is it, my friends? Speak your minds." They hummed and hawed, looked at one another, as if on their neighbours' faces they might discover the purport of their coming, but, all hesitating to begin, finally broke down in a loud laugh.

Manwa Sera, always grave, unless hit dexterously with a joke, hereupon affected anger, and said, "You speak, son of Safeni; verily we act like children! Will the master eat us?"

Wadi, son of Safeni, thus encouraged to perform the spokesman's duty, hesitates exactly two seconds, and then ventures with diplomatic blandness and graciosity. "We have come, master, with words. Listen. It is well we should know every step before we leap. A traveller journeys not without knowing whither he wanders. We have come to ascertain what lands you are bound for."

Imitating the son of Safeni's gracious blandness, and his low tone of voice, as though the information about to be imparted to the intensely interested and eagerly listening group were too important to speak it loud, I described in brief outline the prospective journey, in broken Kiswahili. As country after country was mentioned of which they had hitherto but vague ideas, and river after river, lake after lake named, all of which I hoped with their trusty aid to explore carefully, various ejaculations expressive of wonder and joy, mixed with a little alarm, broke from their lips, but when I concluded, each of the group drew a long breath, and almost simultaneously they uttered admiringly, "Ah, fellows, this is a journey worthy to be called a journey!"

"But, master," said they, after recovering themselves, "this long journey will take years to travel — six, nine, or ten years." "Nonsense," I replied. "Six, nine, or ten years! What can you be thinking of? It takes the Arabs nearly three years to reach Ujiji, it is true, but, if you remember, I was but sixteen months from Zanzibar to Ujiji and back. Is it not so?" "Ay, true," they answered. "Very well, and I assure you I have not come to live in Africa. I have come simply to see those rivers and lakes, and after I have seen them to return home." "Ah, but you know the old master, Livingstone," rejoined Hamoidah, who had followed the veteran traveller nearly eight years, "said he was only going for two years, and you know that he never came back, but died there." "That is true enough, but if I were quick on the first journey, am I likely to be slow now? Am I much older than I was then? Am I less strong? Do I not know what travel is now? Was I not like a boy then, and am I not now a man? You remember while going to Ujiji I permitted the guide to show the way, but when we were returning who was it that led the way? Was it not I, by means of that little compass which could not be like the guide?" "Ay, true, master, true every word." "Very well, then, let us finish the shauri, and go. To-morrow we will make a proper agreement before the consul;" and in Scriptural phrase, "they forthwith arose and did as they were commanded."

Upon receiving information from the coast that there was a very large number of men waiting for me, I became still more fastidious in my choice. But with all my care and gift of selection, I was mortified to discover that many faces and characters had baffled the rigorous scrutiny to which I had subjected them, and that some scores of the most abandoned and depraved characters on the island had been enlisted by me on the Expedition. One man, named Msenna, imposed upon me by assuming such a contrite penitent look, and weeping such copious tears, when I informed him that he had too bad a character to be employed, that my good-nature was prevailed upon to accept his services, upon the understanding that, if he indulged his murderous propensities in Africa, I should return him chained the entire distance to Zanzibar, to be dealt with by his Prince.

The defence of his conduct was something like this: "Bwana, you see these scars on my head and neck. They are from the sabres of the Seyyid's soldiers. Demand of any, Arab or Freeman, why I received them. They will tell you they were inflicted for rebellion against Prince Majid at Melinda. The Arabs hate me because I joined the coast men against their authority. Can any one charge me with worse deeds?" — appealing to the Wangwana. All were silent. "I am a free-born son of the coast, and never did any man or woman who did not molest me the smallest injury. Allah be praised! I am strong, healthy, and contented with my lot, and if you take me you will never have cause to regret it. If you fear that I shall desert, give me no advance pay, but pay me when I come back to Zanzibar according to my deserts."

This appeal was delivered with impassioned accents and lively gestures, which produced a great effect upon the mixed audience who listened to him, and gathering from their faces more than from my own convictions, that poor scarred Msenna was a kind of political refugee, much abused and very much misunderstood, his services were accepted, and as he appeared to be an influential man, he was appointed a junior captain with prospects of promotion and higher pay.

Subsequently, however, on the shores of Lake Victoria it was discovered — -for in Africa people are uncommonly communicative — that Msenna had murdered eight people, that he was a ruffian of the worst sort, and that the merchants of Zanzibar had experienced great relief when they heard that the notorious Msenna was about to bid farewell for a season to the scene of so many of his wild exploits. Msenna was only one of many of his kind, but I have given in detail the manner of his enlistment that my position may be better understood.

Soon after my return from the Rufiji delta, the B. I. S. N. Company's steamer Euphrates had brought the sectional exploring boat, Lady Alice, to Zanzibar. Exceedingly anxious for the portability of the sections, I had them at once, weighed, and great were my vexation and astonishment when I discovered that four of the sections weighed 280 lbs. each, and that one weighed 310 lbs.! She was, it is true, a marvel of workmanship, and an exquisite model of a boat, such, indeed, as few builders in England or America could rival, but in her present condition her carriage through the jungles would necessitate a pioneer force a hundred strong to clear the impediments and obstacles on the road.

While almost plunged into despair, I was informed that there was a very clever English carpenter, named Ferris, about to leave by the Euphrates for England. Mr. Ferris was quickly made acquainted with my difficulty, and for a "consideration" promised, after a personal inspection of the boat, to defer his departure one month, and to do his utmost to make the sections portable without lessening her efficiency. When the boat was exhibited to him, I explained that the narrowness of the path would make her portage absolutely impossible, for since the path was often only 18 inches wide in Africa, and hemmed in on each side with dense jungle, any package 6 feet broad could by no means be conveyed along it. It was therefore necessary that each of the four sections should be subdivided, by which means I should obtain eight portable sections, each three feet wide, and that an afterpiece could easily be made by myself upon arriving at the lakes. Mr. Ferris, perfectly comprehending his instructions, and with the aid given by the young Pococks, furnished me within two weeks with the newly modelled Lady Alice. But it must be understood that her success as a safe exploring boat is due to the conscientious workmanship which the honest and thoroughly reliable boat-builder of Teddington lavished upon her.

The pride which the young Pococks and Frederick Barker entertained in respect to their new duties, in the new and novel career of adventure now opening before them, did not seem to damp that honourable love of country which every Englishman abroad exhibits, and is determined to gratify if he can. Their acquaintance with the shipwright, Mr. Ferris, who had evidently assisted at the ceremony of planting the British flag at the mast-head of many a new and noble structure, destined to plough strange seas, reminded them, during one of the social evening hours which they spent together, that it would be a fine thing if they might also be permitted to hoist a miniature emblem of their nationality over their tent in camp, and over their canoes on the lakes and rivers of Africa.

The Pococks and Barker accordingly, a few days before our departure, formed themselves into a deputation, and Frank, who was the spokesman, surprised me with the following request: —

"My brother, Fred Barker, and myself. Sir, have been emboldened to ask you a favour, which no doubt you will think strange and wrong. But we cannot forget, wherever we go, that we are Englishmen, and we should like to be permitted to take something with us that will always remind us of who we are, and be a comfort to us, even in the darkest hours of trouble, perhaps even encourage us to perform our duties better. We have come to ask you, Sir, if we may be permitted to make a small British flag to hoist above our tent, and over our canoe on the lakes."

"My dear fellow," I replied, "you surprise me by imagining for one moment that I could possibly refuse you. This is not an American Government or a British Government Expedition, and I have neither the power nor the disposition to withhold my sanction to your request. If it will be any pleasure to you, by all means take it, I cannot have the slightest objection to such an innocent proceeding. All that I shall require from you in Africa is such service as you can give, and if you prove yourselves the highly recommended lads you are, I shall not interfere with any innocent pleasure you may feel yourselves at liberty to take. If one British flag is not enough, you may take a thousand so far as I am concerned."

"Thank you kindly. Sir. You may rest assured that we have entered your service with the intention to remember what my old father and our friends strictly enjoined us to do, which was to stick to you through thick and thin."

The young Englishmen were observed soon afterwards busy sewing a tiny flag, about 18 inches square, out of some bunting, and after a pattern that Mr. Ferris procured for them. Whether the complicated colours, red, blue, white, were arranged properly, or the crosses according to the standard, I am ignorant. But I observed that, while they were occupied in the task, they were very much interested, and that, when it was finished, though it was only the size of a lady's handkerchief, they manifested much delight.

Zanzibar possesses its "millionaires" also, and one of the richest merchants in the town is Tarya Topan — a self-made man of Hindustan, singularly honest and just; a devout Muslim, yet liberal in his ideas; a sharp business man, yet charitable. I made Tarya's acquaintance in 1871, and the righteous manner in which he then dealt by me caused me now to proceed to him again for the same purpose as formerly, viz. to sell me cloth, cottons, and kanikis, at reasonable prices, and accept my bills on Mr. Joseph M. Levy, of the Daily Telegraph.

Honest Jetta, as formerly, was employed as my vakeel to purchase the various coloured cloths, fine and coarse, for chiefs and their wives, as well as a large assortment of beads of all sizes, forms, and colours, besides a large quantity of brass wire 1/8 inch in thickness.

The total weight of goods, cloth, beads, wire, stores, medicine, bedding, clothes, tents, ammunition, boat, oars, rudder and thwarts, instruments and stationery, photographic apparatus, dry plates, and miscellaneous articles too numerous to mention, weighed a little over 18,000 lbs., or rather more than 8 tons divided as nearly as possible into loads weighing 60 lbs. each, and requiring therefore the carrying capacity of 300 men. The loads were made more than usually light, in order that we might travel with celerity, and not fatigue the people.

But still further to provide against sickness and weakness, a supernumerary force of forty men were recruited at Bagamoyo, Konduchi, and the Rufiji delta, who were required to assemble in the neighbourhood of the first-mentioned place. Two hundred and thirty men, consisting of Wangwana, Wanyamwezi, and coast people from Mombasa, Tanga, and Saadani, affixed their marks opposite their names before the American Consul, for wages varying from 2 to 10 dollars per month, and rations according to their capacity, strength, and intelligence, with the understanding that they were to serve for two years, or until such time as their services should be no longer required in Africa, and were to perform their duties cheerfully and promptly.

On the day of "signing" the contract, each adult received an advance of 20 dollars, or four months' pay, and each youth 10 dollars, or four months' pay.

Ration money was also paid them from the time of first enlistment, at the rate of 1 dollar per week, up to the day we left the coast. These conditions were, however, not entered into without requiring the presence of each person's friends and relatives to witness and sanction the engagements, so that on this day the parents, uncles, cousins, and near and distant relatives, wives and children, were in attendance, and crowded every room and court at the American Consulate. The entire amount disbursed in cash for advances of pay and rations at Zanzibar and Bagamoyo was 6260 dollars, or nearly £1300,

The obligations, however, were not all on one side. Besides the due payment to them of their wages on demand, and selling them such cloths as they would require for dress while in Africa at reasonable prices, which would be a little above cost price at Zanzibar, I was compelled to bind myself to them, on the word of an "honourable white man," to observe the following conditions as to conduct towards them: —

1st. That I should treat them kindly, and be patient with them.

2nd. That in case of sickness, I should dose them with proper medicine, and see them nourished with the best the country afforded. That if patients were unable to proceed, they should not be abandoned to the mercy of heathen, but were to be conveyed to such places as should be considered safe for their persons and their freedom, and convenient for their return, on convalescence, to their friends. That with all patients thus left behind, I should leave sufficient cloth or beads to pay the native practitioner for his professional attendance, and for the support of the patient.

3rd. That in cases of disagreement between man and man, I should judge justly, honestly, and impartially. That I should do my utmost to prevent the ill-treatment of the weak by the strong, and never permit the oppression of those unable to resist.

4th. That I should act like a "father and mother" to them, and to the best of my ability resist all violence offered to them by "savage natives, and roving and lawless banditti."

They also promised, upon the above conditions being fulfilled, that they would do their duty like men, would honour and respect my instructions, giving me their united support and endeavouring to the best of their ability to be faithful servants, and would never desert me in the hour of need. In short, that they would behave like good and loyal children, and "may the blessing of God," said they, "be upon us."

How we kept this bond of mutual trust and forbearance, and adhered to each other in the hours of sore trouble and distress, faithfully performing our duties to one another: how we encouraged and sustained, cheered and assisted one another, and in all the services and good offices due from man to man, and comrade to comrade, from chief to servants and from servants to chief, how we kept our plighted word of promise, will be best seen in the following chapters, which record the strange and eventful story of our journeys.

Nov. 12. — The fleet of six Arab vessel's which were to bear us away to the west across the Zanzibar Sea were at last brought to anchor a few yards from the wharf of the American Consulate. The day of farewell calls had passed, and ceremoniously we had bidden adieu to the hospitable and courteous Acting British Consul, Captain William F. Prideaux, and his accomplished wife, to friendly and amiable Dr. James Robb and Mrs. Robb, to Dr. Kiddle, and the German and French Consuls. Seyyid Barghash bin Sayid received my thanks for his courtesy, and his never-failing kindness, and my sincere wishes for his lasting prosperity and happiness. Many kind Arab and Hindi friends also received my parting salaams. Grave Sheikh Hashid expressed a hope that we should meet again on earth, Captain Bukhet, the pilot, wished me a quick and safe return from the dread lands of the heathen, and the princely Indian merchant, Tarya Topan, expressed his sincere hopes that I should be prosperous in my undertaking, and come back crowned with success.

The young Englishmen, whose charming, simple manners and manly bearing had won for them a number of true friends at Zanzibar, were not without many hearty well-wishers, and received cheerful farewells from numerous friends.

At the end of Ramadan, the month of abstinence of Mohammedans, the Wangwana, true to their promise that they would be ready, appeared with their bundles and mats, and proceeded to take their places in the vessels waiting for them. As their friends had mustered in strong: force to take their final parting and bestow last useful hints and prudent advice, it was impossible to distinguish among the miscellaneous crowd on the beach those who were present, or to discover who were absent. The greater part of my company were in high spirits, and from this I inferred that they had not forgotten to fortify themselves with stimulants against the critical moment of departure.

As fast as each dhow was reported to be filled, the Nakhuda or Captain was directed to anchor further off shore to await the signal to sail. By 5 P.M. of the 12th of November, 224 men had responded to their names, and five of the Arab vessels, laden with the personnel, cattle, and materiel of the expedition, were impatiently waiting with anchor heaved short, the word of command. One vessel still lay close ashore, to convey myself, and Frederick Barker — in charge of the personal servants — our baggage, and dogs. Turning round to my constant and well-tried friend, Mr. Augustus Sparhawk, I fervently clasped his hand, and with a full heart though halting tongue, attempted to pour out my feelings of gratitude for his kindness and long sustained hospitality, my keen regret at parting and hopes of meeting again. But I was too agitated to be eloquent, and all my forced gaiety could not carry me through the ordeal. So we parted in almost total silence, but I felt assured that he would judge my emotions by his own feelings, and would accept the lame efforts at their expression as though he had listened to the most voluble rehearsal of thanks.

A wave of my hand, and the anchors were hove up and laid within ship, and then, hoisting our latéen sails, we bore away westward to launch ourselves into the arms of Fortune. Many wavings of kerchiefs and hats, parting signals from white hands, and last long looks at friendly white faces, final confused impressions of the grouped figures of our well-wishers, and then the evening breeze had swept us away into mid-sea beyond reach of recognition.

The parting is over! We have said our last words for years, perhaps for ever, to kindly men! The sun sinks fast to the western horizon, and gloomy is the twilight that now deepens and darkens. Thick shadows fall upon the distant land and over the silent sea, and oppress our throbbing, regretful hearts, as we glide away through the dying light towards The Dark Continent.

CHAPTER IV.

Bagamoyo — Taming the dark brother — Bagamoyo in a ferment — An exciting scene — The disturbance quelled — The Universities Mission, its origin, history, decline and present condition — The Rev. Edward Steere — Notre Dame de Bagamoyo — Westward ho! — In marching order — Sub Jose ferrido — Crossing the Kingani — The stolen women.

Bagamoyo, Whindi, and Saadani, East African villages on the mainland near the sea, offer exceptionally good starting points for the unexplored interior, for many reasons. First. Because the explorers and the people are strangers to one another, and a slight knowledge of their power of mutual cohesion, habits, and relative influences, is desirable before launching out into the wilds. Second. The natives of those maritime villages are accustomed to have their normally languid and peaceful life invaded and startled by the bustle of foreigners arriving by sea and from the continent, Arab traders bound for the interior and lengthy native caravans from Unyamwezi. Third, An expedition not fully recruited to its necessary strength at Zanzibar may be easily reinforced at these ports by volunteers from native caravans who are desirous of returning to their homes, and who, day by day, along the route, will straggle in towards it until the list is full and complete.

These, then, were the principal reasons for my selection of Bagamoyo as the initial point, from whence, after inoculating the various untamed spirits who had now enlisted under me, with a respect for order and discipline, obedience and system (the true prophylactic against failure) I should be free to rove where discoveries would be fruitful. This "inoculation" will not, however, commence until after a study of their natures, their deficiencies and weaknesses. The exhibition of force, at this juncture, would be dangerous to our prospects, and all means gentle, patient, and persuasive, have, therefore, to be tried first. Whatever deficiencies, weaknesses, and foibles the people may develop must be so manipulated that, while they are learning the novel lesson of obedience, they may only just suspect that behind all this there lies the strong unbending force which will eventually make men of them, wild things though they now are. For the first few months, then, forbearance is absolutely necessary. The dark brother, wild as a colt, chafing, restless, ferociously impulsive, superstitiously timid, liable to furious demonstrations, suspicious and unreasonable, must be forgiven seventy times seven, until the period of probation is passed. Long before this period is over, such temperate conduct will have enlisted a powerful force, attached to their leader by bonds of good-will and respect, even, perhaps, of love and devotion, and by the moral influence of their support even the most incorrigible mauvais sujet will be restrained, and finally conquered.

Many things will transpire during the first few weeks which will make the explorer sigh and wish that he had not ventured upon what promises to be a hopeless task. Maddened by strong drinks and drugs, jealous of their status in the camp, regretting also, like ourselves, that they had been so hasty in undertaking the journey, brooding over the joys of the island fast receding from them, anxious for the future, susceptible to the first and every influence that assails them with temptations to return to the coast, these people require to be treated with the utmost kindness and consideration, and the intending traveller must be wisely circumspect in his intercourse with them. From my former experiences of such men, it will be readily believed that I had prepared for the scenes which I knew were to follow at Bagamoyo, and that all my precautions had been taken.

Nov. 13. — Upon landing at Bagamoyo on the morning of the 13th, we marched to occupy the old house where we had stayed so long to prepare the First Expedition. The goods were stored, the dogs chained up, the riding asses tethered, the rifles arrayed in the store-room, and the sectional boat laid under a roof close by, on rollers, to prevent injury from the white ants — a precaution which, I need hardly say, we had to observe throughout our journey. Then some more ration money, sufficient for ten days, had to be distributed among the men, the young Pococks were told off to various camp duties to initiate them to exploring life in Africa, and then after the first confusion of arrival had subsided, I began to muster the new engages.

But within three hours Bagamoyo was in a ferment. "The white man has brought all the robbers, ruffians, and murderers of Zanzibar to take possession of the town," was the rumour that ran wildly through all the streets, lanes, courts, and bazaars. Men with bloody faces, wild, bloodshot eyes, bedraggled, rumpled and torn dresses, reeled up to our orderly and nearly silent quarters clamouring for rifles and ammunition. Arabs with drawn swords, and sinewy Baluchis with matchlocks and tinder ready to be ignited, came up threatening, and, following them, a miscellaneous rabble of excited men, while, in the background, seethed a mob of frantic women and mischievous children.

"What is the matter?" I asked, scarcely knowing how to begin to calm this turbulent mass of passionate beings.

"Matter!" was echoed. "What is the matter?" was repeated. "Matter enough. The town is in an uproar. Your men are stealing, murdering, robbing goods from the stores, breaking plates, killing our chickens, assaulting everybody, drawing knives on our women after abusing them, and threatening to burn the town and exterminate everybody. Matter indeed! matter enough! What do you mean by bringing this savage rabble from Zanzibar?" So fumed and sputtered an Arab of some consequence among the magnates of Bagamoyo.

"Dear me, my friend, this is shocking; terrible. Pray sit down, and be patient. Sit down here by me, and let us talk this over like wise men," I said in soothing tones to this enfant terrible, for he really looked in feature, dress, and demeanour, what, had I been an imaginative raw youth, I should have set down as the "incarnate scourge of Africa," and he looked wicked enough with his bare, sinewy arms, his brandished sword, and fierce black eyes, to chop off my innocent head.

The Arab, with a short nod, accepted my proposition and seated himself. "We are about to have a Shauri — a consultation." "Hush there! Silence!" "Words!" "Shauri!" "Words — open your ears!" "Slaves!" "Fools!" "List, Arabs!" "You Baluch there, rein in your tongue!" &c. &c., cried out a wild mixture of voices in a strange mixture of tongues, commanding, or imploring, silence.

The Arab was requested to speak, and to point out, if he knew them, the Wangwana guilty of provoking such astonishing disorder. In an indignant and eloquent strain he rehearsed his special complaint. A man named Mustapha had come to his shop drunk, and had abused him like a low blackguard, and then, snatching up a bolt of cotton cloth, had run away with it, but, being pursued and caught, had drawn a knife, and was about to stab him, when a friend of his opportunely clubbed the miscreant and thus saved his life. By the mouths of several witnesses the complaint was proved, and Mustapha was therefore arrested, disarmed of his knife, and locked up in the dark strong-room, to reflect on his crimes in solitude. Loud approval greeted the sentence.

"Who else?"

A score of people of both sexes advanced towards me with their complaints, and it seemed as though silence could never be restored, but by dint of threatening to leave the burzah from sheer despair, quietness was restored. It is unnecessary to detail the several charges made against them, or to describe the manner of conviction, but, after three hours, peace reigned in Bagamoyo once more, and over twenty of the Wangwana had been secured and impounded in the several rooms of the house, with a dozen of their comrades standing guard over them.

To avoid a repetition of this terrible scene, I despatched a messenger with a polite request to the Governor, Sheikh Mansur bin Suliman, that he would arrest and punish all disorderly Wangwana in my service, as justice should require, but I am sorry to say that the Wali (governor) took such advantage of this request that few of the Wangwana who showed their faces in the streets next day escaped violence. Acting on the principle that desperate diseases require desperate remedies, over thirty had been chained and beaten, and many others had escaped abuse of power only by desperate flight from the myrmidons of the now vengeful sheikh.

Another message was therefore sent to the Governor, imploring him to be as lenient as possible, consistent with equitable justice, and explaining to him the nature and cause of these frantic moods and ebullitions of temper on the part of the Wangwana. I attempted to define to him what "sprees" were, explaining that all men, about to undergo a long absence from their friends and country, thought they were entitled to greater freedom at such a period, but that some weak-headed men, with a natural inclination to be vicious, had, in indulging this privilege, encroached upon the privileges of others, and that hence arose collision and confusion. But the Governor waxed still more tyrannical: beatings, chainings, and extortionate exactions became more frequent and unbearable, until at last the Wangwana appeared in a body before me, and demanded another "Shauri."

The result of this long consultation — after an earnest protest from me against their wild conduct, calculated, as I told them, to seriously compromise me, followed by expostulation with them on their evil course, and a warning that I felt more like abetting the Governor in his treatment of them than seeking its amelioration — was an injunction to be patient and well-behaved during our short stay, and a promise that I would lead them into Africa within two days, when at the first camp pardon should be extended to all, and a new life would be begun in mutual peace and concord, to continue, I hoped, until our return to the sea.

There is an institution at Bagamoyo which ought not to be passed over without remark, but the subject cannot be properly dealt with until I have described the similar institution, of equal importance, at Zanzibar, viz. the Universities Mission. Besides, I have three pupils of the Universities Mission who are about to accompany me into Africa — Robert Feruzi, Andrew, and Dallington. Robert is a stout lad of eighteen years old, formerly a servant to one of the members of Lieutenant Cameron's Expedition, but discharged at Unyanyembe, for not very clear reasons, to find his way back. Andrew is a strong youth of nineteen years, rather reserved, and, I should say, not of a very bright disposition. Dallington is much younger, probably only fifteen, with a face strongly pitted with traces of a violent attack of small-pox, but as bright and intelligent as any boy of his age, white or black.

The Universities Mission is the result of the sensation caused in England by Livingtone's discoveries on the Zambezi and of Lakes Nyassa and Shirwa. It was despatched by the Universities of Oxford and Cambridge in the year 1860, and consisted of Bishop Mackenzie, formerly Archdeacon of Natal, and the Rev. Messrs. Proctor, Scudamore, Burrup, and Rowley. These devoted gentlemen reached the Zambezi river in February 1861.

When the Universities Mission met Livingstone, then engaged in the practical work of developing the discovery of the Zambezi and other neighbouring waters, a consultation was held as to the best locality for mission work to begin at. The Bishop and his followers were advised by Livingstone to ascend the Rovuma river, and march thence overland to some selected spot on Lake Nyassa. But, upon attempting the project, the river was discovered to be falling, and too shallow to admit of such a steamer as the Pioneer, and as much sickness had broken out on board, the Mission sailed to the Comoro Islands to recruit. In July 1861 they reached the foot of the Murchison Cataracts on the Shire. Soon after, while proceeding overland, they encountered a caravan of slaves, whom they liberated, with a zeal that was commendable though impolitic. Subsequently, other slaves were forcibly detained from the caravans until the number collected amounted to 148, and with these the missionaries determined to begin their holy work.

While establishing its quarters at Magomero, the Mission was attacked by the Ajawas; but the reverend gentlemen and their pupils drove off the enemy. Shortly after this, a difference of opinion arising with Livingstone as to the proper policy to be pursued, the latter departed to pursue his explorations, and the Bishop and his party continued to prosecute their work with every promise of success. But in its zeal for the suppression of the slave-trade, the Mission made alliance with the Manganjas, and joined with them in a war against the Ajawas, whom they afterwards discovered to be really a peaceable people. Thus was the character of the Mission almost changed by the complicated politics of the native tribes in which they had meddled without forethought of the consequences. Then came the rainy season with its unhealthiness and fatal results. Worn out with fever and privations, poor Bishop Mackenzie died, and in less than a month the Rev. Mr. Burrup followed him. Messrs. Scudamore, Dickinson, and Rowley removed the Mission to the banks of the Shire, where the two former died, and the few remaining survivors, despairing of success, soon left the country, and the Universities Mission to Central Africa became only a name with which the succeeding Bishop, the Rev. Mr. Tozer, continued to denominate his Mission at Zanzibar.

Nor is the record of this hitherto unfortunate and struggling Mission in the city of Zanzibar, with access to luxuries and comforts, brighter or more assuring than it was at primitive Magomero, surrounded by leagues of fen and morass. Many noble souls of both sexes perished, and the good work seemed far from hopeful. I am reminded, as I write these words, of my personal acquaintance with the venerable figure of Pennell, and the young and ardent West. The latter was alive in 1874, full of ardour, hope, and zealous devotion. When I returned, he had gone the way of his brother martyrs of the Zambezi.

Almost single-handed remains the Rev. Edward Steere, faithful to his post as Bishop and Chief Pastor. He has visited Lake Nyassa, and established a Mission halfway, and another I believe at Lindi; he keeps a watchful eye upon the operations of the Mission House established among the Shambalas; and at the headquarters or home at Kangani, a few miles east of Shangani Point, the old residence, he superintends, and instructs lads and young men as printers, carpenters, blacksmiths, and in the practical knowledge of other useful trades. His quarters represent almost every industrial trade useful in life as occupations for members of the lower classes, and are in the truest sense an industrial and religious establishment for the moral and material welfare of a class of unfortunates who deserve our utmost assistance and sympathy. This extraordinary man, endowed with piety as fervid as ever animated a martyr, looms grander and greater in the imagination as we think of him as the one man who appears to have possessed the faculties and gifts necessary to lift this Mission, with its gloomy history, into the new life upon which it has now entered. With all my soul I wish him and it success, and while he lives, provided he is supported, there need be no fear that the Mission will resume that hopeless position from which he, and he alone, appears to have rescued it.

From the same source that the Universities Missions have drawn their pupils, namely, the youthful victims of the slave-trade, her Majesty's Consul has supplied to a great extent the French Catholic Missions at Zanzibar and Bagamoyo. The Mission in the island which has now been established for years is called the St. Joseph's, that at Bagamoyo bears the title of "Notre Dame de Bagamoyo." The first possesses two priests and four brothers, with one lay professor of music; the other, which is the principal one, consists of four priests, eight brothers, and twelve sisters, with ten lay brothers employed in teaching agriculture. The French fathers superintend the tuition of 250 children, and give employment to about 80 adults; 170 freed slaves were furnished from the slave-captures made by British cruisers. They are taught to earn their own living as soon as they arrive of age, are furnished with comfortable lodgings, clothing, and household utensils.

"Notre Dame de Bagamoyo" is situated about a mile and a half north of Bagamoyo, overlooking the sea, which washes the shores just at the base of the tolerably high ground on which the mission buildings stand. Thrift, order, and that peculiar style of neatness common to the French are its characteristics. The cocoa-nut palm, orange, and mango flourish in this pious settlement, while a variety of garden vegetables and grain are cultivated in the fields; and broad roads, cleanly kept, traverse the estate. During the Superior's last visit to France he obtained a considerable sum for the support of the Mission, and he has lately, during my absence in Africa, established a branch mission at Kidudwe. It is evident that, if supported constantly by his friends in France, the Superior will extend his work still farther into the interior, and it is, therefore, safe to predict that the road to Ujiji will in time possess a chain of mission stations affording the future European trader and traveller safe retreats with the conveniences of civilized life.

There are two other missions on the east coast of Africa, that of the Church Missionary Society, and the Methodist Free Church at Mombasa. The former has occupied this station for over thirty years, and has a branch establishment at Rabbai Mpia, the home of the Dutch missionaries, Krapf, Rebmann, and Erhardt. But these missions have not obtained the success which such long self-abnegation and devotion to the pious service deserved.

It is strange how British philanthropists, clerical and lay, persist in the delusion that the Africans can be satisfied with spiritual improvement only. They should endeavour to impress themselves with the undeniable fact that man, white, yellow, red or black, has also material wants which crave to be understood and supplied. A barbarous man is a pure materialist. He is full of cravings for possessing something that he cannot describe. He is like a child which has not yet acquired the faculty of articulation. The missionary discovers the barbarian almost stupefied with brutish ignorance, with the instincts of a man in him, but yet living the life of a beast. Instead of attempting to develop the qualities of this practical human being, he instantly attempts his transformation by expounding to him the dogmas of the Christian Faith, the doctrine of transubstantiation and other difficult subjects, before the barbarian has had time to articulate his necessities and to explain to him that he is a frail creature requiring to be fed with bread, and not with a stone.

My experience and study of the pagan prove to me, however, that if the missionary can show the poor materialist that religion is allied with substantial benefits and improvement of his degraded condition, the task to which he is about to devote himself will be rendered comparatively easy. For the African once brought in contact with the European becomes docile enough; he is awed by a consciousness of his own immense inferiority, and imbued with a vague hope that he may also rise in time to the level of this superior being who has so challenged his admiration. It is the story of Caliban and Stefano over again. He comes to him with a desire to be taught and, seized with an ambition to aspire to a higher life, becomes docile and tractable, but to his surprise he perceives himself mocked by this being who talks to him about matters that he despairs of ever understanding, and therefore with abashed lace and a still deeper sense of his inferiority, he retires to his den, cavern, or hut with a dogged determination to be contented with the brutish life he was born in.

Nov. 17. — On the morning of the 17th of November, 1874, the first bold step for the interior was taken. The bugle mustered the people to rank themselves before our quarters, and each man's load was given to him according as we judged his power of bearing burthen. To the man of strong sturdy make, with a large development of muscle, the cloth bale of 60 lbs. was given, which would in a couple of months by constant expenditure be reduced to 50 lbs., in six months perhaps to 40 lbs., and in a year to about 30 lbs., provided that all his comrades were faithful to their duties; to the short compactly formed man, the bead sack of 50 lbs. weight; to the light youth of eighteen or twenty years old, the box of 40 lbs., containing stores, ammunition, and sundries. To the steady, respectable, grave-looking men of advanced years, the scientific instruments, thermometers, barometers, watches, sextant, mercury bottles, compasses, pedometers, photographic apparatus, dry plates, stationery, and scientific books, all packed in 40 lb. cases, were distributed; while the man most highly recommended for steadiness and most cautious tread was entrusted with the carriage of the three chronometers which were stowed in balls of cotton, in a light case weighing not more than 25 lbs. The twelve Kirangozis, or guides, tricked out this day in flowing robes of crimson blanket cloth, demanded the privilege of conveying the several loads of brass wire coils, and as they form the second advance guard, and are active, bold youths — some of whom are to be hereafter known as the boat's crew, and to be distinguished by me above all others, except the chiefs — they are armed with Snider rifles, with their respective accoutrements. The boat-carriers are herculean in figure and strength, for they are practised bearers of loads, having resigned their ignoble profession of hamal in Zanzibar to carry sections of the first European-made boat that ever floated on Lakes Victoria and Tanganika and the extreme sources of the Nile and the Livingstone. To each section of the boat there are four men, to relieve one another in couples. They get higher pay than even the chiefs, except the chief captain, Manwa Sera, and, besides receiving double rations, have the privilege of taking their wives along with them. There are six riding asses also in the expedition, all saddled, one for each of the Europeans — the two Pococks, Barker, and myself — and two for the sick: for the latter there are also three of Seydel's net hammocks, with six men to act as a kind of ambulance party.

Though we have not yet received our full complement of men, necessity compels us to move from the vicinity of the Goanese liquor shops, and from under the severe authority of Sheikh Mansur bin Suliman, whose views of justice would soon demoralize any expedition. Accordingly at 9 A.M. of the 17th, five days after leaving Zanzibar, we filed out from the town, receiving some complimentary and not a few uncomplimentary parting words from the inhabitants, male and female, who are out in strong; force to view the procession as follows: Four chiefs a few hundred yards in front; next the twelve guides clad in red robes of Joho, bearing the wire coils; then a long file 270 strong, bearing cloth, wire, beads, and sections of the Lady Alice; after them thirty-six women and ten boys, children of some of the chiefs and boat-bearers, following their mothers and assisting them with trifling loads of utensils, followed by the riding asses, Europeans and gun -bearers; the long line closed by sixteen chiefs who act as rear-guard, and whose duties are to pick up stragglers, and act as supernumeraries until other men can be procured: in all 356 souls connected with the Anglo-American Expedition. The lengthy line occupies nearly half a mile of the path which at the present day is the commercial and exploring highway into the Lake regions.

Edward Pocock is kind enough to act as bugler, because from long practice at the military camps at Aldershot and Chatham he understands the signals. He has familiarized Hamadi, the chief guide, with its notes, so that in case of a halt being required, Hamadi may be informed immediately. The chief guide is also armed with a prodigiously long horn of ivory, his favourite instrument, and one that belongs to his profession, which he has permission to use only when approaching a suitable camping-place, or to notify to us danger in the front. Before Hamadi strides a chubby little boy with a native drum, which is to beat only when in the neighbourhood of villages, to warn them of the advance of a caravan, a caution most requisite, for many villages are scattered in the midst of a dense jungle, and the sudden arrival of a large force of strangers before they had time to hide their little belongings might awake jealousy and distrust.

In this manner we begin our long journey, full of hopes. There is noise and laughter along the ranks, and a hum of gay voices murmuring through the fields, as we rise and descend with the waves of the land and wind with the sinuosities of the path. Motion had restored us all to a sense of satisfaction. We had an intensely bright and fervid sun shining above us, the path was dry, hard, and admirably fit for travel, and during the commencement of our first march nothing could be conceived in better order than the lengthy thin column about to confront the wilderness.

Presently, however, the fervour of the dazzling sun grows overpowering as we descend into the valley of the Kingani river. The ranks become broken and disordered; stragglers are many; the men complain of the terrible heat; the dogs pant in agony. Even we ourselves under our solar topees, with flushed faces and perspiring brows, with handkerchiefs ever in use to wipe away the drops which almost blind us, and our heavy woollens giving us a feeling of semi-asphyxiation, would fain rest, were it not that the sun-bleached levels of the tawny, thirsty valley offer no inducements. The veterans of travel push on towards the river three miles distant, where they may obtain rest and shelter, but the inexperienced are lying prostrate on the ground, exclaiming against the heat, and crying for water, bewailing their folly in leaving Zanzibar. We stop to tell them to rest a while, and then to come on to the river, where they will find us; we advise, encourage, and console the irritated people as best we can, and tell them that it is only the commencement of a journey that is so hard, that all this pain and weariness are always felt by beginners, but that by-and-by it is shaken off, and that those who are steadfast emerge out of the struggle heroes.

Frank and his brother Edward, despatched to the ferry at the beginning of these delays, have now got the sectional boat Lady Alice all ready, and the ferrying of men, goods, asses, and dogs across the Kingani is prosecuted with vigour, and at 3.30 P.M. the boat is again in pieces, slung on the bearing poles, and the Expedition has resumed its journey to Kikoka, the first halting-place.

But before we reach camp, we have acquired a fair idea as to how many of our people are staunch and capable, and how many are too feeble to endure the fatigues of bearing loads. The magnificent prize mastiff dog "Castor" died of heat apoplexy, within two miles of Kikoka, and the other mastiff, "Captain," seems likely to follow soon, and only "Nero," "Bull," and "Jack," though prostrate and breathing hard, show any signs of life.

Nov. 18. — At Kikoka, then, we rest the next day. We discharge two men, who have been taken seriously ill, and several new recruits, who arrive at camp during the night preceding and this day, are engaged.

There are several reasons which can be given, besides heat of the Tropics and inexperience, for the quick collapse of many of the Wangwana on the first march, and the steadiness evinced by the native carriers confirms them. The Wangwana lead very impure lives on the island, and with the importation of opium by the

Banyans and Hindis, the Wangwana and many Arabs have acquired the vicious habit of eating this drug. Chewing betel-nut with lime is another uncleanly and disgusting habit, and one that can hardly benefit the morale of a man; while certainly most deleterious to the physical powers is the almost universal habit of vehemently inhaling the smoke of the Cannabis sativa, or wild hemp. In a light atmosphere, such as we have in hot days in the Tropics, with the thermometer rising to 140° Fahr in the sun, these people, with lungs and vitals injured by excessive indulgence in these destructive habits, discover they have no physical stamina to sustain them. The rigour of a march in a loaded caravan soon tells upon their weakened powers, and one by one they drop from the ranks, betraying their impotence and infirmities.

During the afternoon of this day, as I was preparing my last letters, I was rather astonished by a visit paid to my camp by a detachment of Baluchi soldiers, the chief of whom bore a letter from the governor of Bagamoyo — Mansur bin Suliman — wherein he complained that the Wangwana had induced about fifteen women to abandon their masters, and requested me to return them.

Upon mustering the people, and inquiring into their domestic affairs, it was discovered that a number of women had indeed joined the Expedition during the night. Some of them bore free papers given them by H.M. Political Resident at Zanzibar, but nine were by their own confessions runaways. After being hospitably received by the Sultan and the Arabs of Zanzibar, it was no part of my duty, I considered, unauthorized as I was by any Government, to be even a passive agent in this novel method of liberating slaves. The order was therefore given that these women should return with the soldiers, but as this did not agree with either the views of the women or of their loving abductors, a determined opposition was raised, which bore every appearance of soon culminating in sanguinary strife. The men seized their Snider rifles and Tower muskets, and cartridges, ramrods and locks were handled with looks which boded mischief. Acting upon the principle that as chief of my own camp I had a perfect right to exclude unbidden guests, I called out the "faithfuls" of my first expedition, forty-seven in number, and ranked them on the side of the Sultan's soldiers, to prove to the infuriated men that, if they fired, they must injure their own friends, brothers, and chiefs. Frank Pocock also led a party of twenty in their rear, and then, closing in on the malcontents, we disarmed them, and lashed their guns into bundles, which were delivered up to the charge of Edward Pocock. A small party of faithfuls was then ordered to escort the Sultan's soldiers and the women out of camp, lest some vengeful men should have formed an ambuscade between our camp and the river.

From the details furnished in this and the two preceding chapters, a tolerably correct idea may be gained by the intending traveller, trader, or missionary in these lands, of the proper method of organization, as well as the quality and nature of the men whom he will lead, the manner of preparation and the proportion of articles to be purchased.

As there are so many subjects to be touched upon along the seven thousand miles of explored lines, I propose to be brief with the incidents and descriptive sketches of our route to Ituru, because the country for two-thirds of the way has been sufficiently described in 'How I found Livingstone.'

CHAPTER V.

On the March — Congorido to Rubuti — The hunting-gronnrls of
Kitangeh — Shooting zebra — "Jack's" first prize — Interviewed by lions —
Geology of Mpwapwa — Dudoma "The flood gates of heaven" opened —
Dismal reflections — The Salina — A conspiracy discovered — Desertions —
The path lost — Starvation and deaths — Trouble imminent — Grain huts
plundered — Situation deplorable — Sickness in the camp — Edward Pocock
taken ill — His death and funeral.

The line of march towards the interior, which, after due consideration, we
adopted, runs parallel to the routes known to us, by the writings of many travellers,
but extends as far as thirty miles north of the most northerly of them.

At Rosako the route began to diverge from that which led to Msuwa and Simba-
Mwenni, and opened out on a stretch of beautiful park land, green as an English
lawn, dipping into lovely vales, and rising into gentle ridges. Thin, shallow threads
of water in furrow-like beds or in deep narrow ditches, which expose the
sandstone strata on which the fat ochreous soil rests, run in mazy curves round
forest clumps, or through jungle tangles, and wind about among the higher
elevations, on their way towards the Wami river.

Nov. 23. — On the 23rd, we halted at the base of one of the three cones of
Pongwe, at a village situated at an altitude of 900 feet above the sea. The lesser
Pongwe cone rises about 800 feet higher than the village, and the greater probably
1200 feet. The pedometers marked forty-six miles from Bagamoyo.

Congorido, a populous village, was reached on the 24th. From my hut, the
Pongwe hills were in clear view. The stockade was newly built, and was a good
defensive enclosure. The drinking-water was brackish, but after long search,
something more potable was discovered a short distance to the south-east.

Mfuteh, the next village, was another strong, newly enclosed construction after
the pattern of the architecture of Unyamwezi. The baobab, at this height, began to
flourish, and in the depressions of the land the doum, borassus, and fan-palm were
very numerous. The soil westward of Congorido, I observed, contains considerable
alkali, and it is probable that this substance is favourable to the growth of palms.
The villagers are timid and suspicious. Lions are reported to abound towards the
north.

Westward of Mfuteh we travelled along the right or southern bank of the Wami
for about four miles. Its banks are fringed with umbrageous wooded borders, and
beyond these extends an interesting country. The colossal peak of Kidudu rears its
lofty crown to a great height, and forms a conspicuous landmark, towering above

its less sublime neighbours of Nguru, about fifteen or twenty miles north of the Wami's course.

Nov. 29. — From Mfuteh to Rubuti, a village on the Lugumbwa creek, which we reached on the 29th, game is numerous, but the landscape differs little from that described above. We crossed the Wami three times in one march, the fords being only 2 1/2 feet deep. Granite boulders protruded above the surface, and the boiling points at one of the fords showed a considerable height above the sea. At one of the fords there was a curious suspension bridge over the river, constructed of llianes with great ingenuity by the natives. The banks were at this point 16 feet high above the river, and from bank to bank the distance was only 30 yards: it was evident, therefore, that the river must be a dangerous torrent during the rainy season.

The road thence, skirting a range of mountains, leads across numerous watercourses and some very clear rivers — one, the Mkindo, near Mvomero, being a beautiful stream, and the water of which I thought very invigorating. I certainly imagined I felt in excellent spirits the whole of the day after I had taken a deep draught of it.

Dec. 3. — On the 3rd of December we came to the Mkundi river, a tributary of the Wami, which divides Nguru country from Usagara. Simba-Mwenni, or Simba-Miunyi — the Lion Lord — not the famous man farther south — owns five villages in this neighbourhood. He was generous, and gratified us with a gift of a sheep, some flour, and plantains, accepting with pleasure some cloth in return.

The Wa-Nguru speak the same dialect as the Waseguhha and Wasagara, and affect the same ornaments, being fond of black and white beads and brass wire. They split the lobes of their ears, and introduce such curious things as the necks of gourds or round discs of wood to extend the gash. A medley of strange things are worn round the neck, such as tiny goats' horns, small brass chains, and large egg-like beads. Blue Kanika and the red-barred Barsati are the favourite cloths in this region. The natives dye their faces with ochre, and, probably influenced by the example of Wanyamwezi, dress their hair in long ringlets, which are adorned with pendicles of copper, or white or red beads of the large Sam-sam pattern.

Dec. 4. — Grand and impressive scenery meets the eye as we march to Makubika, the next settlement, where we attain an altitude of 2675 feet above the ocean. Peaks and knolls rise in all directions, for we are now ascending to the eastern front of the Kaouru mountains. The summits of Ukamba are seen to the north, its. slopes famous for the multitude of elephants. The mountain characteristically called the "Back of the Bow" has a small, clear lake near it, and remarkable peaks or mountain crests break the sky line on every side Indeed, some parts of this great mountain range abound in scenery both picturesque and sublime.

Between Mamboya and Kitangeh, I was much struck by the resemblance that many of the scenes bear to others that I had seen in the Alleghanies. Water is abundant, flowing clear as crystal from numerous sources. As we neared Eastern

Kitangeh, villages were beheld clotted over every hill, the inhabitants of which, so often frightened by inroads of the ever marauding Wamasai, have been rendered very timid. Here, for the first time, cattle were observed as we travelled westerly from Bagamoyo.

By a gradual ascent from the fine pastoral basin of Kitangeh, we reached the spine of a hill at 4490 feet, and beheld an extensive plain, stretching north-west and west, with browsing herds of noble game. Camping on its verge, between a lumpy hill and some rocky knolls, near a beautiful pond of crystal-clear water, I proceeded with my gun-bearer, Billali, and the notorious Msenna, in the hope of bringing down something for the Wangwana, and was heartily encouraged thereto by Frank and Ted Pocock.

The plain was broader than I had judged it by the eye from the crest of the hill whence we had first sighted it. It was not until we had walked briskly over a long stretch of tawny grass, crushed by sheer force through a brambly jungle, and trampled down a path through clumps of slender cane stalks, that we came at last in view of a small herd of zebras. These animals are so quick of scent and ear, and so vigilant with their eyes, that, across an open space, it is most difficult to stalk them. But by dint of tremendous exertion, I contrived to approach to within 250 yards, taking advantage of every thin tussock of grass, and, almost at random, fired. One of the herd leaped from the ground, galloped a few short maddened strides, and then, on a sudden, staggered, kneeled, trembled, and fell over, its legs kicking the air. Its companions whinnied shrilly for their mate, and, presently wheeling in circles with graceful motion, advanced nearer, still whinnying, until I dropped another with a crushing ball through the head — much against my wish, for I think zebras were created for better purpose than to be eaten. The remnant of the herd vanished, and the bull-terrier "Jack," now unleashed, was in an instant glorying in his first strange prizes. How the rogue plunged his teeth in their throats! with what ardour he pinned them by the nose! and soon loathing himself in blood, he appeared to be the very Dog of Murder, a miracle of rabid ferocity.

Billali, requested to run to camp to procure Wangwana to carry the meat to camp, was only too happy, knowing what brave cheers and hearty congratulations would greet him. Msenna was already busy skinning one of the animals, some 300 yards from me; Jack was lying at my feet, watchful of the dead zebra on which I was seated, and probably calculating, so I supposed, how large a share would fall to him for his assistance in seizing the noble quarry by the nose. I was fast becoming absorbed in a mental picture of what might possibly lie behind the northern mountain barrier of the plain, when Jack sprang up and looked southward. Turning my head, I made out the form of some tawny animal, that was advancing with a curious long step, and I recognised it to be a lion. I motioned to Msenna, who happened to be looking up, and beckoned him. "What do you think it is, Msenna? " I asked. "Simba (a lion), master," he answered.

Finding my own suspicions verified, we both lay down, and prepared our rifles. Two explosive bullets were slipped into, an elephant rifle, and I felt sure with the perfect rest which the body of the zebra gave for the rifle, that I could drop anything living larger than a cat at the distance of 100 yards; so I awaited his approach with composure. The animal advanced to within 300 yards, and then, giving a quick bound as though surprised, stood still. Shortly afterwards, after a deliberate survey, he turned sharp round and trotted off into a low shrubby jungle, about 800 yards away. Ten minutes elapsed, and then as many animals emerged from the same spot into which the other had disappeared, and approached us in stately column. But it being now dusk, I could not discern them very clearly. We both were, however, quite sure in our own minds that they were lions, or at any rate some animals so like them in the twilight that we could not imagine them to be anything else. When the foremost had come within 100 yards, I fired. It sprang up and fell, and the others disappeared with a dreadful rush. We now heard shouts behind us, for the Wangwana had come; so, taking one or two with me, I endeavoured to discover what I felt to be a prostrate lion, but it could not be found. It occupied us some time to skin and divide our game, and as the camp was far, we did not reach it until 9 P.M., when, of course, we received a sincere welcome from people hungry for meat.

The next day Manwa Sera went out to hunt for the lion-skin, but returned after a long search with only a strong doubt in his mind as to its having been a lion, and a few reddish hairs to prove that it was something which had been eaten by hyenas. This day I succeeded in shooting a small antelope of the springbok kind.

Dec. 11. — We crossed the plain on the 11th of December, and arrived at Tubugwe. It is only six miles in width, but within this distance we counted fourteen human skulls, the mournful relics of some unfortunate travellers, slain by an attack of Wahumba from the northwest. I think it is beyond doubt that this plain, extending, as it does, from the unexplored north-west, and projecting like a bay into a deep mountain fiord south-east of our road, must in former times have been an inlet or creek of the great reservoir of which the Ugombo lake, south of here, is a residuum. The bed of this ancient lake now forms the pastoral plains of the Wahumba, and the broad plain-like expanses visible in the Ugogo country.

Rounding the western extremity of a hilly range near the scene of our adventures, we followed a valley till it sloped into a basin, and finally narrowed to a ravine, along the bottom of which runs a small brackish stream. A bed of rock-salt was discovered on the opposite side.

Two miles farther, at the base of a hilly cone, we arrived at a wooded gully, where very clear and fresh water is found, and from which the path runs west, gradually rising along the slope of a hill until it terminates in a pass 3700 feet above sea-level, whence the basin of Tubugwe appears in view, enclosing twenty-five square, stockaded villages and many low hills, and patched with cultivated fields. A gentle descent of about 400 feet brought us to our camp, on the banks of a small tributary of the Mukondokwa.

Dec. 12. — On the 12th of December, twenty -five days' march from Bagamoyo, we arrived at Mpwapvva.

The region traversed from the eastern slopes of that broad range which we began to skirt soon after passing to the left bank of the Wami river, as far as Chunyu (a few miles west of Mpwapwa), comprises the extreme breadth of the tract distinguished in the work, 'How I found Livingstone,' as the Usagara mountains. The rocks are of the older class, gneiss and schists, but in several localities granite protrudes, besides humpy dykes of trap. From the brackish stream east of Tubugwe, as far as Mpwapwa, there are also several dykes of a feldspathic rock, notably one that overlooks the basin of Tubugwe. The various clear streams coursing towards the Mukondokwa, as we dipped and rose over the highest points of the mountains among which the path led us, reveal beds of granite, shale, and rich porphyritic brown rock, while many loose boulders of a granitic character lie strewn on each side, either standing up half covered with clambering plants in precarious positions upon a denuded base, or lying bare in the beds of the stream, exposed to the action of the running water. Pebbles also, lodged on small shelves of rock in the streams, borne thither by their force during rainy seasons, attest the nature of the formations higher up their course. Among these, we saw varieties of quartz, porphyry, greenstone, dark grey shale, granite, hematite, and purple jasper, chalcedony, and other gravels.

The rock-salt discovered has a large mass exposed to the action of the stream. In its neighbourhood is a greyish tufa, also exposed, with a brown mossy parasite running in threads over its face.

Wood is abundant in large clumps soon after passing Kikoka, and this feature of the landscape obtains as far as Congorido. The Wami has a narrow fringe of palms on either bank; while thinly scattered in the plains and less fertile parts, a low scrubby brushwood, of the acacia species, is also seen, but nowhere dense. Along the base and slopes of the mountains, and in its deep valleys, large trees are very numerous, massing, at times, even into forests. The extreme summits, however, are clothed with only grass and small herbage.

Mpwapwa has also some fine trees, but no forest; the largest being the tamarind, sycamore, Cottonwood, and baobab. The collection of villages denominated by this title lies widely scattered on either side of the Mpwapwa stream, at the base of the southern slope of a range of mountains that extends in a sinuous line from Chanyu to Ugombo. I call it a range because it appeared to be one from Mpwapwa; but in reality it is simply the northern flank of a deep indentation in the great mountain chain that extends from Abyssinia, or even Suez, down to the Cape of Good Hope. At the extreme eastern point of this indentation from the western side lies Lake Ugombo, just twenty-four miles from Mpwapwa.

Desertions from the expedition had been frequent. At first, Kacheche, the chief detective, and his gang of four men, who had received their instructions to follow us a day's journey behind, enabled me to recapture sixteen of the deserters; but the cunning Wangwana and Wanyamwezi soon discovered this resource of mine against their well-known freaks, and, instead of striking east in their departure, absconded either south or north of the track. We then had detectives posted long before dawn, several hundred yards away from the camp, who were bidden to lie in wait in the bush, until the expedition had started, and in this manner we succeeded in repressing to some extent the disposition to desert, and arrested very many men on the point of escaping; but even this was not adequate. Fifty had abandoned us before reaching Mpwapwa, taking with them the advances they had received, and often their guns, on which our safety might depend.

Several feeble men and women also had to be left behind; and it was evident that the very wariest methods failed to bind the people to their duties. The best of treatment and abundance of provisions daily distributed were alike insufficient to induce such faithless natures to be loyal. However, we persisted, and as often as we failed in one way, we tried another. Had all these men remained loyal to their contract and promises, we should have been too strong for any force to attack us, as our numbers must necessarily have commanded respect in lands and among tribes where only power is respected.

One day's march from Mpwapwa, the route skirting a broad arm of the Marenga Mkali desert, which leads to the Ugombo lake, brought us to Chunyu — an exposed and weak settlement, overlooking the desert or wilderness separating Usagara from Ugogo. Close to our right towered the Usagara mountains, and on our left stretched the inhospitable arm of the wilderness. Fifteen or twenty miles distant to the south rose the vast cluster of Rubeho's cones and peaks.

The water at Chunyu is nitrous and bitter to the taste. The natives were once prosperous, but repeated attacks from the Wahehe to the south and the Wahumba to the north have reduced them in numbers, and compelled them to seek refuge on the hill-summits.

Dec. 16. — On the 16th of December, at early dawn, we struck camp, and at an energetic pace descended into the wilderness, and at 7 P.M. the vanguard of the expedition entered Ugogo, camping two or three miles from the frontier village of Kikombo. The next day, at a more moderate pace, we entered the populated district, and took shelter under a mighty baobab a few hundred yards distant from the chiefs village.

The fields, now denuded of the dwarf acacia and gum jungle which is the characteristic feature of the wilderness of Marenga Mkali and its neighbourhood, gave us a clear view of a broad bleak plain, with nothing to break its monotony to the jaundiced eye save a few solitary baobab, some square wattled enclosures within which the inhabitants live, and an occasional herd of cattle or flock of goats that obtain a poor subsistence from the scanty herbage. A few rocky hills rise in the distance on either hand.

Kikombo, or Chikombo, stands at an altitude by aneroid of 2475 feet. The hills proved, as we afterwards ascertained on arriving at Itumbi, Sultan Mpamira's, to be the eastern horn of the watershed that divides the streams flowing south to the Rufiji from those that trend north.

We march under a very hot sun to Mpamira's village; and through the double cover of the tent the heat at Itumbi rose to 96° Fahr. Within an hour of our arrival, the sky, as usual in this season, became overcast, the weather suddenly became cold, and the thermometer descended to 69° Fahr., while startling claps of thunder echoed among the hills, accompanied by vivid flashes of lightning. About three miles to the south-west, we observed a thick fog, and knew that rain was falling, but we only received a few drops. Half an hour later, a broad and dry sandy steam-bed, in which we had commenced to dig for water, was transformed into a swift torrent of 18 inches deep and 50 yards wide, the general direction of which was north by east. Within two or three hours, there were only a few gentle threads of water remaining; the torrent had subsided as quickly as it had risen.

On our road to Leehumwa, we passed over a, greyish calcareous tufa. On either side of us rise hills bare of soil, presenting picturesque summits, some of which are formed by upright masses of yellow feldspar, coloured by the presence of iron and exposure to weather.

The next settlement, Dudoma, is situated on a level terrace to the north of the hills which form the watershed, and from its base extends, to the unknown north, the great plain of Uhumba, a dry, arid, and inhospitable region, but covered with brushwood, and abandoned to elephants, lions, large game, and intractable natives.

Dec. 23. — The rainy season began in earnest on the 23rd of December, while we halted at Dudoma, and next day we struggled through a pelting storm, during an eight miles' march to Zingeh, the plain of which we found already half submerged by rushing yellow streams.

Dec. 25. — The following sketch is a portion of a private letter to a friend, written on Christmas Day at Zingeh: "I am in a centre-pole tent, seven by eight. As it rained all day yesterday, the tent was set over wet ground, which, by the parsing in and out of the servants, was soon trampled into a thick pasty mud bearing the traces of toes, heels, shoe nails, and dogs' paws. The tent walls are disfigured by large splashes of mud, and the tent corners hang down limp and languid, and there is such an air of forlornness and misery about its very set that it increases my own misery, already great at the sight of the doughy muddy ground with its puddlets and strange hieroglyphic traceries and prints. I sit on a bed raised about a foot above the sludge, mournfully reflecting on my condition. Outside, the people have evidently a fellow feeling with me, for they appear to me like beings with strong suicidal intentions or perhaps they mean to lie still, inert until death relieves them. It has been raining heavily the last two or three days, and an impetuous downpour of sheet rain has just ceased. On the march, rain is very disagreeable; it makes the clayey path slippery, and the loads heavier by being saturated, while it half ruins the cloths. It makes us dispirited, wet, and cold, added to which we are hungry — for there is a famine or scarcity of food at this season, and therefore we can only procure half-rations. The native store of grain is consumed during the months of May, June, July, August, September, October, and November. By December, the planting month, there is but little grain left, and for what we are able to procure, we must pay about ten times the ordinary price. The natives, owing to improvidence, have but little left. I myself have not had a piece of meat for ten days. My food is boiled rice, tea, and coffee, and soon I shall be reduced to eating native porridge, like my own people. I weighed 180 lbs. when I left Zanzibar, but under this diet I have been reduced to 134 lbs. within thirty-eight days. The young Englishmen are in the same impoverished condition of body, and unless we reach some more flourishing country than famine-stricken Ugogo, we must soon become mere skeletons.

"Besides the terribly wet weather and the scarcity of food from which we suffer, we are compelled to undergo the tedious and wearisome task of haggling with extortionate chiefs over the amount of black-mail which they demand, and which we must pay. We are compelled, as you may perceive, to draw heavy drafts on the virtues of prudence, patience, and resignation, without which the transit of Ugogo, under such conditions as above described, would be most perilous. Another of my dogs, 'Nero,' the retriever, is dead. Alas! all will die."

Dec. 26. — The next camp westward from Zingeh which we established was at Jiweni, or the Stones, at an altitude above sea-level of 3150 feet; crossing on our march three streams with a trend southerly to the Rufiji. Formerly there had been a settlement here, but in one of the raids of the Wahumba it had been swept away, leaving only such traces of man's occupation as broken pottery, and shallow troughs in the rocks caused probably by generations of female grinders of corn.

Through a scrubby jungle, all of which in past times had been cultivated, we marched from the "Stones" to Kitalalo, the chief of which place became very friendly with me, and, to mark his delight at my leading a caravan to his country — the first, he hoped, of many more — he presented a fat ox to the Wangwana and Wanyamwezi.

The outskirts of Kitalalo are choked with growths of acacia, tamarisk, and gum, while clusters of doum palms are numerous. Further west stretches the broad plain of Mizanza and Mukondoku, with its deceitful mirage, herbless and treeless expanse, and nitrous water.

One Somali youth, Mohammed, deserted just eastward of Kitalalo, and was never afterwards heard of.

Dec. 29. — Early on the 29th of December, guided by Kitalalo's son, we emerged from our camp under the ever rustling doum palms, and a short mile brought us to the broad and almost level Salina, which stretches from Mizanza to the south of the track to the hills of Unyangwira, north.

The hilly range or upland wall which confronted us on the west ever since we left the "Stones," and which extends from Usekke northwards to Machenche, is the natural boundary accepted by the natives as separating Ugogo from Uyanzi — or Ukimbu, as it is now beginning to be called. The slope of the Salina, though slight and imperceptible to the eye, is southerly, and therefore drained by the Rufiji. The greatest breadth of this plain is twenty miles, and its length may be estimated at fifty miles. The march across it was very fatiguing. Not a drop of water was discovered en route, though towards the latter part of the journey a grateful rain shower fell, which revived the caravan, but converted the plain into a quagmire.

On approaching the Mukondoku district, which contains about a hundred, small villages, we sighted the always bellicose natives advancing upon our van with uplifted spears and noisy show of war. This belligerent exhibition did not disturb our equanimity, as we were strangers and had given no cause for hostilities. After manifesting their prowess by a few harmless boasts and much frantic action, they soon subsided into a more pacific demeanour, and permitted us to proceed quietly to our camp under a towering: baobab near the king's village.

This king's name is Chalula, and he is a brother of Masumami of Kitalalo. Unlike his nobler brother, he is crafty and unscrupulous, and levies extortionate tribute on travellers, for which he never deigns to send the smallest present in return. His people are numerous, strong, and bold, and, sharing the overweening pride of their king, are prone to insolence and hostility upon the slightest cause. Being so powerful, he is cordially detested by his royal brothers of Kiwyeh, Khonko, and Mizanza. We experienced therefore much difficulty in preserving the peace, as his people would insist upon filling the camp, and prying into every tent and hut.

A conspiracy was discovered at this place, by which fifty men, who had firmly resolved to abscond, were prevented from carrying out their intention by my securing the ring-leaders and disarming their deluded followers. Twenty men were on the sick list, from fever, sore feet, ophthalmia, and rheumatism. Five succeeded in deserting with their guns and accoutrements, and two men were left at Mukondoku almost blind. Indeed, to record our daily mischances and our losses up to this date in full detail would require half of this volume; but these slight hints will suffice to show that the journey of an expedition into Africa is beset with troubles and disaster.

Frank and Edward Pocock and Frederick Barker rendered me invaluable services while endeavouring to harmonise the large, unruly mob with its many eccentric and unassimilating natures. Quarrels were frequent, sometimes even dangerous, between various members of the Expedition, and at such critical moments only did my personal interference become imperatively necessary. What with taking solar observations and making ethnological notes, negotiating with chiefs about the tribute moneys and attending on the sick, my time was occupied from morning until night. In addition to all this strain on my own physical powers, I was myself frequently sick from fever, and wasted from lack of proper, nourishing food; and if the chief of an expedition be thus distressed, it may readily be believed that the poor fellows depending on him suffer also.

Jan. 1. — Having received our guides from Chalula, king of Mukondoku, on the 1st of January 1875 we struck north, thus leaving for the first time the path to Unyanyembe, the common highway of East Central Africa. We were skirting the eastern base of the upland wall, or hilly range (which, as I have said, we sighted westward from the "Stones"), by a path which connected several Wahumba villages. Though humble to the European eye, these villages owned several herds of humped, short-horned cattle, flocks of sheep and goats, with many strong asses and dogs. Some of the young women were unusually pretty, with regular features, well-formed noses, thin, finely chiselled lips, and graceful forms.

We — the Europeans — were as great curiosities to the natives as though they lived hundreds of miles from the Unyanyembe road. Each of the principal men and women extended to us pressing invitations to stop in their villages, and handsome young chiefs entreated us to become their blood-brothers. Young Keelusu, the son of the chief of Mwenna, even came to my camp at night, and begged me to accept a "small gift from a friend," which he had brought. This gift was a gallon of new milk, still warm from the udder. Such a welcome present was reciprocated with a gilt bracelet, with a great green crystal set in it, a briarwood pipe, stem banded in silver, a gilt chain, and a Sohari cloth, with which he was so overjoyed as almost to weep. His emotions of gratitude were visible in the glistening and dilated eyes, and felt in the fervent grasp he gave my hand. By some magic art with his sandals of cowhide, he predicted success to my journey. As the right sandal after being tossed three times upward, each time turned upside down, my good health and well-being, he said, were assured, without a doubt.

Jan. 2. The next halt was made at Mtiwi, the chief of which was Malewa. The aneroid here indicated an altitude of 2825 feet. Our faithless Wagogo guides having deserted us, we marched a little distance farther north, and ascended the already described "upland wall," where the aneroid at our camp indicated a height of 3800 feet — or about 950 feet above the plain on which Mtiwi, Mwenna, and Mukondoku are situated.

The last night at Mtiwi was a disturbed one. The "floodgates of heaven" seemed literally opened for a period. After an hour's rainfall, 6 inches of water covered our camp, and a slow current ran southerly. Every member of the expedition was distressed, and even the Europeans, lodged in tents, were not exempted from the evils of the night. My tent walls enclosed a little pool, banked by boxes of stores and ammunition. Hearing cries outside, I lit a candle, and my astonishment was great to find that my bed was an island in a shallow river, which, if it increased in depth and current, would assuredly carry me off south towards the Rufiji. My walking boots were miniature barks, floating to and fro on a turbid tide seeking a place of exit to the dark world of waters without. My guns, lashed to the centre pole, were stock deep in water. But the most comical sight was presented by Jack and Bull, perched back to back on the top of an ammunition-box, butting each other rearward, and snarling and growling for that scant portion of comfort.

In the morning, I discovered my fatigue cap several yards outside the tent, and one of my boots sailing down south. The harmonium, a present for Mtesa, a large quantity of gunpowder, tea, rice and sugar, were destroyed. Vengeance appeared to have overtaken us. At 10 A.M. the sun appeared, astonished no doubt at a new lake formed during his absence. By noon the water had considerably decreased, and permitted us to march; and with glad hearts we surmounted the upland of Uyanzi, and from our busy camp, on the afternoon of the 4th of January, gazed upon the spacious plain beneath, and the vast broad region of sterility and thorns which we had known as inhospitable Ugogo.

Jan. 4. — On the upland which we were now about to traverse, we had arrived at an elevation which greatly altered the character of the vegetation. On the plain of Ugogo flourish only dwarf bush, a mongrel and degenerate variety of the noble trees growing in Uyanzi, consisting of acacia, rank-smelling gum-trees, and euphorbias. Here we have the stately myombo or African ash. This tree grows on the loftier ridges and high uplands, flourishing best on loose ferruginous soil. It utterly rejects the rich alluvium, as well as the shady loam. Where the tree assumes its greatest height and girth, we may be sure also that not far off strange freaks of rock will be found in the bosom of the forest, such as gigantic square blocks of granite, of the magnitude of cottages, and at a distance reminding the traveller of miniature castles and other kinds of human dwelling's. Large sheets of hematite and gneiss denuded of soil are also characteristics of this plateau, while still another feature is a succession of low and grandly swelling ridges, or land-waves.

On our road to Muhalala, we met hundreds of fugitives who were escaping from the battle-grounds near Kirurumo, the natives of which were being harassed by Nyungu, son of Mkasiwa of Unyanyembe, for expressing sympathy with Mirambo, the warrior chief of Western Unyamwezi.

Jan. 6. — Muhalala is a small settlement of Wakimbu, the chief of which declares he owes a nominal allegiance to Malewa of Mtiwi. Procuring guides here, on the 6th of January we ascended a ridge, its face rough with many a block of iron ore, and a scabby grey rock, on which torrents and rains had worked wonderful changes, and within two hours arrived at Kashongwa, a village situated on the verge of a trackless wild, peopled by a mixture of Wasukuma, renegade Wangwana, and Wanyamwezi. We were informed by officious Wangwana, who appeared glad to meet their countrymen, that we were but two days' march from Urimi. As they had no provisions to sell, and each man and woman had two days' rations, we resumed our journey, accompanied by one of them as a guide, along a road which, they informed us, would take us the day after to Urimi, and after two hours camped near a small pool.

Jan. 8. — The next day we travelled over a plain which had a gradual uplift towards the north-west, and was covered with dense, low bush. Our path was ill-defined, as only small Wagogo caravans travelled to Urimi, but the guide assured us that he knew the road. In this dense bush there was not one large tree. It formed a vast carpet of scrub and brush, tall enough to permit us to force our way among the lower branches, which were so interwoven one with another that it sickens me almost to write of this day's experience. Though our march was but ten miles, it occupied us as many hours of labour, elbowing and thrusting our way, to the injury of our bodies and the detriment of our clothing. We camped at 5 P.M. near another small pool, at an altitude of 4350 feet above the sea. The next day, on the afternoon of the 8th, we should have reached Urimi, and, in order to be certain of doing so, marched fourteen miles to still another pool at a height of 4550 feet above sea-level. Yet still we saw no limit to this immense bush-field, and our labours had, this day, been increased tenfold. Our guide had lost the path early in the day, and was innocently leading us in an easterly direction!

The responsibility of leading a half-starved expedition — as ours now certainly was — through a dense bush, without knowing whither or for how many days, was great; but I was compelled to undertake it rather than see it wander eastward, where it would be hopeless to expect provisions. The greater number of our people had consumed their rations early in the morning. I had led it northward for hours, when we came to a large tree to the top of which I requested the guide to ascend, to try if he could recognise any familiar feature in the dreary landscape. After a short examination, he declared he saw a ridge that he knew, near which, he said, was situate the village of Uveriveri. This news stimulated our exertions, and, myself leading the van, we travelled briskly until 5 P.M., when we arrived at the third pool.

Meantime Barker and the two Pococks, assisted by twenty chiefs, were bringing up the rear, and we never suspected for a moment that the broad track which we trampled over grass and through bush would be unperceived by those in rear of us. The Europeans and chiefs, assisted by the reports of heavily loaded muskets, were enabled to reach camp successfully at 7 P.M.; but the chiefs then reported that there had not arrived a party of four men, and a donkey boy who was leading an ass loaded with coffee. Of these, however, there was no fear, as they had detailed the chief Simba to oversee them, Simba having a reputation among his fellows for fidelity, courage, and knowledge of travel.

Jan. 9. — The night passed, and the morning of the 9th dawned, and I anxiously asked about the absentees. They had not arrived. But as each hour in the jungle added to the distress of a still greater number of people, we moved on to the miserable little village of Uveriveri. The inhabitants consisted of only two families, who could not spare us one grain! We might as well have remained in the jungle, for no sustenance could be procured here.

In this critical position, many lives hanging on my decision, I resolved to despatch forty of the strongest men — ten chiefs and thirty of the boldest youths — to Suna in Urimi, for the villagers of Uveriveri had of course given us the desired information as to our whereabouts. The distance from Uveriveri to Suna was twenty-eight miles, as we subsequently discovered. Pinched with hunger themselves, the forty volunteers advanced with the resolution to reach Suna that night. They were instructed to purchase 800 lbs. of grain, which would give a light load of 20 lbs. to each man, and urged to return as quickly as possible, for the lives of their women and friends depended on their manliness.

Manwa Sera was also despatched with a party of twenty to hunt up the missing men. Late in the afternoon they returned with the news that three of the missing men were dead. They had lost the road, and, travelling along an elephant track, had struggled on till they perished, of despair, hunger, and exhaustion. Simba and the donkey-boy, the ass and its load of coffee, were never seen or heard of again.

Jan. 10. — With the sad prospect of starvation impending over us, we were at various expedients to sustain life until the food purveyors should return. Early on the morning of the 10th, I travelled far and searched every likely place for game, but though tracks were numerous, we failed to sight a single head. The Wangwana also roamed about the forest — for the Uveriveri ridge was covered with fine myombo trees — in search of edible roots and berries, and examined various trees to discover whether they afforded anything that could allay the grievous and bitter pangs of hunger. Some found a putrid elephant, on which they gorged themselves, and were punished with nausea and sickness. Others found a lion's den, with two lion whelps, which they brought to me. Meanwhile, Frank and I examined the medical stores, and found to our great joy we had sufficient oatmeal to give every soul two cupfuls of thin gruel. A "Torquay dress trunk" of sheet-iron was at once emptied of its contents and filled with 25 gallons of water, into which were put 10 lbs. of oatmeal and four 1 lb. tins of "revalenta arabica." How the people, middle-aged and young, gathered round that trunk, and heaped fuel underneath that it might boil the quicker! How eagerly they watched it lest some calamity should happen, and clamoured, when it was ready, for their share, and how inexpressibly satisfied they seemed as they tried to make the most of what they received, and with what fervour they thanked "God" for his mercies!

At 9 P.M., as we were about to sleep, we heard the faint sound of a gun fired deliberately three times, and we all knew then that our young men with food were not very far from us. The next morning, about 7 A.M., the bold and welcome purveyors arrived in camp with just enough millet-seed to give each soul one good meal. This the people soon despatched, and then demanded that we should resume our journey that afternoon, so that next morning we might reach Suna in time to forage.

Skirting the southern base of the wooded ridge of Uveriveri, we continued to ascend almost imperceptibly for eight miles, when we arrived at another singular series of lofty rocks, called at once by the Wangwaua the Jiweni or "Stones." We camped near a rocky hill 125 feet high, from the summit of which I obtained a view of a green grassy plain stretching towards the north. The altitude of this camp was 5250 feet above sea-level. Towards night I shot a wild boar and a duck, but several of the Wangwana, being strict Muslims, could not be induced to eat the pork. From the "Stones" we came to what we had called a plain from the summit, but what was really, from its marshy nature, more of a quagmire. It appeared to be a great resort for elephants; thousands of the tracks of these great animals ran in all directions. Plunging into another jungle, we reappeared, after marching twenty miles, in the cultivated fields of Suna; and on the verge of a coppice we constructed a strong camp, whence we had a view of the "Stones," which we had left in the morning, no other eminences being visible above what appeared a very ocean of bush.

Jan. 12. — Next morning there was a strange and peculiar air of discontent, like a foreshadowing of trouble, among the natives who appeared before our camp. They did not appear to understand us. They were seen hurrying their women and children away, and deserting their villages, while others hovered round our camp menacingly, carrying in their hands a prodigious quantity of arms — spears, bows and arrows, and knob-sticks. Trouble seemed imminent. To prevent it, if possible, I stepped out to them with empty hands, motioned them to be seated, and, calling an interpreter, likewise unarmed, I attempted to explain the nature of our expedition and a few of its objects, one of which of course was to reach Lake Victoria. To those elders who appeared to have most influence, I gave some beads, as an expression of goodwill and friendship. But nothing seemed to be of avail until, after close questioning, I ascertained they had a grievance. Some of the Wangwana, in their ravenous hunger, had plundered the grain huts, and stolen some chickens. The natives were requested to come and point out the thieves. They did so, and pointed their lingers at Alsassi, a notorious thief and gourmand. Convicted of the crime after a strict examination of his quarters by Kacheche, the chief detective, Alsassi was flogged in their presence, not severely but sufficiently to mark my sense of extreme displeasure. The value of the stolen food was given to the defrauded natives, and peace and tranquillity were restored.

The Warimi are the finest people in physique we saw between their country and the sea. They are robust, tall, manly in bearing, and possess very regular features. As they go stark naked, we perceived that the males had undergone the process of circumcision. Their ornaments are cinctures of brass wire round the loins, armlets and leglets of brass, brass-wire collars, beads plentifully sprinkled over their hair, and about a dozen long necklaces suspended from the neck. The war costumes which they were wearing when I had thought that trouble was near were curious and various. Feathers of the kite and hawk, manes of the zebra and giraffe, encircled their foreheads. Their arms consisted of portentous-looking spears, bows and yard-long arrows, and shields of rhinoceros hide. The women, I imagine, are generally a shade lighter than the men. I failed to see in a day's examination a single flat nose or thick lip, though they were truly negroidal in hair and colour. I ought to have said that many shaved their heads, leaving only a thin wavy line over the forehead.

The rolling plain of Suna was at this season utterly devoid of grass. An immense area was under cultivation; clusters of small villages were sprinkled over all the prospect the eye embraced, and large flocks of goats and sheep and herds of cattle proved that they were a pastoral as well as an agricultural people.

The Warimi appear to have no chief, but submit to direction by the elders, or heads of families, who have acquired importance by judicious alliances, and to whom they refer civil causes. In time of war, however, as we observed the day after we arrived, they have for their elder one who has a military reputation. This fighting elder, to whom I remarked great deference was paid, was certainly 6 1/2 feet in height. The species of beads called Kanyera were, it seemed to me, most in favour; brass wire was also in demand, but all cloth was rejected except the blue Kaniki.

We halted four days at Suna, as our situation was deplorable. A constantly increasing sick list, culminating in the serious illness of Edward Pocock, the evident restlessness of the Warimi at our presence, who most certainly wished us anywhere except in their country, and yet had no excuse for driving us by force from their neighbourhood, the insufficient quantity of food that could be purchased, and the growing importunacy of the healthy Wangwana to be led away from such a churlish and suspicious people, plunged me in perplexity.

We had now over thirty men ailing. Some suffered from dysentery, others from fever, asthma, chest diseases, and heart sickness; lungs were weak, and rheumatism had its victims. Edward Pocock, on the afternoon of the day we arrived at Suna, came to me, and complained of pain in the loins, a throbbing in the head — which I attributed to weariness after our terribly long march — and a slight fever. I suggested to him that he had better lie down and rest. Before I retired, I reminded Frank, his brother, that he should give Edward some alternative medicine. The next day the young man was worse. His tongue was thickly coated with a dark fur, his face fearfully pallid, and he complained of wandering pains in his back and knees, of giddiness and great thirst. I administered to him sweet spirits of nitre with orange water, and a few grains of ipecacuanha as an emetic. The fourth day he was delirious, and we were about to sponge him with cold water, when I observed that small red pimples with white tops covered his chest and abdomen, arms and neck. One or two were very like small-pox pustules, which deceived me for a time into the belief that it was a mild case of small-pox. However, by carefully noticing the symptoms, I perceived that it was unmistakably a case of the dreadful typhus.

Jan. 17. — There were two or three cases of sickness equally dangerous in camp, but far more dangerous was the sickness of temper from which the Warimi suffered. It became imperative that we should keep moving, if only two or three miles a day. Accordingly, on the 17th of January, after rigging up four hammocks, and making one especially comfortable for Edward Pocock, roofed over with canvas, we moved from the camp through the populated district at a very slow pace; Frank Pocock and Fred Barker at the side of the hammock of the sick European, and a chief and four men attending to each suffering Wangwana. Hundreds of natives fully armed kept up with us on either side of our path.

Never since leaving the sea were we weaker in spirit than on this day. Had we been attacked, I doubt if we should have made much resistance. The famine in Ugogo, and that terribly protracted trial of strength through the jungle of Uveriveri, had utterly unmanned us; besides, we had such a long list of sick, and Edward Pocock and three Wangwana were dangerously ill in hammocks. We were an unspeakably miserable and disheartened band; yet, urged by our destiny, we struggled on, though languidly. Our spirits seemed dying, or resolving themselves into weights which oppressed our hearts. Weary, harassed, and feeble creatures, we arrived at Chiwyu, four hundred miles from the sea, and camped near the crest of a hill, which was marked by aneroid as 5400 feet above the level of the ocean.

Edward Pocock was reported by Frank to have muttered in his delirium, "The master has just hit it," and to have said that he felt very comfortable. On arriving at the camp, one of the boat sections was elevated above him as a protection from the sun, until a cool grass hut could be erected. A stockade was being constructed by piling a thick fence of brushwood around a spacious circle, along which grass huts were fast being built, when Frank entreated me to step to his brother's side. I sprang to him — only in time, however, to see him take his last gasp. Frank gave a shriek of sorrow when he realised that the spirit of his brother had fled for ever, and removing the boat section, bent over the corpse and wailed in a paroxysm of agony.

We excavated a grave 4 feet deep at the foot of a hoary acacia with wide-spreading branches, and on its ancient trunk Frank engraved a deep cross, the emblem of the faith we all believe in, and, when folded in its shroud, we laid the body in its final resting-place during the last gleams of sunset.

We read the beautiful prayers of the church service for the dead, and, out of respect for the departed, whose frank, sociable, and winning manners had won their friendship and regard, nearly all the Wangwana were present to pay a last tribute of sighs to poor Edward Pocock.

When the last solemn prayer had been read, we retired to our tents, to brood in sorrow and silence over our irreparable loss.

CHAPTER VI.

From Chiwyu to Vinyata — Kaif Halleck murdered — The magic doctor — Giving away the heart — Deeds of blood — "The white men are only women" — A three days' fight — Punishment of the Wanyatnru — The ubiquitous Mirambo — The plain of the Luwamberri — In a land of plenty — Through the open country — 'I have seen the lake, sir, and it is grand!' — Welcomed at Kagehyi.

Jan. 18. — We have seen no remarkable feature in the landscape since we surmounted that steep wall of the upland which bounds Ugogo on the west. Near its verge, it is true, it rose in steep terraces, until finally it extended westward and northward in a broad jungle-covered plain, which had a gradual rise, culminating in the myombo-clad slopes of the Uveriveri ridge. While standing at Suna, we were in view of that vast waste out of which, after terrible experience, we had emerged as it were only with our lives.

At Chiwyu, we camped near the loftiest altitude of the gradual and almost unbroken rise of upland, at a height of 5400 feet. To the northward of Suna and Chiwyu, the country, however, no longer retained that grand unfurrowed uplift, but presented several isolated hills and short ranges, while to the westward also we saw that it was divided into oval basins, rimmed with low hills. From these same hollows and furrows and basins at the base of the hills, scattered to the north and west of Suna and Chiwyu, issue the first tiny rivulets, which, as we continue our journey to the north-west, gradually converge to one main stream, trending towards Lake Victoria. It is in this region, therefore, that the most extreme southern Sources of the Nile were discovered.

Since leaving Mpwapwa, we have not crossed one perennial stream. All our drinking water has been obtained from pools, or shallow depressions lately filled by rain. Between Suna and Chiwyu was crossed one small rill flowing north-easterly, which soon afterwards joins another and still another, and gathering volume, swerves north, then north-west. These are the furthest springs and head-waters of a river that will presently become known as the Leewumbu, then as the Monangah, and lastly as the Shimeeyu, under which name it enters Lake Victoria on the south-east coast of Speke Gulf.

Descending into the basin of Matongo from Chiwyu with its melancholy associations, we crossed several narrow and shallow furrows, which a few late rains had probably caused, and came to a clear stream flowing north through a deep rocky channel. Near this ravine was a space about a square mile in extent, strangely torn up and exhibiting thousands of boulders and blocks, large and small, with smooth, water-worn tops; and the sides of what is now a small hill in the centre of the basin showed visible traces of the action of furious torrents through centuries of time. The hard granite was worn into cones, the tops of which bore a calcined appearance, proving the effect of intense heat suddenly cooled by rain. The rocky channel of this stream in the Matongo basin was a veritable geological section. The surface consisted of massive granite boulders imbedded in vegetable deposit; below this was a stratum of sand about 3 feet deep, below the sand a stratum of coarse shingle of quartz, feldspar, and porphyry, about 8 feet thick, and below this was alluvium, resting on solid rock.

Jan. 20. — During these days the thermometer had seldom risen higher than 78°; for hours during the day it stood at 66°, while at night the mean was 63°. Seven miles from Chiwyu stand the villages of Mangura on the borders of Ituru. Soon after leaving Mangura we ought to have followed the left-hand road, which, after traversing a forest, would have brought us to Mgongo Tembo, where we should have found Wangwana and Wanyamwezi. We also discovered that we had already lost the regular path to Usukuma at Kashongwa, which would have taken us, we were told, to Utaturu and thence to Mgongo Tembo. But the Mangura natives, though they were otherwise tolerant of our presence and by no means ill-disposed, would not condescend to show us the road, and we were therefore exposed to a series of calamities, which at one time threatened our very existence.

After passing Mangura, we entered Ituru. Streams now became numerous, all flowing northward; but though such a well-watered country, the cattle in it were poor and gaunt in frame, the dogs half starved, and the sheep and goats mere skeletons. Only the human beings seemed to me to be in good condition. Among the birds of this region which attracted our attention, we noted spur-winged geese, small brown short-billed ducks, delicate of flesh and delicious eating, long-legged plover, snipe, cranes, herons, spoonbills, parroquets and jays, and a large greyish-brown bird with short legs resembling a goose, and very shy and difficult of approach.

The language of Ituru is totally distinct from that of Ugogo or of Unyamwezi. Besides possessing large herds of cattle, nearly every village boasts of one or two strong Masai asses. As the Wanyaturu stood in groups indulging their curiosity outside our camps, I observed they had a curious habit of employing themselves in plucking the hair from their faces and armpits. Being extremely distant in their manner, we found it difficult to gain their confidence, though we were assiduous in our attempts to cultivate their goodwill.

Izanjeh was our next camp after Mangura, and the first place we halted at in Ituru. It was 5450 feet above the sea.

On leaving Izanjeh, Kaif Halleck, the bearer of the letter-bag to Livingstone in 1871, was afflicted with asthma, and as we were compelled to travel slowly, I entreated him not to lag behind the Expedition while it traversed such a dangerous country. But I have observed that sick men seldom heed advice. Being obliged to go forward to the front during these evil and trying days, I had to leave the rearguard under Frank Pocock and Fred Barker and the Wangwana chiefs. As my duties would be mainly to introduce and ingratiate our expedition with the natives, I could not possibly know what happened in the rear until we reached camp, and reports were made to me by Frank and Manwa Sera.

Jan. 21. — From the top of a ridge, accompanied by a guide whose goodwill had been secured by me, I descended to the basin of what the Wangwana at Mgongo Tembo call Vinyata, but which the guide, I feel assured, called Niranga. The basin is oval, about twelve miles long by six miles wide, cut through the centre by the Leewumbu, as it flows in a W.N.AV. direction, becoming lost, soon after leaving the basin, in a cluster of woodclad hills. Numbers of villages are sprinkled over it from end to end, and from the summit of the ridge we guessed it to contain a populous and wealthy community. On the evening of the same day, the 21st of January 1875, we arrived at Vinyata.

There was nothing in the horizon of our daily life that the most fearful and timid could have considered ominous. Nevertheless, consistent with custom, the camp was constructed on the summit of a slightly swelling ground, between a forest and the fields in the basin. The people of the small village nearest to us deserted it upon first sight of our party, but they were finally persuaded to return. Everything promised at night to be peaceful, though anxiety began to be felt about the fate of Kaif Halleck. He had not been seen for two days. Some suggested he had deserted, but "faithfuls" rarely desert upon mere impulse, without motive or cause. It was necessary therefore to halt a day at Vinyata to despatch a searching party. Manwa Sera was told to take four staunch men, one of whom was the scout and famous detective, Kacheche, to hunt up the sick "letter-carrier of 1871."

During Manwa Sera's absence, Frank, Barker, and myself were occupied in reducing our loads, and rejecting every article that we could possibly subsist without. Our sick were many, twenty had died, and eighty-nine had deserted, between the coast and Vinyata!

While examining the cloth bales, we discovered that several were wet from the excessive rains of Ugogo, and to save them from being ruined, it was imperative, though impolitic, that we should spread the cloths to dry. In the midst of this work the great magic doctor of Vinyata came to pay me a visit, bringing with him a fine fat ox as a peace offering. Being the first we had received since leaving Kitalalo, we regarded it as a propitious omen, and I showed by my warmth toward the ancient Mganga that I was ready to reciprocate his kindness. He was introduced to my tent, and after being sociably entertained with exceedingly sweet coffee and some of Huntley and Palmer's best and sweetest biscuits, he was presented with fifteen cloths, thirty necklaces, and ten yards of brass wire, which repaid him fourfold for his ox. Trivial things, such as empty sardine boxes, soup and bouilli pots, and empty jam tins, were successively bestowed on him as he begged for them. The horizon appeared clearer than ever, when he entreated me to go through the process of blood-brotherhood, which I underwent with all the ceremonious gravity of a pagan. As he was finally departing, he saw preparations being made to despatch the ox, and he expressed his desire that the heart of the animal should be returned to him. While he stayed for it, I observed with uneasiness that he and his following cast lingering glances upon the cloths which were drying in camp.

During the day the Wangwana received several days' back rations, towards repairing the havoc which the jungle of Uveriveri and famine-stricken Ugogo had effected in their frames, and our intercourse with the natives this day was most friendly. But before retiring for the night, Manwa Sera and his scouts returned with the report that "Kaif Halleck's" dead body had been discovered, gashed with over thirty wounds, on the edge of a wood between Izanjeh and Vinyata!

"We cannot help it, my friends," I said after a little deliberation. "We can mourn for him, but we cannot avenge him. Go and tell the people to take warning from his fate not to venture too far from the camp, and when on the march not to lag behind the caravan; and you, who are the chiefs and in charge of the rear, must not again leave a sick man to find his way unprotected to camp."

Jan. 22. — The next day the magic doctor appeared about 8 A.M. to receive another present, and as he brought with him about a quart of curded milk, he was not disappointed. He also received a few beads for his wife and for each of his children. We parted about 9.30 A.M., after shaking hands many times, apparently mutually pleased with each other. No mention was made to any native of Vinyata of the murder of Kaif Halleck, lest it might be suspected we charged our new friends with being cognisant of, or accessory to, the cruel deed, which would, without doubt, have caused new complications.

Half an hour after the departure of the magic doctor, while many of the Wangwana were absent purchasing grain, and others were in the forest collecting faggots, we heard war-cries. Imagining that they were the muster-call to resist their neighbours of Izanjeh, or of some tribe to the east, we did not pay much attention to them. However, as these peculiar war-cries, which may be phonetically rendered "Hehu-a-hehu," appeared to draw nearer, we mustered a small party on the highest ground of the camp, in an attitude of doubt and inquiry, and presently saw a large body of natives armed with spears, bows and arrows, and shields, appear within a hundred yards on a similar high-ground outside the camp. The sight suggested to us that they had mustered against us, yet I could divine no cause of grievance or subject of complaint to call forth a warlike demonstration.

I despatched two unarmed messengers to them to inquire what their intentions were, and to ascertain the object of this apparently hostile mob. The messengers halted midway between the camp and the crowd, and sitting down, invited two of the natives to advance to them for a "shauri."

We soon discovered upon the return of the messengers that one of the Wangwana had stolen some milk, and that the natives had been aroused to "make war" upon us because of the theft. They were sent back to inform the natives that war was wicked and unjust for such a small crime, and to suggest that they should fix a price upon the milk, and permit us to atone for the wrong with a handsome gift. After some deliberation the proposition was agreed to. A liberal present of cloth was made, and the affair had apparently terminated.

But as this mob was about to retire peacefully, another large force appeared from the north. A consultation ensued, at first quietly enough, but there were one or two prominent figures there, who raised their voices, the loud, sharp, and peremptory tones of which instinctively warned me that their owners would carry the day. There was a bellicose activity about their movements, an emphasis in their gestures, and a determined wrathful fury about the motion of head and pose of body that were unmistakable. They appeared to be quarrelling doggedly with those who had received cloth for the milk, and were evidently ready to fight with them if they persisted in retiring without bloodshed.

In the midst of this, Soudi, a youth of Zanzibar, came hastily upon the scene. He had a javelin gash near the right elbow joint, and a slight cut as though from a flying spear was visible on his left side, while a ghastly wound from a whirling knobstick had laid open his temples. He reported his brother Suliman as lying dead near the forest, to the west of the camp.

We decided, nevertheless, to do nothing. We were strong disciples of the doctrine of forbearance, for it seemed to me then as if Livingstone had taught it to me only the day before. "Keep silence," I said: "even for this last murder I shall not fight; when they attack the camp, it will be time enough then." To Frank I simply said that he might distribute twenty rounds of ammunition without noise to each man, and dispose our party on either side of the gate, ready for a charge should the natives determine upon attacking us.

The loudly arguing mob had not yet settled conclusively what they should do, and possibly hostilities might have been averted, had not the murderers of young Suliman, advancing red-handed and triumphant, extorted from all the unanimous opinion that it would be better after all to fight "the cowardly Wangwana and the white men, who were evidently only women."

They quickly disposed themselves, delivered loud whoops of triumph, prepared their bows, and shot their first arrows. The Wangwana became restless, but I restrained them. Perceiving no sign of life in our camp, the Wanyaturu judged, doubtless, that we were half dead with fright, and advanced boldly to within thirty yards, when the word was given to the Wangwana and Wanyamwesi, who rushed outside and, by the very momentum of the rush, drove the savages to a distance of 200 yards. The Wangwana were then ordered to halt, and deployed as skirmishers.

We still waited without firing. The savages, not comprehending this extraordinary forbearance, advanced once more. The interpreters were requested to warn them that we should delay no longer. They replied, "Ye are women, ye are women; go, ask Mirambo how he fared in Ituru," saying which they twanged their bows. It was only then, perceiving that they were too savage to understand the principles of forbearance, that the final word to "fight" was given. A brisk encounter was maintained for an hour, and then, having driven the savages away, the Wangwana were recalled to camp.

Meanwhile Frank was busy with sixty men armed with axes in constructing a strong stockade, and on the return of the Wangwana they were employed in building marksmen's "nests" at each corner of the camp. We also cleared the ground to the space of 200 yards around the camp. By night our camp was secure, and perfectly defensible.

Jan. 24. — On the morning of the 24th we waited patiently in our camp. Why should we attack? We were wretched enough as it was without seeking to add to our wretchedness. We numbered only seventy effective men, for all the others were invalids, frightened porters, women, donkey-boys, and children. The sick list was alarming, but, try how we might, the number was not to be reduced. While we lived from hand to mouth on a few grains of corn a day, after a month's experience of famine fare, our plight must not only remain pitiable, but become worse. We were therefore in a mood to pray that we might not be attacked, but permitted to leave the camp in safety.

At 9 A.M., however, the enemy appeared, reinforced both in numbers and confidence, for the adjoining districts on the north and east had been summoned to the "war." This word means now, as is evident, daily attacks upon our camp, with forces hourly increasing, until we shall have also perhaps strange tribes to the westward invited to the extermination of the strangers, and ourselves be in the meantime penned in our hold until hunger reduces us to surrender, to be butchered without mercy.

Our position, as strangers in a hostile country, is such that we cannot exist as a corporate expedition, unless we resist with all our might and skill, in order to terminate hostilities and secure access to the western country. We therefore wait until they advance upon our camp, and drive them from its vicinity, as we did the day before. In half an hour our people are back, and organised into four detachments of ten men each under their separate chiefs, two more detachments of ten men each being held in reserve, and one other, of ten also, detailed for the defence of the camp. They are instructed to proceed in skirmishing order in different directions through the hostile country, and to drive the inhabitants out wherever they find them lodged, to a distance of five miles east and north, certain rocky hills, the rendezvous of the foe, being pointed out as the place where they must' converge. Messengers are sent with each detachment to bring me back information.

The left detachment, under chief Farjalla Christie, were soon thrown into disorder, and were killed to a man except the messenger who brought us the news, imploring for the reserve, as the enemy were now concentrated on the second detachment. Manwa Sera was therefore despatched with fifteen men, and arrived at the scene only in time to save eight out of the second detachment. The third plunged boldly on, but lost six of its number; the fourth, under chief Safeni, behaved prudently and well, and, as fast as each enclosed village was taken, set it on fire. But ten other men despatched to the scene retrieved what the third had lost, and strengthened Safeni.

About 4 P.M. the Wangwana returned, bringing with them oxen, goats, and grain for food. Our losses in this day's proceedings were twenty-one soldiers and one messenger killed, and three wounded.

Jan. 25. — On the morning of the 25th we waited until 9 A.M., again hoping that the Wanyaturu would see the impolicy of renewing the fight; but we were disappointed, for they appeared again, and apparently as numerous as ever. After some severe volleys we drove them off again on the third day, but upon the return of the Wangwana, instead of dividing them into detachments I instructed them to proceed in a compact body. Some of the porters volunteered to take the place of the soldiers who perished the previous day, and we were therefore able to show still a formidable front. All the villages in our neighbourhood being first consumed, they continued their march, and finally attacked the rocky hill, which the Wanyaturu had adopted as a stronghold, and drove them flying precipitately into the neighbouring country, where they did not follow them.

We knew now that we should not be disturbed. Some of the guns, lost the day before, we recaptured. On reckoning up our loss on the evening of the third day, we ascertained it to be twenty-two men killed, three men wounded, twelve guns lost, and four cases of ammunition expended. Including Kaif Halleck and Suliman murdered, our losses in Ituru were therefore twenty-four men killed and four wounded, and as we had twenty-five on the sick-list, it may be imagined that to replace these fifty-three men great sacrifices were necessary on the part of the survivors, and much ingenuity had to be exercised. Twelve loads were accordingly placed on the asses, and ten chiefs were detailed to carry baggage until we should arrive at Usukuma. Much miscellaneous property was burned, and on the morning of the 26th, just before daybreak, we resumed our interrupted journey.

The expedition on this day consisted of three Europeans, 206 Wangwana and Wanyamwezi, twenty-five women, and six boys. At 9.30 A.M. we camped at a place which might be called a natural fortress. To our right and left rose two little hills 100 feet high and almost perpendicular. Behind us dropped a steep slope 400 feet down to the Leewumbu river, so that the only way of access was the narrow gap through which we had entered. We soon closed the gateway with a dense wall of brushwood, and in perfect security lay down to rest.

This camp was at an altitude of 5650 feet above the ocean, and due west of Vinyata about ten miles. On one side of us was the deep-wooded valley through which the rapid Leewumbu rushes. Its banks on each side slope steeply upward, and at the top become detached hills clothed with forest; from their base wave the uplands in grand and imposing wooded ridges. North of the Leewumbu the hills are bolder than those to the south.

Jan. 27. — On the 27th, at dawn, we crossed the Leewumbu, and the whole of that day and the day following our route was through a forest of fine myombo, intersected by singular narrow plains, forming at this season of the year so many quagmires. Other features of this region were enormous bare rocks, looming like castles through the forest, and hillocks composed of great fragments of splintered granite and broad heaving humps of grey gneiss. One of these singular features of this part of Africa gives its name to Mgongo Tembo, "The Elephant's Back." Far to the south is a similar hill, which I passed by during the first expedition; and its chief, emigrating to Iramba, has bestowed upon a like feature at the site of his new colony the name of his former village, to remind him of old associations.

Jan. 29. — On the 29th we entered Mgongo Tembo, and became acquainted with the chief, who is also known by the fantastic name which he has given his new quarters, though his real name, is Malewa. He is a strong conservative, dislikes innovations, declares young men nowadays to be too fond of travel, and will not allow his sous — he has sixteen — to visit either Unyanyembe or Zanzibar lest they should learn bad habits. He is a hearty, jovial soul, kindly disposed if let alone. He has lately emerged triumphantly out of a war with Maganga of Rubuga, an ally of the famous Mirambo.

It had been an object with me at one time to steer clear of Mirambo, but as I recognised and became impressed with his ubiquitous powers, I failed to perceive how the system of exploration I had planned could be effected if I wandered great distances out of his way. On the first expedition some of my people perished in a conflict with him, and on returning with Livingstone to Unyanyembe, we heard of him dealing effective blows with extraordinary rapidity on his Arab and native foes. Since leaving Ugogo, we heard daily of him on this expedition. He was one day advancing upon Kirirumo, at another place he was on our flanks somewhere in Utaturu. He fought with Ituru, and, according to Mgongo Tembo's chief, lost 1100 men two months before we entered the country. Mgongo Tembo, who kept a wary eye upon the formidable chief's movements, informed us that Mirambo was in front of us, fighting the Wasukuma. Mgongo Tembo further said, in explanation of the unprovoked attacks of the Wanyaturu upon us, that we ought not to have bestowed the heart of the presented ox upon the magic doctor of Vinyata, as by the loss of that diffuser of blood, the Wanyaturu believed we had left our own bodies weakened and would be an easy prey to them. "The Wanyaturu are robbers, and sons of robbers," said he fiercely, after listening to the recital of our experiences in Ituru.

Feb. 1. — On the 1st of February, after a very necessary halt of two days at Mgongo Tembo, with an addition to our force of eight pagazis and two guides, and encouraged by favourable reports of the country in front, we entered Mangura in Usukuma near a strange valley which contained a forest of borassus palms. In the beds of the several streams we crossed this day we observed granite boulders, blue shale, basalt, porphyry and quartz.

Beyond Mangura, or about six miles west of it, was situate Igira, a sparse settlement overlooking the magnificent plain of Luwamberri, at an altitude by boiling-point of 5350 feet. A camp which we established in this plain, was ascertained with the same apparatus to be 4475 feet. Ten miles farther, near a sluggish ditch-like creek, the boiling-point showed 4250 feet, only 100 feet higher than Lake Victoria.

As far as Igira the myombo flourished, but when we descended into the plain, and the elevation above the sea decreased to 4000 feet, we discovered that the baobab became the principal feature of the vegetation, giving place soon after to thorny acacias and a variety of scrub, succeeded in their turn by a vast expanse of tawny grass.

The Luwamberri plain — with its breadth of nearly forty miles, its indefinite length of level reach towards the N.N.W., its low altitude above the Victorian Lake, the wave-worn slopes of the higher elevations which hem it on the east and the south — appears to me to have been in ancient times a long arm of the great lake which was our prospective goal at this period. About sixteen miles from Igira there is a small sluggish stream with an almost imperceptible current northward, but though it was insignificant at the time of our crossing, there were certain traces on the tall grass to show that during the middle of the rainy season it is nearly a mile broad, and very deep. Several nullahs or ravines with stagnant water, when followed up, prove to have their exit in the broad channel.

In the centre of the level plain rises a curious elevation, like an island crowned with a grove, whither the game with which the plain teems resort during the wet season. At the period of our crossing, however, they roved in countless numbers over the plain — giraffe, zebra, gnu, buffalo, springbok, water-buck, kudu, hartebeest, wild-boar, and several varieties of smaller antelope; while birds abounded, ibis, field-larks, fish-hawks, kingfishers, spur-winged geese, ducks, vultures, flamingos, spoonbills, and cranes.

With such a variety before them, it may readily be conceived that the Wangwana and Wanyamwezi which now numbered, with the accessions to our strength gained at Mangura and Igira, 280 men, earnestly hoped that I should be successful in the sport to which I now devoted myself with the aid of my faithful factotum Billali. One day I shot a giraffe and a small antelope; on the next, in the neighbourhood of the woody elevation in the plain, five zebra; and the third day on the western verge, I shot two gnu, one buffalo, and a zebra, besides bagging two spur-winged geese, four guinea-fowl, and five ducks. Meat was now a drug in our camp. It was cooked in various styles, either stewed, roasted, fried, or pounded for cakes. Some of the Wanyamwezi carried, besides their cloth bale of 60 lbs. weight, nearly 35 lbs. of dried meat.

Feb. 2, — On the western verge of the grassy plain we crossed the Itawa river, a broad but sluggish stream choked with grass, and camped in a locality which seemed to be favourable only to the production of baobab and mimosa. After a few hours' travel west of the Itawa, we crossed the Gogo river with a course N.N.E. towards the Luwamberri plain. Here we arrived at the easternmost of a chain of low hills with truncated tops. These hills, pleasant to the eye, and covered with waving grass and a sprinkling of thin dwarf bush, consisted of silicious feldspathic rock, the stratification of which was vertical, in other parts diagonal, with a dip to the north-west. The slopes of the hills were thickly covered with detached pieces of this rock, and at the base with shingle. The plain beneath, close to the vicinity of the hills, had extensive beds of the same rock, which, in places, rose above it, exposed in great sheets.

Feb. 9. — On the 9th of February we crossed the Nanga ravine, and the next day, by a gradual ascent, arrived at the Seligwa, flowing to the Leewumbu, and, after following it for four miles, reached the hospitable village of Mombiti. We had fairly entered the rich country of Usukuma, where the traveller, if he has resources at his disposal, need never fear starvation.

The products of the rich upland were here laid at our feet, and it must be conceded that the plenteous stores of grain, beans, potatoes, vetches, sesamum, millet, vegetables, such as melons and various garden herbs, honey, and tobacco, which we were enabled to purchase at Mombiti, were merited by the members of the long-enduring expedition. The number of chickens and goats that were slaughtered by the people was enormous. Long arrears of rewards were due to them for the many signal examples of worth they had shown; and here I earned anew the flattering appellation bestowed upon me three years previously in Africa — "The white man with the open hand" — "Huyu Msungu n'u fungua mikono."

With the rewards they received, the Wangwana and Wanyamwezi, men, women, and children, revelled in the delights of repleted stomachs, and the voice of the gaunt monster. Hunger, was finally hushed. In festive rejoicings and inordinate fulness we spent three days at Mombiti.

A fresh troop of porters was here engaged to relieve the long-suffering people, and with renewed spirits and rekindled vigour, and with reserve stores of luxuries on our shoulders, we plunged into the jungle in the direction of the Monangah valley and Usiha, in reference to the ever-troubled route by Usanda, Nguru, and Masari. Mirambo, it was reported, was also in the neighbourhood of Masari, and hovering about our path like a phantom.

Feb. 14. — During the second day's march from Mombiti, Gardner, one of the faithful followers of Livingstone during his last journey, succumbed to a severe attack of typhoid fever. We conveyed the body to camp, and having buried him, raised a cairn of stones over his grave at the junction of two roads, one leading to Usiha, the other to Iramba. His last words were, "I know I am dying. Let my money (370 dollars), which is in charge of Tarya Topan of Zanzibar, be divided. Let a half be given to my friend Chumah, and a half be given to these my friends — pointing to the Wangwana — that they may make the mourning-feast." In honour of this faithful, the camp is called after his name — "Camp Gardner."

A gradual descent from the ridges and wavy upland brought us to the broad, brown valley of the Leewumbu, or the Monangah river, as the Wasukuma now called the river. At the ford in this season the Monangah was 30 yards wide and 3 feet deep, with a current of about a mile an hour, but discoloured marks high above its present level denote a considerable rise during the rainy season. A few hills on the south bank showed the same features of the silicified feld-spathic rock visible near the Gogo stream. Giraffe were numerous, feeding on the dwarf acacia, but the country was too open to permit my approaching them. However, I succeeded in dropping a stray springbok in a hunting excursion which I made in the evening.

On leaving the Monangah, we struck northerly across a pathless country seamed with elephant tracks, rhinoceros wallows, and gullies which contained pools of grey muddy water. Four miles from the river, Kirira Peak bore W.N.W., Usanda west by north, Wanhinni N.N.W., and Samui west by south. A chain of hill-cones ran from Samui to Wanhinni.

Feb. 17. — Surmounting a ridge which bounded the valley of the Monangah on the north, and following its crest westerly, we arrived on the morning of the 17th of February at Eastern Usiha. When in sight of their conical cotes, we despatched one of our native guides ahead, to warn the natives that a caravan of Wangwana was approaching, and to bear messages of peace and goodwill. But in his absence, one of the Kinyamwezi asses set up a terrific braying, which nearly created serious trouble. It appears that on one of his former raids the terrible Mirambo possessed a Kinyamwezi ass which also brayed, and, like the geese of the Roman Capitol, betrayed the foe. Hence the natives insisted, despite the energetic denial of our guide, that this ass must also belong to Mirambo, and for a short period he was in a perilous state. They seized and bound him, and would probably have despatched him had not the village scouts returned laughing heartily at the fright the vicious ass had caused.

Usiha is the commencement of a most beautiful pastoral country, which terminates only in the Victoria Nyanza. From the summit of one of the weird grey rock piles which characterise it, one may enjoy that unspeakable fascination of an apparently boundless horizon. On all sides there stretches toward it the face of a vast circle replete with peculiar features, of detached hills, great crag-masses of riven and sharply angled rock, and outcropping mounds, between which heaves and rolls in low, broad waves a green grassy plain whereon feed thousands of cattle scattered about in small herds.

As fondly as the Wangwana with their suffering vitals lingered over their meals in the days of plenty at Mombiti, so fondly did I gloat over this expanding extent, rich in contrasts and pleasing surprises. Fresh from the tawny plains of Monangah, with its thirsty and sere aspect, I was as gratified as though I possessed the wand of an enchanter, and had raised around me the verdant downs of Sussex. I seated myself apart, on the topmost grey rock. Only my gunbearer was near me, and he always seemed intuitively to know my moods. I revelled therefore undisturbed in the bland and gracious prospect. The voices of the Wangwana came to me now and again faint by distance, and but for this I might, as I sat there, have lost myself in the delusion that all the hideous past and beautiful present was a dream.

After the traveller has performed his six hundred miles from the ocean to Usiha, however phlegmatic he may be, he will surely glow with pleasure when he views this fair scene of promise. The delicious smell of cattle and young grass comes up from the plain quick, and reminds one of home-farm memories, of milk and cheese, and secret dippings into cream-pots, and from the staked bomas and the hedge-encircled villages there rise to my hearing the bleating of young calves, and the lowing of the cows as they looked interested towards the village, and I could see flocks of kids and goats, and sheep with jealously watchful shepherd-boys close by — the whole prospect so peaceful and idyllic that it made a strangely affecting impression on me.

Feb. 19. — Daybreak of the 19th of February saw the refreshed Expedition winding up and down the rolling pasture-land, escorted by hundreds of amiable natives who exchanged pleasant jests with our people, and laughed recklessly and boisterously to show us that they were glad we had visited their country. "Come yet again," said they, as they turned to go back after escorting us three miles on our way. "Come always, and you will be welcome."

We thoroughly enjoyed marching with such a broad prospect on either hand. We felt free, and for the first time enjoyed something of the lordly feeling to which it is said man is born, but to which we had certainly been strangers between the ocean and the grassy plains of Usukuma. One half the distance, it appears to me, we had ploughed our way through the lower regions of vegetation — the dense intermeshed tangle of a full-grown jungle — or we had crawled about like an army of ants, with the ordinary grasses of the maritime lands, the Luwamberri and the Monangah plains, towering like a forest of cane above our heads. The myombo forests of Uveriveri, and wood-clad ridges — drained by the crystal-clear streams and rivulets which supply the furthest waters to Egypt's sacred river — though tolerably open, did not inspire us with such a large, indescribable sense of freedom as the open short-grass lands in which we now found ourselves.

A fair idea of the rugged rock-heaps which relieved a landscape that might otherwise have been monotonous may be obtained from the photograph of Wezi's rocks. They are extremely picturesque from their massiveness and eccentricity, which distance increases and charms into ruined castles or antique human dwellings.

Villages were numerous between Usiha and Wandui. Sweet springs bubbled from all sides, especially from the opposing bases of the granite ridges which, like walls, flank the broad natural avenue, at the upper end of which stands the capital of the king of Usiha, shaded by glorious baobab and bowery masses of milk-weed.

Feb. 20 — As we were marching from Wandui to Mondo, on the 20th of February, we were once again mistaken by the warlike natives for Mirambo, but the mistake went no further than war-cries, long, loud, and melodious, caught up by hundreds of clear voices, and a demonstrative exhibition of how they would have exterminated us had we been really and truly Mirambo. In proportion as Mirambo haunts their vicinity, so do the natives appear to be possessed and disturbed. Wandui and Usiha become suddenly exercised at seeing their cattle run frightened from some prowling beast, and immediately the cry of "Mirambo, Mirambo!" is raised, and from every height the alarming cry is echoed, until from Usiha to Usanda, and from Masari north to Usmau, the dread name is repeated. Then two neighbours, finding it was a mistake, quarrel with each other, and begin fighting, and in the midst of their local war Mirambo veritably appears, as though from the ground, and attacks both.

North of Mondo, as far as Abaddi, or Baddi — sometimes Abatti — the country rolled, clear and open, like a treeless park, with scarcely a single shrub or tree. The grass was only an inch high. The rock-crowned hills were, however, still frequent features. All the male adults of Abaddi stalked about stark naked, but their women were clad with stiff skins and half tanned cowhides. The herds of cattle and flocks of goats and sheep absolutely whitened the glorious park country.

The villages of this part of Usukuma are surrounded by hedges of euphorbias, milk-weed, the juice of which is most acrid, and when a drop is spattered over such a tender organ as the eye, the pain is almost intolerable. My poor bull-terrier "Jack," while chasing a mongoose into one of these hedges, quite lost the use of one eye.

Feb. 22. — Our next camp was Marya, fifteen miles north by east Mag. from Mondo, and 4800 feet above the sea. We were still in view of the beautiful rolling plain, with its rock-crested hills, and herds of cattle, and snug villages, but the people, though Wasukuma, were the noisiest and most impudent of any we had yet met. One of the chiefs insisted on opening the door of the tent while I was resting after the long march. I heard the tent-boys remonstrate with him, but did not interfere until the chief forcibly opened the door, when the bull-dogs "Bull" and "Jack," who were also enjoying a well-earned repose, sprang at him suddenly and pinned his hands. The terror of the chief was indescribable, as he appeared to believe that the white man in the tent had been transformed into two ferocious dogs, so little was he prepared for such a reception. I quickly released him from his position, and won his gratitude and aid in restoring the mob of natives to a more moderate temper.

Feb. 24. — A march of seventeen miles north by west across a waterless jungle brought us on the 24th to South Usmau. Native travellers in this country possess native bells of globular form with which, when setting out on a journey, they ring most alarming though not inharmonious sounds, to waken the women to their daily duties.

The journey to Hulwa in North Usmau was begun by plunging through a small forest at the base of some rocky hills which had been distinctly visible from Marya, thirty-one miles south. A number of monkeys lined their summits, gazing contemptuously at the long string of bipeds condemned to bear loads. We then descended into a broad and populous basin, wherein villages with their milk-weed hedges appeared to be only so many verdant circlets. Great fragments and heaps of riven granite, gneiss, and trap rock, were still seen cresting the hills in irregular forms.

Through a similar scene we travelled to Gambachika in North Usmau, which is at an altitude of 4600 feet above the sea, and fourteen miles from Hulwa. As we approached the settlement, we caught a glimpse to the far north of the mountains of Urirwi, and to the north-east of the Manassa heights which, we were informed by the natives, formed the shores of the Great Lake.

Feb. 27. — On the morning of the 27th of February we rose up early, and braced ourselves for the long march of nineteen miles, which terminated at 4 P.M. at the village of Kagehyi.

The people were as keenly alive to the importance of this day's march, and as fully sensitive to what this final journey to Kagehyi promised their wearied frames, as we Europeans. They, as well as ourselves, looked forward to many weeks of rest from our labours and to an abundance of good food.

When the bugle sounded the signal to "Take the road," the Wanyamwezi and Wangwana responded to it with cheers, and loud cries of "Ay, indeed, ay, indeed, please God;" and their goodwill was contagious. The natives, who had mustered strongly to witness our departure, were affected by it, and stimulated our people by declaring that the lake was not very far off — "but two or three hours' walk."

We dipped into the basins and troughs of the land, surmounted ridge after ridge, crossed watercourses and ravines, passed by cultivated fields, and through villages smelling strongly of cattle, by good-natured groups of natives, until, ascending a long gradual slope, we heard, on a sudden, hurrahing in front, and then we too, with the lagging rear, knew that those in the van were in view of the Great Lake!

Frank Pocock impetuously strode forward until he gained the brow of the hill. He took a long sweeping look at something, waved his hat, and came down towards us, his face beaming with joy, as he shouted out enthusiastically with the fervour of youth and high spirits, "I have seen the Lake, Sir, and it is grand!" Frederick Barker, riding painfully on an ass, and sighing wearily from illness and the length of the journey, lifted his head to smile his thanks to his comrade.

Presently we also reached the brow of the hill, where we found the expedition halted, and the first quick view revealed to us a long broad arm of water, which a dazzling sun transformed into silver, some 600 feet below us, at the distance of three miles.

A more careful and detailed view of the scene showed us that the hill on which we stood sloped gradually to the broad bay or gulf edged by a line of green wavy reeds and thin groves of umbrageous trees scattered along the shore, on which stood several small villages of conical huts. Beyond these, the lake stretched like a silvery plain far to the eastward, and away across to a boundary of dark blue hills and mountains, while several grey rocky islets mocked us at first with an illusion of Arab dhows with white sails.

About half a mile from the villages we were surprised by seeing hundreds of warriors decked with feathered head-dresses and armed to the teeth, advancing on the run towards us, and exhibiting, as they came, their dexterity with bows and arrows and spears. They had at first been alarmed at the long procession filing down the hill, imagining that we were the ubiquitous Mirambo and his force, but, though discovering their error, they still thought it too good an opportunity to be lost for showing their bravery, and therefore amused us with this byplay. Sungoro Tarib, an Arab resident at Kagehyi, also despatched a messenger with words of welcome, and an invitation to us to make Kagehyi our camp, as Prince Kaduma, chief of Kagehi, was his faithful ally.

In a short time we had entered the wretched-looking village, and Kaduma was easily induced by Sungoro to proffer hospitalities to the strangers. A small conical hut about 20 feet in diameter, badly lighted, and with a strong smell of animal matter — its roof swarmed with bold rats, which, with a malicious persistence, kept popping in and out of their nests in the straw roof and rushing over the walls — was placed at my disposal as a store-room. Another small hut was presented to Frank Pocock and Fred Barker as their quarters.

In summing up, during the evening of our arrival at this rude village on the Nyanza, the number of statute miles travelled by us, as measured by two rated pedometers and pocket watch, I ascertained it to be 720. The time occupied — from November 17, 1874, to February 27, 1875, inclusive — was 103 days, divided into 70 marching and 33 halting days, by which it will be perceived that our marches averaged a little over 10 miles per day. But as halts are imperative, the more correct method of ascertaining the rate of travel would be to include the time occupied by halts and marches, and divide the total distance by the number of days occupied. This reduces the rate to 7 miles per diem.

CHAPTER VII.

A burzah held — Paying off recruits — Kagehyi becomes a great trading centre — A Central African "toper" — Prince Kaduma — Hopes of assistance from him relinquished — The boat ready for sea — No volunteers — Selecting my crew — The start for the circumnavigation of Lake Victoria.

Feb. 28. — We all woke up on the morning of the 28th of February with a feeling of intense relief. There were no more marches, no more bugle summons to rouse us up for another fatiguing day, no more fear of hunger — at least for a season.

We Europeans did not rise from bed until 8 A.M., and we then found the Wangwana and Wanyamwezi still extended at their full lengths on their mats and goat-skins, and peacefully reposing after their fatigues; and had I not finally sallied out into the open air at this hour, I believe that Sungoro and Kaduma, who, by the bye, were inseparable friends, would, from motives of delicacy, have refrained from paying a morning call, supposing that I should need many hours of rest.

At 9 A.M. a burzah, or levee, was held. First came Frank and Fred — now quite recovered from fever — to bid me good morning, and to congratulate themselves and me upon the prospective rest before us. Next came the Wangwana and Wanyamwezi chiefs, to express a hope that I had slept well, and after them the bold youths of the Expedition; then came Prince Kaduma and Sungoro, to whom we were bound this day to render an account of the journey and to give the latest news from Zanzibar; and, lastly, the princess and her principal friends — for introductions have to be undergone in this land as in others. The burzah lasted two hours, after which my visitors retired to pursue their respective avocations, which I discovered to be principally confined, on the part of the natives, to gossiping, making or repairing fishing-nets, hatchets, canoes, food-troughs, village fences, and huts; and on the part of our people to arranging plans for building their own grass-huts, being perfectly content to endure a long stay at Kagehyi.

Though the people had only their own small domestic affairs to engage their attentions, and Frank and Fred were for this day relieved from duty, I had much to do — observations to take to ascertain the position of Kagehyi, and its altitude above the sea; to prepare paper, pens, and ink for the morrow's report to the journals which had despatched me to this remote and secluded part of the globe; to make calculations of the time likely to be occupied in a halt at Kagehyi, in preparing and equipping the Lady Alice for sea, and in circumnavigating the great "Nianja," as the Wasukuma call the lake. It was also incumbent upon me to ascertain the political condition of the country before leaving the port and the camp, that my mind might be at rest about its safety during my contemplated absence. Estimates were also to be entered upon as to the quantity of cloth and beads likely to be required for the provisioning of the expeditionary force during my absence, and as to the amount of tribute and presents to be bestowed upon the King of Uchambi — of which Kagehyi was only a small district, and to whom Prince Kaduma was only a subordinate and tributary. In brief, my own personal work was not begun, and pages would not suffice to describe in detail the full extent of the new duties now devolving upon me.

During the afternoon the Wasukma recruits were summoned to receive farewell gifts, and nearly all were discharged. Then 13 doti of cloth were measured for the King of Uchambi, and 10 doti for Prince Kaduma; and beads were also given in proportion — the expectations of these two magnates and their favourite waives being thus satisfactorily realised. These grave affairs were not to be disposed of as mere trivialities, and occupied me many hours of our second day's life at Kagehyi. Meanwhile the Wangwana and Wanyamwezi required me to show my appreciation of their fidelity to me during the march, and chiefs and men received accordingly substantial tokens thereof. Besides new cloths to wear, and beads to purchase luxuries, I was expected to furnish them with meat for a banquet; and in accordance with their just wishes, six bullocks were purchased and slaughtered for their benefit. In addition to which, as a banquet would be rather tame without wine for cheer, twenty gallons of pombe — beer in a state of natural fermentation — were distributed. To satisfy all which demands and expectations, three full bales of cloth and 120 lbs. of beads were disbursed.

March 1 to 8. — On the evening of the second day, I was rewarded for my liberality when I saw the general contentment, and heard on all sides expressions of esteem and renewed loyalty.

Nor were Frank and Fred forgotten, for I gave permission for them to issue for themselves, each day while in camp, four yards of cloth, or two fundo of beads, to be expended as they thought fit, over and above ration money. Small as this may seem, it was really equal to a gift of 4s. per day pocket-money. Though they lived on similar food to that cooked for myself, I observed that they chose to indulge in many things which I could not digest, or for which I had no appetite, such as ground-nuts, ripe bananas, plantains, and parched green corn. Fred Barker was remarkably partial to these things. This extra pocket-money also served to purchase a larger quantity of milk, eggs, chickens, and rice from the Wasukuma and Sungoro. My daily fare at this time consisted principally of chickens, sweet-potatoes, milk, tea and coffee. Pocock and Barker varied this diet with rice, with which Sungoro furnished them, and bread made of Indian corn and millet.

The village of Kagehyi, in the Uchambi district and country of Usukuma, became after our arrival a place of great local importance. It attracted an unusual number of native traders from all sides within a radius of twenty or thirty miles. Fishermen from Ukerewe, whose purple hills we saw across the arm of the lake, came in their canoes, with stores of dried fish; those of Igusa, Sima, and Magu, east of us in Usukuma, brought their cassava, or manioc, and ripe bananas; the herdsmen of Usmau, thirty miles south of Kagehyi, sent their oxen; and the tribes of Muanza — famous historically as being the point whence Speke first saw this broad gulf of Lake Victoria — brought their hoes, iron wire, and salt, besides great plenty of sweet-potatoes and yams.

Reports of us were carried far along the paths of trade to the countries contiguous to the highways of traffic, because we were in a land which had been, from time immemorial, a land of gossip and primitive commerce; and a small band of peaceful natives, accustomed to travel, might explore hundreds of square miles in Usukuma without molestation. But though Unyanyembe, and through it Zanzibar, might receive within a few months reliable information about our movements, there were countries in the immediate neighbourhood of Kagehyi whither traders never venture, which were for ever cut off from the interesting intelligence that there were three white men on the shores of the lake, who were said to be most amiable and sociable. Ujiji, far away on Lake Tanganika, might be set to wondering whether they had come from Masr (Cairo) or from Zanzibar, but Wirigedi, close at hand here, on Speke Gulf, might still be in profound ignorance of the arrival. Mtesa of Uganda might prick up his ears at the gratifying intelligence, and hope they would soon visit him, while Ukara, though only about twenty-five geographical miles from Kagehyi, might be excluded for ever from discussing the strange topic. The natives of Karagwe and their gentle king might be greatly exercised in their minds with the agreeable news, and wonder whether they, in their turn, should ever see the white men, and yet Komeh, 300 miles nearer to us, might only hear of the wonderful event years after our departure! Thus it is that information is only conveyed along the lines of traffic, and does not filter into those countries which are ostracised from common interests and events by the reputed ferocity of their inhabitants and their jealous hostility to strangers, even though they may actually border upon the localities where those interests and events are freely discussed.

Prince Kaduma, truth compels me to state, is a true Central African "toper" — a naturally amiable man, whose natural amiability might be increased to enormous proportions, provided that it was stimulated by endless supplies of pombe. From perpetual indulgence in his favourite vice, he has already attained to that blear-eyed, thick-tongued, husky-voiced state from which only months of total abstinence can redeem a man. In his sober moments — I cannot say hours — which were soon after he rose in the morning, he pretended to manifest an interest in his cattle-yard, and to be deeply alive to the importance of doing something in the way of business whenever opportunities offered. In fact, he would sometimes go so far as to say to his half-dozen elders that he had something in view even then — "but we must have a shauri first." Becoming exceedingly interested, the elders would invite him to speak, and instantly assume that wise, thoughtful, grave respect which you sometimes see in members of Parliament, Congress, Reichstag,

&c. "Ah, but," Kaduma would say, "does a man work when he is hungry? Can he talk when he is thirsty?" The elders slily exchange winks and nods of approval, at which Kaduma bursts into a hoarse chuckle — never a laugh — for Kaduma is remarkable for possessing the conceit of humour. Others may laugh at his dry sayings, but he himself never laughs: he chuckles.

The great jar of froth-topped pombe is then brought up by a naked youth of fourteen or fifteen years, who is exceedingly careful to plant the egg-bottomed jar firmly on the ground lest it should topple over. Beside it is conveniently placed Kaduma's favourite drinking cup, as large as a quart measure, and cut out of a symmetrically shaped gourd. Kaduma is now seated on a favourite low stool, and folds his greasy Sohari cloth about him, while the elders are seated on either side of him on wood chips, or axe handles, or rocks. The foaming jar is ready, and the dusky Ganymede attentive. Kaduma stretches out his hand languidly — it is all affectation, for Kaduma is really thirsty — and Ganymede, with both hands, presents the cup kneeling. The pombe being broached, the valves of the "shauri" are opened. During the hour devoted to the consumption of the pombe, Kaduma may be said to be rational, and even interested in business. Withal he is gay, light-hearted, and pleasant in conversation; grand projects are hinted at; trading expeditions even as far as Ujiji suggested; a trip to Unyanyembe and Zanzibar appears to be in serious contemplation with him. But, alas! the pombe is ended. Kaduma goes to sleep. At three o'clock he expands again into a creature of intelligence. Two or three pots are exhausted between 3 and 6 P.M., and finally Kaduma reels to his cot like the inebriated sot he really is. Alas! for the virtues of a naturally intelligent nature drowned by such intemperance! Alas! for the fine attributes of manhood conquered by vile indulgences! Alas! for the brains muddled by such impurities!

It will be apparent, then, that, though the Prince of Kagehyi is a well-meaning and well-disposed creature, he possessed an infirmity that rendered him incapable of rendering me that service which he had himself suggested to me. He promised that he would accompany me in my exploration of Lake Victoria! It is to be doubted, after acquiring such a knowledge of his character, whether his intentions could be fulfilled. Yet he informed me that he had visited Ukerewe, Ururi, and Ugeyeya, and would, for a consideration, place himself at my disposal. The consideration was ready, but Kaduma, unfortunately for me, I saw, could not be ready within a decade! Hopes of his assistance and influence were therefore relinquished; and, since the chief was not available, it became evident that none of his people could be obtained for the service of exploration. Without this insight into Kaduma's life and manners, it would have been a matter for fair speculation whether his weakness and intemperance, or his dread of the vast lake, were the real causes of his reluctance to accompany me.

The prince was learned in the names of several countries or villages — but which they were, I was then ignorant. But if every name he repeated to my interested ears were the names of real countries, then, I began to think, it might be true, as he himself believed, that the lake was so large that its exploration would occupy years. Nearly all the Wangwana, while the Lady Alice was being prepared for sea, were impressed with the vastness of the enterprise, as Prince Kaduma, his people, Sungoro, and his slaves — who had really only reached Ururi — sketched it to them with their superstitious and crude notions of its size. There were, they said, a people dwelling on its shores who were gifted with tails; another who trained enormous and fierce dogs for war; another a tribe of cannibals, who preferred human flesh to all other kinds of meat. The lake was so large it would take years to trace its shores, and who then at the end of that time would remain alive? Therefore, as I expected, there were no volunteers for the exploration of the Great Lake. Its opposite shores, from their very vagueness of outline, and its people, from the distorting fogs of misrepresentation through which we saw them, only heightened the fears of my men as to the dangers which filled the prospect.

Within seven days the boat was ready, and strengthened for a rough sea life. Provisions of flour and dried fish, bales of cloth and beads of various kinds, odds and ends of small possible necessaries were boxed, and she was declared, at last, to be only waiting for her crew. "Would any one volunteer to accompany me?" A dead silence ensued. "Not for rewards and extra pay?" Another dead silence: no one would volunteer.

"Yet I must," said I, "depart. Will you let me go alone?"

"No."

"What then? Show me my braves — those men who freely enlist to follow their master round the sea."

All were again dumb. Appealed to individually, each said he knew nothing of sea life; each man frankly declared himself a terrible coward on water.

"Then, what am I to do?"

Mauwa Sera said: —

"Master, have done with these questions. Command your party. All your people are your children, and they will not disobey you. While you ask them as a friend, no one will offer his services. Command them, and they will all go."

So I selected a chief, Wadi Safeni — the son of Safeni — and told him to pick out the elect of the young men. Wadi Safeni chose men who knew nothing of boat life. Then I called Kacheche, the detective, and told him to ascertain the names of those young men who were accustomed to sea life, upon which Kacheche informed me that the young guides first selected by me at Bagamoyo were the sailors of the Expedition. After reflecting upon the capacities of the younger men, as they had developed themselves on the road, I made a list of ten sailors and a steersman, to whose fidelity I was willing to entrust myself and fortunes while coasting round the Victorian Sea.

Accordingly, after drawing up instructions for Frank Pocock and Fred Barker on about a score of matters concerning the wellbeing of the Expedition during my absence, and enlisting for them, by an adequate gift, the goodwill of Sungoro and Prince Kaduma, I set sail on the 8th of March, 1875, eastward along the shores of the broad arm of the lake which we first sighted, and which henceforward is known, in honour of its first discoverer, as "Speke Gulf."

CHAPTER VIII.

Afloat on the lake — We catch a guide — Saramba's terror — The Shimeeyu — Pyramid Point — The island of Ukerewe — In the haunt of crocodiles — Shizu Island — The hippopotami — Uriri — The headlands of Goshi — Bridge Island — Volcanoes — U-go-weh — the inebriates of Ugamba — Treachery at Maheta — Primitive man — The art of pleasing — A night at Uvuma — Mobbed by Wavuma — Barmecide fare — Message from Mtesa — "In the Kabaka's name" — Camp on Soweh Island.

March 8. — Afloat on the waters of Speke Gulf! The sky is gloomy and the light grey water has become a dull ashen grey; the rocks are bare and rugged; and the land, sympathising with the gloom above, appears silent and lonely. The people sigh dolorously, their rowing is as that of men who think they are bound to certain death, and now and again wistful looks are thrown towards me as though they expected an order to return. Their hearts are full of misgivings. Slowly, however, we move through the dull, dead waters; slowly we pass by the dull grey rocks of Lutari Point, and still slower do the boatmen row when the rugged rocks shut off the view of Kagehyi and front them with their bare rude masses.

Five miles brought us to Igusa, a settlement doubtless pleasant enough under a fair sky, but bearing this afternoon its share of the universal gloom. Without a guide or interpreter, we bore in for a little reed-lined creek. A fisherman, with a head of hair resembling a thick mop, came down to the boat. He had, it seems, visited Kagehyi two or three days before, and recognised us. A better acquaintance was soon begun, and ended in his becoming captivated with our promises of rewards and offering his services as guide. The boatmen were overjoyed; for the guide, whose name was Saramba, proved to have been one of Sungoro's boatmen in some of that Arab's trading excursions to Ururi. We passed a cheerless night, for the reeds turned out to be the haunt of a multitude of mosquitoes, and the air was cold. However, with Saramba as guide, we promised ourselves better quarters in future.

March 9. — At 6 A.M., after Saramba's appearance, we resumed our voyage, and continued on our way eastward, clinging to the shores of Sima. At 11 A.M. the clouds, which had long been gathering over the horizon to the north-west, discharged both squall and gale, and the scene soon became wild beyond description. We steered from the shore, and were soon involved in the dreadful chaos of watery madness and uproar. The wind swept us over the fierce waves, the Lady Alice bounding forward like a wild courser. It lashed the waters into spray and foam, and hurled them over the devoted crew and boat. With a mere rag presented to the gale, we drove unresistingly along. Strange islets in the neighbourhood of Mashakka became then objects of terror to us, but we passed them in safety and saw the grey hills of Magu far in front of us. The boatmen cowered to windward: Saramba had collapsed in terror, and had resignedly covered his moppy head with his loin-cloth. Zaidi Mganda, the steersman, and myself were the only persons visible above the gunwale, and our united strengths were required to guide the boat over the raging sea. At 2 P.M. we came in view of the Shimeeyu river, and, steering close to the little island of Natwari swept round to leeward, and through a calm water made our way into harbour, opposite the entrance to the river.

March 10. — The next day was beautiful. The wild waters of yesterday were calm as those of a pond. The bold hills of Magu, with all their sere and treeless outlines, stood out in fine relief. Opposite them, at about 1300 yards distant, were the brush-covered tops of the Mazanza heights; while between them lay glittering the broad and noble creek which receives the tribute flood of the Shimeeyu, the extreme southern reach of Nile waters. The total length of the course of this river, as laid out on the chart, is 300 miles, which gives the course of the Nile a length of 4200 miles: thus making it the second longest river in the world. The creek extends to a considerable distance, and then contracts to a width of about 400 yards, through which the Monangah, after uniting with the Luwamberri and the Duma rivers, discharges its brown waters, under the name of the Shimeeyu, into the lake.

After an examination of these features, we continued our journey along the coast of Mazanza, which forms the eastern shore of the bay of Shimeeyu, passing by the boldly rising and wooded hills of Manassa. At 4 P.M. we attempted to land in a small cove, but were driven away by a multitude of audacious hippopotami, who rushed towards us open-mouthed. Perceiving that they were too numerous and bold for us, we were compelled to drop our stone anchors in 40 feet of water, about two miles from shore.

March 11. — On the 11th of March, after rowing nearly the whole day against a head-wind, we arrived at the eastern end of Speke Gulf, which here narrows to about seven miles. On the southern side Manassa extends from Mazanza, its coast-line marked by an almost unbroken ridge about two miles inland, varied here and there by rounded knolls and hills, from whose base there is a gradual slope covered with woods down to the water's edge. The eastern end of the gulf is closed by the land of the Wirigedi or, as Saramba called them, the Wajika. At the north-eastern end begins Sliahshi, consisting of a group of sterile hills, which, as we proceed west along the north side of the gulf, sink down into a naked plain. The Ruana river empties itself into the head of the gulf by two narrow mouths through a low wooded shore.

March 12. — On the 12th we continued to coast along Shahshi's low, bare plain, margined at the water's edge by eschinomenae, and a little farther inland lined by mimosa, thence past Iramba, a similar country to Shahshi, until we reached

Pyramid Point, so christened from the shape of its hills, but on running up into the bay (which has its greatest width at Rugedzi Strait), we found that Pyramid Point really forms the south-western end of a mountain-range. One of the most conspicuous objects we saw, as we stood on the uplands of Usmau, looking towards the N.N.E., was this Pyramid Point, but at that time we had, of course, only a dim idea of its neighbourhood to the lake.

Near the Point is a group of small islands, the principal being Kitaro, on which cattle and goats are found. Though the islanders obtain but a scanty subsistence from the soil, they find reason to congratulate themselves in that they are safe from the periodical raids made by the Wajika, or Wirigedi, a tribe unpleasantly distinguished for the length of their knives and the breadth and weight of their spears. On one of this group, which was uninhabited, we stayed to cook our midday meal. It appeared fair and pleasant enough from without — one mass of deepest verdure, with a cone rising about 100 feet above the lake. Upon exploring it, we found it to be a heap of gigantic rocks, between which the deposit of vegetable matter had given birth to a forest of young trees, the spreading green foliage of which was rendered still more impervious to sunshine by a multitude of parasitical plants and llianes, which had woven the whole into as thick and dense a shade as I ever remember to have seen. Below this mass of tangled branch and leaf the thermometer descends to 70° Fahr.; without, exposed to the blazing sun, it ascends to 115° Fahr.

In the evening we camped on a small island in the middle of the bay of Ukerewe, east of the beautiful isle of Nifuah, which is inhabited and is the home of an industrious colony subject to the king of Ukerewe.

From the summit of Nifuah we could distinguish the tall trees which gave shade to our camp and to Kaduma's village of Kagehyi, across Speke Gulf. Upon coming down to the water's edge, we saw nothing but the blue hills, 600 feet high, situated three miles south of Kagehyi; nor, turning our eyes to the north, could we see anything of the low shore which the Rugedzi Channel cuts. Standing close to the water at Nifuah, we would have imagined that Ukerewe was an island separated by a strait about two miles broad; but turning our boat to the north, a couple of hours' rowing brought us so near that we could see that the opposing point of the mainland is joined to the island, or appears to be joined, by a very low bush -covered neck of land a mile in width, which thus separates the waters of Speke Gulf from the great body of Lake Victoria. A still closer examination, however, reveals the fact that this narrow neck is cut by a shallow channel 6 feet wide and in some places only 3 feet deep. The ground, though extremely low on each side, is firm and compact enough; but here and there it is of a boggy nature. Hence it will be seen that Captain Speke, who called Ukerewe an island, was literally correct.

March 13. — On the 13th we enjoyed a fine six-knot breeze, and were able to make a good day's work, though we still clung to the shore of Ukerewe near enough to note clearly the features of the water-line. A glance at the country of Ukerewe showed it to be exceedingly populous and extensively cultivated. From Matembe to Yambuyah extends a bold ridge about 300 feet above the lake, and beyond this point is a deep indentation, called Ukwya, near the western horn of which we perceived a group of islets named Kiregi. These are the haunts of an immense number of crocodiles, and one nest discovered here contained fifty-eight eggs. At almost every step I took, when walking round one of the reed-lined islets, a specimen of the ugly Saurian tribe sprang with a startling rush into the lake. There appeared also to be as many monitors as there were crocodiles in this infested islet, and all round me, from the little creeks, and sometimes in very close proximity, lowed the hippopotami. I shot one of the monitors, and it measured 7 feet from the tip of the snout to the tip of the tail. One of the boat's crew skinned it, but, not having means or time to preserve it, we were finally compelled to abandon our treasure. Being extremely keen-eyed and agile in its movements, the monitor is a valuable auxiliary to the more indolent crocodile, which it wakes frequently from slumber, and by its impetuous rush at sight of the intruder saves it from becoming a prey to the hunter. In return for its services the greater monster furnishes it with many a delicious meal on its eggs. The enormous number of smaller lizards, skinks, and geckos, which these islets also sustain, prove that the monitors have abundant means of supplies.

From here we sailed round the coast of Wiru, and leaving about four miles on our left the Kuneneh group, we steered N.N. AY. Mag. for the Iraugara Islands, at the north-western extremity of Ukerewe, the shore presenting to our view throughout only a low hill range clothed with woods. Leaving Irangara behind us, we emerged in view of the vast amplitude, as though of ocean, of the Victoria Nyanza.

After sailing past the Kamassi and Kindevi islets, we rounded the hilly point of Masonga, and beheld on our right, as far as Shizu Island, a broad bay, bounded by a crescent-shaped ridge, springing some 300 feet above the lake, and extensively wooded, while on our left lay the large and populous island of Ukara, peopled by an intensely superstitious colony, who cherish the most devout faith in charms and witchcraft.

March 16. — As we rowed past Shizu Island, we beheld the table-topped mountain of Majita rising, massive and grand, to the eastward. On the 16th of March we encamped on one of the bird-rocks about three miles from the base of Majita, which rises probably between 2000 and 3000 feet above the lake. From the northern angle of Majita we sailed, on a north-east course for the district of Wye, across a deep bay distinguished only for the short hill range of Usambara, between which, on either side, extends the low and almost treeless plain of Shahshi to the waters of Speke Gulf.

From Wye we coasted along populous Ururi. The country appears well cultivated, and villages are numerous. Some of the Waruri fishermen informed us we should be eight years circumnavigating the lake! Numerous rocky islands, almost all uninhabited at this period, stud the neighbourhood of the mainland, and the coast is so indented with deep bays and inlets that it requires very careful attention to survey it. Its features are similar to those of Usukuma, namely, swelling and uneven lines of hills, sometimes with slopes extending for three or four miles, more often, as in the case of nearly all the headlands, with points springing abrupt and sheer from the water's edge. Wherever the ridges rise gradually and at a distance from the lake, special advantages for cultivation appear to obtain, for I have noted that all such sites were thickly populated by the tribes of Ururi, Ukerewe, Sima, Magu, or Uchambi. A few of the Burdett-Coutts Islands exhibited traces of having been the resort of fugitives, for on several of them we discovered bananas and other garden plants, and ruined huts. We struck across the bay to Ikungu, and thence across another to picturesque Dobo, nearly opposite Irieni.

March 17. — Having arrived at anchorage at dusk, we were led to seek shelter under the lee of one of the outlying rocks of Dobo. We had moored both by bow and stern, to prevent being swept by the restless surf against the rocks, but about midnight a storm arose from the eastward, exposing us to all its fury. We were swept with great force against the rocks, and should inevitably have been lost had not the oars, which we had lashed outside the boat as fenders, protected it. Through the pelting rain, and amid the thunders of the aroused waves which lashed the reef, we laboured strenuously to save ourselves, and finally succeeded in rowing to the other lee.

Externally, the aspect of these islands on the coast of Ururi is very rugged, bare, and unpromising, but within are many acres of cultivable soil covered with green grass, and the hippopotami, which abound in the neighbourhood of these deserted, grassy islands, here find luxurious pasturage. Like the tribes on the mainland, these amphibiae appear to possess also their respective boundaries and their separate haunts. The hippopotami of Lake Victoria, moreover, are an excessively belligerent species, and the unwary voyager, on approaching their haunts, exposes himself to danger. We were frequently chased by them; and as the boat was not adapted for a combat with such pachyderms, a collision would have been fatal to us. The settlements at Irieni possess large herds of cattle, but the soil does not seem to be highly cultivated. In this respect the people appear to resemble in character the Watusi in Unyamwezi, who live only on the milk of their cattle, and such grain as they are enabled to obtain by its sale.

March 18. — Suspecting, after leaving Irieni, and approaching Mori Bay, that a river of considerable importance emptied into it, we paid particular attention to every indentation on its uneven coast; but on arriving at a lofty though small island at the eastern extremity, and climbing to its summit 150 feet above the lake, we saw that the river was small, and that its course was from south of east. Observation Island was rich in plants, though only a few hundred yards in length.

The wild pine-apple, mimosas, acacia, thorn, gum, vines, euphorbias, eschinomenae, llianes, water-cane, and spear-grass flourished with a luxuriance quite astonishing. As we passed Utiri, we observed that the natives were much interested in our boat, and some fishermen whom we encountered fell into ecstasies of laughter when they saw the novel method we adopted for propelling her. They mocked us good-naturedly, and by their gestures seemed to express contempt for the method in question, as not being equal to paddling. The rudder and its uses also excited unusual astonishment, and when the sail was hoisted, they skurried away as though it were an object of terror.

March 19. — After leaving the hilly coast of Utiri, the lowlands of Shirati and Mohruru rose into view, and the black mountain mass of Ugeyeya appeared to the eastward at the distance of about twenty miles. To the west of it, grim and lofty, loomed the island of Ugingo. Clusters of grey, rocky islets stud the lake along the coast of Shirati, while from the water's edge, to a distance of five or six miles, an uninteresting plain, unenlivened by forest or verdure, slopes slowly up to where the land breaks into groups and masses of irregular hills. This continues to the mouth of a river which the natives call Gori, and which terminates the country of Ururi. On the right bank of the river begins mountainous Ugeyeya, the south-western extremity of which runs out into the lake like a promontory.

Gori is an important and powerful river during the rainy season. It is said to rise in a north-easterly direction near Kavi. Far inland on the east, to a distance of twenty-five days' journey, the country is reported to be a continuous plain, dotted with low hills and containing water only in pools. About fifteen days' journey from the lake, the natives also report a region wherein are "low hills which discharge smoke and sometimes fire from their tops." This district is called Susa, and is a portion of the Masai Land. All concurred in stating that no stream runs north, but that all waters for at least twenty days' journey enter the lake. Beyond that distance lies a small lake which discharges a stream eastward — supposed by me to be the Pangani.

March 21. — On the 21st of March we were passing under the lee — for the wind blew then from the north-east, off the land — of the dark headlands of Goshi, which at first rise steeply from the lake 900 feet and, later, receding from the lake, attain a height of from 2000 to 3000 feet. On our left towered the tall, tree-clad island of Ugingo, extending far to the north-west. Thin blue columns of smoke rising from the depths of its woods announced the presence of man, probably fishermen or fugitives from the mainland. Judging from what I observed of the slopes of this extremity of Ugeyeya, I should say that much of this portion is uninhabited. Bounding the point that confronts the island of Ugingo, we passed between two more uninhabited islands, and then the dome-like hills of Wakuneh burst upon our view. Our impression of the land on this side was that it was a pastoral country, and more thickly populated, for smoke curled more frequently from above depressions and sheltered positions.

At evening we camped on Bridge Island, so named from a natural bridge of basaltic rock which forms an irregular arch of about 24 feet in length by about 12 feet in depth, and under which we were able to pass from one side of the island to the other. The island is covered with brushwood and tall grass, and in the interstices of the rocks, where the vegetable deposit was of great depth, grew several fine mangroves. The height is about 50 feet above the lake, and from its summit we obtained a fine view of Ugingo Island, brooding in its gloomy solitude, and of the steep and high ranges of Ugeyeya, with the level plains of Wagansu and Wigassi extending eastward. To the west stretched an apparently boundless sea, its face ruffled by a strong breeze, and farther northward still loomed upward unknown lands, their contour broken now by rounded domes and again by sharp cones.

March 22. — The number of islands encountered next day proved so troublesome to us that we were compelled to creep cautiously along the shore. As we neared Nakidimo, we observed the water change from its usual clear grey colour to that of a rich brown, and, seeing a creek close by, felt fully assured that we had discovered some important river. As we entered, the creek widened and disclosed picturesque features of outlined hill and wooded slope. We pulled steadily to its farther extremity, but the stream which entered here was small, and oozed through a reedy marsh. We endeavoured for an hour to induce a canoe with three fishermen in it to approach, but all we could make out from Saramba, who, I fear, did not understand them, was that the name of the country was Ugoweh, which sounded so like "You go 'way" that I declined accepting it, until the natives shouted out still more clearly and emphatically, "U-go-weh." It was evident, however, that these natives spoke a language that our guide from the south did not quite comprehend. We continued our keen inspection of the numerous indentations from Ugoweh (?) to Nakidimo Creek, into which an important stream debouches. The hippopotami were numerous, and as bold as those of Speke Gulf.

Emerging once more into the lake, we anchored about a mile from the shore in 6 fathoms, and found that there was a current of about half a knot setting westward. At 2 P.M. we hoisted sail, and with a fair wind were able to hug the mainland and make good progress, within view of a very populous and extensively cultivated shore. This was the land of Maheta, we were told, and the same which we had sighted from the summit of Bridge Island. We flew away with a bellying sail along the coast of Maheta, where we saw a denser population and more clusters of large villages than we had beheld elsewhere. We thought we would make one more effort to learn of the natives the names of some of these villages, and for that purpose steered for a cove on the western shore. We anchored within 50 yards, and so paid out our cable that only a few feet of deep water separated us from the beach. Some half-dozen men, wearing small land-shells above their elbows and a circle of them round their heads, came to the brink. With these we opened a friendly conversation, during which they disclosed the name of the country as

"Mahata" or "Maheta" in Ugeyeya; but more they would not communicate unless we would land. We prepared to do so, but the numbers on the blue shore increased so fast that we were compelled to pull off again until they should moderate their excitement and make room. They seemed to think we were about to pull off altogether, for there suddenly appeared out of the bush on each side of the spot where we had intended to land such a host of spears that we hoisted sail, and left them to try their treachery on some other boat or canoe more imprudent than ours. The discomfited people were seen to consult together on a small ridge behind the bush lining the lake, and no doubt they thought we were about to pass close to a small point at the north end of the cove, for they shouted gleefully at the prospect of a prize; but, lowering sail, we pulled to windward, far out of the reach of bow or sling, and at dusk made for a small island to which we moored our boat, and there camped in security.

March 24. — From our little island off Maheta, we sailed at the dawn of day towards the low shores, and were making good progress, when we bumped over the spine of a rising hippopotamus, who, frightened by this strange and weighty object on his back, gave a furious lunge, and shook the boat until we all thought she would be shaken to pieces. The hippo, after this manifestation of disgust, rose a few feet astern, and loudly roared his defiance; but after experiencing his great strength, we rowed away hard from his neighbourhood.

About 10 A.M. we found ourselves abreast of the cones of Manyara, and discovered the long and lofty promontory which had attracted our attention ever since leaving Maheta to be the island of Usuguru, another, though larger copy of Ugingo. Through a channel two miles broad we entered the bay of Manyara, bounded on the east by the picturesque hills of that country, on the north by the plain of Ugana, and on the west by Muiwanda and the long, narrow promontory of Chaga. This bay forms the extreme north-east corner of Lake Victoria, but strangers, travelling by land, would undoubtedly mistake it for a separate lake, as Usuguru, when looked at from this bay, seems to overlap the points of Chaga and Manyara.

About six miles from the north-eastern extremity of the bay, we anchored on the afternoon of the 24th of March, about 100 yards from the village of Muiwanda. Here we found a people speaking the language of Usoga. A good deal of diplomacy was employed between the natives and ourselves before a friendly intercourse was established, but we were finally successful in inducing the natives to exchange vegetable produce and a sheep for some of the blue glass beads called Mutwida. Neither men nor women wore any covering for their nakedness save a kirtle of green banana-leaves, which appeared to me to resemble in its exceeding primitiveness the fig-leaf costume of Adam and Eve. The men were distinguished, besides, by the absence of the upper and lower front teeth, and by their shaven heads, on which were left only irregular combs or crescents of hair on the top and over the forehead. While we were negotiating for food, a magnificent canoe, painted a reddish brown, came up from the western side of the village, but, despite the loud invitations tendered to them, the strangers kept on their way and proceeded up the bay of Manyara.

March 25. — On the 25th, refreshed by the meat and vegetables we had purchased, we began our voyage along the northern coast of Lake Victoria, and, two hours later, were in conversation with the natives of Chaga or Shaga, who informed us that Murambo, king of Usuguru, was also king of Chaga. I am unable to decide whether Chaga is a promontory or an island, but I believe that there is a narrow channel navigable for canoes (of the same nature as the Rugedzi Channel) separating Chaga from the mainland. Between its southern point and Usuguru Island, there is a strait about three-quarters of a mile wide, through which we passed to Fisherman's Island, where we rested for our noon-day meal. At 2 P.M. we arrived, after an hour's rowing, near Ngevi Island, and when close to it, we were compelled to take shelter from a furious nor'-wester.

We had been at anchor scarcely ten minutes before we saw a small canoe, paddled by two men, boldly approach us from the shore of Ugamba, distant about a mile and a half on our right or to the east of us. In our mildest accents we hailed them, and, after a protracted interval employed by them in curiously scanning us, they permitted us to hear the sound of their voices. But nothing would induce them to come nearer than about 100 yards. In the midst of these vain efforts to win their confidence, a canoe similar in form and colour to that which had won our admiration at Muiwanda advanced towards us. A false prow projected upward, curving in the shape of a bent elbow, from the tip of which to the top of the bow of the canoe was strung a taut line, and along this was suspended some fine grass, which waved like a mane as she charged up, bold and confident, propelled by forty paddlers. Half of this number, who were seated forward, sprang up when they came within 50 yards, and, seizing long tufted lances and shields, began to sway them menacingly. As we made no demonstration of resistance, they advanced cautiously, and when within 20 yards, swerved aside, wheeling round us in a defiant style.

Finally we broke silence, and demanded who they were, and why they came up as though they would attack us. As they did not understand either Kingwana, Kisukuma, or Kiuyamwezi, one of my boatmen attempted Kiganda, a little of which they appeared to understand; and by this means we opened a conversation. They edged towards us a little nearer, and ended by ranging their long canoe alongside of our boat. Our tame, mild manners were in striking contrast to their bullying, overbearing, and insolent demeanour. The paddlers, half of whom were intoxicated, laid their hands with familiar freedom upon every thing. We still smiled, and were as mild and placable as though anger and resentment could never enter our hearts. We were so courteous, indeed, that we permitted them to handle our persons with a degree of freedom which to them appeared unaccountable — unless we were so timid that we feared to give offence. If we had been so many sheep, we could not have borne a milder or a more innocent aspect. Our bold friends, reeling and jostling one another in their eagerness to offend, seized their spears and shields, and began to chant in bacchanalian tones a song that was tipsily discordant. Some seized their slings and flung stones to a great distance, which we applauded. Then one of them, under the influence of wine, and spirits elated by the chant, waxed bolder, and looked as though he would aim at myself, seated observant but mute in the stern of my boat. I made a motion with my hand as though deprecating such an action. The sooty villain seemed to become at once animated by an hysteric passion, and whirled his stone over my head, a loud drunken cheer applauding his boldness.

Perceiving that they were becoming wanton through our apparently mild demeanour, I seized my revolver and fired rapidly into the water, in the direction the stone had been flung, and the effect was painfully ludicrous. The bold, insolent bacchanals at the first shot had sprung overboard, and were swimming for dear life to Ngevi, leaving their canoe in our hands. "Friends, come back, come back; why this fear?" cried out our interpreter; "we simply wished to show you that we had weapons as well as yourselves. Come, take your canoe; see, we push it away for you to seize it." We eventually won them back with smiles. We spoke to them sweetly as before. The natives were more respectful in their demeanour. They laughed, cried out admiringly; imitated the pistol shots; "Boom, boom, boom," they shouted. They then presented me with a bunch of bananas! We became enthusiastic admirers of each other.

Meantime, two more large canoes came up, also bold and confident, for they had not yet been taught a lesson. These new-comers insisted that we should visit their king Kamoydah. We begged to be excused. They became still more urgent in their request. We said it was impossible; they were strangers, and not very well behaved; if they wished to barter with us, they could load their canoes and come to Ngevi, where we would be happy to exchange beads or cloth for their articles. Three other canoes were now seen approaching. We sat, however, extremely still, patient, and placable, and waited for them. The united voices of the 130 natives made a terrible din, but we endured it with saintly meekness and the fortitude of stoics — for a period. We bore the storm of entreaties mixed with rude menace until instinct warned me that it was becoming dangerous. I then delivered some instructions to the boat's crew, and, nodding to the shore, affected to surrender with an indifferent grace. They became suddenly silent. We lifted the stone anchor, and took to our oars, steering to the broken water, ruffled by the nor'-wester, beyond the shelter of the island, convoyed by the six canoes. We accompanied them some hundreds of yards, and then, suddenly hoisting sail, swept by them like an arrow. We preferred the prospect of the lone watery expanse to the company of the perverse inebriates of Ugamba.

We continued sailing for half an hour, and as it was then near sunset, dropped anchor in 75 feet of water. The wind, which had swept in strong gusts from the north-west, suddenly fell, for in the north-east the aspect of the sky had long been threatening. Clouds surged up in thick masses from that direction, and cast a gloom over the wood-clothed slopes and crests of Usuguru, which became almost as black as a velvet pall, while the lake grew as quiet as though vitrified into glass. Soon the piled up cloud-mass grew jagged, and a portentous zigzag line of deep sable hue ran through its centre, from which the storm seemed to issue. I requested the crew to come farther aft, and, fastening a double rope to the stone anchor, prepared every mug and baler for the rain with which we were threatened. The wind then fell, as though from above, upon our bowed heads with an overpowering force, striving against the resistance which it met, as if it would bear us down to the bottom of the lake, and then, repelled by the face of the water, it brushed it into millions of tiny ripples. The temperature fell to 62° Fahr., and with this sudden cold down dropped a severe shower of hailstones of great size, which pelted us with great force, and made our teeth chatter. After this the rain fell in sheets, while the lightning blazed, preceding the most dreadful thunder-claps I remember to have ever heard.

The rain, indeed, fell in such quantities that it required two men for each section to keep the boat sufficiently buoyant to ride the crest of the waves. The crew cried out that the boat was sinking — that, if the rain continued in such volume, nothing could save us. In reply, I only urged them to bale her out faster.

The sable mass of Usuguru — as I observed by the bars of intense light which the lightning flashed almost every second — was still in front, and I knew, therefore, that we were not being swept very fast to sea. Our energies were wholly devoted to keeping our poor pelted selves afloat, and this occupied the crew so much that they half forgot the horrors of the black and dismal night. For two hours this experience lasted, and then, unburdening our breasts with sighs of gladness not unmixed with gratitude, we took our anchor on board, and stole through the darkness to the western side of Ngevi Island, where, after kindling a fire, we dried our clothes and our wetted bodies, and, over a hot potful of Liebig, affected to laugh at our late critical position.

March 26. — In the morning the world appeared re-born, for the sky was a bluish crystal, the shores looked as if fresh painted in green, the lake shone like burnished steel, the atmosphere seemed created for health. Glowing with new life, we emerged out of our wild arbour of cane and mangrove to enjoy the glories of a gracious heaven, and the men relieved their grateful breasts by chanting loudly and melodiously one of their most animating boat-songs.

As we rowed in this bright mood across the bay of Ugamba, we noticed a lofty mount which I should judge to be fully 3000 feet above the lake, towards the north-east. From the natives of Usamu Island, we obtained the name of Marsawa for this the most conspicuous feature of the neighbourhood. After obtaining a clear meridian altitude, on a small island between Usamu and Namungi, we steered for the latter. The art of pleasing was never attempted with such effect as at Namungi.

Though we had great difficulty in even obtaining a hearing, we persisted in the practice of the art with all its amusing variations, until our perseverance was finally rewarded. A young fisherman was despatched to listen from the shore, but the young wretch merely stared at us. We tossed into his canoe a bunch of beads, and he understood their signification. He shouted out to his fellows on the shore, who were burning with curiosity to see closer the strange boat and strange crew, amongst whom they saw a man who was like unto no man they had ever seen or heard, or dreamed of.

A score of canoes loaded with peaceful, harmless souls came towards us, all of whom begged for beads. When we saw that they could be inspired to talk, we suggested to them that, in return for food, abundance of beads might be obtained. They instantly raced for the banana and plantain groves in great excitement. We were so close that we could hear the heavy clusters falling under the native machetes, and within a short time so many bunches were held out to us that we might have sunk under the waves had we purchased all. After storing a sufficient quantity to provision us for three days, of bananas, fowls and eggs, and sweet maramba or banana wine, and eliciting the names of the various islands, capes, and most prominent hills, we attempted to resume our journey. But the people, upon whom our liberality had produced too strong an effect, would not permit us to do so until we had further celebrated our acquaintance with copious draughts of their delicious wine. The Wangwana would have been delighted to have exhausted many days in such a fascinating life, but the coast of the Victoria was lengthy, the winds not always favourable, and we had a large number of friends in Usukuma who might become restless, were we too long absent. We therefore set sail, convoyed a long distance by about thirty canoes, manned by light-hearted guileless creatures in an extreme state of enjoyment and redundant hilarity.

This was altogether a remarkable scene; our exploring boat, with its lug-sail set, dragging about thirty canoes, whose crews were all intoxicated, and whose good-nature was so excessive as to cause them to supply our boat's crew with copious quantities of their wine, until all were in an uncommonly joyous mood. It would be well worth describing in detail, but I am compelled to be brief. After sailing in company a few miles, we finally freed ourselves from our hospitable entertainers, and steering across the channel to the island opposite Neygano, coasted along its well-wooded shores. Perceiving a deep bay farther west, we entered it, and near the extreme eastern end of Uvuma anchored about 150 yards off the village of Mombiti.

Had we been better acquainted with the character of the Wavuma, we probably should have been less inclined to visit their shores, but, ignorant of their ferocity, and zealous to perform our duties, we persevered in attempting to open intercourse with this tribe. We were, however, prudent enough not to rush into danger by taking it for granted that most savages were a guileless, amiable set, who would never dream of injuring or molesting strangers — and this circumspection most likely saved our lives.

After a few minutes' distant conversation, the Wavuma approached us, and we were enabled to purchase fuel for cooking, making a liberal payment. We hoped they would be induced to sell us food also, not that we were really in need of it, but because it furnished us with another motive for continuing our intercourse, and enlarged our opportunities for studying their nature and habits, and obtaining names for the localities around. We had numerous visitors, who appeared to be fine, manly, well-made fellows, but nothing would induce them to bring the smallest quantity of food for sale. We therefore resignedly forbore from troubling them, but inspected them with as much interest as they inspected us. They were evidently people with abundant self-confidence, from the cool complacency with which they regarded us. Their canoes were beautiful specimens, and descriptions and pictures of them will be given hereafter. The shores were bold, irregular in outline, and clothed with a luxuriance of vegetation and many tall trees, between which were seen the banana groves, their pale green colour strongly contrasting with the darker tints of the forest foliage.

The night that followed was wild. At sunset the temperature fell to 70° Fahr., and the wind was charged with a cold drizzle. Being in rather an exposed position, we moved our anchorage near the mouth of the Munulu river, and not a minute too soon, for the wind increased to a gale; and the gale, heralded by a short-lived squall, brought hailstones with it. Preparing to pass the night here, we covered the boat with a sail, under which the sailors slept, though the watch, frequently relieved, was obliged to maintain a strict look-out. Throughout the long hours of darkness, the gale maintained its force; the boat pitched and groaned, and the rain fell in torrents; the seas frequently tossed capfuls of water into us, so that, under such circumstances, we enjoyed no rest.

March 27. — By morning the gale had subsided, and the heavy, sluggish waves were slumbering. After waiting to cook our morning meal, and assisting the restoration of animal heat with draughts of Liebig's extract liquefied, we resumed our journey along the southern coast of Uvuma about 8 A.M.

Upon leaving the bay of Mombiti, we were compelled to pass by a point of land closely covered with tall grass, whither we saw a large force of natives rush to take up advantageous positions. As we slowly neared the point, a few of them advanced to the rocks, and beckoned us to approach nearer. We acceded so far as to approach within a few feet, when the natives called out something, and immediately attacked us with large rocks. We sheered off immediately, when a crowd emerged from their hiding place with slings, with which they flung stones at us, striking the boat and wounding the steersman, who was seated next to me. To prevent further harm, I discharged my revolver rapidly at them, and one of the natives fell: whereupon the others desisted from their attack, and retreated into the grass, leaving us to pursue our way unmolested.

Again edging close to the shore, we continued our investigations of the numerous indentations. The island rose with steep, grassy, treeless slopes to a height of about 300 feet above the lake. Herds of cattle were abundant, and flocks of goats grazed on the hillsides. The villages were many, but unenclosed, and consisted of a few dome-like huts, from which we inferred that the Wavuma were a people who could well defend themselves. At this time the lake was as still as a pond; no clouds hung over any part of the horizon; the sky was of a steel-blue colour, out of which the sun shone with true tropical fervour. But the atmosphere was not clear; a light vapour rose out of the lake, trembling in the heat, rendering islands but five miles distant dim and indistinct.

Arrived in the channel between the tawny, grass-clad island of Bugeyeya and that of Uvuma, we steered midway, that we might take compass bearings. From a small cove in the Uvuma shores, abreast of us, emerged quite a fleet of canoes, thirteen in number. The more advanced held up a handful of sweet-potatoes to our view, and we ceased rowing, but left the sail hoisted, which, with the very slight breeze then blowing, drifted us westward about half a knot an hour.

The Wavuma were permitted to range alongside, and we saw that they were fully armed with spear and shield. We offered several kinds of beads for the potatoes they had offered to sell, but with a gesture of contempt they refused everything, and from their actions and manner we became soon convinced that they had manned their canoes for other purposes than barter; besides, they possessed only about twenty potatoes, which, singularly enough, were all in the first canoe. Strange to say, also, the men of the first canoe were, though disinclined to sell, moderate in their behaviour; but their temper changed as soon as their comrades had arrived, and had taken up their positions in front of our boat, blocking our progress through the water. The Wavuma, now emboldened by their numbers, waxed noisy, then insolent, and finally aggressive. They seized one thing after another with a cunning dexterity, which required all our attention to divine their purpose; and while we were occupied with the truculent rabble in our front, a movement of which we were unaware was being made successfully at the stern; but the guide, Saramba, catching sight of a thief, warned me to cast my eyes behind, and I detected him in the act of robbery. Becoming assured by this time that the Wavuma had arrived in such numbers for the sole purpose of capturing what appeared to them an apparently easy prey, and their manoeuvres were evidently intended to embarrass us and distract our attention, I motioned them to depart with my hand, giving orders at the same time to the boat's crew to make ready their oars. This movement, of necessity, caused them to declare their purposes, and they manifested them by audaciously laying their hands on the oars, and arresting the attempts of the boat's crew to row. Either we were free or we were not. If yet free men, with the power to defend our freedom, we must be permitted to continue our voyage on the sea without let or hindrance. If not free men, we had first to be disarmed. I seized my gun, and motioned them again to depart. With a loud, scornful cry they caught up their spears and shields, and prepared to launch their weapons. To be saved, we must act quickly, and I fired over their heads; and as they fell back from the boat, I bade my men pull away. Forming a line on each side of us, about 30 yards off, they flung their spears, which the boat's crew avoided by dropping into the bottom of the boat. The canoes astern clapped their hands gleefully, showing me a large bunch of Mutunda beads which had been surreptitiously abstracted from the stern of the boat. I seized my repeating rifle and fired in earnest, to right and left. The fellow with the beads was doubled up, and the boldest of those nearest to us was disabled. The big rifle, aimed at the waterline of two or three of the canoes, perforated them through and through, which compelled the crews to pay attention to their sinking crafts, and permitted us to continue our voyage into Napoleon Channel and to examine the Ripon Falls. On an uninhabited point of Usoga, near the falls, we encamped; and on the 29th of March crossed the channel, and coasted along Uganda between numerous islands, the largest of which are densely inhabited.

At Kiwa Island we rested for the day, and were received with the greatest cordiality by the chief, who sent messengers to the island of Kerenge, a distance of three miles, to purchase bananas and jars of maramba wine, for the guest, as he said, of the Kabaka Mtesa. As it was the first time for twenty-two days that we had lived with natives since leaving Kagehi we celebrated, as we were in duty bound, our arrival among friends.

March 30. — The next day, guided and escorted by the chief, we entered Ukafu, where we found a tall handsome young Mtongoleh in command of the district, before whom the chief of Kiwa Island made obeisance as before a great lord. The young Mtongoleh, though professing an ardent interest in us, and voluble of promises, treated us only to Barmecide fare after waiting twenty-four hours. Perceiving that his courtesies, though suavely proffered, failed to satisfy the cravings of our jaded stomachs, we left him still protesting enormous admiration for us, and still volubly assuring us that he was preparing grand hospitalities in our honour, I was staggered when I understood in its full extent the perfect art with which we had been duped. "Could this be Central Africa," I asked myself, "wherein we find such perfect adepts in the art of deception? But two days ago the savagery of the land was intense and real, for every man's hand was raised in ferocity against the stranger. In the land next adjoining we find a people polite, agreeable, and professing the warmest admiration for the stranger, but as inhospitable as any hotel-keeper in London or New York to a penniless guest!"

At a little village in the bay of Buka we discovered we were premature in our judgment. The Mtongoleh at this place invited us to his village, spread out before us a feast of new as well as clotted milk, mellow and ripe bananas, a kid, sweet-potatoes, and eggs, and despatched a messenger instantly to the Kabaka Mtesa to announce the coming of a stranger in the land, declaring, at the same time, his intention not to abandon us until he had brought us face to face with the great monarch of Equatorial Africa, in whom, he smilingly assured us, we should meet a friend, and under whose protection we might sleep secure.

April 1. — We halted one more day to enjoy the bounteous fare of the chief of Buka. My admiration for the land and the people steadily increased, for I experienced with each hour some pleasing civility. The land was in fit accord with the people, and few more interesting prospects could Africa furnish than that which lovingly embraces the bay of Buka. From the margin of the lake, lined by waving water-cane, up to the highest hill-top, all was verdure — of varying shades. The light green of the elegant matete contrasted with the deeper tints of the various species of fig; the satin -sheeny fronds of the graceful plantains were overlapped by clouds of the pale foliage of the tamarind; while between and around all, the young grass of the pastured hillsides spreads its emerald carpet. In free, bold, and yet graceful outline, the hills shut in the scene, swelling upward in full dome-like contour, here sweeping round to enclose within its hollow a gorgeous plantain-grove, there projecting boldly into abrupt, steep headlands, and again receding in a succession of noble terraces into regions as yet unexplored by the white man. One village had a low pebbly beach, that ran in a sinuous light-grey line between the darker grey face of the lake and the living perennial green of a banana plantation. I imagined myself fallen into an estate which I had inherited by right divine and human, or at least I felt something akin to that large feeling which heirs of unencumbered broad lands may be supposed to feel, and attributed such an unusual feeling to an attack of perfect digestion, and a free, unclogged, and undisturbed liver.

April 2. — On the 2nd of April we proceeded, in an amiable, light-hearted mood, the favourites both of men and nature, along the beautiful shore separating Buka Bay from Kadzi Bay, and halted about noon at the village of Kirudo, where we experienced hospitalities similar to those of the day previous. We purposely made our voyages short, in order that the Kabaka might be informed in time of our coming.

April 3. — Just as we were about to depart next morning, we saw six beautiful canoes, crowded with men, coming round a point, and for a very short period were under the impression that they composed another piratical fleet on its way to intercept us, but on surveying them with my glass I saw that several who were seated amidships were dressed in white, like the Wangwana, and our Waganda guides, among whom was our hospitable entertainer of Buka, informed us that they were the Kabaka's people. As they approached us, the commander was seen arraying himself for the occasion. He donned a bead-worked head-dress, above which long white cock's feathers waved, and a snowy white and long-haired goat-skin, while a crimson robe, depending from his shoulders, completed the full dress.

In the middle of the bay of Kadzi we encountered, and a most ceremonious greeting took place. The commander was a fine lusty young man of twenty or thereabouts, and after springing into our boat he knelt down before me, and declared his errand to the following effect: —

"The Kabaka sends me with many salaams to you. He is in great hopes that you will visit him, and has encamped at Usavara, that he may be near the lake when you come. He does not know from what land you have come, but I have a swift messenger with a canoe who will not stop until he gives all the news to the Kabaka. His mother dreamed a dream a few nights ago, and in her dream she saw a white man on this lake in a boat coming this way, and the next morning she told the Kabaka, and, lo! you have come. Give me your answer, that I may send the messenger. Twiyanzi-yanzi-yanzi!" (Thanks, thanks, thanks.)

Whereupon, as the young commander, whose name was Magassa, understood Kiswahili, I delivered the news to him and to his people freely and frankly; and after I had ended, Magassa translated what the information was into Kiganda, and immediately the messenger departed. Meanwhile Magassa implored me to rest for this one day, that he might show me the hospitality of his country, and that I might enter the Kabahas presence in good humour with him. Persuaded also by my boat's crew to consent, we rowed to the village of Kadzi. Magassa was in his glory now. His voice became imperious to his escort of 182 men; even the feathers of his curious head-dress waved prouder, and his robe had a sweeping dignity worthy of a Roman emperor's. Upon landing, Magassa's stick was employed frequently. The sub-chief of Kadzi was compelled to yield implicit obedience to his vice-regal behests.

"Bring out bullocks, sheep, and goat's milk, and the mellowest of your choicest bananas, and great jars of maramba, and let the white man and his boatmen eat, and taste of the hospitalities of Uganda. Shall a white man enter the Kabakas presence with an empty belly? See how sallow and pinched his cheeks are. We want to see whether we cannot show him kindness superior to what the pagans have shown him."

Two bullocks and four goats, a basketful of fat mellow bananas, and four two gallon jars of maramba, were then brought before us, to which extraordinary bounty the boat's crew did ample justice. Nor were the escort of Magassa without supplies. The country was at their mercy. They killed three bullocks for themselves, cut down as many bananas as they wished, and made a raid on the chickens, in accordance with Magassa's serene gracious permission to help themselves.

"A wonderful land!" I thought, "where an entire country can be subjected to such an inordinate bully and vain youth as this Magassa, at the mere mention of the Kabakas name, and very evidently with the Kabakas sanction!" Uganda was new to us then. We were not aware how supreme the Kabaka's authority was; but, having a painful suspicion that the vast country which recognised his power was greatly abused, and grieving that the poor people had to endure such rough treatment for my sake, I did my best to prevent Magassa from extorting to excess.

April 4. — The next day we sallied forth from Kadzi Bay, with Magassa's escort leading the way. We crossed Bazzi Bay, from the middle of which we gained a view of old Sabaganzi's Hill, a square tabular mount, from the summit of which Magassa said we should see the whole of Murchison Bay and Rubaga, one of the Kabaka's capitals. About 10 A.M. we rounded Muvwo Point, and entered Murchison Bay. The entrance is about four miles wide, and naturally guarded by Linant Island, a lofty, dome-shaped island, situated between the opposing points of Muvwo and Umbiru. Upon leaving Muvwo south of us we have a full view of this fine body of water, which reaches its extreme width between Soweh Island and Ukumba. This, the farthest reach of its waters west, is about ten miles across, while its extreme length, from Linant Island to the arm of Monyono Bay, where Mtesa keeps his favourite canoes, cannot be less than fourteen miles.

We encamped, according to Magassa's wish, behind Soweh Island, on the east side of Murchison Bay, whence, the next day, we were to start for Usavara, the Kabaka's hunting village.

CHAPTER IX.

An extraordinary monarch — I am examined — African "chaff " — Mtesa, Emperor of Uganda — Description of Mtesa — A naval review — Arrival at the imperial capital — Mtesa's palace — Fascination of the country — I meet a white man — Col. Linant de Bellefonds — The process of conversion — A grand mission field — A pleasant day with Col. de Bellefonds — Starting for my camp.

April 5. — The little insight we obtained into the manners of Uganda between Soweh Island, Murchison Bay, and Kiwa Island, near Ukafu Bay, impressed us with the consciousness that we were about to become acquainted with an extraordinary monarch and an extraordinary people, as different from the barbarous pirates of Uvuma, and the wild, mop-headed men of Eastern Usukuma, as the British in India are from their Afridi fellow-subjects, or the white Americans of Arkansas from the semi-civilized Choctaws. If politeness could so govern the actions of the men of Kiwa Island, far removed as they were from contact with the Uganda court, and suave duplicity could so well be practised by the Mtongoleh of Ukafu, and such ready, ungrudging hospitality be shown by the chief of Buka, and the Kabaka's orders be so promptly executed by Magassa, the messenger, and the chief of Kadzi, what might we not expect. at the court, and what manner of man might not this "Kabaka" be!

Such were our reflections as Magassa, in his superb canoe, led the way from behind Soweh Island, and his little slave drummed an accompaniment to the droning chant of his canoe-men.

Compared with our lonely voyage from our camp at Usukuma round all the bays and inlets of the much-indented coasts of the Great Lake, these five superb canoes forming line in front of our boat, escorting us to the presence of the great potentate of Equatorial Africa, formed a scene which promised at least novelty, and a view of some extraordinary pomp and ceremony.

When about two miles from Usavara, we saw what we estimated to be thousands of people arranging themselves in order on a gently rising ground. When about a mile from the shore, Magassa gave the order to signal our advance upon it with fire-arms, and was at once obeyed by his dozen musketeers. Half a mile off I saw that the people on the shore had formed themselves into two dense lines, at the ends of which stood several finely-dressed men, arrayed in crimson and black and snowy white. As we neared the beach, volleys of musketry burst out from the long lines. Magassa's canoes steered outward to right and left, while 200 or 300 heavily loaded guns announced to all around that the white man — whom Mtesa's mother had dreamed about — had landed. Numerous kettle and bass drums sounded a noisy welcome, and flags, banners, and bannerets waved, and the people gave a great shout. Very much amazed at all this ceremonious and pompous greeting, I strode up towards the great standard, near which stood a short young man, dressed in a crimson robe which covered an immaculately white dress of bleached cotton, before whom Magassa, who had hurried ashore, kneeled reverently, and turning to me begged me to understand that this short young man was the Katekiro. Not knowing very well who the "Katekiro" was, I only bowed, which, strange to say, was imitated by him, only that his bow was far more profound and stately than mine. I was perplexed, confused, embarrassed, and I believe I blushed inwardly at this regal reception, though I hope I did not betray my embarrassment.

A dozen well-dressed people now came forward, and grasping my hand declared in the Swahili language that I was welcome to Uganda. The Katekiro motioned with his head, and amid a perfect concourse of beaten drums, which drowned all conversation, we walked side by side, and followed by curious thousands, to a courtyard, and a circle of grass-thatched huts surrounding a larger house, which I was told were my quarters.

The Katekiro and several of the chiefs accompanied me to my new hut, and a very sociable conversation took place. There was present a native of Zanzibar, named Tori, whom I shortly discovered to be chief drummer, engineer, and general jack-of-all-trades for the Kabaka. From this clever, ingenious man I obtained the information that the Katekiro was the prime minister, or the Kabaka's deputy, and that the titles of the other chiefs were Chambarango, Kangau, Mkwenda, Sekebobo, Kitunzi, Sabaganzi, Kauta, Saruti. There were several more present, but I must defer mention of them to other chapters.

Waganda, as I found subsequently, are not in the habit of remaining incurious before a stranger. Hosts of questions were fired off at me about my health, my journey, and its aim, Zanzibar, Europe and its people, the seas and the heavens, sun, moon, and stars, angels and devils, doctors, priests, and craftsmen in general; in fact, as the representative of nations who "know everything," I was subjected to a most searching examination, and in one hour and ten minutes it was declared unanimously that I had "passed." Forthwith after the acclamation, the stately bearing became merged into a more friendly one, and long, thin, nervous black hands were pushed into mine enthusiastically, from which I gathered that they applauded me as though I had won the honours of a senior wrangler. Some proceeded direct to the Kabaka and informed him that the white man was a genius, knew everything, and was remarkably polite and sociable, and the Kabaka was said to have "rubbed his hands as though he had just come into the possession of a treasure."

The fruits of the favourable verdict passed upon myself and merits were seen presently in fourteen fat oxen, sixteen goats and sheep, a hundred bunches of bananas, three dozen fowls, four wooden jars of milk, four baskets of sweet-potatoes, fifty ears of green Indian corn, a basket of rice, twenty fresh eggs, and ten pots of maramba wine. Kauta, Mtesa's steward or butler, at the head of the drovers and bearers of these various provisions, fell on his knees before me and said: —

"The Kabaka sends salaams unto his friend who has travelled so far to see him. The Kabaka cannot see the face of his friend until he has eaten and is satisfied. The Kabaka has sent his slave with these few things to his friend that he may eat, and at the ninth hour, after his friend has rested, the Kabaka will send and call for him to appear at the burzah. I have spoken. Twiyanzi-yanzi-yanzi!"

I replied suitably, though my politeness was not so excessive as to induce me to kneel before the courtly butler and thank him for permission to say I thanked him.

My boat's crew were amazed at this imperial bounty, which provided more than a bullock apiece for each member of my following. Saramba, the mop-headed guide from Usukuma, was requested to say what he thought of the Kabaka, who gave bullocks and goats in proportion as the Usukuma chief gave potatoes to his guests. Saramba's wits were all this time under a cloud. He was still dressed in the primitive goatskin of his country, as greasy and dingy as a whaling cook's pan-cloth — the greasiest thing I ever saw. He was stared at, jeered, and flouted by the courtly, cleanly pages of the court, who by this time had taken such keen and complete mental inventories of my features, traits, and points of character as would have put to shame even a Parisian newsmonger.

"What land is this undressed pagan from?" asked the pages, loud enough for poor Saramba to hear.

"Regard the pagan's hair," said another.

"He had better not let the Kabaka see him," said a third.

"He is surely a pagan slave — worth about a goat," remarked a fourth.

"Not he. I would not buy him for a ripe banana," ventured a fifth.

I looked up at Saramba, and half fancied that he paled.

Poor Saramba! "As soon as they are gone, off goes that mop, and we will dress you in white cloth," said Safeni, the coxswain, compassionately.

But Baraka, one of the boatmen, an incorrigible scoffer, said, "What is the use? If we give him cloth, will he wear it? No; he will roll it up and tie it with a piece of string, and save it for his mammy, or sell it in Usukuma for a goat."

To my surprise the boatmen endeavoured to impress the fact on Saramba's mind that the Kabaka was a special personal friend of theirs; that all these cattle, goats, and fowls were the Kabaka's usual gifts to Wangwana, and they endeavoured, with a reckless disregard for accuracy, to enumerate fabulous instances of his generosity to a number of other Safenis, Sarbokos, Barakas, and Zaidis, all natives, like themselves, of Zanzibar. Let Englishmen never henceforth indulge in the illusion, or lay the flattering unction to their self-love, that they are the only people who have studied the art of "chaff." The Zanzibaris are perfect in the art, as the sordid barbarian Saramba discovered to his cost.

The ninth hour of the day approached. We had bathed, brushed, cleaned ourselves, and were prepared externally and mentally for the memorable hour when we should meet the Foremost Man of Equatorial Africa. Two of the Kabaka's pages, clad in a costume semi-Kingwana and semi-Kiganda, came to summon us — the Kingwana part being the long white shirt of Zanzibar, folded with a belt or band about the loins, the Kiganda part being the Sohari doti cloth depending from the right shoulder to the feet. "The Kabaka invites you to the burzah," said they. Forthwith we issue from our courtyard, five of the boat's crew on each side of me armed with Snider rifles. We reach a short broad street, at the end of which is a hut. Here the Kabaka is seated with a multitude of chiefs, Wakungu and Watongoleh, ranked from the throne in two opposing kneeling or seated lines, the ends being closed in by drummers, guards, executioners, pages, &c. &c. As we approached the nearest group, it opened, and the drummers beat mighty sounds; Tori's drumming being conspicuous from its sharper beat. The Foremost Man of Equatorial Africa rises and advances, and all the kneeling and seated lines rise — generals, colonels, chiefs, cooks, butlers, pages, executioners, &c. &c.

The Kabaka, a tall, clean-faced, large-eyed, nervous-looking, thin man, clad in a tarbush, black robe, with a white shirt belted with gold, shook my hands warmly and impressively, and, bowing not ungracefully, invited me to be seated on an iron stool. I waited for him to show the example, and then I and all the others seated ourselves.

He first took a deliberate survey of me, which I returned with interest, for he was as interesting to me as I was to him. His impression of me was that I was younger than Speke, not so tall, but better dressed. This I gathered from his criticisms as confided to his chiefs and favourites.

My impression of him was that he and I would become better acquainted, that I should make a convert of him, and make him useful to Africa — but what other impressions I had may be gathered from the remarks I wrote that evening in my diary: —

"As I had read Speke's book for the sake of its geographical information, I retained but a dim remembrance of his description of his life in Uganda. If I remember rightly, Speke described a youthful prince, vain and heartless, a wholesale murderer and tyrant, one who delighted in fat women. Doubtless he described what he saw, but it is far from being the state of things now. Mtesa has impressed me as being an intelligent and distinguished prince who, if aided in time by virtuous philanthropists, will do more for Central Africa than fifty years of Gospel teaching, unaided by such authority, can do. I think I see in him the light that shall lighten the darkness of this benighted region; a prince well worthy the most hearty sympathies that Europe can give him. In this man I see the possible fruition of Livingstone's hopes, for with his aid the civilisation of Equatorial Africa becomes feasible. I remember the ardour and love which animated

Livingstone when he spoke of Sekeletu; had he seen Mtesa, his ardour and love for him had been tenfold, and his pen and tongue would have been employed in calling all good men to assist him."

Five days later I wrote the following entry: —

"I see that Mtesa is a powerful Emperor, with great influence over his neighbours. I have to-day seen the turbulent Mankorongo, king of Usui, and Mirambo, that terrible phantom who disturbs men's minds in Unyamwezi, through their embassies kneeling and tendering their tribute to him. I saw over 3000 soldiers of Mtesa nearly half civilised. I saw about a hundred chiefs who might be classed in the same scale as the men of Zanzibar and Oman, clad in as rich robes, and armed in the same fashion, and have witnessed with astonishment such order and law as is obtainable in semi-civilised countries. All this is the result of a poor Muslim's labour; his name is Muley bin Salim. He it was who first began teaching here the doctrines of Islam. False and contemptible as these doctrines are, they are preferable to the ruthless instincts of a savage despot, whom Speke and Grant left wallowing in the blood of women, and I honour the memory of Muley bin Salim — Muslim and slave-trader though he be — the poor priest who has wrought this happy change. With a strong desire to improve still more the character of Mtesa, I shall begin building on the foundation stones laid by Muley bin Salim. I shall destroy his belief in Islam, and teach the doctrines of Jesus of Nazareth."

It may easily be gathered from these entries that a feeling of admiration for Mtesa must have begun very early, and that either Mtesa is a very admirable man, or that I am a very impressionable traveller, or that Mtesa is so perfect in the art of duplicity and acted so clever a part, that I became his dupe.

The chief reason for admiration lay, probably, in the surprise with which I viewed the man whom Speke had beheld as a boy — and who was described by him through about two hundred pages of his book as a vain, foolish, peevish, headstrong youth and a murderous despot — sedate and composed in manner, intelligent in his questions and remarks beyond anything I expected to meet in Africa. That I should see him so well dressed, the centre of a court equally well dressed and intelligent, that he should have obtained supremacy over a great region into which moneyed strangers and soldiers from Cairo and Zanzibar flocked for the sake of its supreme head, that his subjects should speak of him with respect, and his guests, so far as I could gather, honour him, were minor causes, which, I venture to consider, were sufficient to win my favourable judgment. That he should have been so royally liberal in his supplies to me, have proffered other courtesies in a tone of sincerity, and have appeared to me a kindly, friendly soul, who affected all the dignity of one who entertains a vast respect for himself and his position without affronting or giving wanton offence to those around him who also have wants, hopes, and self-respect, may also be offered as reasons which contributed not a little towards creating a favourable impression on me. I am aware that there are negrophobists who may attribute this conduct of Mtesa to a natural gift for duplicity. He is undoubtedly a man who possesses great natural talents, but he also shows sometimes the waywardness, petulance, and withal the frank, exuberant, joyous moods, of youth. I will also admit that Mtesa can be politic, as, indeed, future pages will show, but he has also a child's unstudied ease of manner. I soon saw that he was highly clever, and possessed of the abilities to govern, but his cleverness and ability lacked the mannerisms of a European's.

Whether or no I became Mtesa's dupe will be seen in the chapters on Uganda. Meanwhile, he appeared to me to be a generous prince and a frank and intelligent man, and one whose character was well worth studying for its novel intensity and extreme originality, and also as one whom I judged could be made to subserve higher ends than he suspected he was fashioned for. I met his friendly advances with the utmost cordiality, and the burzah concluded at sunset, with the same ceremony that had inaugurated it, leaving Mtesa and myself mutually pleased and gratified with our acquaintance.

A description of Mtesa's person was written in my diary on the third evening of my visit to him, from which I quote: —

"April 7. — ln person Mtesa is tall, probably 6 feet 1 inch, and slender. He has very intelligent and agreeable features, reminding me of some of the faces of the great stone images at Thebes, and of the statues in the Museum at Cairo. He has the same fulness of lips, but their grossness is relieved by the general expression of amiability blended with dignity that pervades his face, and the large, lustrous, lambent eyes that lend it a strange beauty, and are typical of the race from which I believe him to have sprung. His colour is of a dark red brown, of a wonderfully smooth surface. When not engaged in council, he throws off unreservedly the bearing that characterises him when on the throne, and gives rein to his humour, indulging in hearty peals of laughter. He seems to be interested in the discussion of the manners and customs of European courts, and to be enamoured of hearing of the wonders of civilisation. He is ambitious to imitate as much as lies in his power the ways of the white man. When any piece of information is given him, he takes upon himself the task of translating it to his wives and chiefs, though many of the latter understand the Swahili language as well as he does himself."

On this day I recorded an interesting event which occurred in the morning. Mtesa, about 7 A.M., sallied out of his quarters, accompanied by a host of guards, pages, standard bearers, fifers, drummers, chiefs, native guests, claimants, &c., and about two hundred women of his household, and as he passed by my courtyard, he sent one of his pages to request my presence. While he passed on, I paid some attention to my toilet, and made as presentable an appearance as my clothes-bag enabled me, and then, accompanied by two of my boat's crew as gunbearers, followed the court to the lake. Mtesa was seated on an iron stool, the centre of a large group of admiring women, who, as soon as I appeared, focussed about two hundred pairs of lustrous, humid eyes on my person, at which he laughed.

"You see, 'Stamlee,'" said he, "how my women look at you; they expected to see you accompanied by a woman of your own colour. I am not jealous though. Come and sit down."

Presently Mtesa whispered an order to a page, who sprang to obey, and responding to his summons, there darted into view from the bend in Murchison Bay west of Usavara forty magnificent canoes, all painted an ochreous brown, which I perceived to be the universally favourite colour. En passant, I have wondered whether they admire this colour from an idea that it resembles the dark bronze of their own bodies. For pure Waganda are not black by any means. The women and chiefs of Mtesa, who may furnish the best specimens of Waganda, are nearly all of a bronze or a dark reddish brown, with peculiar smooth, soft skins, rendered still more tender and velvety to the touch by their habit of shampooing with butter. Some of the women, I observed, were of a very light red-gold colour, while one or two verged on white. The native cloths — the national dress — which depended from the right shoulders of the larger number of those not immediately connected with the court were of a light brown also. It struck me, when I saw the brown skins, brown robes, and brown canoes, that brown must be the national colour.

These forty canoes, which now rode on the calm grey-green waters of Murchison Bay, contained in the aggregate about 1200 men. The captain of each canoe was dressed in a white cotton shirt and a cloth head-cover, neatly folded turban-fashion, while the admiral wore over his shirt a crimson jacket, profusely decorated with gold braid, and on his head the red fez of Zanzibar. Each captain, as he passed us, seized shield and spear, and, with the bravado of a matador addressing the Judge of the Plaza to behold his prowess, went through the performance of defence and attack by water. The admiral won the greatest applause, for he was the Hector of the fleet, and his actions, though not remarkably graceful, were certainly remarkably extravagant. The naval review over, Mtesa commanded one of the captains of the canoes to try and discover a crocodile or a hippopotamus. After fifteen minutes he returned with the report that there was a young crocodile asleep on a rock about 200 yards away. "Now, Stamlee," said Mtesa, "show my women how white men can shoot." To represent all the sons of Japhet, on this occasion, was a great responsibility, but I am happy to say that — whether owing to the gracious influence of some unseen divinity who has the guardianship of their interests or whether from mere luck — nearly severed the head of the young crocodile from its body at a distance of 100 yards with a three-ounce ball, which was accepted as conclusive proof that all white men are dead shots.

In the afternoon we amused ourselves with target practice, at which an accident occurred that might have produced grave results. A No. 8 double-barrelled rifle was fractured in Mtesa's hands at the second shot, but fortunately without injuring either him or the page on whose shoulder it rested. General alarm prevailed for a short time, until that, seeing it was about to be accepted as a bad omen, I examined the rifle and showed Mtesa an ancient flaw in the barrel, which his good sense perceived had led to the fracture. The gun was a very old one, and had evidently seen much service.

April 10. — On the 10th of April the court broke up its hunting lodges at Usavara, on Murchison Bay, and moved to the capital, whither I was strongly urged to follow. Mtesa, escorted by about two hundred musketeers and the great Wakungu and their armed retainers, travelled quickly, but owing to my being obliged to house my boat from the hot sun, I did not reach the capital until 1 P.M.

The road had been prepared for his Imperial Majesty's hunting excursion, and was 8 feet wide, through jungle and garden, forest and field. Beautiful landscapes were thus enjoyed of rolling land and placid lake, of gigantic tamarinds and gum-trees, of extensive banana groves and plantations of the ficus, from the bark of which the national dress or mbugu, is made. The peculiar dome-like huts, each with an attempt at a portico, were buried deep in dense bowers of plantains which filled the air with the odour of their mellow rich fruit.

The road wound upward to the summits of green hills which commanded exquisite prospects, and down again into the sheltered bosoms of woody nooks, and vales, and tree-embowered ravines. Streams of clear water murmured through these depressions as they flowed towards Murchison Bay. The verdure was of a brilliant green, freshened by the unfailing rains of the Equator; the sky was of the bluest, and the heat, though great, was tempered by the hill breezes, and frequently by the dense foliage overhead.

Within three hours' march from Usavara, we saw the capital crowning the summit of a smooth rounded hill — a large cluster of tall conical grass huts, in the centre of which rose a spacious, lofty, barn-like structure. The large building, we were told, was the palace! the hill, Rubaga; the cluster of huts, the imperial capital!

From each side of the tall cane fence enclosing the grass huts on Rubaga hill radiated very broad avenues, imperial enough in width. Arriving at the base of the hill, and crossing by a "corduroy" road over a broad slimy ooze, we came up to one of these avenues, the ground of which was a reddish clay strongly mixed with the detritus of hematite. It gave a clear breadth of 100 feet of prepared ground, and led by a gradual ascent to the circular road which made the circuit of the hill outside the palace enclosure. Once on the dome-like height, we saw that we had arrived by the back avenue, for the best view of this capital of magnificent distances was that which was obtained by looking from the burzah of the palace, and carrying the eye over the broad front highway, on each side of which, as far as could be defined from the shadows of the burzah, the Wakungu had their respective courts and houses, embowered in gardens of banana and fig. Like the enclosure round the palace courts and quarters, each avenue was fenced with tall matete (water-cane) neatly set very close together in uniform rows. The by-streets leading from one avenue to another were narrow and crooked.

While I stood admiring the view, a page came up, and, kneeling, announced that he had been despatched by the Emperor to show me my house. Following him, I was ushered within a corner lot of the fenced square, between two avenues, into what I might appropriately term a "garden villa" of Uganda. My house, standing in the centre of a plantain garden about 100 feet square, was 20 feet long, and of a marquee shape, with a miniature portico or eave projecting like a bonnet over the doorway, and was divided into two apartments. Close by, about 30 feet off, were three dome-like huts for the boat's crew and the kitchen, and in a corner of the garden was a railed space for our bullocks and goats. Were it not that I was ever anxious about my distant camp in Usukuma, I possessed almost everything requisite to render a month's stay very agreeable, and for the time I was as proud of my tiny villa as a London merchant is of his country house.

In the afternoon I was invited to the palace. A number of people in brown robes, or white dresses, some with white goatskins over their brown robes, others with cords folded like a turban round their heads, which I heard were distinguishing marks of the executioners, were also ascending to the burzah. Court after court was passed until we finally stood upon the level top in front of the great house of cane and straw, which the Waganda fondly term Kibuga, or the Palace. The space at least was of aulic extent, and the prospect gained at every point was also worthy of the imperial eyes of the African monarch.

On all sides rolled in grand waves a voluptuous land of sunshine, and plenty, and early summer verdure, cooled by soft breezes from the great equatorial freshwater sea. Isolated hill-cones, similar to that of Rubaga, or square tabular masses, rose up from the beautiful landscape to attract, like mysteries, the curious stranger's observation, and villages and banana groves of still fresher green, far removed on the crest of distant swelling ridges, announced that Mtesa owned a land worth loving. Dark sinuous lines traced the winding courses of deep ravines filled with trees, and grassy extents of gently undulating ground marked the pastures; broader depressions suggested the cultivated gardens and the grain fields, while on the far verge of the horizon we saw the beauty and the charm of the land melting into the blues of distance.

There is a singular fascination about this country. The land would be loved for its glorious diversified prospects, even though it were a howling wilderness; but it owes a great deal of the power which it exercises over the imagination to the consciousness that in it dwells a people peculiarly fascinating also. "How comes it," one asks, "that this barbarous, uneducated, and superstitious monarch builds upon this height?" Not for protection, surely, for he has smoothed the uneven ground and formed broad avenues to approach it, and a single torch would suffice to level all his fences? Does he, then, care for the charms of the prospect? Has he also an eye to the beauties of nature?

Were this monarch as barbarous as other African chiefs whom I had met between Zanzibar and Napoleon Channel, he would have sought a basin, or the slope of some ridge, or some portion of the shores of the lake where his cattle might best graze, and would there have constructed his grass dwellings. But this man builds upon a hill that he may look abroad, and take a large imperial view of his land. He loves ample room; his house is an African palace, spacious and lofty; large clean courtyards surround it; he has spacious quarters for his harem, and courtyards round those; he has spacious quarters for his guards, and extensive courtyards round those; a cane enclosure surrounds all, and beyond the enclosure again is a wide avenue running round the palace fences. His people, great and small, imitate him as much as lies in their power. They are well dressed, and immodesty is a crime in the land. Yet I am still in Africa, and only yesterday, as it were, I saw naked men and naked women. It may be that such a monarch and people fascinate me as much as their land. The human figures in the landscape have, indeed, as much interest for me as the gracious landscape itself.

The drums sounded. Mtesa had seated himself on the throne, and we hastened to take our seats.

Since the 5th of April, I had enjoyed ten interviews with Mtesa, and during all I had taken occasion to introduce topics which would lead up to the subject of Christianity. Nothing (recurred in my presence but I contrived to turn it towards effecting that which had become an object to me, viz., his conversion. There was no attempt made to confuse him with the details of any particular doctrine. I simply drew for him the image of the Son of God humbling Himself for the good of all mankind, white and black, and told him how, while He was in man's disguise. He was seized and crucified by wicked people who scorned His divinity, and yet out of His great love for them, while yet suffering on the cross, He asked His great Father to forgive them. I showed the difference in character between Him whom white men love and adore, and Mohammed, whom the Arabs revere; how Jesus endeavoured to teach mankind that we should love all men, excepting none, while Mohammed taught his followers that the slaying of the pagan and the unbeliever was an act that merited Paradise. I left it to Mtesa and his chiefs to decide which was the worthier character. I also sketched in brief the history of religious belief from Adam to Mohammed. I had also begun to translate to him the Ten Commandments, and Idi, the Emperor's writer, transcribed in Kiganda the words of the Law as given to him in choice Swahili by Robert Feruzi, one of my boat's crew, and a pupil of the Universities Mission at Zanzibar,

The enthusiasm with which I launched into this work of teaching was soon communicated to Mtesa and some of his principal chiefs, who became so absorbingly interested in the story as I gave it to them that little of other business was done. The political burzah and seat of justice had now become an alcove, where only the moral and religious laws were discussed.

Before we broke up our meeting Mtesa informed me that I should meet a white man at his palace the next day.

"A white man, or a Turk?"

"A white man like yourself," repeated Mtesa.

"No; impossible!"

"Yes, you will see. He comes from Masr (Cairo), from Gordoom (Gordon) Pasha."

"Ah, very well, I shall be glad to see him, and if he is really a white man I may probably stay with you four or five days longer," said I to Mtesa, as I shook hands with him, and bade him good-night.

April 11. — The "white man," reported to be coming the next day, arrived at noon with great eclat and flourishes of trumpets, the sound of which could be heard all over the capital. Mtesa hurried off a page to invite me to his burzah. I hastened up by a private entrance. Mtesa and all his chiefs, guards, pages, executioners, claimants, guests, drummers and fifers were already there, en grande tenue.

Mtesa was in a fever, as I could see by the paling of the colour under his eyes and his glowing eyeballs. The chiefs shared their master's excitement.

"What shall we do," he asked, "to welcome him?"

"Oh, form your troops in line from the entrance to the burzah down to the gate of the outer court, and present arms, and as he comes within the gate, let your drums and fifes sound a loud welcome."

"Beautiful! " said Mtesa. "Hurry Tori, Chambarango, Sekebobo; form them in two lines just as Stamlee says. Oh, that is beautiful! And shall we fire guns, Stamlee?"

"No, not until you shake hands with him; and as he is a soldier, let the guards fire, then they will not injure anyone."

Mtesa's flutter of excitement on this occasion made me think that there must have been a somewhat similar scene before my landing at Usavara, and that Tori must have been consulted frequently upon the form of ceremony to be adopted.

What followed upon the arrival of the white man at the outer gate had best be told as an interlude by the stranger himself:

"At two o'clock, the weather having cleared up, Mtesa sent a messenger to inform me that he was ready to receive me. Notice is given in the camp; every one puts on his finest clothes; at last we are ready; my brave Soudanians look quite smart in their red jackets and white trousers. I place myself at their heads; trumpets flourish and drums sound as we follow an avenue from eighty-five to a hundred yards wide, running direct north and south, and terminating at Mtesa's palace." . . .

"On entering this court, I am greeted with a frightful uproar; a thousand instruments, each one more outlandish than the other, produce the most discordant and deafening sounds. Mtesa's bodyguard, carrying guns, present arms on my appearance; the king is standing at the entrance of the reception hall. I approach and bow to him a la turque. He holds out his hand, which I press; I immediately perceive a sunburnt European to the left of the king, a traveller, whom I imagine to be Cameron. We exchange glances without speaking.

"Mtesa enters the reception room, and we follow him. It is a narrow hall about 60 feet long by 15 feet wide, the ceiling of which, sloping down at the entrance, is supported by a double row of wooden pillars which divide the room into two aisles. The principal and central room is unoccupied, and leads to the king's throne; the two aisles are filled with the great dignitaries and chief officers. At each pillar stands one of the king's guard, wearing a long red mantle, a white turban ornamented with monkey skin, white trousers and black blouse with a red band. All are armed with guns.

"Mtesa takes his place on his throne, which is a wooden seat in the shape of an office arm-chair; his feet rest upon a cushion; the whole placed on a leopard's skin spread over a Smyrna carpet. Before the king is a highly polished elephant's tusk, and at his feet are two boxes containing fetishes; on either side the throne is a lance (one copper, the other steel), each held by a guard; these are the insignia of Uganda; the dog which Speke mentions has been done away with. Crouching at the foot of the king are the vizier and two scribes.

"Mtesa is dignified in his manner, and does not lack a certain natural air of distinction; his dress is elegant: a white conflan finished with a red band, stockings, shippers, vest of black cloth embroidered with gold, and a tarbouche with a silver plate on the top. He wears a sword with ivory-inlaid hilt (a Zanzibar weapon), and a staff.

"I exhibited my presents, which Mtesa scarcely pretended to see, his dignity forbidding him to show any curiosity.

"I address the traveller, who sits in front of me, on the left of the king: 'Have I the honour of speaking to Mr. Cameron?'

"Stanley. 'No, sir; Mr. Stanley.'

"Myself. 'M. Linant de Bellefonds, member of the Gordon-Pasha Expedition.'

"We bow low to each other, as though we had met in a drawing-room, and our conversation is at an end for the moment.

"This meeting with Mr. Stanley greatly surprises me. Stanley was far from my thoughts; I was totally ignorant of the object of his Expedition.

"I take leave of the king, who meanwhile has been amusing himself by making my unlucky soldiers parade and flourish their trumpets. I shake hands with Mr. Stanley, and ask him to honour me with his presence at dinner.

"I had scarcely been more than a few minutes in my hut when Mr. Stanley arrived. After having mutually expressed the pleasure our meeting gave us, Mr. Stanley informed me that Cameron had written from Ujiji that he was starting for the Congo. Mr. Cameron, he told me, must have been much embarrassed by the question of money, having exceeded the amount allowed by the Royal Geographical Society. At Ujiji, he would have lost all his companions, and would be actually alone. Mr. Stanley was loud in his praises of Cameron, and hoped that he would succeed in his expedition." . . .

"Leaving his expedition at Usukuma, Mr. Stanley embarked with eleven men on the Victoria Lake, in a small boat which he had brought with him; he explored all the eastern part of the lake, penetrating into all the bays, gulfs, and creeks, and taking the bearings of islands and capes. I saw Mr. Stanley's work, which is very extensive. He showed me some curious sketches of islands he had seen; the islands of the Bridge, the Grotto, and the Sphinx. The first is a natural bridge of granite, with all the appearance of a bridge made by the hand of man; the second is like the grotto of the enchantress Calypso; the third greatly resembles the Egyptian Sphinx." . . .

Colonel Linant de Bellefonds having thus described our meeting, there remains but little for me to add.

As soon as I saw him approaching the burzah, I recognised him to be a Frenchman. Not being introduced to him — and as I was then but a mere guest of Mtesa, with whom it was M. Linant's first desire to converse — I simply bowed to him, until he had concluded addressing the Emperor, when our introduction took place as he has described.

I was delighted at seeing him, and much more delighted when I discovered that M. Linant was a very agreeable man. I observed that there was a vast difference between his treatment of his men and the manner in which I treated mine, and that his intercourse with the Waganda was conducted after exactly opposite principles to those which governed my conduct. He adopted a half military style which the Waganda ill brooked, and many things uncomplimentary to him were uttered by them. He stationed guards at the entrance to his courtyard to keep the Waganda at a distance, except those bearing messages from Mtesa, while my courtyard was nearly full of Watongolehs, soldiers, pages, children, with many a dark-brown woman listening with open ears to my conversation with the Waganda. In fact, my courtyard from morning to night swarmed with all classes, for I loved to draw the natives to talk, so that perfect confidence might be established between us, and I might gain an insight into their real natures. By this freer converse with them I became, it seemed, a universal favourite, and obtained information sufficient to fill two octavo volumes.

M. Linant passed many pleasant hours with me. Though he had started from Cairo previous to my departure from Zanzibar, and consequently could communicate no news from Europe, I still felt that for a brief period I enjoyed civilised life. His cuisine was after the French fashion. He possessed French beans and olive oil, various potted meats of Paris brands, pates de foie gras and Bologna sausage, sardines and Marseilles biscuits, white sugar, coffee, cocoa, chocolate, and tea. If we add to this list the articles that the natives and Mtesa's bounty furnished — milk, beef, kid, green and ripe bananas, eggs, sweet-potatoes, tomatoes, melons, and cassava flour — it will be seen that his cook had abundance of material wherewith to supply and satisfy our moderate gastronomic tastes. The pleasure we mutually felt in each other's company, and the exceptional good health which blessed us, sharpened our appetites and improved our digestion. The religious conversations which I had begun with Mtesa were maintained in the presence of M. Linant de Bellefonds, who, fortunately for the cause I had in view, was a Protestant. For when questioned by Mtesa about the facts which I had uttered, and which had been faithfully transcribed, M. Linant, to Mtesa's astonishment, employed nearly the same words, and delivered the same responses. The remarkable fact that two white men, who had never met before, one having arrived from the south-east, the other having emerged from the north, should nevertheless both know the same things, and respond in the same words, charmed the popular mind without the burzah as a wonder, and was treasured in Mtesa's memory as being miraculous.

The period of my stay with Mtesa drew to a close, and I requested leave to depart, begging the fulfilment of a promise he had made to me that he would furnish me with transport sufficient to convey the Expedition by water from Kagehyi in Usukuma to Uganda. Nothing loth, since one white man would continue his residence with him till my return, and being eager to see the gifts I told him were safe at Usukuma, he crave his permission, and commanded Magassa to collect thirty canoes, and to accompany me to my camp.

April 15. — On the 15th of April, then, escorted by Magassa and his Watongolehs, and also by M. Linant and ten of his Nubian soldiers, we left Rubaga.

We arrived at Usavara about 10 A.M., and I imagined, foolishly enough, that Magassa would be ready for the voyage. But the Magassa of the 15th of April was several grades higher in his own estimation than the Magassa of the 1st of April. Fifteen days' life in the Emperor's favour and promotion to an admiralship had intoxicated the youth. Magassa could not be ready for two days.

"Not if I send a messenger back to Mtesa with this information?" I asked.

"Ah, yes, perhaps to-morrow morning."

"Only a few hours longer, M. Linant; so it does not matter much. Meantime we will take possession of our old quarters at Usavara, and pass the evening in a ramble along the shores of the bay, or a sail in the boat." To which suggestion M. Linant assented.

There was matter sufficient to engage us in conversation. The rich region we trod, landscapes steeped in most vivid green, the splendour of the forest foliage, the magnificent lake of Equatorial Africa, studded with a thousand isles, the broad and now placid arm known as Murchison Bay, the diversity of scenery, the nature of the rocks, the variety of the plants, ourselves met upon this far strand of the inland sea, to part perhaps for ever — a continuous chain of topics which, with an intelligent and sympathetic companion like M. Linant, might have served to make our rambles and our evenings in the hut enjoyable for weeks.

In the evening I concluded my letters dated 14th of April 1875, which were sent to the Daily Telegraph and the New York Herald, the English and American journals I represented here, appealing for a Christian mission to be sent to Mtesa.

The appeal written hurriedly, and included in the letter left at Usavara, was as follows: —

"I have, indeed, undermined Islamism so much here that Mtesa has determined henceforth, until he is better informed, to observe the Christian Sabbath as well as the Muslim Sabbath, and the great captains have unanimously consented to this. He has further caused the Ten Commandments of Moses to be written on a board for his daily perusal — for Mtesa can read Arabic — as well as the Lord's Prayer and the golden commandment of our Saviour, 'Thou shalt love thy neighbour as thyself.' This is great progress for the sew days that I have remained with him, and, though I am no missionary, I shall begin to think that I might become one if such success is feasible. But oh! that some pious, practical missionary would come here! What a field and harvest ripe for the sickle of civilisation! Mtesa would give him anything he desired — houses, lands, cattle, ivory, etc.! he might call a province his own in one day. It is not the mere preacher, however, that is wanted, here. The bishops of Great Britain collected, with all the classic youth of Oxford and Cambridge, would effect nothing by mere talk with the intelligent people of Uganda. It is the practical Christian tutor, who can teach people how to become Christians, cure their diseases, construct dwellings, understand and exemplify agriculture, and turn his hand to anything, like a sailor -this is the man who is wanted. Such an one, if he can be found, would become the saviour of Africa He must be tied to no church or sect, but profess God and His Son and the moral law, and live a blameless Christian, inspired by liberal principles, charity to all men, and devout faith in Heaven. He must belong to no nation in particular, but to the entire white race. Such a man or men, Mtesa, Emperor of Uganda, Usogo, Unyoro, and Karagwe — an empire 360 geographical miles in length, by 50 in breadth — invites to repair to him. He has begged me to tell the white men that, if they will only come to him, he will give them all they want. Now, where is there in all the pagan world a more promising field for a mission than Uganda? Colonel Linant de Bellefonds is my witness that I speak the truth, and I know he wall corroborate all I say. The Colonel, though a Frenchman, is a Calvinist, and has become as ardent a well-wisher for the Waganda as I am. Then why further spend needlessly vast sums upon black pagans of Africa who have no example of their own people becoming Christians before them? I speak to the Universities Mission at Zanzibar and to the Free Methodists at Mombasa, to the leading philanthropists, and the pious people of England. 'Here, gentlemen, is your opportunity — embrace it! The people on the shores of the Nyanza call upon you. Obey your own generous instincts, and listen to them; and I assure you that in one year you will have more converts to Christianity than all other missionaries united can number. The population of Mtesa's kingdom is very dense; I estimate the number of his subjects at 2,000,000. You need not fear to spend money upon such a mission, as Mtesa is sole ruler, and will repay its cost tenfold with ivory, coffee, otter skins of a very fine quality, or even in cattle, for the wealth of this country in all these products is immense. The road here is by the Nile, or via Zanzibar, Ugogo, and Unyanyembe. The former route, so long as Colonel Gordon governs the countries of the Upper Nile, seems the most feasible.'"

When the letters were written and sealed, I committed them to the charge of Colonel Linant. My friend promised he would await my return from Usukuma; meanwhile he lent me a powerful field-glass, as mine, being considerably injured, had been given to Mtesa.

Magassa was not ready on the second day of our arrival. One of his women had absconded, or some of Mtesa's chiefs had seized her. Only ten canoes had arrived by the evening of the 16th.

April 17. — The parting between M. Linant and myself, I shall allow him to describe:

"At 5 A.M. drums are beaten: the boats going with Stanley are collecting together.

"Mr. Stanley and myself are soon ready. The Lady Alice is unmoored; luggage, sheep, goats, and poultry are already stowed away in their places. There is nothing to be done except to hoist the American flag and head the boat southwards. I accompany Stanley to his boat; we shake hands and commend each other to the care of Gnd. Stanley takes the helm; the Lady Alice immediately swerves like a spirited horse, and bounds forward, lashing the water of the Nyanza into foam. The starry flag is hoisted, and floats proudly in the breeze; I immediately raise a loud hurrah with such hearty good will as perhaps never before greeted the traveller's ears.

"The Lady Alice is already far away. We wave our handkerchiefs as a last farewell; my heart is full; I have just lost a brother. I had grown used to feeing Stanley, the open-hearted, sympathetic man and friend and admirable traveller. With him I forgot my fatigue; this meeting had been like a return to my own country. His engaging instructive conversation made the hours pass like minute? I hope I may see him again, and have the happiness of spending several days with him."

CHAPTER X.

Parting with Colonel Linant — Magassa's vanity and disloyalty — The sailor's island — Jumba's Cove — Uganga — Dumo — The Alexandra Nile — Lupassi Point — In danger at Makongo — Alone with Nature — Insect life — Dreams of a happier future — A dark secret — Murabo and the fish — Alice Island — A night never to be forgotten — The treachery of Bumbireh — Saved! — Refuge Island — Wiru — "Go and die in the Nyanza!" — Back in camp — Sad news.

April 17. — "Adieu! adieu! mon ami Linant! Remember my words, I shall return within a month; if not, present my compliments to your friends at Ismailia (Gondokoro), and tell them they may see me on the Albert Nyanza," were the last words I said to M. Linant de Bellefonds, as I seated myself in my boat on the morning of the 17th of April.

We had scarcely gone three miles on our voyage, before the vanity of the youth Magassa exceeded all bounds. Deeming it prudent — before it was too late — to lecture him, and hold out prospects of a reward conditional upon good behaviour, I called to him to approach me, as I had something to say to him. He would not come, but continued on his way with a slight grimace and a saucy inclination of the head. I reserved the lecture until we should arrive in camp.

At noon I took observations for latitude at the entrance to Murchison Bay, and during the afternoon we rowed hard upon our voyage, reaching Chiwanuko Island near sunset. Magassa soon followed me, and as I landed, I laid hold of him gently but firmly, and seating him by my side, employed myself in holding forth grand expectations before him, only, however, on the condition that he obeyed Mtesa's orders, behaved well, and acted in unison with me. Magassa promised faithfully, and as a sign that he was sincere, begged to be permitted to continue his voyage to Sesse, a large island where Mtesa's canoes were beached, to procure the full quota of thirty promised to me. Leaving five canoes in charge of Sentum and Sentageya, two of his Watongolehs, he departed by night, which I thought was a remarkable instance of energy. The truth was, however, that he only proceeded two miles, and slept at a village, where he abused his authority by seizing a woman, and binding the chief.

April 20. — The next day we proceeded with the Watongolehs, Sentum and Sentageya, and camped at Jumba's Cove. Jumba is the hereditary title of one of the junior admirals in command of a section of the imperial canoe fleet, to whom is awarded the district of Unjaku, a headland abutting on the left or north bank of the Katonga river. It is an exceedingly fertile district, separating Gabunga's, or the chief admiral's, district from Sambuzi's, a sub-chief of Kitunzi.

The whole of the north coast from Murchison Bay presents a panorama of beautiful views, of square table-topped mounts, rounded hills, and cones forming low ranges, which run in all directions, but with a general inclination east and west, and form, as it were, a natural boundary to the lake on the north. These masses of mountain, forming irregular ranges, suggest to the observer that no rivers of importance issue into the lake from the north side. They are terminated suddenly at the Katonga, and from the northwest along their base the river flows sluggishly into the lake. On the right or southern bank the land appears to be very low, as far as the hills of Uddu, four miles off. The Katonga river at this mouth is about 400 yards wide, but its current is very slow, almost imperceptible.

Uganda is a lowland district lying at the mouth of the Katonga, on the south or right bank, whence a large bay with well-wooded shores rounds from this river to the southward in a crescent form, to Bwiru, from which point we begin to trace the coast of Uddu. Uganda proper extends only as far as the Katonga river; from its bank Uddu begins, and stretched as far as the Alexandra Nile or Kagera.

Sesse Island extends from a point six miles south of Kibonga, westward to a point seven miles south of Jumba's village, and southward — parallel almost with the coast of Uddu — to a distance of about twenty-three miles. Its extreme length is about forty-two miles, while its extreme breadth must be about twenty miles. The principal canoe builders and the greater number of the sailors of Mtesa's empire dwell in Sesse, and because of their coal-black colour, timidity, superstition, and general uncleanly life, are regarded as the helots of Uganda.

April 21. — On the 21st we made a tedious, eventless voyage along the low, swampy, and jungly shores of Ujaju to Dumo, a village situated on the mainland nearly opposite the extreme southern end of Sesse Island. From a curious stony hill near Dumo, which bears traces of ancient effects of water, we obtained a distant view of the outskirts of a pastoral plateau rising westward.

Magassa appeared in the evening from his unsuccessful quest for canoes. He gave a graphic account of the dangers he had encountered at Sesse, whose inhabitants declared they would rather be beheaded by the Kabaka than risk themselves on an endless voyage on the stormy sea, but he had obtained a promise from Magura, the admiral in charge of the naval yards at Sesse, that he would endeavour to despatch fourteen canoes after us. Meanwhile, Magassa had left me at Chiwanuko with five canoes, but returned with only two, alleging that the other three leaked so much that they were not seaworthy. He suggested also that, as Magura might cause great delay if left alone, I should proceed with Sentum and Sentageya, and leave him in charge of five. Having witnessed his vanity and heard of his atrocious conduct near Chiwanuko, I strongly suspected him of desiring to effect some more mischief at Dumo, but I was powerless to interpose the strong arm, and therefore left him to answer for his shortcomings to Mtesa, who would doubtless hear of them before long.

After leaving Dumo and Sesse north of us, we had a boundless horizon of water on the east, while on the west stretched a crescent-shaped bay, bordered by a dense forest, ending south at Chawasimba Point. From here another broad bay extends southwards, and is terminated by the northernmost headland of Uzongora. Into this bay issues the Alexandra Nile in one powerful deep stream, which, from its volume and dark iron colour, may be traced several miles out. At its mouth it is about 150 yards wide, and at two miles above narrows to about 100 yards. We attempted to ascend higher, but the current was so strong that we made but slow progress, and after an ascent of three miles were obliged to abandon it. The plain on either side has a breadth of from five to ten miles, which during the rainy season is inundated throughout its whole extent. The deepest soundings we obtained were 85 feet. I know no other river to equal this in magnitude among the affluents of the Victoria Nyanza. The Shimeeyu river thus becomes the second largest affluent of the lake, and the two united would form a river equal to that which has its exit by the Ripon Falls.

The Waganda Watongolehs, Sentum and Sentageya, call the Alexandra Nile the "Mother of the River at Jinja," or the Ripon Falls.

The Alexandra Nile constitutes a natural boundary between the sovereignty of Uganda and its subject kingdoms of Karagwe and Uzongora, which begin south of the river. The plain of the Alexandra stretches south a few miles to an irregular line of grassy and treeless mountains, which are the characteristics of the fine pastoral countries of Uzongora and Karagwe. At Lupassi Point the mountains project steeply, almost cliff-like, into the lake, with heights varying from 200 feet to 500 feet. The steep slopes bristle at many points with grey gneiss rocks — massy debris from the mountain brows. Near this point I discovered a stream which had a fall of 3 feet issuing from an orifice in a rocky cliff, though above it there was not the faintest sign of a watercourse. In the gullies and clefts of the cliff-sides most beautiful ferns abounded.

I managed to climb to the top of the bluffs, and to my surprise overlooked a plateau, with a grandly rolling surface, covered with pasture and almost treeless, except near the villages, where grew dense groves of bananas. Further west, however, the plateau heaves upwards into mountain masses of the same naked character. Looking towards the east, directly in front of North Uzongora, stretches an apparently illimitable silvery sea; but towards the south one or two lofty islands are visible, situated about twenty-five miles from the mainland, serene and royal in their lone exclusiveness.

The first village we halted at on the coast of Uzongora was Makongo. It nestles in a sheltered nook in a bay-like indentation of the lofty mountain wall crowded with banana groves and huts scattered under their impenetrable shades — with a strip of grey gravel beach gently sloping from the water's edge about 40 feet upward to where it meets the prodigious luxury of the grove. There were about a dozen natives clad in dingy goat-skins seated on the beach, sucking the potent maramba from gourds when we came up, and without question we hauled our boat and two canoes high and dry. To our greetings the natives responded readily and civilly enough. With rather glazed eyes they offered us some of the equatorial nectar. The voyage had been long on this day, and we were tired, and it might be that we sighed for such cordial refreshing drink as was now proferred to us. At any rate, we accepted their hospitable gift, and sucked heartily, with bland approval of the delicacy of the liquid, and cordial thanks for their courtesy. An observation for longitude was taken, the natives looking on pleased and gratified. To all our questions as to the names of the localities and islands in view they replied like friends.

Sunset came. We bade each other good-night. At midnight there was a fearful drumming heard, which kept us all 'awake from the sheer violence of the sound. "Is anything wrong?" we demanded of Sentum and Sentageya. "Oh, no!" they answered. Still the drumming sounded hoarsely through the dark night, and the desire for sleep fled.

My men were all up before dawn, impatient for the day. Instinct, startled by that ominous drumming, warned them that something was wrong. I was still in my boat with drawn curtains, though able to communicate with my people. At sight of the natives Safeni, the coxswain, hailed me. As I was dressed, I arranged my guns and soon stepped out, and my astonishment was great when I perceived that there were between 200 and 300 natives, all in war costume and armed with spears, and bows and arrows, and long-handled cleaver-like weapons, with ample and long cane shields for defence, so close to us. For this terrible looking body of men stood only about thirty paces off, regarding us steadfastly. It was such a singular position, so unusual and so strangely theatrical, that, feeling embarrassed, I hastened to break the silence, and advanced towards a man whom I recognised as the elder who had given me some native wine on the previous evening.

"What means this, my friend?" I asked. "Is anything wrong?"

He replied rapidly, but briefly and sternly, in the Kinyambu language, which as I did not understand, I called the Mtongoleh Sentum to translate for me.

"What do you mean by drawing your canoes on our beach?" I was told he asked.

"Tell him we drew them up lest the surf should batter them to pieces during the night. The winds are rough sometimes, and waves rise high. Our canoes are our homes, and we are far from our friends who are waiting for us. Were our canoes injured or broken how should we return to our friends?"

He next demanded, "Know you this is our country?" "Yes, but are we doing wrong? Is the beach so soft that it can be hurt by our canoes? Have we cut down your bananas, or entered into your houses? Have we molested any of your people? Do you not see our fires by which we slept exposed to the cold night?"

"Well, you must leave this place at once. We do not want you here. Go!"

"That is easily done," I answered; "and had you told us last night that our presence was not welcome to you, we should have camped on yonder island."

"What did you come here for?"

"We came to rest for the night, and to buy food, and is that a crime? Do you not travel in your canoes? Supposing people received you as you received us this morning, what would you say? Would you not say they were bad? Ah, my friend, I did not expect that you who were so good yesterday would turn out thus! But never mind; we will go away quickly and quietly, and the Kabaka Mtesa shall hear of this, and judge between us."

"If you wish food, I will send some bananas to yonder island, but you must go away from this, lest the people, who wish to fight you, should break out."

We soon shoved the boat and two canoes into the water, and I and my boat's crew embarked and rowed away a few yards. But Sentum was angry with the people, and instead of quietly departing, was loudly expostulating with them. To prevent mischief and the massacre of his entire party, I shouted to Sentum, commanding him to embark at once, which after a short time he obeyed, growling.

We steered for Musira Island, about three miles from Makongo, where we found four or five canoes from Kamiru's country loaded with coffee and butter. The Waganda, Sentum and Sentageya, with feelings embittered against the natives, seized upon several packages of coffee, which drew a loud remonstrance from the natives. The Waganda sailors, ever ready for a scramble, followed their chiefs' example, and assisted in despoiling the natives, which caused one of them to appeal to me. I was busy directing my boat's crew to set my tent, when I was thus made acquainted with the conduct of the Waganda. The property taken from them was restored immediately, and Sentum and Sentageya were threatened with punishment if they molested them further, and the natives were advised to leave for another island about five miles north of us, as soon as the lake should become calm.

About 10 A.M. the chief of Makongo, true to his promise, sent us ten bunches of green bananas, sufficient for one day's provisions for the sixty-two men, Waganda and Wangwana, of whom our party consisted.

After these events I strolled alone into the dense and tangled luxuriance of the jungle woods which lay behind our camp. Knowing that the people would be discussing their bananas, that no foe could molest them, and that they could not quarrel with any natives — there being nobody else on the island of Musira but ourselves — I was able to leave them to pass the time as they might deem most agreeable. Therefore, with all the ardour of a boy, I began my solitary exploration. Besides, it was so rare for me to enjoy solitude and silence in such perfect safety as was here promised to me. My freedom in these woods, though I was alone, none could endanger or attempt to restrain; my right to climb trees, or explore hollows, or stand on my head, or roll about on the leaves or ruins of branch and bark, or laugh or sing, who could oppose? Being thus absolute monarch and supreme arbiter over myself, I should enjoy for a brief period perfect felicity.

That impulse to jump, to bound, to spring upward and cling to branches overhead, which is the characteristic of a strong green age, I gave free rein to. Unfettered for a time from all conventionalisms, and absolved from that sobriety and steadiness which my position as a leader of half wild men compelled me to assume in their presence, all my natural elasticity of body came back to me. I dived under the obstructing bough or sprang over the prostrate trunk, squeezed into almost impossible places, crawled and writhed like a serpent through the tangled undergrowth, plunged down into formidable depths of dense foliage, and burrowed and struggled with frantic energy among shadowing pyramids of vines and creepers, which had become woven and plaited by their numbers into a solid mass.

What eccentricities of creation I became acquainted with in this truanting in the wild woods! Ants, red, black, yellow, grey, white, and parti-coloured, peopling a miniature world with unknown emmet races. Here were some members of the belligerent warrior caste always threatening the harmless, and seeking whom they might annoy, and there the ferocious food-providers, active for the attack, ranging bole, bough, twigs and leaf for prey; the meek and industrious artisans absorbed in defending the poor privilege of a short existence; the frugal neuters tugging enormous loads towards their cunningly constructed nests; sentries on watch at the doors to defend the approaches to their fastnesses. They swarmed among the foliage in columns of foraging and plundering marauders and countless hordes of ruthless destroyers. In the decaying vegetation I heard all around me the xylophagous larvae of great beetles hard at work by thousands, and saw myriads of termites destroying with industrious fury everything that lay in their path, whether animal or vegetable. Armies of psyllae and moths innumerable were startled from the bushes, and from every bough shrilled the tiresome cicada, ever noisy. Here the relentless ant-lions prepared their pitfalls, and there the ghostly mantis, green or grey, stood waiting for unwary insects. Diamond beetles abounded, and many other species, uncouth and horrid, scrambled away from before my feet. Nor are these a thousandth part of the insect nations that I disturbed; the secluded island was a world of infinite activities.

Beyond the flats I came at last to where the ground sloped upward rapidly, though still clothed with tall trees and their parasitical plants and undergrowth; and in spite of the intense heat, I continued my exploration, determined to view the upper regions. Clambering up the steep side, I had a large choice of supports; here a tamarind and next a bombax, now a projecting branch of mimosa and now a thick lliane, hung down, inviting me to haul myself upward and forward: the young and pliant teak sapling or slender jasmine bent as I seized them to assist my labouring feet, and at last I emerged above the trees and the tangle of meshed undergrowth, and stood upright on the curious spiky grass, studded with wild pineapple, ground orchids and aloes, which covered the summit.

After a general look around the island, I discovered it was in the form of a rudely shaped boot-last, lying east and west, the lowest parts being the flats through which I had just struggled. It was about three-quarters of a mile long and about 200 yards wide. The heel was formed by a narrow projecting ledge rising about 50 feet nearly perpendicularly from the water. From this ledge rose the rock 80 feet above it, and 130 feet therefore above the water.

I gazed long on the grand encircling prospect. A halcyon calm brooded on the lake, eastward, northward, and southward, until the clear sky and stainless silver water met, the clear bounds of both veiled by a gauzy vapour, suggesting infinity. In a bold, majestic mass to the south-east rose Alice Island, while a few miles south-east of it appeared the Bumbireh group. Opposite me, to the west, and two miles from where I stood, was the long cliffy front of the plateau of Uzongora, its slowly-rising summit gemmed with patches of evergreen banana, until it became banked in the distance by lines of hazy blue mountains.

It is a spot from which, undisturbed, the eye may rove over one of the strangest yet fairest portions of Africa — hundreds of square miles of beautiful lake scenes — a great length of grey plateau wall, upright and steep, but indented with exquisite inlets, half surrounded by embowering plantains — hundreds of square miles of pastoral upland dotted thickly with villages and groves of banana. From my lofty eyrie I can see herds upon herds of cattle, and many minute specks, white and black, which can be nothing but flocks of sheep and goats. I can also see pale blue columns of ascending smoke from the fires, and upright thin figures moving about. Secure on my lofty throne, I can view their movements and laugh at the ferocity of the savage hearts which beat in those thin dark figures; for I am a part of Nature now, and for the present as invulnerable as itself. As little do they know that human eyes survey their forms from the summit of this lake-girt isle as that the eyes of the Supreme in heaven are upon them. How long, I wonder, shall the people of these lands remain thus ignorant of Him who created the gorgeous sunlit world they look upon each day from their lofty upland! How long shall their untamed ferocity be a barrier to the Gospel, and how long shall they remain unvisited by the Teacher!

What a land they possess! and what an inland sea! How steamers afloat on the lake might cause Ururi to shake hands with Uzongora, and Uganda with Usukuma, make the wild Wavuma friends with the Wazinza, and unite the Wakerewe with the Wagana! A great trading port might then spring up on the Shimeeyu, whence the coffee of Uzongora, the ivory, sheep, and goats of Ugeyeya, Usoga, Uvuma, and Uganda, the cattle of Uwya, Karagwe, Usagara, Ihangiro, and Usukuma, the myrrh, cassia, and furs and hides of Uganda and Uddu, the rice of Ukerewe, and the grain of Uzinza, might be exchanged for the fabrics brought from the coast; all the land be redeemed from wildness, the industry and energy of the natives stimulated, the havoc of the slave-trade stopped, and all the countries round about permeated with the nobler ethics of a higher humanity. But at present the hands of the people are lifted — murder in their hearts — one against the other; ferocity is kindled at sight of the wayfarer; piracy is the acknowledged profession of the Wavuma; the people of Ugeyeya and Wasoga go stark naked; Mtesa impales, burns, and maims his victims; the Wirigedi lie in wait along their shores for the stranger, and the slingers of the islands practise their art against him; the Wakara poison anew, their deadly arrows at sight of a canoe; and each tribe, with rage and hate in its heart, remains aloof from the other. "Verily, the dark places of the earth are full of the habitations of cruelty."

Oh for the hour when a band of philanthropic capitalists shall vow to rescue these beautiful lands, and supply the means to enable the Gospel messengers to come and quench the murderous hate with which man beholds man in the beautiful lands around Lake Victoria!

I descended from the lofty height, the summit of Musira Island, by another way, which disclosed to me the character of the rocky island, and exposed to my view the precipitous walls of shale, rifted and indented by ages of atmospheric influences; that surround the island upon all sides but the western. After great difficulty I succeeded in getting upon the top of a portion of an upper ledge that had fallen on the north-east corner and now formed a separate projection about 30 feet high. In a cavernous recess upon the summit of it, I discovered six human bodies in a state of decomposition, half covered with grass and debris of rock. One of the skulls showed the mark of a hatchet, which made me suspect that a tragedy had occurred here but a short time before. No doubt the horrible event took place on the island on the ground occupied by our camp, for there was no other spot where such a deed could have been wrought, and probably the victims were taken in canoes, and deposited in this hidden recess, that strangers might not be alarmed at the sight of the bodies, or of such evidence of violence as the hatchet-cleft skull. Probably, also, these strangers were murdered for their cargo of coffee or of butter by the natives of the mainland, or by a later arrival of strangers like my own Waganda, who because of their numerical superiority had begun their molestation and robbery of the coffee traders, without other cause than that they were strong and the traders weak.

About 5 P.M., having long before returned to camp, I saw on the horizon Magassa's fleet of canoes, and counted fourteen. I despatched Safeni and some of the Waganda in a canoe to the small islands we passed just before reaching Makongo, begging Magassa to hasten and join me early next morning, as we were short of provisions, and starvation would ensue if we were delayed in our voyage. Safeni returned about 9 P.M. with a request from Magassa that I would go on as early as I wished, and a promise that he would follow me to camp.

April 26. — I waited, however, for Magassa until 10 A.M., and as Alice Island — which Sentum and Sentageya advised me was the best place to touch at in order to make a short course for Usukuma — was about thirty miles from Musira, I could delay no longer. It was then agreed that Sentum should stay at Musira Island until Magassa arrived, and inform him of the direction which Sentageya and I had taken.

We had proceeded on our voyage but three miles when Sentageya turned back with all speed towards Musira, waving his hand to me to continue my journey. Imagining that he had merely forgotten something, I did as he directed.

We reached Alice Island about 9 P.M., for we had been delayed by a strong head wind since 4 P.M. As it was pitch-dark, we were guided to a camping-place by a flickering light which we saw on the shore. The light for which we steered was that of a fire kindled by two men and a boy, who were drying fish in a cavern the entrance of which opened on the lake. Though the fishermen were rather frightened at first, they were discreet enough to remain passive; and to calm their fears, I assumed an air of extreme blandness and amiability. It being late, I prepared to rest in the stern-sheets of my boat, but as I was about to lie down, I heard the natives expostulating. I knew by this that the boat's crew must be committing depredations on their fish stores; so I sprang out — and only just in time to save them a serious loss. Murabo had already made himself master of half-a-dozen large fish, when I came up with naked feet behind him, announcing my arrival by a staggering blow, which convinced the fishermen better than any amount of blandness and affectation of amiability could have done, that I was sincere, and convinced the Wangwana also that injustice would not be permitted. The fishermen received a handful of beads as an atonement for the attempted spoliation, and to secure the Wangwana against further temptation, I gave them double rations.

April 27. — The next morning, when I woke, I found that we were camped under the shadow of a basaltic cliff, about 50 feet high, at the base of which was the fishermen's cavern, extending about 15 feet within. The island was lofty, about 400 feet above the lake at its highest part, nearly four miles in length, and a mile and a half across at its greatest breadth. The inhabitants consisted of about forty families from Ukerewe, and owned King Lukongeh as their liege lord.

The summit of Alice Island is clothed with an abundance of coarse grass, and the ravines and hollows are choked with a luxuriance of vegetable life — trees, plants, ferns, ground orchids, and wild pine-apples: along the water's edge there waves a thin strip of water-cane. The people became fast friends with us, but their keen trading instincts impelled them to demand such exorbitant prices for every article, that we were unable to purchase more than a few ears of corn. I obtained a view from the summit with my field-glass, but I could distinguish nothing east or south-east. South-west we saw the Bumbireh group, and to purchase food we were compelled to proceed thither — disagreeably convinced that we had lost a whole day by calling at Alice Island, whereas, had we kept a direct course to the south, we might have reached the Bumbireh group in a few hours.

April 28. — As we started only at noon from Alice Island, being delayed by expectations of seeing Magassa, and also by the necessity for purchasing something even at high prices to prevent starvation, we did not reach Barker's Island — the easternmost of the Bumbireh group — until night, which we passed most miserably in a little cove surrounded by impenetrable brushwood. It was one downpour of rain throughout the whole night, which compelled us to sit up shivering and supperless, for, to crown our discomforts, we had absolutely nothing to eat. No more abject objects can be imagined than the human beings that occupied the boat through the hours of darkness. There were my crew all sitting as closely as possible, back to back or side by side, on the oars and boards which they had arranged like a platform on the thwarts, and I sitting alone under the awning in the stern sheets, wearily trying to outline their figures, or vaguely taking mental notes of the irregularities of the bush, with occasional hasty glances at the gloomy sky, or at Bumbireh, whose black mass looked grim and lofty in the dark, and all the time the rain kept pouring down with a steady malignant impetuosity. I doubt if even the happiest hours which may fall to my lot in the future will ever obliterate from my memory that dismal night of discomfort and hunger.

But as it generally happens, the dismal night was followed by a beautiful, bright morning. Every inch of nature that we could scan seemed revivified, refreshed, and gay, except the little world which the boat contained. We were eager to renew our acquaintance with humanity, for only by contact with others could we live. We accordingly sailed for Bumbireh, which lay about two miles from Barker's Island, and ran down the coast in search of a cove and haven for our boat, while we should be bartering our beads for edibles.

Bumbireh Island is about eleven miles in extreme length by two miles greatest breadth. It is in appearance a hilly range, with a tolerably even and softly rolling summit line clothed with short grass. Its slopes are generally steep, yet grassy or cultivated. It contains probably fifty small villages, averaging about twenty huts to a village, and if we calculate four souls to each hut, we have a population of about 4000 including all ages.

Herds of cattle grazed on the summit and slopes; a tolerably large acreage here and there showed a brown soil upturned for planting, while extensive banana groves marked most of the village sites. There was a kindly and prosperous aspect about the island.

As soon as we had sailed a little distance along the coast, we caught sight of a few figures which broke the even and smooth outline of the grassy summit, and heard the well-known melodious war-cries employed by most of the Central African tribes, "Hehu-a-hehu-u-u-u!" loud, long-drawn, and ringing.

The figures increased in number, and fresh voices joined in the defiant and alarming note. Still, hungry wretches as we were, environed by difficulties of all kinds, just beginning to feel warm after the cold and wet of the night before, with famine gnawing at our vitals, leagues upon leagues of sea between us and our friends at Usukuma, and nothing eatable in our boat, we were obliged to risk something, reminding ourselves "that there are no circumstances so desperate which Providence may not relieve."

At 9 A.M. we discovered a cove near the south-east end of the long island, and pulled slowly into it. Immediately the natives rushed down the slopes, shouting war-cries and uttering fierce ejaculations. When about 50 yards from the shore, I bade the men cease rowing, but Safeni and Baraka became eloquent, and said, "It is almost always the case, master, with savages. They cry out, and threaten, and look big, but you will see that all that noise will cease as soon as they hear us speak. Besides, if we leave here without food, where shall we obtain it?"

The last argument was unanswerable, and though I gave no orders to resume their oars, four of the men impelled the boat on slowly, while Safeni and Baraka prepared themselves to explain to the natives, who were now close within hearing, as they came rushing to the water's edge. I saw some lift great stones, while others prepared their bows.

We were now about 10 yards from the beach, and Safeni and Baraka spoke, earnestly pointing to their mouths, and by gestures explaining that their bellies were empty. They smiled with insinuating faces; uttered the words "brothers," "friends," "good fellows," most volubly; cunningly interpolated the words Mtesa — the Kabaka — Uganda, and Antari king of Ihanoiro, to whom Bumbireh belongs Safeni and Baraka's pleasant volubility seemed to have produced a good effect, for the stones were dropped, the bows were unstrung, and the lifted spears lowered to assist the steady, slow-walking pace with which they now advanced.

Safeni and Baraka turned to me triumphantly and asked, "What did we say, master?" and then, with engaging frankness, invited the natives, who were now about two hundred in number, to come closer. The natives consulted a little while, and several — now smiling pleasantly themselves — advanced leisurely into the water until they touched the boat's prow. They stood a few seconds talking sweetly, when suddenly with a rush they ran the boat ashore, and then all the others, seizing hawser and gunwale, dragged her about 20 yards over the rocky beach high and dry, leaving us almost stupefied with astonishment!

Then ensued a scene which beggars description. Pandemonium — all its devils armed — raged around us. A forest of spears was levelled; thirty or forty bows were drawn taut; as many barbed arrows seemed already on the wing; thick, knotty clubs waved above our heads; two hundred screaming black demons jostled with each other and struggled for room to vent their fury, or for an opportunity to deliver one crushing blow or thrust at us.

In the meantime, as soon as the first symptoms of this manifestation of violence had been observed, I had sprung to my feet, each hand armed with a loaded self-cocking revolver, to kill and be killed. But the apparent hopelessness of inflicting much injury upon such a large crowd restrained me, and Safeni turned to me, though almost cowed to dumbness by the loud fury around us, and pleaded with me to be patient. I complied, seeing that I should get no aid from my crew; but, while bitterly blaming myself for my imprudence in having yielded — against my instincts — to placing myself in the power of such savages, I vowed that, if I escaped this once, my own judgment should guide my actions for the future.

I assumed a resigned air, though I still retained my revolvers. My crew also bore the first outburst of the tempest of shrieking rage which assailed them with almost sublime imperturbability. Safeni crossed his arms with the meekness of a saint. Baraka held his hands palms outward, asking with serene benignity, "What, my friends, ails you? Do you fear empty hands and smiling people like us? We are friends, we came as friends to buy food, two or three bananas, a few mouthfuls of grain, or potatoes, or muhogo (cassava), and, if you permit us, we shall depart as friends."

Our demeanour had a great effect. The riot and noise seemed to be subsiding, when some fifty new-comers rekindled the smouldering fury. Again the forest of spears swayed on the launch, again the knotty clubs were whirled aloft, again the bows were drawn, and again the barbed arrows seemed flying. Safeni received a push which sent him tumbling, little Kirango received a blow on the head with a spear-staff, Saramba gave a cry as a club descended on his back.

I sprang up this time to remonstrate, with the two revolvers in my left hand. I addressed myself to an elder, who seemed to be restraining the people from proceeding too far. I showed him beads, cloth, wire, and invoked the names of Mtesi, and Antari their king.

The sight of the heaps of beads and cloth I exposed awakened, however, the more deliberate passions of selfishness and greed in each heart. An attempt at massacre, they began to argue, would certainly entail the loss of some of themselves. "Guns might be seized and handled with terrible effect even by dying men, and who knows what those little iron things in the white man's hands are?" they seemed to be asking themselves. The elder, whatever he thought, responded with an affectation of indignation, raised his stick, and to right and left of him drove back the demoniac crowd. Other prominent men now assisted this elder, whom we subsequently discovered to be Shekka, the king of Bumbireh.

Shekka then, having thus bestirred himself, beckoned to half-a-dozen men and walked away a few yards behind the mass. It was the "shauri," dear to a free and independent African's heart, that was about to be held. Half the crowd followed the king and his council, while the other half remained to indulge their violent, vituperative tongues on us, and to continually menace us with either club or spear. An audacious party came round the stern of the boat and, with superlatively hideous gestures, affronted me; one of them even gave a tug at my hair, thinking it was a wig. I avenged myself by seizing his hand, and suddenly bending it back almost dislocated it, causing him to howl with pain. His comrades swayed their lances, but I smilingly looked at them, for all idea of self-preservation had now almost fled.

The issue had surely arrived. There had been just one brief moment of agony when I reflected how unlovely death appears in such guise as that in which it then threatened me. What would my people think as they anxiously waited for the never returning master! What would Pocock and Barker say when they heard of the tragedy of Bumbireh! And my friends in America and Europe! "Tut, it is only a brief moment of pain, and then what can the ferocious dogs do more? It is a consolation that, if anything, it will be short, sharp, sudden — a gasp, and then a silence — for ever and ever!" And after that I was ready for the fight and for death.

"Now, my black friends, do your worst; anything you choose; I am ready."

A messenger from the king and the council arrives, and beckons Safeni. I said to him, "Safeni, use your wit."

"Please God, master," he replied.

Safeni drew nearly all the crowd after him, for curiosity is strong in the African. I saw him pose himself. A born diplomatist was Safeni. His hands moved up and down, outward and inward; a cordial frankness sat naturally on his face; his gestures were graceful; the man was an orator, pleading for mercy and justice.

Safeni returned, his face radiant. "It is all right, master, there is no fear. They say we must stop here until tomorrow."

"Will they sell us food? "

"Oh, yes, as soon as they settle their shauri."

While Safeni was speaking, six men rushed up and seized the oars.

Safeni, though hitherto politic, lost temper at this, and endeavoured to prevent them. They raised their clubs to strike him. I shouted, "Let them go, Safeni."

A loud cheer greeted the seizure of the oars. I became convinced now that this one little act would lead to others; for man is the same all over the world. Set a beggar on horseback, and he will ride to the devil; give a slave an inch, and he will take an ell; if a man submit once, he must be prepared to submit again.

The "shauri" proceeded. Another messenger came, demanding five cloths and five fundo of necklaces. They were delivered. But as it was now near noon, and they were assured we could not escape, the savages withdrew to their nearest village to refresh themselves with wine and food.

After the warriors had departed, some women came to look at us. We spoke kindly to them, and in return they gave us the consoling assurance that we should be killed; but they said that if we could induce Shekka to make blood-brotherhood, or to eat honey with one of us, we should be safe. If we failed, there was only flight or death. We thanked them, but we would wait.

About 3 P.M. we heard a number of drums beaten. Safeni was told that if the natives collected again he must endeavour to induce Shekka with gifts to go through the process of blood-brotherhood.

A long line of natives in full war costume appeared on the crest of the terrace, on which the banana grove and village of Kajurri stood. Their faces were smeared with black and white pigments. Almost all of them bore the peculiar shields of Usongora. Their actions were such as the dullest-witted of us recognised as indicating hostilities.

Even Safeni and Baraka were astounded, and their first words were, "Prepare, master. Truly, this is trouble."

"Never mind me," I replied, "I have been ready these three hours. Are you ready, your guns and revolvers loaded, and your ears open this time?"

"We are," they all firmly answered.

"Don't be afraid; be quite cool. We will try, while they are collecting together, the woman's suggestion. Go frankly and smilingly, Safeni, up to Shekka, on the top of that hill, and offer him these three fundo of beads, and ask him to exchange blood with you."

Safeni proceeded readily on his errand, for there was no danger to him bodily while we were there within 150 yards, and their full power as yet unprepared. For ten minutes he conversed with them, while the drums kept beating, and numbers of men bepainted for war were increasing Shekka's force. Some of them entertained us by demonstrating with their spears how they fought; others whirled their clubs like tipsy Irishmen at Donnybrook fair. Their gestures were wild, their voices were shrill and fierce, they were kindling themselves into a fighting fever.

Safeni returned. Shekka had refused the pledge of peace. The natives now mustered over 300.

Presently fifty bold fellows came rushing down, uttering a shrill cry. Without hesitation they came straight to the boat, and, hissing something to us, seized our Kiganda drum. It was such a small affair we did not resist; still the manner in which it was taken completely undeceived us, if any small hope of peace remained. Loud applause greeted the act of gallantry.

Then two men came towards us, and began to drive some cows away that were grazing between us and the men on the hill. Safeni asked one them, "Why do you do that?"

"Because we are going to begin fighting presently, and if you are men, you may begin to prepare yourselves," he said scornfully.

"Thanks, my bold friend," I muttered to myself. "Those are the truest words we have heard to-day."

The two men were retiring up the hill. "Here Safeni," I said, "take these two fine red cloths in your hand; walk slowly up after them a little way, and the minute you hear my voice run back; and you, my boys, this is for life and death, mind; range yourselves on each side of the boat, lay your hands on it carelessly, but with a firm grip, and when I give the word, push it with the force of a hundred men down the hill into the water. Are you all ready, and do you think you can do it? Otherwise we might as well begin fighting where we are."

"Yes, Inshallah Master," they cried out with one voice.

"Go, Safeni!"

I waited until he had walked fifty yards away, and saw that he acted precisely as I had instructed him.

"Push, my boys; push for your lives!"

The crew bent their heads and strained their arms; the boat began to move, and there was a hissing, grinding noise below me. I seized my double-barrelled elephant rifle and shouted, "Safeni! Safeni, return!"

The natives were quick-eyed. They saw the boat moving, and with one accord they swept down the hill uttering the most fearful cries.

My boat was at the water's edge. "Shoot her into the lake, my men; never mind the water"; and clear of all obstructions she darted out upon the lake.

Safeni stood for an instant on the water's edge, with the cloths in his hand. The foremost of a crowd of natives was about twenty yards from him. He raised his spear and balanced himself.

"Spring into the water, man, head first," I cried.

The balanced spear was about to fly, and another man was preparing his weapon for a deadly cast, when I raised my gun and the bullet ploughed through him and through the second. The bowmen halted and drew their bows. I sent two charges of duck-shot into their midst with terrible effect. The natives retreated from the beach on which the boat had lately lain.

Having checked the natives, I assisted one of my men into the boat, and ordered him to lend a hand to the others, while I reloaded my big guns, keeping my eyes on the natives. There was a point about 100 yards in length on the east, which sheltered the cove. Some of the natives made a rush for this, but my guns commanded the exposed position, and they were obliged to retire.

The crew seized their rifles, but I told them to leave them alone, and to tear the bottom-boards out of the boat and use them as paddles; for there were two hippopotami advancing upon us open-mouthed, and it seemed as if we were to be crushed in the water after such a narrow escape from the ferocious people ashore. I permitted one of the hippos to approach within ten yards, and, aiming between his eyes, perforated his skull with a three-ounce ball, and the second received such a wound that we were not molested by him.

Meanwhile the savages, baffled and furious at seeing their prey escape, had rushed, after a short consultation, to man two canoes that were drawn up on the beach at the north-west corner of the cove. Twice I dropped men as they endeavoured to launch the boats; but they persisted, and finally, launching them, pursued us vigorously. Two other canoes were seen coming down the coast from the eastern side of the island.

Unable to escape, we stopped after we had got out of the cove, and waited for them.

My elephant rifle was loaded with explosive balls for this occasion. Four shots killed five men and sank two of the canoes. The two others retired to assist their friends out of the water. They attempted nothing further, but some of those on shore had managed to reach the point, and as we resumed our paddles, we heard a voice cry out, "Go and die in the Nyanza!" and saw them shoot their arrows, which fell harmlessly a few yards behind us. We were saved!

It was 5 P.M. We had only four bananas in the boat, and we were twelve hungry men. If we had a strong fair breeze, a day and a night would suffice to enable us to reach our camp. But if we had head-winds, the journey might occupy a month. Meanwhile, after the experience of Makongo, Alice Island, and Bumbireh, where should we apply for food? Fresh water we had in abundance, sufficient to satisfy the thirst of all the armies of the world for a century. But food? Whither should we turn for it?

A gentle breeze came from the island. We raised the lug sail, hoping that it would continue fair for a south-east course. But at 7 P.M. it fell a dead calm. We resumed our extemporized paddles — those thin weak bottom-boards. Our progress was about three-quarters of a mile per hour.

Throughout the night we laboured, cheering one another. In the morning not a speck of land was visible: all was a boundless circle of grey water.

April 29. — About 9 A.M. a squall came fair and drove us about eight miles to the south; about 10.30 it became calm again, but still we paddled unceasingly. At night we found ourselves about seven miles away from an island to the southward of us, and we made noble efforts to reach it. But a gale came up from the south-west, against which it was useless to contend. The crew were fatigued and weakened after paddling forty -nine hours without food.

We resigned ourselves to the waves and the rain that was falling in sheets, and the driving tempest. Up and down we rose and sank on the great waves, battered from side to side, swung round, plunged in dark hollows, and bathed in spray. We baled the boat out, and again sat down. At midnight the gale moderated and the moon rose, throwing a weird light upon the face of the lake and its long heaving billows, which still showed high crests whitened with foam. Up and down we rose and plunged. The moon now shone clear upon the boat and her wretched crew, ghastlily lighting up the crouching, wearied, despairing forms, from which there sometimes rose deep sighs that wrung my heart. "Cheer up, my lads, think nothing of the curse of those of Bumbireh; bad men's curses sometimes turn out blessings," I said, to encourage them. One of the thwarts was chopped up, and we made a fire, and with some of the coffee which I had obtained from Colonel Linant at Mtesa's we felt somewhat refreshed. And then, completely wearied out, they all slept, but I watched, busy with my thoughts.

April 30. — The morning came, the morning of the 30th of April, and though my men had only eaten four bananas between them and tasted, besides, a cup of coffee since 10 A.M. of the 27th, they nevertheless, sixty-eight hours afterwards, when I urged them to resume their paddles that we might reach an island twelve miles south of us, rallied to my appeal with a manliness which won my admiration, responding with heroic will but, alas! with little strength.

At 2 A.M. — seventy-six hours after leaving Alice Island — we approached a cove in an uninhabited island, which I have distinguished on the chart by the name of "Refuge." We crawled out of the boat, and each of us thanked God for even this little mercy and lay down on the glowing sand to rest.

But food must be obtained before night. Baraka and Safeni were sent to explore the interior in one direction, Murabo and Marzouk in another. Robert and Hamoidah were set to kindle a fire, and I took my shot-gun to shoot birds. Within half an hour I had obtained a brace of large fat ducks; Baraka and Safeni returned each with two bunches of young green bananas, and Murabo and his comrade had discovered some luscious berries like cherries.

And what glad souls were we that evening around our camp fire with this gracious abundance to which a benignant Providence had led us, storm-tossed, bruised, and hungry creatures that we were but a few hours before! Bananas, ducks, berries, and coffee! The tobacco gourd and pipe closed one of the most delicious evenings I ever remember to have passed. No wonder that before retiring, feeling ourselves indebted to the Supreme Being, who had preserved us through so many troubles, we thanked Him for His mercies and His bounties.

May 2. — We rested another day on Refuge Island to make oars; and further explorations enabled us to procure half-a-dozen more bunches of bananas. Our appetites were so keen that there was but little left next morning by the time we were ready to start afresh. With oar and sail we set out for Singo Island. Perceiving it was uninhabited, we steered for Ito Island, the slopes of which were rich with plantains, but the natives slung stones at us, and we were therefore obliged to continue on our way to the Kuneneh group, near the peninsula of Ukerewe.

May 4. — On the afternoon of the 4th of May, a stormy head-wind rising, we were compelled to turn into the cove of Wiru, where, through the influence of Saramba the guide, who was at home in this country, we were hospitably received, and meat, potatoes, milk, honey, bananas both ripe and green, eggs and poultry, were freely sold to us. We cooked these delicacies on board, and ate them with such relish and appetite as only half-starved men can appreciate.

May 5. — Hoping to reach our camp next morning, we set sail at 9 P.M., steering across Speke Gulf. But about 3 A.M., when we were nearly in mid-gulf, the fickle wind failed us, and then, as if resolved we should taste to the uttermost the extreme of suffering, it met us with a tempest from the N.N.E., as fearful in other respects as that which we experienced at Usuguru, but with the fresh torments added of hailstones as large as filberts. The sky was robed in inky blackness, not a star was visible, vivid lightnings flashed accompanied by loud thunder crashes, and furious waves tossed us about as though we were imprisoned in a gourd, the elements thus combining to multiply the terrors of our situation. Again we resigned the boat to wind and wave, as all our efforts to keep our course were unavailing.

We began to think that the curse of the people of Bumbireh, "Go and die in the Nyanza," might be realized after all — though I had much faith in the staunch craft which Messenger of Teddington so conscientiously constructed.

May 6. — A grey, cheerless morning dawned at last, and we discovered ourselves to be ten miles north of Rwoma, and about twenty miles north-west of Kagehyi. We put forth our best efforts, hoisted sail, and though the wind was but little in our favour at first, it soon veered round, and sent us sailing merrily over the tall weaves, and along the coast of Usukuma, straight towards camp.

Shouts of welcome greeted us from shore, for the people had recognized us by our sail when miles away, and as we drew nearer the shouts changed to volleys of musketry, and the waving of flags, and the land seemed alive with leaping forms of the glad-hearted men. For we had been fifty-seven days away from our people, and many a false rumour had reached them of our deaths, strengthened each day that our return was deferred and our absence grew longer. But the sight of the exploring boat sailing towards Kagehyi dissipated all alarm, concern, and fear.

As the keel grounded, fifty men bounded into the water, dragged me from the boat, and danced me round the camp on their shoulders, amid much laughter, and clapping of hands, grotesque wriggling of forms, and real Saxon hurrahing.

Frank Pocock was there, his face lit up by fulness of joy, but when I asked him where Frederick Barker was, and why he did not come to welcome me, Frank's face clouded with the sudden recollection of our loss, as he answered, "Because he died twelve days ago. Sir, and he lies there," pointing gravely to a low mound of earth by the lake!

CHAPTER XI.

Barker's illness and death — Other deaths — Traitors in the camp — Rest!
— Sickness — Rwoma blocks our passage by land — Magassa fails us by
water — A periods dilemma — Lukongeh comes to the rescue — History of
Ukerewe — Educated amphibians — Leaving Kagehyi with half the
Expedition — The foundering canoes — All saved — Ito conciliates us —
Arrival at Refuge Island with half the Expedition — I return for the rest — A
murderous outbreak in camp — Final departure from Kagehyi — All
encamped on Refuge Island — We ally ourselves with Komeh — A dance of
kings — Mahyiga Island (in the Bumbireh group) — Interviewed by Iroba
canoes — Our friendship scorned — The king of Bumbireh a hostage — The
massacre of the Kytawa chief and his crew — The punishment of the
murderers — Its salutary effect upon their neighbours — We arrive in
Uganda.

May 6. — When the hysterical congratulations of the Expedition had somewhat slackened, Prince Kaduma and the friends of Saramba, the guide (who was now quite a hero), and Frank accompanied me to my hut — the dogs Jack and Bull following — to give me a brief narrative of the events that had transpired.

Fred Barker, according to Frank, had good health till the middle of April; after which he began to experience aguish fits. On the 22nd he had enjoyed a hippopotamus hunt on the shore between Kagehyi and Lutari, and on the morning of the 23rd had bathed in the lake and eaten a hearty early breakfast. At 9 A.M., however, he complained of feeling ill, and lay down. Almost immediately a cold fit seized him, and his blood seemed to stagnate in its veins, Frank and Barker's servants employed their utmost art to increase the warmth of his body. They administered brandy and hot tea, put heated stones to his feet, and piled blanket after blanket upon him, but the congealed blood would not run, and at 11 A.M. the poor young man was dead.

"At 3 P.M. we buried him," said Frank, "close to the Nyanza. Poor fellow I many and many a time he said during the last few days, 'I wish the master would come back. I should then feel as if there were some chance of life for me, but I shall die stagnating and rotting here if he does not come.' I think, Sir, he would have pulled through had you been here."

I missed young Barker very much. He had begun to endear himself to me by his bright intelligence and valuable services. When ill, my least wish was immediately gratified: he understood the least motion or sign. He was also a good writer, and he kept the accounts of the various stores, cloths, and beads. He was an admirable companion to Frank, and the two young men were good company for me; they had also won the hearts of the Wangwana by their gentle, amiable conduct. An oath or a profane word I seldom heard from either of them; and when angry, their anger at the stupidity or insolence of the people was of the passive kind; they never resorted to violence without appealing to me.

But Frank had other bad news to tell. Mabruki Speke, whom Burton called the bull-headed — the faithful servant of Burton and Speke, Speke and Grant, of myself on the first expedition, of Livingstone on his last journey, and one of the most trusted men of my present following from Zanzibar to Lake Victoria — was dead. Jabiri (one of the stout boat-bearers) was dead, and so was old Akida, besides three others. All had died of dysentery. Msenna the "bully of Zanzibar" had broken out once more, after nearly six months of good behaviour. I arrived at Kagehyi on the 5th of May from the exploration of the lake; on the 6th he was to have led a body of sixty men to Unyanyembe, if the master did not return!

Kipingiri, chief of Lutari, and brother of Kaduma, chief of Kagehyi, had formed a conspiracy with Kurrereh, chief of Kyenzi, and the chief of Igusa, to unite their forces to attack and plunder the camp. But the Wangwana chiefs, Manwa Sera and Kacheche, had discovered the plot, and Frank and Fred Barker, after sounding Kaduma, had distributed ammunition, with every intention of employing their best abilities to resist the attack. Prince Kaduma's loyalty to his absent friend, and Frank and Fred's bold conduct, with the sudden death of the chief of Igusa, had caused Kipingiri to abandon the wicked conspiracy.

Frank informed me also that he had suffered one or two slight attacks of fever, but that he had "easily shaken them off." The Wangwana were wonderfully recovered from the miserable attenuation which the scant fare of Ugogo and Urimi had wrought in their frames, and some were so robust and fat that I scarcely knew them. Upon examining the stock of goods left in the store-room, I was gratified to discover that Frank had been extremely economical. I found him in perfect accord with Prince Kaduma, good friends with Sungoro, and respected by the Wangwana; and on inspecting his work, there was nothing in his conduct that did not deserve hearty approval and commendation.

May 7. — Our return to Kagehyi was followed by Sabbath repose and rest, fairly earned and much needed. When I placed myself under the spring-balance scales, I found I weighed only 115 lbs., just 63 lbs. less than when leaving Zanzibar. Frank Pocock weighed 162 lbs.! I saved this excessive reduction of flesh to scant fare and days of hunger, not to sickness.

Sweet were those first days of rest! Frank was eager to hear all that had befallen us, in our 1000 miles' sail round the lake, and the Wangwana formed circles many deep, to hear the Iliad of our woes. What hearty sympathisers what these poor, black, untutored men were! Kaduma was all amazement, and Sungoro never ceased to express his wonder as to how we managed to go round the lake in the "little boat." The Wasukuma extemporized songs in her honour, which they sang in the evenings; and the naked urchins made miniature boats out of the stem of the banana, with twigs as masts and leaves for sails. The influence of one example had, it seemed to me, already produced fruit here, and the efforts of the little ones proved to me that the natives needed but one or two more such examples to stimulate them to similar enterprises. Future explorers will find many ready to imitate bold Saramba's conduct as guides, and the Wasukuma may become in future as docile boatmen as they are capable porters and steady travellers on land.

Then came sickness. The African fever having found my frame weakened from privations attacked me vigorously one day after another. Three fevers reduced me 7 lbs. in weight. But I quininized myself thoroughly from dawn of day to set of sun, and on the fifth day stepped out, sallow, pale, weak, and trembling, it is true, with jaundiced eyes, palpitating heart, and ringing ears — but the fever had been conquered.

Where was Magassa with his canoes? Day after day we hoped and wished he would appear, but his canoes were never sighted on the horizon, and we finally abandoned all hope of seeing him, or of being able to reach Uganda by water. We prepared therefore to march overland by way of Mwere through King Rwoma's country. We made no secret of it. Kaduma was informed, and he communicated it to every one, and it soon came to Rwoma's ears.

But King Rwoma, being an ally of Mirambo, entertained a strong objection to Wangwana, and he had exaggerated ideas of the appearance of the white men who were at Kagehyi. Some silly child of nature had told him there was a white man at Kagehyi with "long red hair, and great red eyes" — it was probably Frank, though a libellous caricature of him certainly — and the report induced Rwoma to send an embassy to Kagehyi. He said, "Rwoma sends salaams to the white man. He does not want the white man's cloth, beads, or wire, and the white man must not pass through his country; Rwoma does not want to see him or any other white man with long red hair down to his shoulders, white face, and big red eyes; Rwoma is not afraid of him, but if the white man comes near his country, Rwoma and Mirambo will fight him." To this bold but frank challenge the Wasukuma added other reasons to prove that the overland route was impassable. The road between Muanza and Mwere was closed by factious tribes. Rwoma was an ally of Mirambo; Kijaju, his neighbour, was an ally of the predatory Watuta; the chief of Nchoza, hard by him, was at war with the Watuta; Antari, king of Ihangiro and Bumbireh, would naturally resent our approach; Mankorongo, successor of Swarora of Usui, could only be appeased with such tribute as would be absolutely ruinous. If I proceeded south to Unyanyembe the Wangwana could never be held together, and the Expedition would dissolve like snow.

By water, what was the outlook? Magassa and his fleet were not to be heard of. He had probably returned from Musira Island, afraid to risk his canoes in the great waste of waters between Musira Island and Alice Island, for Waganda canoes made of plank and sewn together with fibre of cane sometimes founder in bad weather, and the lake in the rainy season is dangerous to such. The Wasukuma possessed no canoes, and I but one boat capable of carrying fifteen men in rough weather. Yet my duty urged me to proceed to Uganda. Lake Albert must be visited, for I had given my word of honour that I would attempt it. Yet the land route was impassable, and to all appearance so also was the lake route!

While explaining my difficulties to Sungoro, he informed me, after responding to various other questions, that Lukongeh, king of Ukerewe, possessed numerous canoes, but he doubted if he would lend them to me. "However," said he, "he is an agreeable man, and a good friend if he takes a fancy to one." I thought of Lukongeh, but another attack of fever cut short my deliberations. My system was much injured by exposure and privations, and in my delirium I fancied myself pleading with the king, and throughout each day's sick vagaries, "Lukongeh, Lukongeh," nothing but Lukongeh, flitted through my brain.

May 15. — On the 15th of May I was convalescent, and arranged that Prince Kaduma, Sungoro's carpenter, and Frank Pocock should proceed together to Lukongeh, bearing ten fine cloths, ten fundo of beads, and five fathom of brass wire, to open negotiations either for the sale or hire of canoes.

May 28. — On the 28th, Frank and his party returned with fifty canoes and their crews, under the command of two chiefs and the "premier" of Ukerewe. I gripped Frank's hand with ardour, but was dismayed when I was told that these canoes were to convey the Expedition to Ukerewe! This was by no means a desirable thing, for its progress might be delayed for months by caprice, or by any future ill will arising from a too intimate acquaintance between the Wangwana and the natives. I refused, and told the chiefs they could accompany me back to Ukerewe, as I would see Lukongeh myself.

May 29. — Accordingly, on the 29th, after providing myself with presents such as might win any African's goodwill — fine rugs, blankets, crimson cloth, and striped cloths of Kutch and Muscat, besides beads of a rare quality, and other things too numerous to mention, equal to about 800 dollars' worth — I started for Msossi, Lukongeh 's capital on the north side of Ukerewe.

May 30. — We halted a few hours at Wezi, and its curious granite rocks were photographed by me, and in the -afternoon continued our journey, arriving at Kisorya at 4 P.M., where we camped. The next morning, about 9 A.M., we passed through Rugedzi Channel, which connects Speke Gulf with Majita Bay. It was 6 feet wide in some places, and if left undisturbed there was every indication from the grasses and water-plants which grew in it that it would soon be choked, but by vigorous punting with poles we succeeded ill getting through. Some of the Wakerewe say that Majita mountain is separated from the mainland by a similar channel, at which I should not be surprised. We reached Msossi, and received a hut to house ourselves in, an ox for meat, bananas for vegetables, and milk for drink.

May 31. — At 9 A.M. of the 31st we advanced upon the aulic council of Ukerewe, which, seated on some rising rocks on a plain, was quite picturesque, with the gay figure of Lukongeh in the centre, round which the lesser lights revolved. The king, a handsome, open-faced, light coloured young man of twenty-six or twenty-eight years old, merely gazed his fill; and his chiefs Msiwa, Mosota, Mgeyeya, and Wakoreh, followed his example, as well as the lesser chiefs, men, boys, and women.

From his questions I perceived that Lukongeh would be quite as much influenced by conversations about Europe as Mtesa of Uganda, and I soon saw in him as eligible a convert to Christianity, though the future was too fraught with anxiety for me to attempt it. No business could be commenced on this day. We were to eat and rest, and the next, if the king felt in good health, we might begin the negotiations.

On the second day Lukongeh was fortunately in excellent health and spirits, and I felt so also, and with the greatest possible suavity I proposed that he should either sell or lend me thirty canoes. All his objections were met and overruled by the exhibition of my presents. But when he saw me thus publicly expose the gorgeous cloths in broad daylight, he trembled, and made me cover them up quickly, saying that he would visit me in my hut at night, and that I might rest assured he would do his best for me. On the evening of the 4th of June, he stole into my hut at night, in company with his faithful premier, and four principal chiefs, and here I presented him with two fine rugs, one Scotch plaid, two red blankets, ornaments of copper, thirty fine cloths, fifty fundo of beads, and two coils of brass wire, besides various other things, such as dishes, plates, tin pots. &c. His chiefs received five cloths each and five fundo (a fundo consists of ten necklaces) of beads, and two fathoms each of brass wire. For these munificent presents, I should obtain my answer shortly; but in the meantime I must enjoy myself. "Feed and get fat," said Lukongeh, as he withdrew happy with his wealth.

The Wakerewe, following the example of their king, treated us with consideration. We had to undergo a narrow inspection, and a keen analysis of physiognomy, that they might compare us with the Arab Sungoro; but we had long become accustomed to this, and therefore bore it with unconcern.

There are representatives of many tribes in Ukerewe — such as Wataturu, Wa-hya, Watambara, Wasumbwa, Waruri, Wakwya and Waziuja.

The elders, to whom are entrusted the traditions of the country, furnished me with a list of the following kings:

1. Ruhinda I.
2. Kasessa.
3. Kytuwa.
4. Kahana I.
5. Gurta I.
6. Nagu.
7. Mebigo I.
8. Mebigo II.

9. Kahana II.

10. Gurta II.

11. Ruhinda II.

12. Kahana III.

13. Iwanda

14. Machunda.

15. Lukongeh, the present king.

The founder of Ukerewe, Ruhinda I, is the king whose memory is most revered. He brought his people in canoes from Usongora and Ihangiro, which was known in old times by the name of U-wya. He it was who introduced the plantain and banana plants into Ukerewe. The aborigines, whom he conquered, were called Wa-kwya — another name for the inhabitants of Majita Mount. A small remnant of the tribe still live on the south coast of Ukerewe, opposite Kagehyi.

The royal sepulchre is at Kitari. The hill on which it is situated is seen in the photograph of the boat at the landing-place of Msossi, and an eminent chief of Ukerewe has the charge of it to protect it inviolate. The kings are all buried in a sitting posture.

Lukongeh's dominions east of Rugedzi Channel were acquired by the forcible dispossession of Wataturu shepherds, after a fierce battle, which lasted five days, during which many of the Wakerewe were slain by the poisoned arrows of the shepherds. Though they live harmoniously together now, there is as much difference between the Wakerewe and the Wataturu as exists between a Nubian and a Syrian Arab. The Wataturu are light-coloured, straight, thin-nosed and thin-lipped, while the Wakerewe are a mixture of the Ethiopic and negro type.

The king is supposed to be endowed with supernatural power, and Lukongeh seizes every opportunity to heighten this belief. He is believed to be enabled to create a drought at pleasure, and to cause the land to be drenched with rain. It is fortunate that, since his accession to power, rain has been regular and copious in its season. The king has not been slow to point out this immense advantage which Ukerewe has gained since he succeeded his father; he is therefore beloved and feared.

Aware of the value of a reputation as rain-maker, he was ambitious to add to it that of "great medicine man," and besought me earnestly to impart to him some of the grand secrets of Europe — such as how to transform men into lions and leopards, to cause the rains to fall or cease, the winds to blow, to give fruitfulness to women and virility to men. Demands of this character are commonly made by African chiefs. When I stated my inability to comply with his requests, he whispered to his chiefs: —

"He will not give me what I ask, because he is afraid he will not get the canoes; but you will see when my men return from Uganda, he will give me all I ask."

The custom of greeting the king is a most curious one, differing from any I have observed elsewhere. His people, after advancing close to him, clap their hands and kneel to him. If the king is pleased, he reveals his pleasure by blowing and spitting into their hands, with which they affect to anoint their faces and eyes. They seem to believe that the king's saliva is a collyrium for the eyes.

To each other the Wakerewe kneel, clap hands, and cry, "Wache! wache!" "Wache sug!" Mohoro!" "Eg sura?" which, translated, signifies, "Morning! morning!" "Good-morning!" "A good day!" "Are you well?"

The stories current in this country about the witchcraft practised by the people of Ukara Island prove that those islanders have been at pains to spread abroad a good repute for themselves, that they are cunning, and, aware that superstition is a weakness of human nature, have sought to thrive upon it. Their power — according to the Wakerewe — over the amphibiae is wonderful. One Khamis, son of Hamadi, the carpenter of Sungoro, having been a long time constructing a dhow, or sailing vessel, for his employer, shared most thoroughly in these delusions.

Khamis averred, with an oath, that there was a crocodile who lived in the house of the chief of Ukara, which fed from his hands, and was as docile and obedient to his master as a dog, and as intelligent as a man. Lukongeh had once a pretty woman in his harem, who was coveted by the Ukara chief, but the latter could devise no means to possess her for a long time until he thought of his crocodile. He instantly communicated his desire to the reptile, and bade him lie in wait in the rushes near Msossi until the woman should approach the lake to bathe, as was her custom daily, and then seize and convey her without injury across the eight-mile channel to Ukara. The next day. at noon, the woman was in the Ukara chiefs house.

When I expressed a doubt about the veracity of the marvellous tale, Khamis said, indignantly, "What, you doubt me? Ask Lukongeh, and he will confirm what I have told you."

He then added, "Machunda, Lukongeh's father, owned a crocodile that stole an Arab's wife, and carried her across the country to the king's house!" To Khamis, and the Wangwana who listened to him, this last was conclusive evidence that the crocodiles of Ukai'a were most astonishing creatures.

The Wakerewe also believe that, if a hawk seizes a fish belonging to the Wakara, it is sure to die in the very act!

Kaduma Kagehyi, according to Khamis, possessed a hippopotamus which came to him each morning, for a long period, to be milked!

It requires twelve goats and three hoes to purchase a wife in Ukerewe from her parents. Sungoro, the Arab, was obliged to pay Lukongeh 350 lbs. of assorted beads and 300 yards of good cloth before he succeeded in obtaining one of his young sisters in marriage. If the lover is so poor that he has neither goats nor hoes, he supplies such articles as spears, or bows and arrows, but he cannot obtain a wife until he furnishes a sufficient dowry to please her parents. If the parents or older relatives are grasping, and impose hard conditions, the state of the lover is hard indeed, as frequently after marriage demands are made for cattle, sheep, goats, &c., a refusal of which renders the marriage void until children have been born, when all connection with her blood relatives ceases.

Thieves, adulterers, and murderers are put to death by decapitation. They may escape death, however, by becoming the slaves of the party they have wronged.

Coils of brass wire are much coveted by the Wakerewe, for the adornment of their wives, who wear it in such numerous circlets round their necks as to give them at a distance an appearance of wearing ruffs. Wristlets of copper and brass and iron, and anklets of the same metal, besides armlets of ivory, are the favourite decorations of the males.

Families in mourning are distinguished by bands of plantain leaf round their heads, and by a sable pigment of a mixture of pulverized charcoal and butter. The matrons who have fallen into the sere of life are peculiar for their unnatural length of breasts, which, depending like pouches down to the navel, are bound to their bodies by cords. The dresses of men and women consist of half dressed ox-hides, goat-skins, or a cincture of banana leaves, or kirtles of a coarsely made grass cloth.

June 6. — On the 6th of June, Lukongeh, having issued instructions to his chiefs how to assist me, called on me at night, accompanied by his premier, to impart his decisions and plans.

Said he, "My people are very timid in strange lands. They are no travellers like the Wangwana. I am obliged therefore to act in the dark with them, otherwise I could not help you. I am going to give you twenty-three canoes and their paddles. They are not worth much, and if they give you trouble, you must not blame me. I am telling my people you are coming back to Ukerewe. Don't deny it, and don't talk about it, or they will be sure to run away back here. If you are clever, they will follow you to Usukuma. Once there, take the canoes and paddles, because I give them to you; and here are my young nephew and cousin, who will follow you to Uganda, and make friends with the Wazinja, as far as Ihangiro, for you. When you reach Uganda, I wish you to make Mtesa and myself brothers, and we will exchange gifts. You must also remember to send my young men back from Uganda. Good-bye. I have said all."

I was also enjoined to send to Lukongeh by his young nephew and cousin two suits of crimson and blue flannels, medicine for rheumatism and headache, one revolver and ammunition, one bale of cloth, beads of various kinds to the amount of 50 lbs., two fezes, one English rug, one Kiganda canoe, capable of carrying forty men, two tusks of ivory, Usoga goat-skins, otter furs, and iron and brass wire — all of which of course I promised most faithfully to send.

June 7. — Lukongeh and his chiefs were out early on the morning of the 7th of June to bid me farewell. But there were only five small canoes ready! "How is this, Lukongeh?" I asked. "Never mind, go on; and remember what I have said to you, my brother. Lukongeh is true," he replied, with dignity.

"Wonderful man," I thought, "to have a respect for truth in this country. He is assuredly one of the first. However, we shall see."

We punted our boat through the narrow Rugedzi Channel, and rowed to Kisorya. Lukongeh's premier, his nephew and cousin, who were to be our guides, were with us.

June 11. — From the hills of Kisorya I obtained a capital photograph of the deep bay which leads from Speke Gulf to Rugedzi Channel, and of the mountains of Urirwi, across the bay. From Kisorya we moved to Ugoma, where we halted, a sore trial to our patience, until the 11th of June, on which day, with twenty-seven canoes of Ukerewe, we rowed to Wezi Island, situate nearly midway in Speke Gulf between Ukerewe and Kagehyi.

June 12. — The next day, upon landing at Kagehyi, I whispered instructions to Frank and Manwa Sera to haul up the canoes to a distance of eighty yards on land, and with the aid of Lukongeh's premier and the king's relatives induced the Wakerewe canoe-men, 216 in number, to store their paddles in my hut.

The Wakerewe were then apprised of the strategy of their king, and told that there were four canoes left to them to return to Ukerewe, and that, as it would occupy four days to transport their entire party back, beads would be given for ten days' provisions. At this the Wakerewe were naturally very much surprised, and the uproar became tremendous. They seized the premier, but he audaciously shuffled the fault upon the young relatives, so releasing him they bound Lukongeh's relatives, and would undoubtedly have murdered them then and there but for the precautions I had taken. A nod to Frank and Manwa Sera, and fifty Wangwana had dashed up to the rescue and, charging on the excited mob with the muzzles of their guns, drove them clear out of the village of Kagehyi.

When the Wakerewe were outside, we held a palaver with them, at which it was explained that we should wait six days at Kagehyi, during which time they could communicate with Lukongeh, and if the king repented of his promise, the canoes should be sent back, or that, if they pleased, they could return and, by manning the canoes for us, would be sure of earning each man his reward, but that the relatives of Lukongeh, being in my camp and in my service, must not be molested, as I was bound to protect them.

This firm decision being fully explained to them, forty-five took the four canoes given and returned to Ukerewe, to communicate with Lukongeh. Six additional canoes, despatched by their friends the next day, assisted in the transport of the natives of Ukerewe back to their country; and on the third day our camp was emptied of almost all of them, but though we waited seven days at Kagehyi, no further communication came from Lukongeh, and therefore the premier and his five servants departed.

Meanwhile I had despatched messengers to all the districts around to summon the people to a grain market, whereat all grain brought to Kagehyi would be purchased, at the rate of eight measures (similar to pecks) at the rate of one doti or four yards of blue, white, or coloured cloth. By the 19th of June, 12,000 lbs. of grain, sesamum, millet, and Indian corn, and 500 lbs. of rice had been purchased and stowed in cloth sacks, each containing about 100 lbs.

As the canoes were so rotten, the crews of each were detailed under the supervision of Lukanjah, the nephew, and Mikoudo, the cousin of Lukongeh, to repair them. This was done by re-sewing many of the planks with cane-fibre and caulking them with the bruised stalk of the banana.

June 20. — At early dawn we began the embarkation of 150 men, women, and children, with 100 loads of cloth, beads, and wire, 88 sacks of grain, and 30 cases of ammunition; and as I could not delegate to others the care of the flotilla without feeling uncontrollable anxiety about it, the Lady Alice, loaded with most of the ammunition, led the way at 9 A.M. to Mabibi. These islets are three miles westward of Wezi, six miles from Ukerewe, and about nine miles from Kagehyi.

To my great satisfaction I perceived that the Wangwana would soon acquire the art of paddling, though many were exceedingly timid on the water. Until they gained confidence in their new duties, our plan was to avail ourselves of the calm periods, and not to risk so many lives and so much property in a tempestuous sea.

A strong breeze from the north-west lasted all the morning, but at noon it moderated, and two hours afterwards, taking advantage of the calm, we pushed off from Mabibi, and, rounding the south-west corner of the Ukerewe peninsula, pulled for the Kunneneh islets, which we reached without loss or accident. Again the north-west breeze blew strong, and, as it had power over a greater expanse of water, the waves did not subside until 2 P.M. It was tough labour rowing against the heavy swell, and the distance to the Miandereh Islands was long. By persevering, however, we made good progress, yet at sunset Miandereh islets were not in sight.

Intense darkness set in. We could not see one another, though we could hear the measured, rhythmic beat and splash of oar and paddle, but no voices. Now and then I flashed a waxlight over the dark waste as a beacon to the thoughtless and unwary. By this means, and by threats of punishment to those who strayed from the line, the canoes were kept together.

We had proceeded quietly for three hours in the darkness, when suddenly shrill cries were heard for "the boat." Hurrying to the spot, I managed to distinguish, to my astonishment, round dark objects floating on the water, which we found to be the heads of men who were swimming towards us from a foundered canoe. We took the frightened people on board, and picked up four bales of cloth, but a box of ammunition and 400 lbs. of grain had sunk.

We moved forward again, but had scarcely gone half a mile when again piercing cries from the deep gloom startled us. "The boat, oh, the boat!" was screamed in frenzied accents.

As we steered for the spot, I lit a wax taper and set fire to the leaves of a book I had been reading during the afternoon, to lighten up the scene. Heads of struggling men and bales were found here likewise in the water, and a canoe turned bottom up with a large rent in its side; and while distributing these among the other canoes, we heard to our alarm that five guns had sunk, but fortunately no lives were lost or other property, except four sacks of grain.

My boat was now up to her gunwale with twenty-two men and thirty loads, and if a breeze rose, she would, unless we lightened her of property, inevitably sink.

Through the darkness I shouted out to the frightened men, that if any more canoes collapsed, the crews should at once empty out the grain and beads, but on no account abandon their boats, as they would float and sustain them until I could return to save them.

I had scarcely finished speaking before the alarming cries were raised again: "Master, the canoe is sinking! Quick, come here. Oh, master, we cannot swim!"

Again I hurried up to the cries, and distinguished two men paddling vigorously, while five were baling. I was thinking how I could possibly assist them, when other cries broke out: "The boat! Bring the boat here! Oh, hurry — the boat, the boat!" Then another broke out, "And we are sinking — the water is up to our knees. Come to us, master, or we die! Bring the boat, my master!"

It was evident that a panic was raging amongst the timid souls, that the people were rapidly becoming utterly unnerved. In reply to their frenzied cries, and as the only way to save us all, I shouted out sternly: "You who would save yourselves, follow me to the islets as fast as you can: and you who are crying out, cling to your canoes until we return."

We rowed hard. The moon rose also, and cheered us in half an hour with a sight of Miandereh, for which we steered. Her brightness had also the effect of rousing up the spirits of the Wangwana; but still the piteous cries were heard far behind: "Master! oh, master! bring your boat — the boat."

"Hark to them, my boys — hark," I sang out to my crew, and they responded to my appeal by causing the Lady Alice to fly through the water, though the waves almost curled over her sides. "Pull, my men; break your oars; shoot her through the water; life and death hang on your efforts. Pull like heroes." She hissed through the waves, as ten men, bending with the wildest, most desperate effort, spurred her with their oars.

Miandereh islets rose larger and clearer into view. "Hurrah, my boys, here is our island! pull and defy the black water — your brothers are drowning!"

We reached Miandereh — shot the goods out, lightened her of the wrecked men, and flew back again, skimming over the dark surface.

There were two brothers who had been made coxswains of canoes, who came prominently into notice on this terrible night. Each had his special crew, friends and people of the same tribe, and their names were Uledi and Shumari; the former about twenty-five years old, the latter eighteen.

As I was returning with my boat to the scene, two canoes passed me like arrows. "Who go there?" I demanded.

"Uledi and Shumari's canoes," replied somebody.

"Return instantly, after unloading, to save the people."

"It is what we intend to do, Inshallah!" answered a voice.

"Fine fellows those, I warrant them," I thought. "Their very action and tone reveal their brave spirits."

Away we flew to the rescue, blowing the bugle to announce our approach. We passed three or four canoes, racing by us to the islets. Thank Heaven, the lake was calm, and the moon shone clear and strong, casting a golden light upon the waters.

"You are brave fellows; pull, my sons; think of those poor men in the lake in sinking canoes." Responding to my prayers, the crew almost cracked their hearts in the mighty efforts they made; their quick-swaying figures, the deep sighs which burst from their breasts, the careering boat, the excited helmsman, everything sympathized with me. I seized one of the oars myself to relieve a lad, and to assist the force which now dashed the boat over the water. She seemed instinct with life.

We now heard the cries for aid, "Oh, the boat! Master, bring the boat!" come once more pealing over the golden lake from the foundering canoes.

"Do you hear, men? break the oars — lift the boat over the water. We will save them yet. It is to-night or never!"

With fresh force she bounded upward. Every fibre of our straining bodies and the full strength of our energies were roused, and in five minutes we ran alongside first one canoe, then a second and a third — until again the boat was down in the water to within an inch of her gunwale. But all the people — men, women, and children — were saved. The light material of which the canoes were constructed had sufficed to float the loads that were in them.

We rested until help should arrive, and presently Uledi's and Shumari's canoes were seen advancing side by side, with lines of pale foam flashing from each bow, as they were driven with the force of strong men towards us. With loud, glad cries they stopped their furious career alongside, and the first words they uttered were, "Are all safe?"

"Yes all," we replied

"El hamd-ul'-illah!" ("Thanks be to God!"), they answered fervently.

With the aid of these two canoes we were able to return to the islets with the thirty-two men, women, and children, and the entire property safe. Our loss during this fearful night was five canoes, five guns, one case of ammunition, and twelve hundred pounds of grain.

June 21. — The next morning, leaving a third of the party and goods at Miandereh, we departed for Singo, which we reached at 9 A.M. A few canoes were then hastened back to Miandereh for the remainder.

It will be remembered that, while the boat was returning from Uganda and passing by Ito, an island situated half a mile south-west of Singo, the natives of Ito drove us away by slinging stones at us. Such a force as we now numbered could not be received with such rudeness: at the same time they were secure from molestation by us. I despatched therefore Lukanjah and Mikondo, the Wakerewe guides, to the Island of Ito, to explain to the natives who we were, and to remove all fears of reprisal. Lukanjah was extremely successful, and brought the chief of Ito, who, as some atonement for our previous treatment, had furnished himself with peace-offerings in the shape of a couple of fat kids, and several bunches of mellow plantains. The large island of Komeh also, on the next day, sent its king to rejoice with us over numerous jars of potent beer and many slaughtered goats. The king of Komeh sold us besides four good, almost new, canoes of sufficient capacity to render us secure from further anxiety.

The Wangwana, after their terrible experiences while crossing the entrance to Speke Gulf, were awakened to the necessity of narrowly inspecting and carefully repairing their canoes. At Kagehyi the repairs had been extremely superficial, but the men were now fully alive to the importance of good caulking and a thorough replacing of the planks together, while Frank, Lukanjah, and I superintended their work.

June 24. — Seven hours' paddling on the 24th of June brought us to Refuge Island, and on its south side we proceeded to establish a small camp. The 25th was employed in constructing one large store hut for the grain, and another for the property of the Expedition; and the huts of the garrison were built with due regard to the strict watch of the camp.

After selecting forty-four men as garrison, and appointing Frank Pocock captain and Manwa Sera his lieutenant, with the two guides, Lukanjah and Mikondo, as interpreters in case of visitors, and leaving four canoes for the garrison to communicate, if they wished, with the natives of Itawagumba on the mainland, I began my return to Usukuma on the 26th with the boat, seventeen canoes, and 106 men.

July 1. — Four days afterwards we reached Kagehyi, at 3 P.M. But as the voyage had been extremely rough, only fourteen canoes were mustered in the cove.

When five days had passed, and we received no tidings of the three canoes and their crews of thirteen men which were still absent, I despatched a canoe with two Wangwana and eight Wasukuma to Lukongeh, the king, requesting him to hunt up the laggards, who no doubt had either deserted or had been captured by the Wakerewe.

On this day also I purchased from Kipingiri, for 40 yards of cloth, a large canoe capable of carrying thirty men, which the Wangwana, on account of her uncouth shape, called the "Hippopotamus." The wood of which she was made was sycamore, and she was so rotten at the stern that one thrust of my foot kicked a hole in her 9 inches in diameter. Though she was an ancient craft, and heavy with saturation, she might, I thought, be still made serviceable for the transport of the riding asses.

Whilst Uledi and Salaam Allah, the carpenters, and two or three chiefs, were assisting me to repair the venerable "Hippo" in a hollow close to the water's edge, a man came rushing down, crying, "Quick! quick I Master, the Wangwana are murdering one another! They are all dead men!"

Leaving one man to look after our tools, we ran up the hill, and witnessed a most horrible scene. About thirty men armed with guns were threatening one another in an excited manner; others brandished clubs or knobsticks; some held spears menacingly, while several flourished knives. A frenzy seemed to have possessed the hitherto well-behaved people. One man was already dead with a ghastly knife-wound in his heart, another lay prostrate with a fractured skull from a knobstick, and the author of this deed was even then striding with sweeping flourishes of a long club through the ranks of a turbulent crowd, delivering sounding blows on their heads and shoulders.

Snatching a stout stick, I rapped the ruffian so vigorously over his knuckles that he dropped his club and was secured by my assistants, and then, calling the chiefs to my aid, we disarmed the infuriates. This summary proceeding soon quelled the disturbance, and then, perceiving that pombe — beer — was at the bottom of the mischief, all who were sober were ordered to fall into line, by which we discovered that fifty-three were quite intoxicated.

Upon examination it was found that the murderer of Membe, one of the stoutest of our boat-bearers, was Fundi Rehani, and that he who had fractured the other man's skull was Rehani, the brother of Membe. Both were immediately secured for trial before Prince Kaduma, the Arab Sungoro, and the Wangwana chiefs. The jars of pombe were broken, and diligent search made in every place for beer.

This bloodshed upon the soil of Usukuma had to be paid for out of my cloth stores to mollify Prince Kaduma, and further payment was required for the privilege of burial.

The jury which I convened to adjudge the case sentenced the murderer to death; but, as I would not consent to this extreme measure, the sentence was changed to two hundred lashes and the chain, until his arrival at Zanzibar, when he might be rendered to his prince. The drunken madman Rehani, though he had been inspired to the fury which led him to fracture a man's skull by the sight of his dead brother, was also condemned by the jury, for endangering the life of a perfectly innocent man, to fifty lashes. These sentences, faithfully executed with due ceremony in presence of all the Wangwana, affected them greatly, and I took advantage of this scene to call the attention of the bully Msenna, and others who had distinguished themselves in the previous day's ebullition of madness, to the punishment which must assuredly follow the commission of such dreadful acts.

July 5. — On the 5th of July, to my great joy, the scouts sent to Lukongeh in search of the missing canoes returned with two of them, but of the third we received no news, until a year later — after our arrival at Ujiji — when we heard that they had deserted and had proceeded direct to Unyanyambe with their guns.

The crews of the two canoes, now happily restored to us, informed me that they had been driven by the gale to seek shelter on the mainland of Ukerewe, where they were instantly seized and conveyed to Lukongeh, when, instead of being slain, as the natives expected the captives would be, they were kindly treated by the king, proving to the islanders that the white man had only acted by his orders.

July 6. — On the 6th of July, after giving farewell presents to Prince Kaduma and his clever, genial princess, to the Arab Sungoro, Prince Kipingiri of Lutari, and Kurereh — though the two latter little deserved them — as well as to many others, I embarked all the people, animals, and effects of the Expedition, and by ten o'clock we were safely clear of Kipingiri's power and vicious intents, and, for the last time, of Kagehyi.

There was not one feeling of regret in my breast at leaving this place, where the Expedition had found a camp for over four months. Not that the village was in any way destitute of comforts, for these it afforded, nor that the natives were in any manner repugnant to me, for they were not; but the objects for which we came into the land could never be attained by unnecessary residence at any one spot. The time had simply arrived to begin our travels again, and I was glad of it, for the bold and bad Kipingiri was, I suspected, ever exercising an evil influence over Kaduma.

July 11. — On the 11th of July we arrived safely and without accident at Refuge Island, where I found the garrison thriving admirably. Through the influence of young Lukanjah — the cousin of the king of Ukerewe — the natives of the mainland had been induced to exchange their churlish disposition for one of cordial welcome, and the process of blood-brotherhood had been formally gone through between Maawa Sera, on my part, and Kijaju, king of Komeh, and the king of Itawagumba on the other part.

Lukanjah, aware of the respect paid by his dusky brothers to power, had deftly exaggerated my influence and the numbers of my force, until a friendly alliance with one so powerful became a cherished project with Kijaju, and caused him to seek it by a tribute of three fat oxen, six goats, and fifty bunches of bananas, besides a store of delectable maramba, upon which I found that the garrison had been subsisting during my absence from Refuge Island.

I deputed Frank to repay with cloths, beads, and wire Kijaju's generosity, for the constant anxiety which I suffered during the passages between Refuge Island and Kagehyi, for the safety of my people and effects, had induced such a serious illness, that for five days I was unable to leave my hut on the island.

July 17. — On the sixth day, however, I left my bed and strolled over the island on which, on that terrible day of our escape from Bumbireh, we had found a refuge and relief in our distress, and now an asylum for half of the Expedition for about a month. The younger portion of the garrison knew every nook and cranny of our island home, and had become quite attached to it. On the eastern side about fifteen fruit trees had been discovered by them, laden with delicious berries, the flavour of which seemed something of a mixture of custard apple and a ripe gooseberry. The stones of this small fruit were two in number, like small date-stones. The leaves of the tree resemble those of the peach; its fruit are smooth-surfaced, and hang in threes; its wood is tough and. flexible. It is no doubt a species of the Verbenaceae. The garrison had failed to consume half the quantity found, so that, when I arrived with a reinforcement of 150 men, there was a sufficient quantity left to cause them all to remember the sweet fruit of Refuge Island.

On this day, Kijaju, king of Komeh, visited me, to our mutual satisfaction. He furnished me with two guides to accompany me to Uganda, who were to be returned to Komeh along with Lukanjah and Mikondo. Their assistance was valuable only as the means of furnishing me with the names of localities between Refuge Island and Uzongora.

In the same manner that we had left Kagehyi, we departed from Refuge Island, viz. by embarking the garrison, and leaving those who had stayed at Kagehyi to rest upon Refuge Island until we should return for them.

The night was passed with a wild dance under the moonlight, at which three kings were present, who participated with all the light-hearted gaiety of children in the joyous sport.

Old Kijaju distinguished himself on the wild "fantastic toe" most extraordinarily. Itawagumba, jealous of his uncle's performance, exerted himself with mad vigour, and the stalwart chief of Bwina bounded upward as though performing on the flying trapeze. Young Lukanjah of Ukerewe, and his royal relative Mikondo, with all the suppleness of acrobats, made their debut on this night with great spirit, and the hundred warriors from the mainland sang to the dance with such force of lungs as startled the colossal rocks of Refuge Island into echoing the wild harmony. The Wangwana, headed by Frank and the gallant Manwa Sera, enlarged the vast circle with 150 men and 20 women, and all voices chimed to the song which old Kijaju sang to celebrate the day on which the white chief made brotherhood with the king of Komeh.

Refreshments were not wanting to cheer the dancers. Great masses of beef were roasted over glorious fires, and many jars of beer and maramba, brought from Bwina and Komeh, invited the special attention of the thirsty.

July 18. — As we left Refuge Island, on the morning of the 18th of July, the guides furnished by Kijaju, king of Komeh, propitiated the genius of the lake with beads given to him for the occasion, and adjured it by saying: —

"Be kind to the white M'kama, O Nianja, I charge thee! Give him a safe and prosperous voyage across thy wide waters."

From Kazaradzi Island, on which we rested for the night, we beheld a most glorious sunset. The western sky, halfway up to the zenith, was all aglow for about an hour with resplendent gold, which tinted mountain, hill, plain, and lake with the reflection of the lustrous hue.

July 19. — Next day we sailed for Wawizua Island; and on the 20th, passing by the picturesque islands of Mysomeh and Kumondo — every canoe hoisting small lug-sails, made of the loin-cloths of the crew, in order to benefit by the strong south-easter — we steered for Nameterre Island, where we arrived without accident.

July 21. — On the 21st of July we arrived at the southernmost of the dreaded Bumbireh group, Mahyiga Island, which I ascertained, after careful survey, was not inhabited.

At a little cove on the western side we discovered relics of a large camp, which, by the shape of the dome-like huts and bonneted doorways had, we were assured, been constructed by Waganda. Yet what force of Waganda could have penetrated thus far to the south?

As we were now in a dangerous neighbourhood, it behoved us to form a proper camp, as a small party would be compelled to remain upon this island until the remainder of the Expedition could be brought from Refuge Island. For this purpose, every hand was employed to clear the scrub and bush for a distance of 200 yards from the cove, and a road 12 feet wide was cut from the south side of Mahyiga Island to the north end.

About 5 P.M. while we were still at work, two large canoes approached cautiously from the direction of Iroba Island towards our cove. They took great pains to ascertain the number of our canoes, and we could see that they endeavoured to reckon up the number of men on the island before they spoke a word. Finally they hailed us, and Lukanjah, of Ukerewe, and Kijaju's man were requested to reply to them.

Our conversation, which was of great interest to us, as we burned to know what to expect from Bumbireh, was as follows: —

"Is this the white chief who was at Bumbireh?"

"Yes."

"Oh, he was not lost on the Nianja then?"

"No, he lives, and has returned."

"Oh. The white chief must not be angry with Iroba. We did not trouble him, therefore he has no quarrel with us The people of Bumbireh are bad. What has the white chief come for?"

"He is going to Uganda."

"How can he go to Uganda? Does he not know that Bumbireh is in the way, and Ihangiro's eyes will be upon him? Will he fly? "

"No; he will proceed by water in his canoes. Tell Bumbireh the white chief is not afraid; his young men are many in number. If the men of Bumbireh wish to make friends, let Shekka send the oars he stole, and the white chief will be glad."

"Magassa," replied they, "who camped on that island you are on, received the oars from Shekka, and he took them away to Uganda, believing you were lost in the Nianja."

"The white chief was not lost; he is here. If it is true that the oars are gone to Uganda, let Shekka make friends with the white chief, and send him two or three men to go with him to Makongo, in Uzongora, or to Uganda, as Lukongeh of Ukerewe and Kijaju of Komeh have done, and there will be no more words between them."

"Shekka is very strong, and the men of Bumbireh are bold. Antari of Ihanghiro, the great king, is stronger, and Shekka is his son. All this Nianja about here is his water, and they will not let you pass. What will the white chief do?"

"Tell Shekka and Antari, his father, that the white chief will remain here for many days. He will be glad to hear good words from them. When he is ready to go away, he will let them know. If the king of Iroba is the white chief's friend, let him send food here to sell."

After promising to perform all that we required, and to bring food the next day, the two canoes paddled away, two or three of their crews laughing ostentatiously.

July 23. — On the morning of the 23rd, about 10 A.M., another canoe, containing fifteen men, approached us from Iroba, in a bold, defiant manner. We asked their crew if they brought food for sale. They replied, "No; but you will get food in plenty by-and-by." After taking a searching look at our camp, they turned away, giving expression to their contempt by a method which obtains all round the Uvuma, Uganda, Uzongora, and Ukerewe coasts, viz. by throwing up water behind them in the air with their paddles, which is as well understood as the British youth's gesture of placing a thumb to his nose.

Lukanjah smiled when he saw this, and when requested to give me his thoughts, he said significantly, "Those people mean something."

July 24. — On the morning of the 24th, long before dawn, in order that the Iroba or Bumbireh people might not espy their departure, I despatched sixteen of the largest canoes under Manwa Sera, to return to Refuge Island for the remainder of the Expedition, after many injunctions to be cautious, and not to commit any folly.

Our camp was now in perfect condition, and presented as clean and orderly an appearance as two days' labour could render it. Watch-huts were also erected upon the highest part of the island, and five men under a chief were detached for the duty of observation. The garrison left with me upon the island consisted of forty-five men and the four guides from my friends Lukongeh and the Kijaju.

On this day also canoes came from Iroba, to the crews of which, as they rested in the water, we exhibited beads and cloth, copper bracelets and bright brass wire. In return for our professions of friendliness and our proffers of gifts, they spurned the water towards us, and replied with mockery,

July 25. — On the 25th, when the Iroba natives came, I adopted, after due forethought, a sterner tone, perceiving that amiability was liable to contempt and misconstruction. I told them that the king of Iroba must prove his friendship by sending food for sale by noon of the next day; and that as I was assured he was in communication with the king of Bumbireh, his neighbour, I should expect either the return of the oars or two or three men as sureties and pledges of peace. I knew the mainland was hostile, and since I was compelled to proceed to Uganda, I resolved to be assured, before venturing the lives of the women and children in rotten and crowded canoes, that I should be permitted to proceed in peace, and not be attacked midway between Bumbireh and the mainland.

The natives, cowed a little by the tone of voice, promised that there should be no delay in sending provisions, bananas, milk, honey, chickens, even oxen, for the white M'kama.

July 26. — On the morning of the 26th, the men at the observation-post reported that they saw a great many canoes proceeding from the mainland towards the great island of Bumbireh. I ascended the road to the summit, and with my glass I counted eighteen canoes, heavily laden with men, and watched them till they had passed round Iroba's western most point towards Bumbireh. It was evident that mischief was brewing, but how or in what shape I could not tell. It was probable that they would attack the island by night, knowing we were not very strong in numbers at the time. It was a very possible feat, for the islanders, as we had experienced, were not dull-witted, and were resolute and brave. Meantime, what should I do in such a case?

I waited until 3 P.M. for the king of Iroba. He did not come. Instant action on my part was therefore imperative.

I manned my boat and four of the canoes with thirty-five men, leaving only Safeni with fourteen men in charge of the camp and island, and proceeded to Iroba to make a reconnaissance. As we came up, I observed a flutter of excitement on the shore. I steered straight for the beach opposite a village, and landed. Twenty-five of the men were deployed as skirmishers along the shore, to give due effect to what I purposed. Lukanjah of Ukerewe was told to request the king of Iroba and elders to approach, or we should begin fighting.

They came to us, about fifteen in number. "Tell him, Lukanjah," I said, "that Iroba has behaved badly by sending his young men to laugh at us. Since he has lied so many times to me, he himself and two of his chiefs must depart with me to my camp. He will not be hurt, but he must stay with me until Shekka of Bumbireh is in my hands, or peace is made as I suggested."

There was no violence used, and the king of Iroba and two chiefs quietly walked into the boat. When they were seated, the king was requested to give instructions to his young men how to capture Shekka of Bumbireh and two Bumbireh chiefs; and a solemn promise was given that on their appearance the king of Iroba and his friends would be released. The natives of Iroba, who were collected by this time on the beach, entered into the project with animation. They declared that next day Shekka should be in my hands.

July 27. — On the morning of the 27th, a canoe from Iroba came with provisions for the king and chiefs, and to report their failure at Bumbireh. One of the young men, said to be the king's son, offered to remain in his father's place, while he himself should try to obtain possession of Shekka's person. This touching confidence so affected me that, after inducing the king of Iroba to go through the process of blood-brotherhood with one of the Wangwana, he was released.

At 5 P.M., faithful to his promise that he would perform what I wished, the king of Iroba brought the treacherous king of Bumbireh with two of his chiefs, whose appearance, after he had landed at Mahyiga and been recognised, was hailed with a loud shout by the Wangwana. He was about to be maltreated, and had I not been present at the time, there is no doubt that he would have been murdered by the enraged boat's crew. But they calmed down when they were told that his life and services were necessary to us, and that good treatment might secure his friendship and peace with Bumbireh.

My purpose in possessing myself of the person of the king of Bumbireh and his two chiefs may easily be divined. It must have been perceived that weakness and irresolution — or, in other words, over-gentleness and want of firmness — had proved harmful on several previous occasions. Thus, the hesitation to act immediately after the commission of murder by the Wanyaturu led them to imagine that it was fear which withheld us; the forbearance exhibited at Ngevi Island only brought upon us more annoyance; our mildness at Mombiti in Uvuma suggested the attack upon us by stoning; our long-suffering temper at the straits between Uvuma and Ugeyeya induced the Wavuma to proceed to piracy and violence; our patient bearing at Bumbireh led the natives to think we might be murdered like lambs; our placability merited and received the contempt of the natives of Iroba; and a hundred times afterwards did I see that the savage only respects force, power, boldness, and decision; and that he is totally ignorant of the principles which govern the conduct of Christian man to man. Forbearance is to him cowardice: mildness, patience, and an equable temper are, in his undeveloped and unreasoning mind, only evidences of effeminacy. But the murderous Wanyaturu, when we finally turned out of our camp, learned, when it was too late, that our womanly gentleness covered power; the audacious Wakamba at Ngevi Island were only brought to their senses when they heard the startling reports of the revolver; the intention of the daring Wavuma to murder was only checked by quick and energetic action; the treacherous rock-slingers of Mombiti only desisted when fired upon; the ferocious Wa-Bumbireh only respected us after our successful escape; the cunning king of Iroba only became really friendly when we quietly showed our power, and his rapidly growing insolence was only cowed by the exhibition of sternness.

But the exercise of power without magnanimity is simply brutality, and has only a transient effect. If, therefore, I could only show the king of Bumbireh and his people that the first white man they had seen was extremely gentle in his manner until aroused, but, though strong and powerful when angered, was magnanimous afterwards, I should, I felt, leave a lasting good effect upon their minds. Though Shekka's capture was necessary, in order to ensure the passage of the Expedition between Bumbireh and Ihangiro in peace and safety, his good treatment and after release were none the less necessary also — provided that nothing serious occurred in the meantime to prevent the exhibition of clemency towards him.

Perceiving himself to be in the power of those whom he had outraged with a wanton ferocity, and whom he had compelled to risk the terrors of the stormy sea without the means of subsistence, or means to seek shelter from the gales and tempests which prevail during the rainy season, Shekka's behaviour became as abject as it had been ferocious when our positions were reversed. But he was informed in mild tones that we sought not his life, but our own safety; that he was captured to secure ourselves from violence by the possession of his person; that, while he was a prisoner with us, there would be no fear that Antari of Ihangiro and the people of Bumbireh would attack us by night, as they must know that we possessed the means of retaliation through him.

He was pleased to be communicative on this assurance, and informed us that Antari was collecting a vast force on Bumbireh, by day and night, for the purpose of attacking us on the island of Mahyiga. He imparted to us also the narrative of how Antari's father, in conjunction with Kytawa in the days of old, had successfully defied for a long period the full power of the great Suna of Uganda, and he was curious to know how a small body of men like ourselves could hope to escape from Antari — or "the Lion" — of Iliangiro.

Shekka was advised that, as we knew how to defend ourselves when attacked, he had better send word to Bumbireh and to Antari that we did not seek trouble, but were desirous of establishing peaceful relations between the Wangwana and the natives. Three of the ordinary natives of Bumbireh, who had been brought with Shekka and his two chiefs, were therefore permitted to depart with the king of Iroba and his friends.

July 28. — At 9 A.M. the king of Iroba appeared again, this time with gifts of milk, honey, bananas, and a fat kid, which kindness we liberally reciprocated, not without much politic ostentation for the advantage of Shekka and the natives.

At noon he reappeared with three large canoes, containing twenty men each, from Ihangiro, under the command of Antari's chief elder. They were permitted to land, though they were numerically superior to the garrison on the island. But before I had given them permission to that effect, Frank was requested to hold thirty men under arms to prevent treachery and surprise.

Our greeting was friendly, though there was a certain proud reserve in their manner.

"What says the king Antari?" I asked through Lukanjah.

"Antari asks, 'Why have you come to his waters and camped on his island?'"

"We have come because we must pass through to Uganda, and have rested on Mahyiga to wait for our people. As I have not sufficient canoes to carry my people and property in one passage, I must leave some here, while I proceed to Uganda with the first half of the party. I wish to be assured by Antari that in my passage by

Bumbireh we shall not be attacked, nor the party which must be left in my absence on this island be molested. What say you?"

"Antari says he is a great and strong king. All the mainland which you see from Rumondo to Kytawa's is his, so are all these islands and waters. He has never seen strangers before travelling by sea; they always went by land. He says, 'You must go back.'"

"We cannot go back, tell him," I replied. "This water belongs to every stranger, as much as the wind. The island may be his, but no one dwells on Mahyiga, and we will not injure the rocks."

"Antari says he will make peace only if you go back. He sends these three bunches of bananas to you, and this woman and child."

"We do not deal in slaves, and three bunches of bananas are of no use to us. We want permission to pass quietly and peacefully through to Uganda, and if Antari will send many bananas to us, we will buy them, as we have many mouths with us."

"Then Antari says he will make war on you, and kill you all."

"Ah, does he say those words?"

"Yes, Antari says those words."

I whispered to Frank to bring Shekka, who was immediately brought to their presence. When they saw him, they all rose to a man with threatening actions. We all rose also, in a prepared attitude, which convinced them that violence was useless. I said to the elders —

"Sit down, and carry my words to Antari. Open your ears wide, and understand. Antari is Mtesa's slave; I am Mtesa's friend. Antari's people rob and try to murder Mtesa's friend, but he escapes, and has now come back on his way to Mtesa. Again, Antari and his people are busy preparing war against Mtesa's — Antari's master's — friend. He sends many canoes and hundreds of men to Bumbireh. He also sends three canoes to tell me that he is about to fight me, and perhaps — you know best — to rescue Shekka, who is my means for securing my safety. Tell Antari that the white man is not a woman, and that lying words will not be swallowed by him. He means to go to Uganda, whether Antari will let him or not. If Antari fights, tell him to remember how the white man escaped from Bumbireh. The white man wants peace, but he is not afraid of Antari. Now go, and carry every word to Antari, and to-morrow, by noon, I must have his answer, or I shall carry Shekka and his two chiefs to Uganda, and deliver them up to Mtesa."

Without giving them time to consider further, we urged them towards their canoes, not violently, but firmly. When the principal elder had recovered his senses, which he did not until he felt himself safe in his canoe, it seemed to dawn on his mind that I was purposely avoiding violence, and he said —

"Let the white man rest in peace. You have Antari's son, Shekka, in your hands. Antari will not fight you. I will speak to him truly, and when the sun is high I shall return with words of peace."

"It is well. Tell Antari his son shall not be hurt, and will be delivered over to his people as soon as we shall have passed Bumbireh safely."

Those were days which required caution, for the first false or weak step would have ensured the destruction of the Expedition, the members of which I was bound by every principle of honour to protect and defend to the best of my ability. They had pledged themselves to me only upon the condition that I should secure their safety, and they looked to me to watch and guard their lives with paternal care. In my opinion, considering all the circumstances, I could not have better avoided trouble than — while the savages were actively preparing and offensively boasting — by acting as I did.

About 4 P.M. a small fleet of six beautiful canoes, painted a brown colour, were seen approaching us, having travelled mid-channel between Bumbireh and Ihangiro. We soon made them out to be Waganda, and when the chief, who was received with loud and warm greetings, had landed, he gave his name as Sabadu.

He soon informed us that he was on a double errand, one of which was to proceed to Kagehyi in Usukuma to convey the Arab Sungoro to Uganda, and the other was to hunt up news of myself. He said also that I had been reported by the long-lost Magassa, on his return to Uganda, to have been either murdered by the savages of Bumbireh or to have foundered in the lake. He had returned with the oars and drum to Mtesa, who was much shocked at the sight of them, for he believed that, as the oars were our "feet," we were murdered. But as nothing else was found, such as traces or parts of the boat, Mtesa was in doubt; he had therefore enjoined Sabadu to make strict inquiries at all points about me, and had despatched Magassa with a strong force by land to Uzongora and Ihangiro, and a Mtongoleh, called M'kwanga, with a fleet of eight canoes, to prosecute a more rigid search by water along all the coasts. Sabadu said also that, while he was at Kytawa's with M'kwanga, on the mainland, he had heard of our danger, and had hurried up to assist us, and that M'kwanga would appear on the morrow with eight canoes, manned by Waganda, and five canoes manned by Kytawa's people under two chiefs, who, by their influence with Antari, might negotiate a successful peace.

Sabadu, upon delivering his news, was, as may well be imagined, heartily welcomed, and was readily induced, upon my taking the responsibility, to remain with me, to assist in the transport of the Expedition to Uganda, for which his canoes, with those of M'kwanga and Kytawa, would prove amply sufficient. He was also informed in his turn of the state of affairs at Bumbireh and Ihangiro, at which he expressed great indignation; but both he and Bugomba — a youth of sixteen, the brother of the Katekiro, or Premier, of Uganda — were confident that, when they should proceed to Bumbireh to treat with the natives through the assistance of Kytawa's chiefs, they would be able to persuade them to abandon their hostile attitude. My experience of the people of Bumbireh, however, would not permit me to entertain this feeling of assurance.

July 29. — About 11 A.M. M'kwanga's search expedition, consisting of eight large canoes, accompanied by five of a smaller size, under two chiefs of Kytawa, arrived at Mahyiga Island, containing about 250 Waganda and 50 Wazongora. Including the crews of Sabadu's canoes, the garrison of Mahyiga, and the natives of Komeh and Ukerewe, I had now a force of 470 men. There was no fear of the issue of an attack on the island now, but a fear of famine remained.

The king of Iroba was appealed to, and for an adequate remuneration he promised to supply the Waganda with bananas; while we possessed sufficient grain upon which the Wangwana might subsist for a few days longer. The king of Iroba again confirmed the information that Antari was collecting a large force of canoes, and about sunset a single canoe, powerfully manned, dashed up opposite our camp, and one man stood up with spear and shield, and delivered a stout defiance, after which the canoe as hastily departed for Bumbireh, without paying any attention to Kytawa's chiefs.

It was apparent that our departure for Uganda would be hotly contested, but of the result there could be but one opinion. What kind of canoes Antari possessed I knew by the specimens which Kytawa, who was neighbour to him, sent to us at Mahyiga. Their number would be probably a hundred, which, with a crew of ten men in each, would amount to a thousand. Allowing six bowmen in each canoe, this would make the fighting force about 600 strong, against which I could offer 70 guns and about 350 effective spearmen of Uganda.

August 2. — However, it was my duty to persist in avoiding the bloody conflict, as it would assuredly be by water, and employ all my efforts towards bringing Antari and the natives of Bumbireh to a sense of the inutility of hostile demonstrations. Messages of a peaceful nature accordingly passed between us. Antari's elders visited us once more, on the 2nd of August, this time with an assurance that we should not be molested, as a proof of which they said that Antari had given orders to the people of Bumbireh to sell us provisions upon the condition that we should deliver Shekka, Antari's son, and two other chiefs to Kytawa, the day we should arrive on the mainland.

This news was received with shouts of applause by all, and no one was more sincerely glad that the trouble was over than myself, though there was something in the manner of the delivery, in the sly exchange of looks between Antari's elders and the prisoners, that I did not like. It may have been that a slight suspicion still lurked in my mind, but I did not permit any sign of doubt to escape me, but treated the elders affably and courteously.

Sabadu — who was of a sanguine disposition — and young Bugomba were for testing the truth of this manifestation of friendship at once, but I restrained them for this day, as we possessed sufficient food for the time being. The Waganda also were eager to remind me that they were a people decidedly averse to scarcity, and they obtained my promise that next morning they should have cloths and beads wherewith to purchase food.

August 3. — Accordingly the next day Sabadu was despatched with beads, cowries, and cloths to Kajurri, from the cove of which we had made our escape in April. They were absent about six hours, during which time I was very anxious, as the event would decide our future.

"What is the news, Sabadu?" I asked eagerly as he stepped on the shore near our camp with gloomy looks. "Anything wrong?"

"Ah," he sighed; "the people of Bumbireh are bad, wicked people. We went on shore at Kajurri, saw some twenty people there, and Kytawa's chief talked with them. They said we might go and cut as many bananas as we wanted, and they would talk afterwards about the price we should have to pay. The Waganda left their spears, and, taking only their mundu — bill-hooks — proceeded to cut the fruit while I remained in the canoe. Suddenly I heard a shout and a rustling in the banana grove, and the Waganda came running back, and pushing the canoes into the water, plunged in, and got on board. Kytawa's chief had his left arm chopped clean off, and then they cut him on the head, which killed him. Eight of the Waganda have been badly hurt. They will be carried on shore presently, and you shall see them. Bumbireh! ah, ah! Bumbireh is bad!" he said emphatically.

The wounded men were brought on shore with ghastly wounds from spears, and one or two from arrows, at the sight of which a grand rush was made upon the captives by two or three hundred excited Waganda and Wazongora, but with the aid of the Wangwana and Frank we saved them.

"Gently, gently, friends," we cried; "these men are not they who are guilty of this deed. Do not ill-use them; they are innocent."

M'kwanga, the chief of the search expedition of Waganda, was furious. He seized his shield and three spears, and called his men together, telling them to arm, as he would lead them through and through Bumbireh, and then would proceed to Antari and slay him in his house, would cut down every banana, burn down every hut, and scorch Ihangiro to a cinder, &c.

But M'kwanga was persuaded to be patient, and not foolishly throw more lives away. We should, I told him, consult together, and if I found, after consideration, that my duty was to avenge this deed, I should do it.

Said he: "If you do not assist me to punish this treachery, you need never expect to see Mtesa's face or Uganda again. The Waganda came to do you service; they came to seek you while Mtesa believed you were lost. The Waganda, with myself and Sabadu, promised to stand by you when we heard you were in danger. The Waganda left your camp with your consent to go and get food for you as well as for us. Kytawa's chief is dead, and here are eight wounded men. What will you do?"

"Only what I think is right, and after proper consideration. If I do not assist you, it will not prevent you from going to fight them to-morrow."

" But," said M'kwanga, "if I go to fight to-morrow by myself, I shall never return to Mahyiga."

He stalked away sullenly, and the Waganda became cold and distant towards us, as though we were to blame for the sad event. The Wazongora bewailed their chief aloud, and the strangely mournful tones of their lamentations produced a powerful impression on all who heard them.

Before many minutes had elapsed, I had manned my boat and five canoes, and was on my way to Iroba before the intelligence could be spread, simply with the view to ascertain how far the king of Iroba was involved in this affair. I found him to be perfectly innocent of all knowledge of anything that had occurred at Bumbireh since morning. Upon asking him if any natives of Ihangiro were there, he answered that one of Antari's youngest sons was there. We proceeded to the hut, and the young man was secured and conveyed into the boat, and the king of Iroba was instructed to convey the intelligence to Bumbireh to the chiefs of Antari's people, and to tell them that, if they intended to make peace, they must be quick, and send me word of it before noon of the next day, as I should not be able to restrain the Waganda or defer my departure another day.

The arrival of messengers from the post of observation on the summit of the island announcing that the canoes of the Expedition were seen coming from the south, distracted the attention of all for a period, and soon the summit was lined with the figures of the anxious Wangwana, some of whom had wives and children, besides relatives and friends in the little fleet that was bearing towards the island with miniature sails set.

By sunset they were answering their safe arrival close to us with cheer after cheer, and soon had landed amid hearty greetings.

But Manwa Sera, to cap the day's dismal and tragic record, had to report the loss of two men, who were drowned by the collapse of one of the rotten canoes, which added another cause for grief. The riding asses also were in a pitiable condition, for the poor things, being obliged to be bound in the small canoes, were terribly chafed even to the quick, and could scarcely stand. The rest of the force were in good condition, and no property had been lost or other accident occurred.

That evening, while the sorrowing Wazongora made the camp doleful with their loud mournful cries for the dead chief, Frank and all the Wangwana chiefs were summoned to my tent to discuss our future. I only wished to hear their views, to discover their sentiments, not to disclose my own. The unanimous opinion of the party was that we were bound to fight. All I could say on the other side availed nothing to shake the decision they had arrived at. Then they were dismissed with a promise that I should impart my resolution in the morning. I also enjoined on Frank to double the guard over the captives, lest they might be injured during the night.

Alone with myself, I began to discuss seriously the strict line of duty. If it were a military Expedition that I commanded, duty would have pointed out the obvious course to follow; but though the Expedition was governed for its own well-being after military principles, it was an expedition organized solely for the purposes of exploration, with a view to search out new avenues of commerce to the mutual advantage of civilization and such strange lands as we found suitable for commercial and missionary enterprise. But whatever its character, its members possessed the privilege of self-defence, and might justly adopt any measures, after due deliberation, for self-protection. The principles of right and justice every educated Christian professes to understand, and may be credited with a desire to observe, but in addition to these, it was desirable in a person in my position — knowing how frequently it is necessary to exercise them in barbarous lands — to remember charity and forbearance, in order to ensure the objects in view, and to create good impressions for the benefit of those who might succeed the pioneer.

Thirteen days had elapsed since our arrival at Mahyiga, and the thirteenth day was signalized by this bloody attack upon people entrapped to their death maliciously, and evidently by a preconcerted arrangement between Antari's elders and the chiefs of Bumbireh. Sabadu said also that the last words he had heard as the Waganda paddled away from Bumbireh were, "Look out for mischief to-morrow," which no doubt meant that the war "shauri" was nearly terminated, and that all were by this time worked up into proper fighting spirit.

The Expedition was now ready to move towards Uganda, but the water-way had first to be opened; whatever plot was on hand must be frustrated, and treachery punished; otherwise impunity would inspire an audacity which might be dangerous to our safety.

Apart, therefore, from a duty owing to the wounded Waganda and the dead chief of Kytawa, as well as to our respect for and gratitude to Mtesa and Kytawa — apart from the justice which, according to all laws human and divine, savage and civilized, demands that blood shall atone for blood, especially when committed with malice prepense, and the memory of our narrow escape from their almost fatal wiles, and the days of agony we had suffered — there lay the vital, absolute, and imperative necessity of meeting the savages lest they should meet us. For they were by this time reinforced by about 2000 auxiliaries from the mainland; they were flushed with triumph at their success in the snare they had set for the unsuspecting Waganda, and the sight of their dead victim would only inspire them with a desire for more blood.

As I could not see any way to avoid the conflict, I resolved to meet them on their own island, and by one decisive stroke break this overweening savage spirit. I should, however, wait the result of my last message, for it might be that the capture of one of Antari's sons might induce them to embrace peaceful proposals.

August 4. — Accordingly next morning a couple of ammunition boxes were opened, and twenty rounds distributed to each man who bore a rifle or musket; 230 spearmen and fifty musketeers were detailed for a fighting party, and eighteen canoes were prepared to convey them to Bumbireh.

I waited until noon, having gazed through a field-glass many times in the direction of Bumbireh, but nothing was observed approaching Mahyiga.

The force was therefore mustered, and I addressed it to this effect —

"My friends and Wangwana, — We must have the sea clear. Whatever mischief these people have meditated must be found out by us, and must be prevented. I am about to go and punish them for the treacherous murder of our friends. I shall not destroy them, therefore none of you are to land unless we find their canoes, which we must break up. We must fight till they or we give in, for it can only be decided in this manner. While in the fight you will do exactly as I tell you, for I shall be able to judge whether their fierce spirit is broken, or whether we shall have to fight on land."

As the distance between Bumbireh and Mahyiga was about eight miles, we did not arrive until 2 P.M. before the former island. It was evident that the savages had expected us, for the heights of the hilly ridge were crowded with large masses, and every point was manned with watchmen.

Through my field-glass I observed messengers running fast to a thick plantain grove which crowned the southernmost hill, and commanded a view of all approach to a cove that penetrated to its base. It was clear that the main force of the natives was ready in the shadows of the grove. Calling the canoes together, I told the chiefs to follow my boat, and to steer exactly as I did. We made a feint of entering into this cove, but when near the point, perceiving that we were hidden by the lofty hill from the observation of those in the grove and of the look-outs, we swerved to the left, and, clinging to the land, pulled vigorously until we came to a cape, after rounding which we came in view of a fine and noble bay to our right.

By this manoeuvre the enemy was revealed in all his strength. The savages were massed behind the plantains as I had suspected, and from their great numbers proved much too strong to be attacked under cover. All the eastern and northern sides of the bay were surrounded by lofty hills, which sloped steeply to within a few feet of the water's edge, and were covered with small shingly rocks and thin short grass. The low shelf of land that lay between the hill base and the water was margined with tall cane-grass.

We steered straight east towards the more exposed hill slopes. The savages, imagining we were about to effect a landing there, hurried from their coverts, between 2000 and 3000 in number. I examined the shores carefully, to see if I could discover the canoes which had conveyed this great number of warriors from the mainland. Meanwhile we pulled slowly, to afford them time to arrange themselves.

Arrived within 100 yards of the land, we anchored in line, the stone anchors being dropped from midships that the broadsides might front the shore. I told Lukanjah of Ukerewe to ask the men of Bumbireh if they would make peace, whether we should be friends, or whether we should fight.

"Nangu, nangu, nangu!" (" No, no, no! ") they answered loudly, while they flourished spears and shields.

"Will they not do anything to save Shekka?"

"Nangu, nangu! Keep Shekka; he is nobody. We have another M'kama" (king).

"Will they do nothing to save Antari's son?"

"Nangu, nangu. Antari has many sons. We will do nothing but fight. If you had not come here, we should have come to you."

"You will be sorry for it afterwards."

"Huh," incredulously. "Come on; we are ready."

Further parley was useless; so each man having taken aim was directed to fire into a group of fifty or thereabouts. The result was several killed and wounded.

The savages, perceiving the disastrous effect of our fire on a compact body, scattered, and came bounding down to the water's edge, some of the boldest advancing until they were hip-deep in water; others, more cautious, sought the shelter of the cane-grass, whence they discharged many sheaves of arrows, all of which fell short of us.

We then moved to within 50 yards of the shore, to fire at close quarters, and each man was permitted to exercise himself as he best could. The savages gallantly held the water-line for an hour, and slung their stones with better effect than they shot their arrows. The spirit which animated them proved what they might have done had they succeeded in effecting a landing at Mahyiga by night, but here, however, the spear, with which they generally fight, was quite useless.

Perceiving that their spirit was abating, we drew the canoes together, and made a feint as though we were about to make a precipitate landing, which caused them to rush forward by hundreds with their spears on the launch. The canoes were then suddenly halted, and a volley was fired into the spearmen, which quite crushed their courage, causing them to retreat up the hill far away from the scene. Our work of chastisement was complete.

The Waganda spearmen (230 strong), who had been, up to this time, only interested spectators, now clamoured loudly to be permitted to land and complete the work of vengeance. M'kwanga was fierce in his demands; the Wangwana seconded the Waganda, and in their hot ardour several of the canoes rushed on the shore, but as this extremity was not my object, I resisted them, and when, despite my refusal, they persisted in their attempts to land, I threatened to fire upon the first man, Mgwana or Mgwanda, who set foot upon the shore, and this threat restored order.

Lukanjah was again told to warn the natives of Bumbireh that, if they had not had enough of fighting, we should return next day, but that we would allow them a night to think over it.

It was dark when we arrived at our camp; but we did not omit, while passing Iroba, to comfort the friendly king with the assurance that he need not fear trouble, as he was not involved in the atrocious acts of Bumbireh.

August 5. — Having thus shown sufficient boldness in meeting the enemy and demonstrated our ability for the encounter, it was now clear that the passage of the channel, with the women and children and property of the Expedition, might be performed without danger. Accordingly, on the 5th of August, at early dawn, we began the embarkation. The fourteen Kiganda canoes were large, with ample storage room, and all the goods, ammunition, and asses, and all the timid, men, women, children, and Wanyamwezi, were placed in these. Our eighteen canoes of Ukerewe and Komeh and five lent us by generous Kytawa proved sufficient to transport the remainder, consisting of the more active members of the party, who were directed, in the event of trouble, to range on either side.

At the tap of M'kwanga's drum, without which no party of Waganda march, and a cheery blast from Hamadi's bugle, the thirty-seven canoes and boat, containing 685 souls, departed from our island cove towards Bumbireh.

About 9 A.M. we were abreast of Bumbireh, and when, on coming to the bay, we saw hundreds of people lining the topmost ridges, I deemed it expedient to make a demonstration once more in order to discover the effect of the previous day's engagement. On arriving near the shore, a shot was fired, the effect of which was to cause about a hundred to scamper away hastily. Others, whom we distinguished as elders, after hailing us, came down towards us.

Lukanjah was requested to ask, "If we were to begin the fight again?"

"Nangu, nangu, M'kama." ("No, no, king.")

"The trouble is over then?"

"There are no more words between us."

"If we go away quietly, will you interfere with us any more?"

"Nangu, nangu."

"You will leave strangers alone in future?"

"Yes, yes."

"You will not murder people who come to buy food again?"

"Nangu, nangu."

I then told them that, having murdered one and wounded eight of Mtesa's people, it would be my duty to convey Shekka and his friends to him, but I should intercede for them, and they would probably be back in two moons. Advantage was also taken to point out the contrast between the conduct of Bumbireh and that of Ukerewe, Komeh, Itawagumba, Kytawa, and Kamiru, and to adorn the brief speech with a moral.

Turning away, we coasted along the much indented shores of the savage island, and several times had opportunities of distinguishing the altered demeanour of the natives and to observe that their fierce temper had abated.

King Kamiru received us with princely magnificence. The Wazongora who were with us extolled me as a father and begged his permission to accompany me to Uganda. Kamiru, a bluff, hearty old man, kindly consented, and furnished us with canoes to replace four of the most rotten of the vessels from Ukerewe, which required constant caulking and baling to prevent their foundering. The generous king supplied Frank and myself with such a quantity of milk and honey that several potfuls broke, and a section of the boat was a couple of inches deep with the luscious mixture, which the boat's crew licked up with broad grins of satisfaction.

A bay separates Ihangiro from King Kamiru's land. We were encamped on the north side, which belongs to Kamiru; had we ventured on the south side, we should have been in the enemy's country. Desirous of showing some kindness to Shekka and his friends, I made proposals to Kamiru to accept them on behalf of Mtesa and to negotiate with Antari for their release, but the king peremptorily refused, saying that he would be unable to protect them, and that as they were Mtesa's subjects, they ought to be given up to him.

August 8. — On the 8th of August we arrived once more on the little island of Musira, whither we had before been driven by the natives of Makongo, in King Kytawa's country. The elders of all the villages along his coast greeted us with acclamation. Makongo outdid the generosity of Kamiru, for it sent four oxen besides 200 bunches of bananas. Kytawa despatched quite a little army to bear his salaams and gifts of provisions and messages, thanking me for avenging the death of his chief, and making an offer of twenty canoes if I were short of vessels.

Inspired by the effect on the Wazongora which the punishment of the natives of Bumbireh had created, Sabadu hinted that it would be desirable to threaten Kyozza, the king of northern Uzongora, but he was speedily made to understand that white men only fought in self-defence.

As we proceeded by Kyozza's villages, Kagya, Weza, and Bugavu, the inhabitants lined the shores without arms and loudly greeted us; and when we stopped for our midday meal at a village near Weza, a messenger from Kyozza came and promised us ten oxen if we would wait for that day and accept his hospitalities. We returned a courteous reply, but refused, upon the ground that we were in a hurry to proceed to Uganda.

August 12. — We halted at Mezinda, and on the 12th of August, passing by the mouth of the Alexandra Nile and Chawasimba Point, directed our course for Dumo, in Uganda, at which place we arrived in the afternoon without further incident of interest.

The next day was devoted to preparing a camp, arranging for supplies with the neighbouring Watongoleh of Mtesa during my absence, and writing letters to the Daily Telegraph and New York Herald, giving in brief an account of the events which are described in detail in this chapter, a copy of which was left with Frank to send to the coast by way of Karagwe and Unyanyembe.

A score of small matters employed my attention until midnight, of a similar nature to those arranged before setting out from Kagehyi on the exploration by circumnavigation of Lake Victoria in March. Before retiring, messengers arrived in camp from Magassa — the dilatory admiral of the canoe fleet despatched as my convoy in April — entreating me to wait a couple of days for him before setting out for the capital of Uganda. But as every hour was now precious, I was not able to defer my departure.

CHAPTER XII.

We find Mtesa at war — "Jack's Mount" — Meeting with Mtesa — The Waganda army in camp and on the march — The imperial harem — In sight of the enemy — The Waganda fleet — Preliminary skirmishing — The causeway — The massacre of Mtesas peace party — "What do you know of angels?" — Mtesa's education proceeds in the intervals of war — Translating the Bible — Jesus or Mohammed? — Mtesa's decision — The royal proselyte.

August 13. — At Dumo rumour and gossip were busy about a war and a mighty preparation which Mtesa, the Emperor of Uganda, was making for an expedition against the Wavuma. He had not been as yet actually engaged, it was said, though it was expected he would be shortly. In the hope, then, of finding him at his capital, I resolved to be speedy in reaching him, so that, without much delay, I might be able to return and prosecute my journey to Lake Albert.

The first day, favoured by a gale from the north-west, the Lady Alice left the fastest of the Waganda canoes far behind, but, obliged to halt for her company, put in for the night among the mosquito-haunted papyrus of Bwiru. The next day, after sailing across Sesse Channel, and passing the mouth of the Katonga, we rested at Jumba's Cove in Unjaku. From this cove runs a wide road constructed by Mtesa about two years before, when he undertook to invade Ankori and punish Mtambuko, the king of that shepherd state. Though untouched during two years, it is still sufficiently clear of grass to define its width and illustrate the energy of Mtesa when aroused.

August 18. — On the 18th of August we sailed to Ntewi, where we learned two reliable facts. The king had already marched towards Usoga, and had an engagement with his enemies, the Wavuma. When I heard this news, I felt more than half inclined to turn back, for I knew by experience that African wars are tedious things, and I was not in the humour to be delayed long; but on reflection, and after much importunity from the Waganda, I adhered to the first intention, by which I thought that probably, though delayed, I might reach the Albert Nyanza by a short route, which would in a manner balance the delay occasioned by visiting Mtesa.

We also heard that the Wavuma were abroad on the lake in hundreds of canoes searching for prey, and, not wishing the Lady Alice, which had already done me such good service, to fall into their hands, we conveyed the boat into the centre of the village, where we stored her and her appurtenances — oars, sails, rudder, &c. I also heard that the oars, which Magassa had received from Bumbireh, were in the chief of Ntewi's house, and had the satisfaction of seeing them once more under the charge of the boat-keeper. We halted at Ntewi one day, by which I was enabled not only to house the boat properly and to receive the oars, but to meet the two soldiers left as guard of honour with Magassa and to receive salaams from Mtesa, and more guards to ensure my welcome and comfort en route to him.

August 20. — Under the auspices of a considerable addition to our convoy, we left Ntewi, and, paddling vigorously during the afternoon of the 20th, arrived at Nankuma, in the bay of Buka. Here we left the canoes, and the next day prosecuted our journey overland to avoid the Wavuma, and camped at Ziba, at the base of "Jack's Mount."

This name is derived from a fatal accident to my faithful companion Jack, a bull-terrier of remarkable intelligence and affection which accompanied me from England. A wild cow given by the Mtongoleh for the subsistence of the king's stranger, being rather obstreperous in her behaviour, was assaulted by Jack, but the cow in her turn tossed the unfortunate dog and gored him to death. He died "regretted by all who knew his many good qualities." His companion, "Bull," the last of five English dogs, when he beheld his poor mate stretched out still and dead, also expressed, as clearly as canine nature would allow, his great sorrow at his lamentable fate. Grave and deliberate from years and long travel, he walked round the body two or three times, examining it carefully, and then advanced to me with his honest eyes wide open as if to ask, "What has caused this?" Receiving no answer, he went aside and sat down with his back to me, solemn and sad, as though he were ruminating despondingly on the evils which beset dog and man alike in this harsh and wicked world.

August 22. — The next day, marching in an east by north direction from Jack's Mount, we crossed the Zedziwa, a stream rising at the base of a hill situated but two miles from the north-western extremity of "Grant Bay," which I believe to be the "Luajerri," a stream Speke sketched on his map as issuing from the Victoria and forming a second outlet into the Nile.

Having explored by water all the coast washed by the Victoria Nyanza and having since travelled on foot the entire distance between Nakaranga Cape and Buku Bay, I can state positively that there is but one outlet from the lake, viz. the Ripon Falls. There are three rivers, one on the Usoga side of Napoleon Channel, called the Nagombwa, and two on the Uganda side — the Zedziwa, rising in Makindo near Grant Bay, and the Mwerango, rising west of Mtesa's capital — any of which, seen by travellers journeying at a little distance from the lake, might be supposed by them to be outlets of Lake Victoria. The Nagombwa empties into the Victoria Nile not far from Urondogani; the Zedziwa empties into the Victoria Nile near Urondogani, and the Mwerango flows into the Mianja, the Mianja flows into the Kafu, and the Kafu into the Victoria Nile, somewhere in the neighbourhood of Rionga's Island.

At Makindo I received the Emperor's salaams for the fifth time since arriving in Uganda, and his walking-stick, as a token that it really was Mtesa who sent the repeated messages of welcome. By sea and by land his messengers of welcome had met me, and each stage was supplied with an "augmented greeting" with many manifestations of his regard. I was well convinced, from the repeated expeditions sent by land and water to hunt up news of me when Magassa reported me as dead, that the friendship conceived for me by Mtesa was something more than in name.

August 23. — Arriving next day at Ugungu, opposite Jinja, or the Ripon Falls, two more messengers came up breathless from the imperial camp — which I could see covering many miles of ground — with yet an additional welcome, and pointed out on the opposite side Mtesa and his chiefs, most picturesque in their white dresses and red caps, with a large concourse of attendants, waiting to see my party cross the channel. Five large canoes were in readiness at the ferry, and also soldiers of the royal guard to escort us through the vast crowds on the other side of the channel.

Far different was the scene on this day around the Falls to that which Speke had gazed upon in 1863, and to that which I had seen five months before when I entered this channel after a skirmish with the Wavuma. For now the channel swarmed with large canoes, and the shores of Ugungu and Jinja were covered with thousands of men, women, and children; while then all was silent and lonely, and the monotonous noise of falling waters was the only sound that was heard.

Crossing the channel amid the noise and bustle of many thousands, we soon found ourselves in the midst of the vast army that Mtesa had collected from all parts of his empire. Natives of Karagwe, lean, lank-bodied, and straight-nosed, with their deficiencies of calf made up for by a preposterous fulness of ankle, caused by hundreds of coils of fine iron wire, gathered round us with as much curiosity as the ferocious Wakedi, who intruded their bodies, naked as when they were born, among the clean-robed Waganda, reckless of the laughter and jeering which their nudity provoked. The vain Wasoga also seemed to forget, while they gazed on us, that they were as much objects of curiosity to the rustic yet unabashed natives of Sesse, who stood by them, as we were to them; for, indeed, look where I might, the undisguised vanity of the Wasoga made them extremely conspicuous. Though amidst such a large army of sable warriors, a solah topee, European complexion, and boots wonderfully created of some kind of leather, might well be deemed curiosities; yet lambskins of all colours, stuffed with grass, and standing erect on men's heads, and long white-haired goat-skin for robes and loin coverings, were not a whit less curious to the canoe-building natives of Sesse, who until now had never, it seemed, witnessed such things. But, taking advantage of the quiet complacency with which we permitted these warriors to gaze on us, they began to press on us more closely than was convenient, until they were scattered by the mighty sticks of the guards, who felled them to right and left without remorse, and Wasoga, Wanyambu, Wakedi, Wazongora, and Waganda were compelled to be more careful of their bones than curious to see us.

A short time afterwards, near the imperial quarters, I met the great chiefs of Uganda with whom I had struck up an acquaintance on my first visit, among whom I recognized tall and handsome Chambarango, the king's steward Kauta, Sambuzi, and lastly the Katekiro — the Premier — brilliant in his scarlet robe, white dress, and fez, attended by a retinue almost regal. They all expressed their satisfaction at seeing me alive and safe, and were all anxious to hear how we had escaped from Bumbireh.

August 24. — The next day at the usual levee hour of Mtesa — 8 A.M. — the drums announced the levee as begun, and half an hour later the pages came to conduct me to the presence of Mtesa. The imperial quarters covered an area of about 200 yards square, and though but temporarily put up, few Europeans could have constructed such commodious houses and neat courts with such means, as the Waganda had prepared for their sovereign.

The gates of the outer court were thronged with representatives of many countries, anxious to get a glimpse of the great monarch in his state; but the guards were merciless, and with gunstock and baton rudely thrust or beat back the intrusive nameless, and were as flint-hearted in their office as London policemen are on a similar occasion. For me the pages sufficed. Their presence cleared a broad road to the gate, which was drawn widely open to allow our procession to go by. One court was passed, and when the gate of the levee court was drawn back, a most picturesque scene was disclosed. In the centre rose a conical hut at the broad doorway of which sat a silent figure; on either side were standard-bearers and the hereditary guards, while, forming a broad crescent in the front rank, were the chiefs and important captains of the Empire seated on mats. In the background the bodyguards of Mtesa stood at "shoulder arms" in double ranks; in one corner were arranged the drummers and musicians, while scattered here and there in the open space before the monarch stood groups of claimants and courtiers.

As I advanced, Mtesa rose, and came to the edge of the leopard-rug, on which his feet rested while seated, and there was even greater warmth in this greeting than on the former occasion at Usavara. After a short pause, Sabadu, the chief who had conducted me from Bumbireh, was called forward to relate the incidents of our meeting, our fight with Bumbireh, and other events of the journey, which he did with a most wonderful minuteness of detail. He then in my name presented the captives of Bumbireh to the king, with an intercession that he would not slay them, but keep them in durance until their ransom was paid by Antari. Mtesa was then informed of the purpose of my coming, which was to obtain the guides he had promised me on my first visit, to show me the road to Muta Nzige; and I begged he would furnish them without much delay, as I had already lost considerable time from his canoes having failed me.

Mtesa replied that he was now engaged in a war with the rebellious people of Uvuma, who insolently refused to pay their tribute, harassed the coast of Chagwe, and abducted his people, "selling them afterwards for a few bunches of bananas," and that it was not customary in Uganda to permit strangers to proceed on their journeys while the Kabaka was engaged in war, but that the war would soon be over, when, if I would wait, he would send a chief with an army to conduct me to the Nyanza (Muta Nzige) by the shortest road.

"Besides," said he, "a small force cannot reach that lake. Kabba Rega of Unyoro is at present at war with the whites of Kaniessa (Gondokoro), and the people of Ankori do not admit strangers into their territory for trade or otherwise, and all the roads to the lake run through their countries."

After this intelligence I saw that I had either to renounce the project of exploring the Albert, and proceed at once to the Tanganika — which, after coming so far out of the way, would perhaps have been regarded in Europe as madness — or to wait patiently until the war was over, and then make up by forced marches for lost time. But being again assured that the war would not last long, I resolved to stay and witness it as a novelty, and to take advantage of the time to acquire information about the country and its people.

August 27. — On the 27th of August, Mtesa struck his camp, and began the march to Nakaranga, a point of land lying within 700 yards of the island of Ingira, which had been chosen by the Wavuma as their depot and stronghold. He had collected an army numbering 150,000 warriors, as it was expected that he would have to fight the rebellious Wasoga as well as the Wavuma. Besides this great army must be reckoned nearly 50,000 women, and about as many children and slaves of both sexes, so that at a rough guess, after looking at all the camps and various tributary nations which at Mtesa's command had contributed their quotas, I estimated the number of souls in Mtesa's camp to be about 250,000!

This large total may seem startling, but not more so to those acquainted with the customs and population of Uganda and the nature and extent of Mtesa's authority, than the five millions and a quarter said to have started with Xerxes in his invasion of Greece. I myself, though I saw the vast area which the several camps occupied, did not believe it possible, until one day I asked Mtesa, for the sake of satisfying my curiosity, to permit me to make a muster-roll of his chiefs. Always affable and willing to please white men, for whom he entertains profound respect, he called together all his principal chiefs and officers (who in Uganda are distinguished by the titles of Wakungu and Watongoleh), and commanded them to bring the respective numbers of their sub-chiefs.

These sub-chiefs command followers numbering from 50 to 3000, and Mtesa's bodyguard, though claiming twenty-three Watongoleh, must not be estimated at a less number than 3000 in the aggregate. Now, roughly calculating the native Waganda force at 125,000, we have to add the quotas furnished by Karagwe, Uzongora, Ukedi, Usoga, Sesse, and the islands of the lake, Irwaji, Lulamba, Kiwa, Uziri, Kihibi, &c., also all the Arabs and Wangwana guests who came with their guns to assist Mtesa, and 25,000 seems to me to be a reasonable estimate of the force drawn from these sources.

The advance-guard had departed too early for me to see them, but, curious to see the main body of this great army pass, I stationed myself at an early hour at the extreme limit of the camp.

First with his legion came Mkwenda, who guards the frontier between the Katonga valley and Willimiesi against the Wanyoro. He is a stout, burly young man, brave as a lion, having much experience of wars, and cunning and adroit in their conduct, accomplished with the spear, and possessing, besides, other excellent fighting qualities, I noticed that the Waganda chiefs, though Muslimized, clung to their war-paints and national charms, for each warrior, as he passed by on the trot, was most villainously bedaubed with ochre and pipe-clay. The force under the command of Mkwenda might be roughly numbered at 30,000 warriors and camp-followers, and though the path yesterday was a mere goat-track, the rush of this legion on the half-trot soon crushed out a broad avenue.

The old general Kangau, who defends the country between Willimiesi and the Victoria Nile, came next with his following, their banners flying, drums beating and pipes playing, he and. his warriors stripped for action, their bodies and faces daubed with white, black, and ochreous war-paint.

Next came a rush of about 2000 chosen warriors, all tall men, expert with spear and shield, lithe of body and nimble of foot, shouting as they trotted past their war-cry of "Kavya, kavya" (the two last syllables of Mtesa's title when young — Mukavya, "king"), and rattling their spears. Behind them at a quick march came the musket-armed body-guard of the Emperor, about two hundred in front, a hundred on either side of the road, enclosing Mtesa and his Katekiro, and two hundred bringing up the rear, with their drums beating, pipes playing, and standards flying, and forming quite an imposing and warlike procession.

Mtesa marched on foot, bare-headed, and clad in a dress of blue check cloth, with a black belt of English make round his waist, and — like the Roman emperors, who, when returning in triumph, painted their faces a deep vermilion — his face dyed a bright red. The Katekiro preceded him, and wore a dark grey cashmere coat, which M. de Bellefonds had given him. I think this arrangement was made to deceive any assassin who might be lurking in the bushes. If this was the case, the precaution seemed wholly unnecessary, as the march was so quick that nothing but a gun would have been effective, and the Wavuma and Wasoga have no such weapons.

After Mtesa's bodyguard had passed by, chief after chief, legion after legion, followed, each distinguished to the native ear by its different and peculiar drum-beat. They came on at an extraordinary pace, more like warriors hurrying up into action than on the march, and it is their custom, I am told, to move always at a trot when on an enterprise of a warlike nature.

About two hours after the main body began its march, Kasuju, the guardian of the young princes and Mtesa's women, preceded by a thousand spears and followed by a similar number, trotted by. The women numbered about 5000, but not more than 500 can be styled the Emperor's concubines; the others were for the duties of the household.

If beautiful women of sable complexion are to be found in Africa, it must, I thought, be in the household of such a powerful despot as Mtesa, who has the pick of the flower of so many lands. Accordingly I looked sharply amongst the concubines, that I might become acquainted with the style of pure African beauty. Nor was I quite disappointed, though I had imagined that his wives would have all been of superior personal charms. But Mtesa apparently differs widely from Europeans in his tastes. There were not more than twenty out of all the five hundred worthy of a glance of admiration from a white man with any eye for style and beauty, and certainly not more than three deserving of many glances. These three, the most comely among the twenty beauties of Mtesa's court, were of the Wahuma race, no doubt from Ankori. They had the complexion of quadroons, were straight-nosed and thin-lipped, with large lustrous eyes. In the other graces of a beautiful form they excelled, and Hafiz might have said with poetic rapture that they were "straight as palm-trees and beautiful as moons." The only drawback was their hair — the short crisp hair of the negro race — but in all other points they might be exhibited as the perfection of beauty which Central Africa can produce. Mtesa, however, does not believe them to be superior, or even equal, to his well-fleshed, unctuous-bodied, flat-nosed wives: indeed, when I pointed them out to him one day at a private audience, he even regarded them with a sneer. Speke, if I remember rightly, declares that fatness in womankind is synonymous with beauty in Uganda. This may once have been the case, but it is certainly not so now, for in few women regarded with favour by Mtesa or his chiefs have I seen any gross corpulence of body. Naturally, where there is abundance of good digestible food, and the climate is agreeable, humanity of the respectable class will generally be found to be well clothed in flesh, be it in Uganda or in England, but it is somewhat unreasonable to state that the respectable class therefore considers superfluous rotundity to be an element of beauty.

After the royal harem followed Mtesa's uncle, ancient and well-featured Sabaganzi, whom, as regards the multitude of women that followed him, I looked upon for a long time as a very Solomon among the Waganda, until one day I learned that large possessions of womankind mean wealth in Uganda, for all of them have a market value, and are saleable for wares of any kind, be they cloth, cows, beads, or guns. Still I cannot quite acquit the old gentleman of the imputation of gallantry, for one night, at Nakaranga, he slew with his own hand a lover who had come to serenade one of his numerous Dulcineas. Besides the character I have credited him with, I must dub him as a jealous, vindictive, choleric old pagan, despite his fine features and smooth tongue.

Wearied with gazing on the vast multitude, which rolled by steadily in wave after wave, a living tide of warriors, and having gained sufficient insight into their numbers and method of travel, I left my post of observation and struck into the line of march behind Sabaganzi's rear-guard, where, to say the least, I was much annoyed by the rush of hurrying warriors, all of whom thought it necessary to push on to the front in spite of all obstacles. The guards given to me by Mtesa to conduct me on the road did their utmost to check the furious, persistent impetuosity of the on-coming warriors, and used their stout staffs with angry violence. The blows, however, were quite harmless, as they were warded off by ample shields of wood and cane.

Perceiving it useless to contend against such a weight of numbers and such well-established custom, I submitted to the annoyance patiently, as the march to Nakaranga would not occupy more than two or three days.

At Mpani, where we camped that night, we learned that the Wavuma, soon after our departure from Jinja, or the "Stones," had paid a visit to it, and set the abandoned imperial quarters and the camp on fire, besides spearing some five or six unfortunates before the chief appointed to guard the camp was aware of their presence. At sunset we saw the canoes of the Wavuma, some two or three hundred in number, returning in triumph to their island.

Sept. 1. — Four days afterwards, or on the 1st of September, the army of Mtesa occupied Nakaranga, where it commenced to construct its camp, each chief surrounded by the men of his own command in the position assigned to him by the Katekiro.

The legion commanded by the officers of the queen-mother occupied the ground east of Cape Nakaranga; the chief Ankori and his fantastically dressed Wasoga camped north of Nana Masurie's people; to the gallant Mkwenda with his formidable legion was assigned the entire north of the camp; and to the redoubtable Sekebobo, when he should arrive from Namagongo Point, was appointed the lake side, from Mkwenda to the end of Nakaranga Cape. The imperial quarters occupied an area of 400 yards square in the centre of the vast camp, and was jealously guarded by the bodyguard, the legions of the Katekiro, Chambarango, and Kimbugwe, by Kasuju with the guard of the imperial family, and the bluff, outspoken Kitunzi, chief of the Katonga valley.

The following rough sketch may assist the reader to understand better the locality which at this period was of such importance to Uganda. By sunset the army was comfortably housed in some 30,000 dome-like huts, above which here and there rose a few of a conical shape and taller than the rest, showing the temporary residences of the various chiefs.

Amid all the hurry and bustle the white stranger "Stamlee" (as all the Waganda now called me) was not forgotten. Commodious quarters were erected and allotted to him and his boat's crew, by express orders from Mtesa, near the great broadway which the Katekiro constructed, leading from the imperial quarters to the point of Cape Nakaranga.

Anxious to see what chances Mtesa possessed of victory over his rebellious subjects, I proceeded along the road over the mountain to a position which commanded a clear view of Ingira Island, whither the rebels had betaken themselves, their families, and a few herds of cattle. Considered as being in possession of some twenty thousand savages, whose only weapons of war were the spear and the sling, Ingira Island presented no very formidable obstacle to a power such as the Emperor of Uganda had amassed on this cape, only 700 yards from it. In length it was barely a mile, and only half a mile in width from the base of the mountain which confronted the cape to the water's edge on the Uvuma side. The mountain rose on all sides with rather a steep slope, but was easy of ascent to the nimble-footed and deep-chested natives. The Wavuma, however, were not without allies to assist them in averting the punishment that Mtesa threatened them with, and the common danger, as well as a common hate of the dread monarch, had drawn together, for one strong effort to win their freedom, the inhabitants of Ugeyeya and Utamba Islands, as well as Kitenteh — famous in the annals of Uganda for its long but unfortunate struggle with the Emperor Suna, the father of Mtesa.

The people of the entire coast of Usoga from Nakaranga to Uganda had voluntarily enlisted in the cause of Uvuma, and had despatched over 150 large canoes fully manned to the war. The confederates, in arranging their plan of action, had chosen Ingira Island as the rendezvous of the united fleets of canoes. Mtesa's plan was to capture this island, and to cross over from Ingira to the next, and then to Uvuma, when, of course, only immediate and complete submission would save them; and I rejoiced that I was present, for I was in hopes that at such a period my influence might be sufficient to avert the horrors that generally attend victory in Africa. Though I had no reason to love the Wavuma, and for the time was a warm ally of Mtesa, I was resolved that no massacre of the submissive should take place while I was present.

The redoubtable Sekebobo, commanding twenty-four Watongoleh, or colonels, and a force of about 50,000, occupied Namagongo, and the fleet of Mtesa was under his charge, waiting orders to cross the bay with them.

The Uganda war fleet numbered 325 large and small canoes, out of which only 230 might be said to be really effective for war. One-half of these were manned by Wasesse, natives of the large island of Sesse; the other half by the courageous natives of the Irwaji and Lulamba Islands, by picked men collected from the coast between Usavara and Buka Bay under the command of Chikwata, the Vice-Admiral, by crews of Unjaku under Vice-Admiral Jumba, and by the naval brigade of Gabunga, the Admiral of the Fleet.

Gabunga, though entitled to be called Grand Admiral of the Fleet, because under his charge were placed all the canoes of Uganda, numbering perhaps 500 altogether, must not be supposed to exercise supreme command in action. His duty was simply to convey the orders of the fighting general to his captains and lieutenants, for the sailors, as in England in former times — except in desperate extremity — seldom fight.

The fighting men of each canoe owe obedience only to their General-in-chief; the sailors or paddlers obey Gabunga, the Grand Admiral of the Fleet, who, again, is controlled by the General-in-chief.

Many readers, unless detained to consider the naval force of Mtesa, might be contented with the mere figures giving the numerical strength of his war-vessels. But let us for the sake of curiosity calculate the number of men required to man these 230 effective war-canoes.

The largest canoe seen by me in this fleet measured 72 feet in length, 7 feet 3 inches in breadth, and was four feet deep within, from keel to gunwale. The thwarts were 32 in number, to seat 64 paddlers besides the pilot. There were probably over 100 canoes between 50 and 70 feet in length, and about 50 between 30 and 50 feet long; the remaining 80 fighting-boats were of all sizes, from 18 to 30 feet long. The rest. of the fleet consisted of small boats fit only to carry from three to six men.

The largest class — 100 in number — would require on an average fifty men each to man them, which would be equal in the aggregate to 5000. The second class would require on an average forty men each, or 2000 to man the fifty canoes. The third class would average twenty men each, and being eighty in number, would require 1600 men to man them, the sum total standing therefore at 8600.

A very respectable figure for a naval force, most men would think. But in a battle on the lake, or for such an occasion as the present, when the resources of the empire were mustered for an important war, they would be further required to carry a strong force to assault Ingira Island. The canoes for the assault would therefore lie crammed with fighting men, the largest class carrying from 60 to 100 men exclusive of their crews; so that the actual fact is that Mtesa can float a force of from 16,000 to 20,000 on Lake Victoria for purposes of war.

Of the spirit with which the Wavuma intended to fight the Waganda, we had proof enough on the second day of our arrival. They dashed up close to the shore, and back again into the lake, three or four times, before the Waganda remembered that they had means at hand in the shape of muskets to purge them of this bravado. As the shots were fired at the canoes, most of the Wavuma bent their heads low and paddled their canoes with one hand, but a few of the boldest stood up exhibiting for our benefit their dexterity in the use of the spear, and to show how well they could maintain their footing on the thwarts of their narrow canoes. Their bravado was not without its effect on many of the Waganda, for I heard several remark that the Wavuma would be hard to conquer.

On the third morning Sekebobo, having been instructed during the night, began to cross the bay of Nakaranga with the imperial fleet. Mtesa had sent a messenger to inform me that the chief was about to start, and I hastened up to the beach to witness the sight. I found that almost all the Waganda were animated with the same curiosity, for the beach was lined for three or four miles with dense masses of people, almost all clad in the national brown, bark-cloth robes.

The Wavuma meanwhile kept their eyes on Sekebobo, and from the summit of their mountain island discerned, almost as well as if they had been told by Mtesa, what was about to be done; and to frustrate this, if possible, or at least to gather booty, they hastily manned 100 canoes or thereabouts, and darted out like so many crocodiles towards Namagongo. Before Sekebobo could arrange the fleet in order, the Wavuma were in the middle of the bay to dispute his passage, and calmly awaiting his coming into deep water.

A hundred canoes against 325 was rather an unequal contest, and so the Wavuma thought, for as the fleet of Mtesa approached in a compact, tolerably well-arranged mass, the Wavuma opened their line to right and left, and permitted their foe to pass them. The Waganda, encouraged by this sign, began to cheer, but scarcely had the first sounds of self-gratulation escaped them when the Wavuma paddles were seen to strike the water into foam, and, lo! into the midst of the mass from either flank the gallant islanders dashed, sending dismay and consternation into the whole Uganda army.

What work those desperate Wavuma might have done, I know not, but Mtesa at the sight leaped up high, and shouted his war-cry, "Kavya, kavya!" and the army, men, women, and children, screamed "Kavya, kavya!" and the approaching fleet, hearing the cry, echoed it fiercely, and turned itself on the enemy with spirit. But the Wavuma, having made fourteen good prizes, did not wish, so unequally matched, to meet the Waganda in a pitched fight, and accordingly hastened away — contented for the time — into deeper water, whither, strangely enough, the Waganda fleet did not dare to follow them.

This short but spirited scene caused me to reflect deeply, and to ask myself why, if the Wavuma were so courageous, I was permitted to escape from their hands; and why one boat and a double-barreled elephant-rifle were sufficient to release us, in our voyage of discovery, from thirteen well-manned Wavuma canoes. Some answers to this question were derived subsequently from observation of events.

A pause of two or three days without incident followed the arrival of Sekebobo's legion and Mtesa's fleet. Then Mtesa sent for me, and was pleased to impart some of his ideas on the probable issue of the war to me, in something like the following words: —

"Stamlee, I want your advice. All white men are very clever, and appear to know everything. I want to know from you what you think I may expect from this war. Shall I have victory or not? It is my opinion we must be clever, and make head work take that island."

Smiling at his naive, candid manner, I replied that it would require a prophet to be able to foretell the issue of the war, and that I was far from being a prophet; that headwork, were it the best in the world, could not take Ingira Island unassisted by valour.

He then said, "I know that the Waganda will not fight well on the water; they are not accustomed to it. They are always victorious on land, but when they go in canoes, they are afraid of being upset; and most of the warriors come from the interior, and do not know now how to swim. The Wavuma and Wasoga are very expert in the water, and swim like fish. If we could devise some means to take the Waganda over to the island without risking them in the canoes, I should be sure of victory."

I replied, "You have men, women, and children here in this camp as numerous as grass. Command every soul able to walk to take up a stone and cast into the water, and you will make a great difference in its depth; but if each person carries fifty stones a day, I will warrant you that in a few days you will walk on dry land to Ingira."

Mtesa at this slapped his thighs in approval, and forthwith commanded the Katekiro to muster two legions and set them to work, and very soon the face of the rocky mountain was covered with about 40,000 warriors, or about a sixth of the multitude at the cape, toiling at the unusual work of making a rocky causeway to connect Nakaranga with Ingira Island. After they had been at work three hours, I proceeded to view the progress they were making, and saw that they were expending their energies in making a causeway about 100 feet wide. I told the Katekiro that it would take a year to finish such a work, but if he would limit the width to 10 feet, and form the people into rows, he would have the satisfaction of setting foot on Ingira Island without danger. But though the Premier and first lord of Uganda lost none of his politeness, and never forgot that Mtesa, his master, was pleased to call me his friend, I was not slow in perceiving that he would not accept friendly advice from a stranger and a foreigner. It was not by words, or even a hint or unfriendly gesture, that the fact was betrayed, but simply by inattention to my advice. The most courtly European could not have excelled the Uganda Premier. He offered in the same friendly manner a gourdful of the honey-sweet wine of the plantain, talked sociably upon various matters, invited verbal sketches of European life, and smiled in an aristocratically insolent manner. Nevertheless, under this urbane mask, I detected a proud spirit, unbending as steel. With such an unruffled, composed, smiling patrician of Uganda, what could I do but groan inwardly that good, brave, excellent Mtesa should be served by such men? At the same time, I could not help smiling at the diplomatic insouciance of this man, who indeed represented in only a too perfect degree the character of the Waganda chiefs.

For two days the work was carried on in the way I had described, namely, with rocks, and then Mtesa thought that filling the passage with trees would be a speedier method, and the Katekiro was so instructed. For three days the Waganda were at work felling trees, and a whole forest was levelled and carried to Nakaranga Point, where they were lashed to one another with bark-rope, and sunk.

On the morning of the fifth day Mtesa came down to the point to view the causeway, and was glad to see that we were nearer by 130 yards to Ingira Island. While viewing the island, he asked me what I thought of sending a peace party over to ascertain the feeling of the Wavuma. I replied that it would be a good and wise thing in Europe, but not in Central Africa, as I feared the Wavuma would massacre the entire party. Mtesa, however, advised by the chiefs or one of the Wagwana, persisted in the idea, and a favourite page, named Webba, was about to be sent in a large canoe with fifty men to open negotiations for peace with the Wavuma, when I entreated that he would listen to me, and send a small, rotten canoe instead. He listened to me so far as to send a canoe manned with only fifteen men. As they were paddling on, unthinking and undreading danger, I cried out to Mtesa, who was about twenty yards from me, "Say farewell to Webba, for you will see little Webba no more."

The Katekiro and two or three of his chiefs smiled as if this was most absurd. I felt precisely at this moment as I felt the first time I saw a bull-fight: a cold shiver of horror crept over me. I was helpless and unable to avert the tragedy which instinct warned me would be enacted.

The entire Uganda army was concentrated on the slope of Nakaranga mountain, and the eyes of the vast multitude were fastened upon this scene; and no doubt they thought as I did, that it was a moment of thrilling interest. The men of the Uganda canoe fleet were in their camps, and the canoes were all beached near them.

The peace party held on its way until near Ingira, when one of them opened a conversation with the Wavuma, the result of which was an invitation to take their canoe in-shore. As they paddled the canoe gently in among the rushes that lined the island, I observed that all the Wavuma gathered together near the place where the Waganda were expected to land, and that several Wavuma canoes pushed out in order that the Waganda might have no chance of escape.

We waited only a few seconds for what was about to happen. The canoe of the peace party had scarcely touched their island before we heard the shrieks of the unfortunates pealing across the water, and then the triumphant shouts of the Wavuma; and soon we saw men rushing to the point of their island nearest the causeway, and with jeers and scoffing they showed the bloody heads of the unfortunates to Mtesa, and tossed them into the lake. Mtesa rose gloomy and disconcerted, and returned to his quarters much depressed in spirits, but he gave instructions to his Katekiro to continue the work on the causeway.

The Katekiro, placidly obedient, instructed two chiefs, the two chiefs instructed their Watongoleh, the Watongoleh instructed their men, and the result of these several instructions was, that about 100 men out of 150,000 were seen lounging idly on the causeway and that was all, for the novelty of the idea had now worn off.

Nothing more was heard of the bridge, for Mtesa had conceived a new idea, which was, to be instructed in the sciences of Europe. I was to be a scientific encyclopaedia to him. Not wishing to deny him, I tried, during the afternoon of the massacre, to expound the secrets of nature and the works of Providence, the wonders of the heavens, the air, and the earth. We gossiped about the nature of rocks and metals, and their many appliances, which the cunning of the Europeans had invented to manufacture the innumerable variety of things for which they are renowned. The dread despot sat with wide-dilated eyes and an all-devouring attention, and, in deference to his own excitable feelings, his chiefs affected to be as interested as himself, though I have no doubt several ancients, such as Kangau and Sabaganzi, thought the whole affair decidedly tedious, and the white man a "bore." The more polite and courtly Katekiro, Chambarango, and Kauta vied with each other in expressing open-mouthed and large-eyed interest in this encyclopaedic talk. I drifted from mechanics to divinity, for my purpose in this respect was not changed. During my extemporised lectures, I happened to mention angels. On hearing the word, Mtesa screamed with joy, and to my great astonishment the patricians of Uganda chorused, "Ah-ah-ah!" as if they had heard an exceedingly good thing. Having appeared so learned all the afternoon, 1 dared not condescend to inquire what all this wild joy meant, but prudently waited until the exciting cries and slapping of thighs were ended.

The boisterous period over, Mtesa said, "Stamlee, I have always told my chiefs that the white men know everything, and are skilful in all things. A great many Arabs, some Turks, and four white men have visited me, and I have examined and heard them all talk, and for wisdom and goodness the white men excel all the others. Why do the Arabs and Turks come to Uganda? Is it not for ivory and slaves? Why do the white men come? They come to see this lake, our rivers and mountains. The Arabs bring cloth, beads, and wire, to buy ivory and slaves; they also bring powder and guns; but who made all these things the Arabs bring here for trade? The Arabs themselves say the white men made them, and I have seen nothing yet of all they have brought that the white men did not make. Therefore, I say, give me the white men, because if you want knowledge, you must talk with them to get it. Now, Stamlee, tell me and my chiefs what you know of the angels."

Verily the question was a difficult one, and my answer would not have satisfied Europeans. Remembering, however, St. Paul's confession that he was all things to all men, I attempted to give as vivid a description of what angels are generally believed to be like, and as Michael Angelo and Gustave Dore have laboured to illustrate them, and with the aid of Ezekiel's and Milton's descriptions I believe I succeeded in satisfying and astonishing the king and his court; and in order to show him that I had authority for what I said, I sent to my camp for the Bible, and translated to him what Ezekiel and St. John said of angels.

This little incident, trivial as it may appear, had very interesting results. Encyclopaedic talk was forgotten in the grander and more sublime themes which Scripture and divinity contributed. The Emperor cast covetous eyes on the Bible and my Church of England Prayer Book, and perceiving his wish, I introduced to him a boy named Dallington, a pupil of the Universities Mission at Zanzibar, who could translate the Bible into Kiswahili for him, and otherwise communicate to him what I wished to say.

Henceforth, during the intervals of leisure that the war gave us, we were to be seen — the king, court, Dallington, and I — engaged in the translation of an abstract of the Holy Scriptures. There were readers enough of these translations, but Mtesa himself was an assiduous and earnest student.

Having abundance of writing-paper with me, I made a large book for him, into which the translations were fairly copied by a writer called Idi. When completed, Mtesa possessed an abridged Protestant Bible in Kiswahili, embracing all the principal events from the Creation to the Crucifixion of Christ. St. Luke's Gospel was translated entire, as giving a more complete history of the Saviour's life.

When the abridged Bible was completed, Mtesa called all his chiefs together, as well as the officers of his guard, and when all were assembled, he began to state that when he succeeded his father he was a Mshensi (a heathen), and delighted in shedding blood because he knew no better, and was only following the customs of his fathers; but that when an Arab trader, who was also a Mwalim (priest), taught him the creed of Islam, he had renounced the example of his fathers, and executions became less frequent, and no man could say, since that day, that he had seen Mtesa drunk with pombe. But there were a great many things he could not understand, such as, why circumcision was necessary to gain Paradise, and how it was possible that men having died could enjoy earth's pleasures in heaven, and how men could walk along a bridge of the breadth of a hair, for such were some of the things the sons of Islam taught. He could not comprehend all these things, as his sense condemned them, and there was no one in Uganda able to enlighten him better. But as it was in his heart to be good, he hoped God would overlook his follies and forgive him, and send men who knew what was right to Uganda. "Meanwhile," said he with a smile, "I refused to be circumcised, though the Arabs say it is the first thing that should be done to become a true son of Islam. Now, God be thanked, a white man, 'Stamlee,' has come to Uganda with a book older than the Koran of Mohammed, and Stamlee says that Mohammed was a liar, and much of his book taken from this; and this boy and Idi have read to me all that Stamlee has read to them from this book, and I find that it is a great deal better than the book of Mohammed, besides, it is the first and oldest book. The prophet Moses wrote some of it a long, long time before Mohammed was even heard of, and the book was finished long before Mohammed was born. As Kintu, our first king, was a long time before me, so Moses was before Mohammed. Now I want you, my chiefs and soldiers, to tell me what we shall do. Shall we believe in Isa (Jesus) and Musa (Moses) or in Mohammed? "

Chambarango replied, "Let us take that which is the best."

The Katekiro said, "We know not which is the best. The Arabs say their book is the best, and the white men say their book is the best — how then can we know which speaks the truth?"

Kauta, the imperial steward, said, "When Mtesa became a son of Islam, he taught me, and I became one; if my master says he taught me wrong, having got more knowledge, he can now teach me right. I am waiting to hear his words."

Mtesa smiled and said, "Kauta speaks well. If I taught him how to become a Muslim, I did it because I believed it to be good. Chambarango says, 'Let us take that which is best.' True, I want that which is the best, and I want the true book; but Katekiro asks, 'How are we to know which is true?' and I will answer him. Listen to me: The Arabs and the white men behave exactly as they are taught by their books, do they not? The Arabs come here for ivory and slaves, and we have seen that they do not always speak the truth, and that they buy men of their own colour, and treat them badly, putting them in chains and beating them. The white men, when offered slaves, refuse them, saying, 'Shall we make our brothers slaves? No; we are all sons of God.' I have not heard a white man tell a lie yet. Speke came here, behaved well, and went his way home with his brother Grant. They bought no slaves, and the time they were in Uganda they were very good. Stamlee came here, and he would take no slaves. Abdul Aziz Bey (M. Linant Bellefonds) has been here, and is gone, and he took no slaves. What Arab would have refused slaves like these white men? Though we deal in slaves, it is no reason why it should not be bad; and when I think that the Arabs and the white men do as they are taught, I say that the white men are greatly superior to the Arabs, and I think therefore that their book must be a better book than Mohammed's, and of all that Stamlee has read from his book I see nothing too hard for me to believe. The book begins from the very beginning of this world, tells us how it was made, and in how many days; gives us the words of God Himself, and of Moses, and the prophet Solomon, and Jesus, the son of Mary. I have listened to it all well pleased, and now I ask you, shall we accept this book or Mohammed's book as our guide?"

To which question, no doubt seeing the evident bent of Mtesa's own mind, they all replied, "We will take the white man's book"; and at hearing their answer a manifest glow of pleasure lighted up the Emperor's face.

In this manner Mtesa renounced Islamism, and professed himself a convert to the Christian Faith, and he now announced his determination to adhere to his new religion, to build a church, and to do all in his power to promote the propagation of Christian sentiments among his people, and to conform to the best of his ability to the holy precepts contained in the Bible.

I, on the other hand, proud of my convert, with whom I had diligently laboured during three months, promised that, since Dalliiigton wished it, I would release him from my service, that he might assist to confirm him in his new faith, that he might read the Bible for him, and perform the service of a Bible reader until the good people of Europe should send a priest to baptize him and teach him the duties of the. Christian religion.

"Stamlee," said Mtesa to me, as we parted, nearly two months after the massacre of the peace party, "say to the white people, when you write to them, that I am like a man sitting in darkness, or born blind, and that all I ask is that I may be taught how to see, and I shall continue a Christian while I live."

CHAPTER XIII.

The war-drum beaten — The wizards play their part — In full war-paint — Bullets against spears — The Wavuma baulked — Mtesa's fury — Victory or the stake! — Hard fighting — The captive chief: a struggle between the pagan and the Christian — A floating mystery — "Return, spirit! the war is ended!" — The camp on fire: a race for life.

Sept. 14. — On the 14th of September the Emperor of Uganda decided to give battle to the Wavuma, who were daily becoming bolder and more boastful. In the morning, in accordance with Mtesa's orders, forty Waganda canoes sallied out from the beach in front of our camps to Nakaranga Point, where they formed in line of battle before the causeway, with the sterns of their canoes fronting Ingira, and their bows towards Nakaranga Point.

Mtesa was followed by about three-fourths of his army when he proceeded to the point to view the battle, and with him went the great war-drums, to the number of fifty or thereabouts, and fifes about a hundred, and a great number of men shaking gourds filled with pebbles, and the court criers and mad charmers against evil were not wanting to create din and noise, and celebrate victory,

A hut of ample size had been erected on the mountain slope overlooking the strait, into which Mtesa and his favourite women retired. When the Emperor was seated, the "prophets of Baal," or the priests or priestesses of the Muzimu, or witchcraft, came up, more than a hundred in number, and offered the charms to Mtesa one after another in a most tedious, ceremonious way, and to all of them Mtesa condescended to point his imperial forefinger.

The chief priest was a most fantastically dressed madman. It is customary before commencing a battle to carry all the potent medicines or charms of Uganda (thus propitiating the dreadful Muzimu or evil spirits) to the monarch, that he may touch or point his forefinger at them. They consist of dead lizards, bits of wood, hide, nails of dead people, claws of animals, and beaks of birds, a hideous miscellany, with mysterious compounds of herbs and leaves carefully enclosed in vessels ornamented with vari-coloured beads.

During the battle these wizards and witches chant their incantations, and exhibit their medicines on high before the foe, while the gourd-and-pebble bearers sound a hideous alarum, enough to cause the nerves of any man except an African to relax at once,

Mtesa and his array were in full war-paint, and the principal men wore splendid leopard skins over their backs, but the Wasoga bore the palm for splendour of dress and ornate equipments.

Ankori the chief and his officers were wonderfully gay. Snow-white ostrich plumes decorated their heads, and lion and leopard skins covered their backs, while their loins were girded with snow-white, long-haired monkey and goat skins; even the staves of their lances were ornamented with feathers and rings of white monkey skin.

There was ample time afforded to observe all these things, and to be exceedingly amused and interested in what promised to be an animating scene, before all attention was drawn to and engaged by the battle. The spectators were seated, safe from harm or danger, on the slope of Nakaranga mountain, from the water's edge to the mountain summit, tier above tier, and rank above rank, in thousands upon thousands.

The canoes, having formed line, slowly moved sternwise towards Ingira. The Wavuma were not inactive spectators of this manoeuvre, but as yet their warriors had not embarked. They were busy mustering, while those appointed to garrison the island, with the women and children, several thousands in number, sate down on the slopes of the opposite mountain of Ingira Island. The rushes and weeds lining the water's edge were too tall and thick to enable us to estimate exactly the number of the enemy's war-canoes, but the brown-coloured prows, long and curving, of a great many were seen thrust out from among the vivid green banana plantations, or arranged on the rising beach of the island beyond its reedy margin.

Having advanced with the utmost regularity of line, near enough to the island to make their "Brown Bess" muskets effective, the Waganda began to open fire in a steady, deliberate manner, and succeeded after a while in annoying the foe and arousing him to action. At a given signal from their chiefs, forth from the reeds and rushes shot the prows of the Wavuma canoes; and then, giving utterance to most shrill war-cries, the rowers impelled them from all quarters, to the number of 194, with an extraordinary velocity upon the Waganda line, which now began to retire slowly towards the causeway.

On the causeway at its farthest extremity were assembled a force of a hundred musketeers and four small boat howitzers under the command of the Katekiro and Mtesa's factotum Tori.

The furious advance of the Wavuma soon caused the Waganda to hurry their movements, and on approaching the causeway they parted their line, rushing on either side of it, giving the Katekiro and Tori ample opportunity to wreak their will on the pursuers. But owing to the want of skill of the cannoniers, and the nervousness of the musketeers, very little damage was inflicted on the Wavuma, but the noise and whirring of lead and iron sufficed to check them, and caused them to withdraw with much of the baffled aspect of hungry crocodiles cheated of their prey. This was all the battle — but, short as it was, it had sufficed to prove to me that Mtesa would be unable to take Ingira Island, garrisoned and defended as it was by such a determined foe. After a while Mtesa withdrew from the scene, the army returned to its quarters, and the canoes of the Waganda, closely hugging the

Nakaranga shore, went back to their rendezvous, leaving the Wavuma masters of the situation.

During the afternoon of this day Mtesa held a grand levee, and when all were assembled, he addressed them publicly to the effect that in a few days another battle would be fought, but as he had heard very important news, he intended to wait a while to ascertain if it was true.

Work progressed but languidly at the causeway. It was very tedious waiting, but my time was principally occupied in teaching Mtesa and his principal chiefs, and in gleaning such information as might enable me to understand the complicated politics of the empire.

Sept. 18. — Suddenly on the 18th of September, at early dawn, orders were communicated to the chiefs to prepare for battle. The first intelligence of it that I received was from the huge war-drums which summoned both sailors and warriors to action.

But first a burzah, or council, was held. Though eager to learn the news, I dared not appear too much interested in the war. Sabadu, who would be present on guard, would be sure to relate to me all the details of whatever transpired.

At night, though I interpolate it here for the benefit of the narrative, gossipy Sabadu, whose retentive brain I knew I could trust, conveyed to me a faithful report of the proceedings; and I cannot do better than give it to the reader in Sabadu's language.

"Ah! master, you have missed a sight. I never saw Mtesa as he was to-day. Oh, it was awful! His eyes were as large as my fists. They jumped from their sockets, and they were glowing as fire. Didn't the chiefs tremble! They were as children, whimpering and crying for forgiveness. He said to them, 'Wherein have I been unkind to you, that you will not fight for me, for my slaves who were sent to Usoga have returned saying there was not a man but either had joined me or had already joined the Wavuma? Who gave you those clothes that you wear? Who gave you those guns that you have? Was it not I? Did Suna my father give his chiefs such fine things as I give? No; yet they fought for him, and the boldest of them would not have dared to advise him to fly, as you have done me. Am I not Kabaka? Is this not Uganda, as well as my capital? Have I not my army here? And you, Katekiro, were you not a peasant before I dressed you and set you up as a chief of Uddu? And you, Chambarango, who made you a chief? And you, Mkwenda, and you, Sekebobo, and you, Kimbugwe, Kitunzi, Kaeema, Kangau, Kagu, speak, was it not Mtesa who made you chiefs? Were you princes, that you came to be made chiefs, or peasants whom it was my pleasure to make chiefs? Ah, ha! I shall see to-day who will not fight; I will see to-day who dares to run away from the Wavuma. By the grave of my father, I will burn the man over a slow fire who runs away or turns his back, and the peasant who distinguishes himself to-day shall eat his land. Look out for yourselves, chiefs. I will sit down to-day and watch for the coward, and the coward I will burn. I swear it.' Instantly the Katekiro fell on his face to the earth, and cried, 'Kabaka' (emperor), 'send me to-day to fight, watch my flag, and if I turn my back to the Wavuma, then take and burn me or cut me to little pieces.' The example of the Katekiro was followed by the other chiefs, and they all swore to be desperately brave."

About 8.30 A.M., while I was at the point of Nakaranga, the sound of drums approached me, and I knew that the council was ended, and that the battle would soon begin. Mtesa appeared anything but a Christian, judging from his looks. Fires of fury shot from his eyes; and pages, women, chiefs, and all seemed awe-stricken. I was then ignorant of what had taken place, but when I observed the absence of Chambarango, and several of the great Wakungu, or generals, I felt assured that Mtesa had lately been in the midst of a scene.

Presently other drums sounded from the water-side, and soon the beautiful canoes of Uganda appeared in view. The entire war-fleet of 230 vessels rode gracefully on the calm grey waters of the channel.

The line of battle, I observed, was formed by Chambarango, in command of the right flank, with fifty canoes; Sambuzi, Mukavya, Chikwata, and Saruti, all sub-chiefs, were ranged with 100 canoes under the command of Kauta, the imperial steward, to form the centre; the left flank was in charge of the gallant Mkwenda, who had eighty canoes. Tori commanded a force of musketeers, and with his four howitzers was stationed on the causeway, which was by this time 200 yards from the shore.

In the above manner the fleet of vessels, containing some 16,000 men, moved to the attack upon Ingira. The centre, defended by the flanks, which were to menace the rear of the Wavuma should they approach near the causeway, resolutely advanced to within thirty yards of Ingira, and poured in a most murderous fire among the slingers of the island, who, imagining that the Waganda meant to carry the island by storm, boldly stood exposed, resolved to fight. But they were unable to maintain that courageous behaviour long. Mkwenda then moved up from the left, and attacked with his musketeers the Wavuma on the right, riddling their canoes, and making matters specially hot for them in that quarter.

The Wavuma, seeing matters approaching a crisis, and not wishing to die tamely, manned their canoes, and 196 dashed impetuously, as at first, from the rushes of Ingira with loud shrill yells, and the Waganda lines moved backward to the centre of the channel, where they bravely and coolly maintained their position. As the centre of the Uganda line parted in front of the causeway and disclosed the hotly advancing enemy, Tori aimed the howitzers and fired at a group of about twenty canoes, completely shattering more than half of them, and reloading quickly, he discharged several bolts of iron three inches long among them with terrible effect. Before this cool bearing of the Waganda, the Wavuma retired to their island again, and we saw numbers of canoes discharging their dead and wounded, and the Waganda were summoned to Nakaranga shore to receive the congratulations of the Emperor and the applause of the vast multitude. Mtesa went down to the water's edge to express his satisfaction at their behaviour.

"Go at them again," said he, "and show them what lighting is." And the line of battle was again formed, and again the Wavuma darted from the cover of the reeds and water-cane, with the swiftness of hungry sharks; beating the water into foam with their paddles, and rending the air with their piercing yells. It was one of the most exciting and animating scenes I ever beheld; but, owing to the terror of the stake with which their dread monarch had threatened them, the Waganda distinguished themselves for coolness and method, and the Wavuma, as on a former occasion, for intrepidity and desperate courage.

A third time the Waganda were urged to the battle, and a third time the unconquerable and desperate enemy dashed on them, to be smitten and wounded sore in a battle where they had not the least chance of returning blow for blow without danger of being swept by the cannon and muskets on the causeway.

A third battle was fought a few days after between 178 Wavuma canoes and 122 Waganda; but had the Waganda possessed the spirit and dash of their enemies, they might have decided the war on this day, for the Wavuma were greatly dispirited.

A fourth battle was fought the next day by 214 Waganda canoes and 203 Wavuma canoes, after the usual delay and premonitory provocation. The Wavuma obtained the victory most signally, chasing the Waganda within 40 yards of Nakaranga Cape, and being only driven from their prey by the musketeers and the howitzers on the causeway, which inflicted great execution on them at such close quarters. The Waganda did not attempt a second trial this day, for they were disorganized and dispirited after the signal defeat they had experienced.

The fleet of the Waganda returned to their rendezvous with the jeers and scoffs of the intrepid Wavuma ringing in their ears. On enquiring into the cause of the disaster, I learned that Mtesa's gunpowder was almost exhausted, and that he had scarcely a round left for each musket. This fact alarmed him, and compelled him to request me to lend him my powder in the camp at Dumo, which was refused in such a decided tone that he never repeated the request.

Oct. 5. — It was now the 5th of October, and I had left my camp on the 12th of August. It was necessary that I should participate in some manner in the war and end it. Yet I scarcely knew how I should act effectively to produce results beneficial to all parties. For though my own interests and the welfare of the Expedition were involved and in a manner staked on the success of the Waganda, and though a passive partisan of Mtesa, yet the brave Wavuma, by their magnificent daring and superb courage, had challenged my fullest sympathies. My energies and thoughts were bent, therefore, upon discovering a solution of the problem how to injure none, yet satisfy all.

It was clear that the Wavuma would not surrender without a frightful waste of life; it was equally evident that Mtesa would not relax his hold upon them without some compensation or satisfaction, nor assist me in my projects of exploration unless I aided him in some manner.

At length I devised a plan which I thought would succeed; but before I was enabled to perfect my scheme an incident occurred which called for my immediate intervention.

Mtesa, by means of his scouts, had succeeded in capturing one of the principal chiefs of the Wavuma, and his Wakungu and principal strangers had been invited to be present to witness the execution of this chief at the stake.

When I arrived at the scene, a large quantity of faggots had already been collected to burn him. By this mode of punishment, Mtesa thought he would be able to strike terror into the souls of the Wavuma.

Mtesa was in high glee when I entered the council: he was unable to hide the triumph he felt at the terrible vengeance he was about to take for the massacre of Webba, his favourite page, and the peace party.

"Now, Stamlee," he said, "when the chief is at the stake," — he was an old man of sixty or thereabouts — "you shall see how a chief of Uvuma dies. He is about to be burnt. The Wavuma will tremble when they hear of the manner of his death."

"Ah, Mtesa," I said, "have you forgotten the words of the good book which I have read to you so often? 'If thy brother offend thee, thou shalt forgive him many times.' 'Love thy enemies.' 'Do good to them that hate you.' 'Thou shalt love thy neighbour as thyself.' 'Forgive us our trespasses, as we forgive them that trespass against us.'"

"But this man is a native of Uvuma, and the Wavuma are at war with me. Have you forgotten Webba?"

"No, I remember poor little Webba. I saw him die, and I was very sorry."

"Shall this man not die, Stamlee? Shall I not have blood for him, Stamlee?"

"No."

"But I shall, Stamlee. I will burn this man to ashes. I will burn every soul I catch. I will have blood! blood I the blood of all in Uvuma."

"No, Mtesa! no more blood. It is time the war was ended."

"What!" said Mtesa, bursting into one of those paroxysms of fury which Sabadu had so graphically described. "I will slay every soul in Uvuma, will cut down every plantain, and burn every man, woman, and child on that island. By the grave of my father Suna, I will."

"No, Mtesa, you must stop this wild pagan way of thinking. It is only a pagan who always dreams of blood and talks of shedding blood as you do. It is only the pagan boy Mtesa who speaks now. It is not the man Mtesa whom I saw, and whom I made a friend. It is not 'Mtesa the Good,' whom you said your people loved. It is not Mtesa the Christian, it is the savage. Bah! I have had enough of you, I know you now."

"Stamlee! Stamlee! Wait a short time, and you will see. What are you waiting for?" he said, suddenly turning round to the executioners, who were watching his looks.

Instantly the poor old man was bound; but, suddenly rising, I said to Mtesa, "Listen to one word. The white man speaks but once. Listen to me for the last time. You remember the tale of Kintu which you told me the other day. He left the land of Uganda because it stank with blood. As Kintu left Uganda in the old, old days, I shall leave it, never to return. To-day Kintu is looking down upon you from the spirit-land, and as he rebuked Ma'anda for murdering his faithful servant, so is he rebuking you to-day through me. Yes, kill that poor old man, and I shall leave you to-day, unless you kill me too, and from Zanzibar to Cairo I shall tell every Arab I meet what a murderous beast you are, and through all the white man's land I shall tell with a loud voice what wicked act I saw Mtesa do, and how the other day he wanted to run away because he heard a silly old woman say the Wasoga were marching upon him. How grand old Kamanya must have wept in the spirit-land when he heard of Mtesa about to run away. How the lion-hearted Suna must have groaned when he saw Mtesa shiver in terror because an old woman had had a bad dream. Good-bye, Mtesa. You may kill the Mvuma chief, but I am going, and shall not see it."

Mtesa's face had been a picture wherein the passions of brutish fury and thirsty murder were portrayed most faithfully; but at the mention of Suna and Kamanya in the spirit-land looking down upon him, the tears began to well in his eyes, and finally, while they rolled in large drops down his face, he sobbed loudly like a child, while the chiefs and executioners, maintaining a deathly silence, looked very uncomfortable. Tori the cannonier and Kauta the steward, however, sprang up, and, unrolling their head-dresses, officiously wiped Mtesa's face, while the poor wayward man murmured audibly as I walked away from the scene: —

"Did not Stamlee talk about the spirit-land, and say that Suna was angry with me? Oh, he speaks too true, too true! Oh father, forgive me, forgive me." After which, I was told he suddenly broke away from the council.

An hour afterwards I was summoned by a page to his presence, and Mtesa said: —

"Stamlee will not say Mtesa is bad now, for he has forgiven the Mvuma chief, and will not hurt him. Will Stamlee say that Mtesa is good now? And does he think Suna is glad now?"

"Mtesa is very good," and I clasped his hand warmly. "Be patient, all shall come out right, and Kintu and Suna must be glad when they see that Mtesa is kind to his guests. I have something to tell you. I have thought over your trouble here, and I want to finish this war for your good without any more trouble. I will build a structure which shall terrify the Wavuma, and make them glad of a peace, but you must give me plenty of men to help me, and in three days I shall be ready.

Meantime shout out to the Wavuma from the causeway that you have something which will be so terrible that it will finish the war at once."

"Take everybody, do anything you like; I will give you Sekebobo and all his men."

Oct 6. — The next morning Sekebobo brought about 2000 men before my quarters, and requested to know my will. I told him to despatch 1000 men to cut long poles 1 inch thick, 300 to cut poles 3 inches thick and 7 feet long, 100 to cut straight long trees 4 inches thick, and 100 to disbark all these, and make bark rope. Himself and 500 men I wished to assist me at the beach. The chief communicated my instructions and urged them to be speedy, as it was the Emperor's command, and himself accompanied me to the canoe fleet.

I selected three of the strongest-built canoes, each 70 feet long and 6 ½ feet wide, and, after preparing a space of ground near the water's edge, had them drawn up parallel with one another, and 4 feet apart from each other. With these three canoes I began to construct a floating platform, laying the tall trees across the canoes, and lashing them firmly to the thwarts, and as fast as the 7-foot poles came, I had them lashed in an upright position to the thwarts of the outer canoes, and as fast as the inch poles arrived, I had them twisted in among these uprights, so that, when completed, it resembled an oblong stockade, 70 feet long by 27 feet wide, which the spears of the enemy could not penetrate.

Oct. 7. — On the afternoon of the second day, the floating fort was finished, and Mtesa and his chiefs came down to the beach to see it launched and navigated for a trial trip. The chiefs, when they saw it, began to say it would sink, and communicated their fears to Mtesa, who half believed them. But the Emperor's women said to him: "Leave Stamlee alone; he would not make such a thing if he did not know that it would float."

Oct. 8. — On receiving orders to launch it, I selected sixty paddlers and 150 musketeers of the bodyguard to stand by to embark as soon as it should be afloat, and appointed Tori and one of my own best men to superintend its navigation, and told them to close the gate of the fort as soon as they pushed off from the land. About 1000 men were then set to work to launch it, and soon it was floating in the water, and when the crew and garrison, 214 souls, were in it, it was evident to all that it rode the waves of the lake easily and safely —

"The invention all admired, and each how he

To be the inventor missed, so easy it seemed

Once found, which yet unfound most would have thought

Impossible " —

and a burst of applause from the army rewarded the inventor.

Several long blue Kaniki and white and red cloths were hoisted above this curious structure, which, when closed up all round, appeared to move of its own accord in a very mysterious manner, and to conceal within its silent and impenetrable walls some dread thing, well calculated to strike terror into the mind of the ignorant savage.

Oct. 13. — At eight o'clock on the morning of the 13th of October the army was assembled at Nakaranga with unusual display, and it was proclaimed across the strait from the extremity of the causeway that a terrible thing was approaching which would blow them into atoms if they did not make peace at once and acknowledge the power of Mtesa; and I believe that they declared that all the Muzimus and the charms of Uganda were within, for I heard something said about Muzimu and Uganda. The old Mvuma chief was also placed in prominent view, and induced to urge them to accept the terms which Mtesa offered, viz. pardon to all, provided they went through the form of submission. After this announcement, which was made with all gravity, the awful mysterious structure appeared, while the drums beat a tremendous sound, and the multitude of horns blew a deafening blast.

It was a moment of anxiety to me, for manifold reasons. The fort, perfectly defensible in itself against the most furious assaults by men armed with spears, steadily approached the point, then steered direct for the island of Ingira, until it was within fifty yards.

"Speak," said a stentorian voice amid a deathly silence within. "What will you do? Will you make peace and submit to Mtesa, or shall we blow up the island? Be quick and answer."

There was a moment's consultation among the awe-stricken Wavuma. Immediate decision was imperative. The structure was vast, totally unlike anything that was ever visible on the waters of their sea. There was no person visible, yet a voice spoke clear and loud. Was it a spirit, the Wazimu of all Uganda, more propitious to their enemy's prayers than those of the Wavuma? It might contain some devilish, awful thing, something similar to the evil spirits which in their hours of melancholy and gloom their imagination invoked. There was an audacity and confidence in its movements that was perfectly appalling.

"Speak," repeated the stern voice; "we cannot wait longer."

Immediately, to our relief, a man, evidently a chief, answered, "Enough, let Mtesa be satisfied. We will collect the tribute to-day, and will come to Mtesa. Return, spirit, the war is ended!" At which the mysterious structure solemnly began its return back to the cove where it had been constructed, and the quarter of a million of savage human beings, spectators of the extraordinary scene, gave a shout that seemed to split the very sky, and Ingira's bold height repeated the shock of sound back to Nakaranga.

Three hours afterwards a canoe came from Ingira Island, bearing fifty men, some of whom were chiefs. They brought with them several tusks of ivory, and two young girls, daughters of the two principal chiefs of Uvuma. These were the tribute. The ivory was delivered over to the charge of the steward, and the young girls were admitted to the harem of Mtesa, into the mystery of which no man dare penetrate and live. The old Mvuma chief was surrendered to his tribe, and thus the long war terminated on the evening of the 10th of October, 1875.

Glad shouts from both sides announced all parties equally pleased. The same afternoon the canoe fleet of Uganda, which had by this time been reduced to 275 in number, was escorted as far as Jinja by twenty Wavuma canoes, and after it had departed and rounded Namagongo Point, releasing their late foe from all fear of treachery, the Wavuma canoes presented us with a peaceful exhibition of their dexterity, and gave us an opportunity of viewing them more distinctly than we had previously been able to do through the smoke of gunpowder.

Oct. 15. — We set out next morning, the 15th of October, at three o'clock. We were wakened by the tremendous "Jojussu," the great king of war-drums. Instantly we began to pack up, but I was scarcely dressed before my people rushed up to me, crying that the immense camp was fired in a hundred different places. I rushed out of my hut, and was astounded to see that the flames devoured the grass huts so fast that, unless we instantly departed, we should be burnt along with them. Hastily snatching my pistols, I bade the Waugwana shoulder the goods and follow me as they valued their lives.

The great road from Mtesa's quarters to Nakaranga Point, though 100 feet wide, was rendered impassable by furious, overlapping weaves of fire. There was only one way left, which was up the slope of Nakaranga mountain, and through the camp of the Wasoga. We were not alone in the attempt to escape by this way, for about 60,000 human beings had sought the same path, and were wedged into an almost solid mass, so great was the danger and the anxiety to be away from the cruel sea of fire below.

It was a grand scene, but a truly terrible one; and I thought, as I looked down on it, that the Waganda were now avenging the dead Wavuma with their own hands, for out of a quarter of a million human beings there must have been an immense number of sick unable to move. Besides these, what numbers of witless women and little ones having lost presence of mind must have perished; and how many must have been trampled down by the rush of such a vast number to escape the conflagration! The wide-leaping, far-reaching tongues of flame voraciously eating the dry, tindery material of the huts, and blown by a strong breeze from the lake, almost took my breath away, and several times I felt as if my very vitals were being scorched; but with heads bent low we charged on blindly, knowing no guide save the instinct of self-preservation.

As soon as an opportunity permitted, I looked after the laggards of my party, and by dint of severity kept them together, but three or four were more than half inclined to give in before we breathed cooler air, and could congratulate ourselves upon our safety.

Indignant at such a murderous course, for I mentally taxed Mtesa with this criminal folly, I marched my party far from the route of the Waganda army, and though repeatedly urged by Mtesa to attach myself to his party, I declined to do so until he should explain to me why he had commanded the camp to be fired without giving warning to his people or to myself, his guest. His messenger at once acquitted him of such gross recklessness, and declared that he had arrested several persons suspected of having fired the camp, and that he himself had suffered the loss of goods and women in the flames. I thereupon, glad that he was not the author of the catastrophe, sent my salaams, and a promise to rejoin him at Ugungu, on the Uganda side of the Ripon Falls, which I did on the 18th of October.

CHAPTER XIV.

The Legend of the Blameless Priest — The heroes of Uganda — Chwa — Kimera, the giant — Nakivingi — Kibaga, the flying warrior — Ma'anda — Wakinguru, the champion — Kamanya, the conqueror of the Wakedi — Suna, the cruel — His massacre of the Wasoga — Namujnrilwa, the Achilles of Uganda — Setuba and his lions — Kasindula the hero, peasant, and premier — Mtesa the mild eyed.

Having arrived safely in Uganda, through most extraordinary and novel scenes, I may be permitted to leave the direct narrative of our travels and our life in Uganda in order to inform the reader on certain points of the history of Mtesa's country, beginning with Kiutu, Priest, Patriarch, and first King of Uganda.

Whatever of the incredible or marvellous may be discovered by the learned critic in this chapter must not be debited against the author, but against Sabadu and the elders who are responsible for the tale of Kintu, the wars of Kamanya, Suna, and Mtesa, and the feats of Namujurilwa, Setuba, and Kasindula the heroes, while Mtesa himself furnished me with the names of the kings his forefathers, with many other facts contained in this chapter.

For my part I regret only that want of space compels me to compress what I have gathered of the history of this interesting country into a few pages, but brief as it is, I venture to believe that it will not be without interest to a large class of readers.

Uganda, then, was first peopled by immigrants from the north, about the thirteenth or fourteenth century. But the date at which I thus fix the arrival of the patriarch Kintu may be wrong; he may have arrived at a much early period, and the names of a large number of his successors may have sunk into oblivion.

Tradition, as well as it has been able, has faithfully preserved the memory of the acts of the first of these immigrants, though it has contemptuously omitted the acts of his successors, and, as usual, has contrived to endow its favourites, here as elsewhere, with marvellous power and extraordinary attributes.

Kintu, the first immigrant and the founder of Uganda, came from the north, and perhaps derived his descent from some African Arab or ancient Ethiopia family. He was a mild, humane, and blameless man, and from his character was probably a priest of some old and long forgotten order. He brought with him one wife, one cow, one goat, one sheep, one banana-root, and a sweet potato; and, journeying in search of a suitable land to dwell in, established himself finally on the western bank of the Mwerango river, at Magonga, near the present frontier of Unyoro. He found the country uninhabited, for not a single soul then dwelt in all the land lying between the lakes Victoria and Albert and Muta Nzige. Usoga was a wilderness, Ukedi a desolate plain, and the fertile valleys of Unyoro were unpeopled.

The priest Kintu was alone in his kingdom. But these countries were not destined to remain desolate long, for his wife was remarkably prolific. She brought forth four children at a birth each year, and each male issued into the world with an incipient beard and the powers of lusty prime youth; and the female children at two years of age bore children, who at an equally early age conceived and bore sons and daughters, until the land began to be fully peopled, the forests to be cut down, the land to be cultivated, and planted with bananas and corn.

The single cow, goat, sheep, and chicken increased after their kind by some extraordinary manner, until they grew so numerous that each of the offspring of Kintu soon possessed large herds of cattle, and flocks of sheep and goats, and numerous chickens. The banana-root also, once planted in the soil of Uganda by the holy hands of Kintu, sprang up almost instantly into a stalk of vast girth, from the top of which hung pendent such a cluster of fruit as is not seen in Uganda nowadays, and the root spread itself over a large area, from which hundreds of bananas shot upward with great stalks and all the leafy luxuriance of a large plantation. The potato-plant also vied with the banana, for so great was its vitality that it appeared to crawl over the ground so fast was its growth,

When his offspring had grown so numerous that they crowded Magonga, Kintu cut portions of the original banana-root and potato-plant and gave to each family a portion, and having taught them how "to sow the glebe and plant the generous vine," bade them seek each a home, and establish themselves in the land round about him. Those who received the banana established their home south of Magonga, while those who received the sweet potato-plant migrated to the north of Magonga, and dwelt in the valleys of Unyoro. Hence it is that to this day the people of Uganda, south, and all about Magonga, prefer the banana for food, while the people of Wanyoro have such a predilection for sweet potatoes.

Being a priest, Kintu entertained a special aversion to the shedding of blood, whether of man, animal, bird, or insect, but he did not instruct his offspring to abstain from shedding the blood of beasts. If any animal was to be slain for food, it was ordained that it should be taken far from the neighbourhood of his house, and if a man was to be executed for murder, the executioner dare not slay his victim near Kintu or his house or his garden, neither might the man of blood at any time approach the patriarch's person. If the culprit on his way to execution could contrive to make his way to Kintu's presence and touch his feet or his garments, or were the patriarch even to cast his eyes on him, his life was safe.

When the good patriarch became old, his children forgot to follow his pious example, for from the banana they had discovered the art of making wine and strong drinks, with which they debauched themselves, and, being daily intoxicated, committed indecencies, became violent in language, reckless and hardened in impiety, and, worse than all, so rebellious as to threaten to depose and kill him. Kintu bore this conduct in his unloving children with meekness and sorrow for a long time, but warned them that their impiety and violence would be punished some day; but they heeded him not, for the wine had maddened them.

After a time, finding his admonitions of no avail, he said to his wife, "See my sons whom I brought into this world have become wicked and hard of heart, and they threaten to drive their father away or kill him, for they say I am become old and useless. I am like a hateful stranger amongst my own children. They shed the blood of their brothers daily, and there is nothing but killing and bloodshed now, until I am sick of blood. It is time for us to get away and depart elsewhere. Come, let us go." And in the night Kintu and his wife departed, taking with them their original cow, goat, sheep, chicken, a banana-root, and a sweet potato-plant.

In the morning it became known that their father Kintu was not in his house, nor to be found anywhere, that he had left the country with all the things which he had brought thither when he first arrived. Then all were filled with sorrow, and great lamentation was made throughout the land.

After three days, during which search was instituted far and wide for the lost patriarch, Chwa, the eldest son, took his spear and shield in his hand and said, "I am the first-born, and it is my right to sit in the place of my father. Now you, my brothers, be good and beware of my spear"; and Chwa being strong, his brothers feared him, and paid homage to him as their king.

Chwa did not abandon the search for his father, though he had attained the regal power. He seems to have cherished a hope that in some distant country his father would be discovered, whither he might be able to proceed to him and ask his forgiveness.

A rumour sometimes reached Chwa that his father had been seen, but none of his several messengers succeeded in seeing him, and he at last died without the hope being gratified.

Chwa was succeeded by his son Kamiera, a name to this day retained by the members of the imperial family. Like his father Chwa, Kamiera searched for the patriarch Kintu until his own death, without success.

Kamiera was succeeded by his gigantic son Kimera, who distinguished himself as a hunter. He first introduced dogs for the chase, and was so fond of them that he always led one by the cord wherever he went. It was from this king that his successors inherited their partiality for the canine race, and in the memory of many yet living Suna is remembered for his extraordinary attachment to dogs, for the special subsistence of which he surrendered whole districts. Mtesa was also seen by Speke showing great fondness for a dog, but the present monarch has long ago abandoned this traditional predilection, and he now prohibits their presence in his court.

Kimera was of such size, strength, and weight that his feet made marks in rocks, and the impress of one of his feet is shown to this day by the antiquarians of Uganda in a rock situated not far from the capital, Ulagalla. It is said that this mark was made by one of his feet slipping while he was in the act of launching his spear at an elephant. Kimera also explored countries remote and near, searching all the forests, the wilderness, the plains, the fastnesses of the mountains, the summits of hills and the caves, and travelled along all the river-banks in vain quest for the lost Kintu.

The fact seemed to be impressed on the minds of all that Kintu was only lost, not dead, that he was immortal, and Kimera, even more than his predecessors, was indefatigable in his efforts to verify this belief. He led in person large expeditions, and offered great rewards to peasants, promising to make him who discovered Kintu next to the king in power — the Katekiro of Uganda. But he likewise failed in the search, and finally died.

Almass (which name, if Arabic, rendered into English, means "Diamond") succeeded Kimera the hunter. This king's name is a favourite one among the Arabs, which I take to be further evidence that the founder of the Uganda monarchy had Asiatic blood in his veins. Of Almass, tradition says nothing save that, like his father, he hoped to find Kintu. On his death he was succeeded by his son Tembo.

After Tembo came Kigara, Wanpaudia, Kaeema, and Nakivingi, the last being remembered for his heroic valour and many conquests.

Nakivingi fought and subjected the Wanyoro, who, from their predilection for sweet potatoes, may have deemed themselves long ago a separate people from the Waganda, a theory by no means supported by the authority of venerable tradition.

After Nakivingi we have a long list of kings, about whom tradition, fable, and history are all alike silent. Morondo succeeded Nakivingi — the Charlemagne of Uganda — and after him followed Sekamanya, Jemba, Suna I., Kimbugwe, Katerega, Ntewi, and Juko. This last, it is said, had a headstrong, violent, and disobedient son, named Kyemba, whom he was obliged to pacify with the island of Uvuma, whence afterwards he appeared in Uganda, deposed his father Juko, and, slaying him, reigned in his stead.

One of the heroes of Nakivingi was a warrior named Kibaga, who possessed the power of flying. When the king warred with the Wanyoro, he sent Kibaga into the air to ascertain the whereabouts of the foe, who, when discovered by this extraordinary being, were attacked on land in their hiding-places by Nakivingi, and from above by the active and faithful Kibaga, who showered great rocks on them, and by these means slew a vast number.

It happened that among the captives of Unyoro Kibaga saw a beautiful woman, who was solicited by the king in marriage. As Nakivingi was greatly indebted to Kibaga for his unique services, he gave her to Kibaga as wife, with a warning, however, not to impart the knowledge of his power to her, lest she should betray him. For a long time after marriage his wife knew nothing of his power, but suspecting something strange in him from his repeated sudden absences and reappearances at his home, she set herself to watch him, and one morning as he left his hut she was surprised to see him suddenly mount into the air with a burden of rocks slung on his back. On seeing this she remembered the Wanyoro complaining that more of their people were killed by some means from above than by the spears of Nakivingi, and, Delilah-like, loving her race and her people more than she loved her husband, she hastened to her people's camp, and communicated, to the surprise of the Wanyoro, what she had that day learned.

To avenge themselves on Kibaga, the Wanyoro set archers in ambush on the summits of each lofty hill, with instructions to confine themselves to watching the air and listening for the brushing of his wings, and to shoot their arrows in the direction of the sound, whether anything was seen or not. By this means on a certain day, as Nakivingi marched to the battle, Kibaga was wounded to the death by an arrow, and upon the road large drops of blood were seen falling, and on coming to a tall tree the king detected a dead body entangled in its branches. When the tree was cut down, Nakivingi saw to his infinite sorrow that it was the body of his faithful flying warrior Kibaga.

Succeeding Kyemba came Tibandeke, Mdowra, Kaguru, Kikuruwe, and Ma'anda. It was the fortune of this last king to discover news of the lost Kintu, after a most remarkable and romantic manner.

Though history and fable are silent respecting the acts of many of Ma'anda's predecessors, we may well believe that each king made efforts to discover the missing Kintu, as the belief that he was still alive obtained as firm credence in the reign of Ma'anda as in the days of Chwa and Kimera. With Ma'anda this belief was very strong, and spurred by the hope that some day it would be his happy fortune to be successful, he was ardent in the chase, penetrating great forests, and traversing extensive plains and valleys, ostensibly to hunt game, but really to hunt up news of Kintu.

It happened one day, after returning to his capital from one of these expeditions, that a peasant living not far off was compelled from lack of fuel for his family to enter a forest to cut wood. Having over-exerted himself, and being very much fatigued, and his home being far, he resolved to sleep in the forest, near his wood pile. For the sake of security and uninterrupted sleep he constructed a rude hut, and fenced it round with the branches of the prostrate trees, and when it was completed he laid himself down and slept.

And a sound sleep it was, we may imagine, induced by hard labour and fatigue, though not a dreamless one. For in his sleep, it is said, he dreamed a strange dream, wherein he thought he heard a voice, which said, "Go to a place in this forest, where the trees are very thick, round an open space near a stream running by, and you will there see something which will give you great wealth, and make you a great chief." Three times the dream was repeated. These words caused the heart of the sleeping peasant to bound for joy; so much so that it woke him, and then he began to regret that the good which was promised him was but a dream and a mockery. But reflecting that he knew the place described, for he had often been there, and that it was not very far off, he thought he might as well obey the voice in the dream, if only for the sake of satisfying his curiosity. He had dreamed the same dream thrice, and each time the voice had been emphatic and precise, and he thought that there might be something of truth conveyed in it.

After a few hours' hurried travel, he approached the place described, and his movements towards the spot became now very cautious, lest some event might occur quite the reverse of his hopes, as dreams sometimes go by contraries. He heard the murmur and gurgle of the stream, and the soughing of the branches of the forest overhead in such a solitary place filled his heart with awe. He began to feel frightened, though he knew not at what, and was more than half inclined to turn hack. Yet this eerie feeling and alarm might be causeless; he therefore advanced into the open space, and suddenly he saw there a sight that almost petrified him.

Ranged in two rows, on either side of a venerable man, who reclined on a kind of throne, were many warriors seated on mats. They held spears and shields in their hands, and the complexion of these men was so light as to resemble that of white men. The central figure on the throne was that of an old man, whose long beard was white with age, and his complexion was similar to the warriors seated on the mats. All were clothed in spotless white robes.

For a time no man spoke, though all eyes were turned on the astonished and awed peasant, and regarded him with a stern and awful gaze. Finally, the silence was broken by the voice of the old man, which sounded to the peasant like that which he had heard in the dream, and it said, "Peasant, tell me what country this is."

The peasant answered, trembling, and perspiring through excessive fear, "Eh, don't you know? This is Uganda."

"And who was the first king?" demanded the old man. "Come tell me his name?"

"Kintu," answered the peasant.

"True," said the old man. "Now tell me the name of the present king."

"Ma'anda," replied the peasant.

"Well then, depart instantly, and haste to Ma'anda the king, and bid him come to Kintu, who shall be here to meet him, for Ma'anda has long searched for Kintu, and Kintu has somewhat to tell Ma'anda. Bid him come hither accompanied only by his mother and thyself, and mark me, not even his dog must follow him. Haste and tell King Ma'anda all thou hast seen and heard, and if thou art faithful, thy reward shall be great."

The peasant needed to hear no more, but turned and fled away with the speed of an antelope, and early at dawn next day arrived at the capital, and proceeded direct to the Katekiro, to whom he said, "I have news to tell King Ma'anda, and no man else must hear it. Take me to the king without delay."

The man's manner, though he was mean in appearance, was peremptory, and the Katekiro dared not refuse his request, but rose and conducted him to the king.

It happened, strangely enough, that at the same moment Ma'anda was relating to his mother, whom he had sent for, the story of a strange dream he had dreamed during the night. He had scarcely finished its relation when the Katekiro was announced, who said to him, "King, here is a strange man, a peasant, I believe, who states that he has important news to tell thee, and thee alone," which when the king heard, and had seen the peasant, he said to his mother, "Lo! now, this is the very man I saw in my dream, who told me such wonderful news."

Then turning eagerly to the peasant, he said to him, "Speak, man what is it thou hast to say to me?"

"O, king," he replied, "I may not speak except to thee and thy mother, for so have I been commanded."

Then Ma'anda impatiently commanded the Katekiro to retire and, that they might not be disturbed, to set a guard at the outer gate, so that on no account either man, woman, or child might enter the inner court.

When they were quite alone, the peasant began to unfold to Ma'anda his story from the beginning to the end, just as it is told here, concluding with the old man's words: "Bid the king come with his mother and thyself, and, mark me. not even his dog must follow him."

On hearing this news, Ma'anda said, "Come, let us go, only us three, for so the old man said," and taking his spear and shield, the king strode out of the inner court through a private gate followed by his mother and the peasant without communicating to a soul else whither he was going.

Despite this secrecy, however, it soon became publicly known that King Ma'anda and his mother had left the palace, accompanied by a peasant, and that they had taken the direction of the forest, towards which they had been seen travelling with rapid steps by one who communicated the information to the Katekiro.

This news plunged the principal chief of the kingdom into a state of perplexity. He was for a moment at a loss what to do, for had his master desired any other company he would undoubtedly have made it known; but, on the other hand, this conduct was inexplicable, and the king might have been lured by some cunning plausible tale to proceed in this manner, whereby he might be destroyed without detection.

As the thought of treachery to the king flashed through his mind, he instantly resolved to follow him and watch after his safety, and should the peasant mean harm to him, he would be at hand, though unsuspected, to assist his master. He therefore seized his spear and shield, and sped away after the king in stealthy pursuit. Soon he discovered the king, the king's mother, and the peasant, and, slackening his steps, sought only to keep them in view, and to elude the quick, searching glances which he saw the king frequently dart behind him. They travelled in this manner all that day and half of the next day, when the peasant informed the king that they were approaching the appointed place.

The king, to assure himself that they had not been followed by any one, looked keenly around once more, and having satisfied himself that they were alone, he commanded the peasant to move on and point out the meeting-place. Gliding under the shadows of the dense grove surrounding the open space, they soon emerged from them, and were in front of the extraordinary assembly, who appeared to have preserved the same posture and attitude since the departure of the peasant on his errand to the king.

As the three advanced near the extremity of the rows of seated warriors, the old man on the throne asked the king, who was in advance, and gazing on the scene with the greatest astonishment, "Who art thou?"

"I am Ma'anda," he replied.

"Art thou the king?"

"I am."

"And who is that woman with thee?" the old man demanded.

"My mother," the king answered.

"It is well," said he; "but how is it you did not observe what I commanded? Why came ye not alone?"

"We have done exactly as we were told," said the king.

"There are only my mother and this peasant with me, for no one knew of my departure."

"But I have seen another man behind thee," persisted the old man. "Tell me who he is?"

"Rest assured," said Ma'anda, "there is no man save this peasant with me, for yesterday and to-day I looked several times behind me to make sure that I was not followed."

"Who was the first king of Uganda?" suddenly asked the old man.

"Kintu," answered Ma'anda.

"Thou sayest truly," said the old man slowly and deliberately; "and Kintu was good. He injured no man, beast, bird, or insect, and no living thing had cause to complain of him. He never even struck a man with a stick, or caused him pain in any manner, for he loved his children like a kind father should; but his sons grew exceedingly wicked, headstrong, disobedient, and utterly unmanageable. They loved to shed blood. They first slaughtered beasts, and became so accustomed to blood that at last they slew their brothers and sisters. They became so madly in love with blood that they wished to shed that of their good father Kintu. Then Kintu saw that Uganda was no more a land for him, that it was unfit for him to live in, and, oh! when he looked on the face of the land at first, it was so fair and pure that it delighted his eyes, but when it became red and filthy with the blood of innocent men and women and children, it became hateful to Kintu, and he departed from the horrid, cruel land. From Chwa down to Ma'anda each king has sought to find Kintu, though in vain. Thou, Ma'anda, shalt see Kintu face to face, and thou shalt hear him speak; but first I have somewhat to tell thee from him. Listen, and mark well his words — but tell me who was that man that followed thee hither?" he suddenly asked.

Ma'anda, well pleased that he of all his predecessors was selected to see and converse with Kintu, had become all attention, and every fibre and nerve quivered to hear the prelude to the introduction; but when interrogated by the old man again upon a subject already satisfactorily answered, he asked impatiently, "Why dost thou ask again when I have already told thee that no man followed me here, because no man could have known whither I went?"

"But I," said the old man calmly, "saw a man follow thee step by step. Why didst thou let him come, when I expressly told thee thou must come only with thy mother and this peasant?"

The king's mother and the peasant declared that Ma'anda had spoken truly, and that no man followed them.

"I saw him behind that tree listening. Behold! there he stands," said the old man, suddenly pointing to the Katekiro, who, perceiving that he was discovered, now came forward.

The three turned their eyes on hearing the words of the old man, and at the sight of the Katekiro, Ma'anda grew desperately enraged, and with passionate fury he seized his spear, launched it, and pierced his faithful servant through the heart, who with a short, sharp shriek, fell dead at his feet.

But, lo! when King Ma'anda and his companions turned to discover what effect this scene had upon the old man and the seated warriors, they found that they had vanished, and that not even the slightest trace of them was left; at which the three stared at one another in the wildest astonishment. Then the king, recovering from his surprise, fell upon the ground and wept aloud, calling upon the name of Kintu; and the king's mother and the peasant added their cries to his, and wept as if their hearts would break. But no blood-hating Kintu answered to them, only the tall deep woods echoed their cries, "Kintu, Kintu-u, Kintu-u-u-u," as if in mockery of their sorrow.

All night they kept watch, breaking out now and then into moaning and wailings for the last loss of the great father of Uganda. But Kintu, after this scene, never more appeared in Uganda, and to this day he has not been seen or heard of by any man.

After Ma'anda's death succeeded Msangi, Namugara, and Chabagu. In the time of this latter king flourished Wakinguru, a hero, whose name history, cherished within the memories of admiring men, has preserved for his unparalleled deeds. When Chabagu invaded Usoga, it appears that the Wasoga were very numerous, and, having as yet never been reduced to submission by the Waganda, very bold and fearless. The people of Usoga mocked the victorious Waganda until Chabagu was roused to declare war upon them; and to show them the prowess of the people whom they had so insolently defied Chabagu permitted Wakinguru to cross over to Jinja alone, that he might exhibit the warlike qualities of his nation in his own person.

Wakinguru, we are led to believe, was a man of herculean frame, and we may well suppose him gifted with more than common courage. He marched to the height of Jinja with a large bundle of spears on his back, and his shield was so ample and thick that it required two ordinary men to lift it.

Arriving at a place where he could command a clear view of the Wasoga camp, he shouted out a bold challenge to any man, or to all at once, to approach him, that he might show them what manner of men were those who had been so frequently insulted by them. Several of the Wasoga, responding to the challenge, rushed up to try his mettle, but Wakinguru's spears were so formidable, and his strength so great, that long before any of the foe came within distance permitting an ordinary man to launch his spear, they were all dead men. The hero then plucked his spears from the corpses, and prepared to meet the next party, who came up in hot haste to avenge the deaths of their friends. Again the redoubtable man launched his fatal spears, and again the Wasoga had to lament the deaths of their champions.

Enraged by this, the Wasoga at length advanced in a body, and formed a large circle round him; but Wakinguru only laughed at this manoeuvre, and continued remorselessly slaying, launching his whirring lengthy shafts with the most deadly effect; and then, picking up the spears of his enemies, with which the ground near him was plentifully strewn, he returned their own weapons to them, launching them with the swiftness and certainty of arrows. His strength sustained him in this unequal contest from sunrise to sunset, when it was discovered that Wakinguru had slain 600 men with his own hand! At night he crossed Jinja (or the Falls) to Ugungu unharmed, where he refreshed himself with the bananas and milk and water of Uganda, and where he received the warmest congratulations from King Chabagu and his army.

Next morning Wakinguru renewed the battle, and it continued throughout the whole of the second day, during which time the hero slew a similar number; and on the third day also he fought with the same success, until at last the Wasoga confessed that they were unable to meet him.

Then King Chabagu crossed the water above Jinja (Napoleon Channel), and completed the conquest of Usoga.

After Chabagu succeeded Junju, Waseje, and Kamanya. This last king, grandfather of the present monarch, is remembered for his victories over the Wakedi a most ferocious and warlike people occupying country north of Usoga. The Wakedi, it is said, wore armour, and employed in their wars an immense number of great dogs, as large as young lions. Besides, the country of the Wakedi was surrounded by broad rivers or small lakes, and these several advantages had made the Wakedi rather feared by the Waganda. But vexed by the repeated forays made by them into the very heart of his country, and the impunity with which they carried them, Kamanya determined to prosecute a war against them until one side or the other should be declared beyond doubt the stronger. For this purpose he assembled his chiefs, and, having stated the advantages of situation which Ukedi enjoyed against attack, commanded them to advise him as to the means and ways of conducting the campaign.

Stimulated by large rewards, the chiefs proposed various tactics for retaliating upon the enemy; but it was the plan of the grandfather of Sabadu the historian that was deemed the best. This person advised Kamanya to command 100 canoes to proceed by water to Jinja, where they might be taken to pieces and conveyed overland through Usoga to the Nagombwa river, whence, after reconstruction, they could proceed to attack the Wakedi in the rear, while the king himself could proceed with his army to Urondogani, along the western bank of the Victoria Nile, and menace Ukedi from that side. This wise counsel was loudly applauded and at once adopted, the charge of the canoes being given to Sabadu's grandfather himself.

The Wakedi, as might be imagined, attacked in such an unlooked-for direction, were greatly surprised and discouraged. They fled for refuge to their fenced villages, leaving their cattle in the hands of the Waganda, who drove them across the Nagombwa to Usoga. The vengeance of the Waganda not being yet complete, they proceeded to attack the Wakedi in their fenced villages, using red-hot arrows wrapped in bark cloth, by which the straw huts were set on fire, and the inhabitants driven out to meet the spears of the Waganda.

Perceiving that the presence of Kamanya on the opposite bank of the Nile was only a ruse, the Wakedi concentrated their forces to drive the Waganda who had come by way of the Nagombwa out of the country. When the two nations met, a desperate battle ensued, rather to the disadvantage of the Waganda, for the enemy wore iron armour, which their spears could not penetrate.

After consultation, it was decided by the Waganda that at the next battle they would not waste their time in launching their spears, but would rush on the foe with naked hands and capture and bind them.

Having received large reinforcements, the Waganda resumed the battle, but instead of throwing their spears they simply defended their bodies with their shields, and rushing on their encumbered adversaries, seized and bound them with cords. Perceiving that affairs were becoming desperate for them, the Wakedi mustered all their war-hounds, which, while the Waganda were engaged with their masters, rushed upon them from all sides, with their large mouths wide open, barking tremendously, and bit and tore them in such a manner that the Waganda became stricken with panic, and fled to their canoes. The hounds, with their fury unappeased, rushed after the canoes into the water, where an immense number of them were easily slaughtered by the Waganda, whose senses, it appears, were by this time collected. Fearing that they would lose all their faithful war-hounds, the Wakedi recalled their dogs, paid tribute, and acknowledged the superiority and supremacy of the Waganda, and to this day the Wakedi have been true to their allegiance.

As we arrive nearer our own times, the history of Uganda becomes, of course, more precise and trustworthy. Thus, when we come to Suna II., the son of Kamanya, and predecessor and father of Mtesa, we are told that he was about sixteen years of age when he succeeded to his father, and about forty when he died, and that he reigned, therefore, twenty-four years. As Mtesa ascended the throne in his nineteenth year, and as he has already reigned fifteen years (up to 1875), Suna must have been born in 1820, begun to reign in 1836, and died in 1860.

Suna, so his intimate friends still alive told me, was short of stature and of very compact build, most despotic and cruel, but brave and warlike.

He had a peculiar habit, it is said, of sitting with his head bent low, seldom looking up. His attitude seemed to be that of one intently tracing designs on the ground, though in reality he was keenly alive to all that was transpiring around him. He frequently beheaded his people by hundreds. It is reported that one day he executed 800 people of Uganda for a single crime committed. Other punishments which he inflicted were dreadful, such as gouging out eyes, and slitting ears, noses, and lips. It is said that he so seldom lifted his eyes from the ground that whenever he did look up at a person, the executioners, called "Lords of the Cord," understood it as a sign of condemnation.

Any messenger arriving with news was compelled to crawl on his knees, and in this position to whisper it into the king's ears. Whenever he passed along a path, the announcement, "Suna is coming," sufficed to send the people flying in a panic from the neighbourhood.

To strangers from other countries he was most liberal and hospitable, and many Arab traders have had cause to bless the good fortune that conducted them to Uganda in the days of Suna.

This Emperor, or Kabaka, as the rulers of Uganda, after their vast conquest, were styled, was also exceedingly fond of dogs. For the sustenance of one of his pets he caused an entire district to be cultivated and planted with the sweet potato, which was its favourite diet; and when it died, he caused each chief to contribute bark-cloths for its burial.

He also kept a lion and a leopard, and another animal which, from its description, I take to have been either a species of wolf or lynx; the two former became quite tame, but the latter was so incorrigibly fierce that he finally ordered it to be destroyed.

From such a disposition as that of Suna, it was natural that he should engage in frequent wars, and from his determined and resolute character we cannot be surprised to hear that they were most bloody and terrible. He conquered Ankori, overran Unyoro and Usoga, and was the first to conquer the united nations of Uzongora. The lion-hearted Wavuma owned him as their liege lord; even distant

Ruanda heard of his name, tried him in battle, and became convinced of his greatness. The details of the two last wars in which Suna was engaged I have collected, and present them here, as told by Sabadu, from which the reader may perceive for himself the character of this monarch and the general nature of wars in Central Africa.

Suna heard that Usoga had rebelled and refused to pay tribute to him, whereupon, after rendering homage and dues to the Muzimu, or spirits, he levied a vast army and marched to Jinja, or the rocks overlooking the Ripon Falls, where he rested four days. The Wasoga, upon Suna's advance, fled to Kitenteh Island (situate in the channel between Uvuma and Usoga, about seven miles from Nakaranga Cape). On this island the Wasooa placed their women and children, and large herds of cattle, and it was evident from the measures they adopted that they intended to make a desperate and prolonged resistance.

After marching through Usoga, he camped on the mainland, about half a mile from Kitenteh Island. The Wavuma, responding to his command to muster their canoes for the war, supplied him with over 100, manned by natives of Uziri, Wema, and Kibibi; Lulamba, Irwaji, and Sesse Islands supplied him with 200; while from the Uganda coast he obtained 200 more; so that, in all, Suna had 500 canoes for the war.

Usoga, an extensive country of itself, did its best to meet the monarch of Uganda with a large and powerful fleet, and, assisted by its islands, Namungi and Neygano; as also by Usuguru, Chaga, Muiwanda, and Ugana, was able to match Suna's fleet, canoe for canoe.

But the spirit which animated the warriors of the two nations differed greatly. On the one side was the determination to win freedom; on the other a monarch resolved to retain in subjection, but lacking people to meet the Wasoga on the water, and only able to compel his warriors to fight at all on that element by the most horrible threats and the inspiration of terror.

Having assembled his fleet, Suna ordered the assault; but the Wasoga met the Waganda in the channel, and after a desperate battle drove the Waganda in precipitate retreat to the mainland. For the period of a month repeated efforts were made to effect a landing on the island, but the Wasoga, with great spirit and bravery, repelled the Waganda with severe loss. The Wasoga also, adding insult to injury, were accustomed to approach the mainland and taunt the king with bitter words, telling him to seek the graves of Kaguru and Kamanya, and bury himself there for very shame. At length, enraged by these taunts, Suna called his chiefs to him, and in assembly assailed them with bitter reproaches, and asking them if he was not the Emperor, and if Emperor, why the Wasoga were permitted to taunt him, and stung to frenzy by the memory of the insults lately received, commanded his chiefs to man their canoes on the morrow and assault the island, threatening them, if they failed, with roasting, decapitation, and utter destruction.

The chiefs prostrated themselves one after another, and swore to set their feet on Kitenteh Island the next day. The morrow came, and each chief was in his canoe with his most chosen warriors. The battle ensued, but only four chiefs were true to their promise — the Katekiro, Namujurilwa, and two others of equal bravery and eminence. The Katekiro on landing killed two with his spear at one thrust, so great was the throng of Wasoga who rushed against him. Namujurilwa's spear was plunged through three at a time, but unable to draw his weapon out, he was attacked by a Msoga, who with his javelin pinned both his arms, and he was only saved by a rush of his own men, who bore him away to his canoe. The two other chiefs slew two men each, and were obliged to retire, being unsupported by their people. Many other chiefs distinguished themselves, and many died fighting in the attempt to land on the island.

The Wasoga had formed themselves into four ranks on this day. The first comprised the slingers, and the second the spearmen, the third, on higher ground, slingers again, and the fourth a reserve of spearmen, for the final and supreme struggle.

For three successive days the chiefs of Uganda led in person the Waganda to the assault, until finally the queen's father requested Suna not to sacrifice all his chiefs while the peasants were standing idle spectators. Suna yielded to his request, and perceiving that bravery was of no avail against the desperate Wasoga, he adopted the plan of surrounding the island day and night with his canoes, and starving the rebels into submission. What food the unfortunate Wasoga were able to obtain was inadequate for their wants, and colt them much trouble and many lives, both on shore, in distant parts of the coast, and in the channel, for Suna had constructed large camps along the coast of Usoga, and his canoes kept strict watch and ward over Kitenteh Island.

For two months the Wasoga endured this state of things, but at the end of that period, being reduced to the verge of absolute starvation, four of their chiefs approached the camp of Suna with offers of submission. Suna refused to see them, but gave them thirty head of cattle to convey to the island, with a request to the chiefs to eat, and think well first of what they offered, promising that, if on the fourth day they were still of the same mind, he would be willing to talk with them.

At the end of the fourth day twenty chiefs came over from Kitenteh Island, stating that they were willing to submit to Suna, to pay tribute, and to render service. He received them graciously, and ordered them to commence the next day, with the assistance of his own canoes, the transportation of the Wasoga to his camp, in order that they might all render their submission to him.

For three days, it is said, the Waganda and Wasoga canoes were engaged in this service, and as fast as the Wasoga arrived they were conducted to a large stockade erected expressly for them during the night of the surrender. On the fourth day, his late enemies being all in his camp, surrounded by his own people, he called their chiefs and told them he would be gratified if they and their warriors would perform their war-dance before him next day. Unsuspecting evil, they willingly promised.

Suna after their departure to the stockade instructed the Waganda chiefs to bring all their people, early next morning, each man supplied with a cord, and to form them in two ranks four deep, and when he gave the signal, to fall upon the Wasoga and bind them. On the morning of the fifth day the Waganda were all drawn up as instructed, and the Wasoga, seeing nothing in this but Suna's desire of showing his power and pomp, and without the least idea what this war-dance portended to them, marched within the fatal lines, armed only with sticks, as had been agreed — upon the cunning plea that the Waganda might take offence at seeing them play with edged weapons before Suna. They were the more completely thrown off their guard by the kindness shown to them by the Emperor and by the liberal supplies of cattle and bananas supplied to them since their surrender.

We can imagine how the unhappy Wasoga advanced smiling into Suna's presence on this great day, and how, wishing to please the fearful despot, they danced to the best of their power. But on a sudden, while they were exerting their voices (30,000 is the number given) into a grand swelling chorus at the triumphal finale of the fictitious war which they had been representing, Suna gave the signal, and 100,000 Waganda warriors fell upon them, and despite their fearful, desperate struggles — when all too late the treachery of Suna became apparent — bound them hand and foot.

Out of this immense number of prisoners, sixty of the principal chiefs were selected and placed before Suna, who said to them: — "For three months you have kept me and my people waiting for your submission; you rebelled against my authority, and attempted to throw off your allegiance; you have slain more than half of my principal chiefs, and you have vexed me with taunts, telling me to go and seek the graves of Kaguru and Kamanya, and to hide myself there for shame. You have mocked me — me who am called Suna — Suna, the Emperor (Kabaka). I go to my grave by-and-by, but by the grave of my father Kamanya you shall die to-day, and you may tell your fathers that Suna the Emperor sent you to them."

Then turning to the Waganda, he fiercely shouted, "Cut them to little pieces, and pile their remains on the plain without the camp." As Suna commanded, so was it done, and the Waganda were employed on this monstrous work for five days, for they obeyed his command literally, and, beginning at the legs and arms, hacked their victims to pieces without taking the trouble to despatch them first.

Usoga, upon hearing of this terrible deed, sent all its principal men and chiefs to implore pardon and proffer submission and allegiance, which Suna was pleased to accept. This event closed the war, and Suna returned to his palace in Uganda with a train of 5000 female captives and 8000 children.

Soon after his return to Uganda the Wasoga rebelled a second time under the leadership of Eura, chief of Nakaranga, upon hearing which Suna smiled grimly and said, "Eura has taken much time to make up his mind; since he has waited so long let him wait a little longer, and I will show him who his master is."

Meantime Namujurilwa, chief of Uddu, after returning to visit his home, heard that his neighbour the king of Ankori or Usagara was preparing to invade his country with a mighty force. Ever prompt for mischief and war, Namujurilwa did not wait to meet the Wasagara on his own soil, but beat his war-drum, and, mustering his followers, marched through Bwera and penetrated into the very heart of Ankori, and there surprised his enemies, assembled under five princes, in their own camp.

Namujurilwa fell upon them with a ferocity and vigour that the numerical superiority of his enemies could not equal. For five hours the battle lasted without intermission or advantage to either side, when Namujurilwa was accidentally met by one of the princes of Ankori.

"Not dead yet, Namujurilwa?" cried the prince. "Wait a little for me," saying which he took a bow from one of his servants and shot an arrow which hit the border of the tough double bull-hide shield which the chief of Uddu generally carried.

Namujurilwa did not wait for a second arrow, but bounded forward, crying out, "No, not dead yet, prince" (Mlanglra), "and shall not die until I have killed you," and forthwith launched his dirk-pointed spear, which pinned both the shield and body of the unfortunate youth.

Another prince coming up and observing his brother fall, shot an arrow, and pierced the leopard-skin of the Uddu chief, who returned the compliment with one of his long spears, which penetrated his body and protruded far through his back. The death of these two princes decided the battle, for the Wasagara became panic-stricken and fled, leaving a vast spoil of cattle and effects in the conqueror's hands.

Upon returning to Uddu from the war, the victorious chief sent 300 women, 600 children of both sexes, and 1000 head of cattle to the Emperor Suna, as his share of the spoil, who on viewing the magnificent gift said to his chiefs in assembly, "Truly, Namujurilwa is brave, there is none like him in Uganda."

Setuba, a great chief, holding under Suna an extensive tract of country bordering upon Unyoro, whispered to his neighbour, "H'm, you hear how Suna praises Namujurilwa; let us go to Unyoro and show Suna that he has other chiefs as brave as Namujurilwa."

Requesting and obtaining leave of the Emperor to visit his own country, Setuba soon left the capital, and after arriving at his chief village, beat his war-drum and summoned his people to war.

Taking with him 300 head of cattle, he crossed the frontier of Unyoru, where he slew his cattle and made his followers eat beef to make themselves strong. Having devoured the meat, his people informed Setuba that they were now as strong as lions and all prepared for war.

Setuba smiled and said to them, "I have given you 300 head of my own cattle; go and bring me 3000 head and I shall consider that you have paid me for what you have eaten."

The warriors responded to Setuba's words with a shout, and at once set out to collect spoil from the Wanyoro, while Setuba and a chosen band remained in camp. The Waganda, however, were promptly met by the Wanyoro in considerable numbers, and after a few hours were defeated and pursued as far as Setuba's camp.

The chief received the fugitives sternly and said, "Where are those lions whom I lately fed with, my cattle? Are you about to return to Uganda with empty hands? Yes, go on, and as you fly proclaim that Setuba, your chief, is dead." Saying which Setuba seized his spears and shield, and followed by his chosen band bounded out of his camp to meet the advancing Wanyora.

Fired with indignation and shame, Setuba soon met the Wanyora, and began flinging his spears with splendid effect. With his first spear he killed three, with the second he slew two more. The fugitives, seeing the vigour and courage of their chief, halted, and began to ask of one another, "Who dares go and tell Suna that Setuba is dead? Let us fight and die with Setuba."

The word "Setuba, tuba, tuba!" became a war-cry, echoed fiercely far and near, turning the fugitives on their pursuers, who in a short time became the pursued. For two days the Waganda rioted in the blood of the now terror-stricken Wanyora, who were finally compelled to fly to the summit of the mountains for refuge, leaving their families and cattle in the valleys to be swept away by the fierce Waganda.

On returning to Uganda Setuba sent 2000 women, 4000 children, and 2000 heads of cattle, besides goats and sheep without number, to the Emperor as his share, and Setuba heard Suna declare proudly that he knew of no monarch who could show heroes to equal Setuba and Namujurilwa, and that his heart was big with pride.

There stood that day, when the Emperor publicly mentioned with praise the names of Setuba and Namujurilwa, a young man listening to him, who from that moment resolved to eclipse both chiefs. His name was Kasindula, a sub-chief or Mtongoleh of the great Sekebobo's country of Chagwe, who had neither pride of birth nor riches to boast of. He was a mere worthy young fellow, who had distinguished himself in a few engagements under Sekebobo, for which the old chief had promoted him from a peasant (kopi) to be a sub-chief (mtongoleh).

A few days after the great levee of Suna, Kasindula proceeded to Sekebobo, and requested him to ask permission of the Emperor that he should be allowed to rebuild his majesty's camp at Jinja, as many of the huts were in a most ruinous state, and many of Suna's women were compelled to sleep in the open air.

Sekebobo introduced Kasindula to the Emperor, and preferred his request to him, who graciously acceded to it, adding that it was not every day that men came to ask leave to do him a service: they generally asked him for some gift or other.

Kasindula was profuse in his thanks, and then departed with 2000 men from Sekebobo to assist him in the work of reconstructing the imperial camp at Jinja, and the kind old chief also gave him several large canoes, to transport the working force across Napoleon Channel.

The young chief lost no time after his arrival at Jinja, but industriously set to work, and in a few days had entirely rebuilt the houses, and surrounded them with their respective courts, and had cleared the whole camp from much accumulated rubbish, until the camp would have pleased even fastidious Suna himself.

He then caused the war-drum to be sounded, and, responding to its ominous call, all who were capable of lifting the spear, dwelling in the neighbourhood of Jinja, gathered round Kasindula, who said: —

"Warriors of Uganda and children of Suna, listen to me. You know how, after Suna slew the rebellious Wasoga before Kitenteh Island, that the chiefs of Usoga all came and swore allegiance to him; and how, when Suna had returned to Uganda, the Wasoga chief Kura headed another rebellion, and challenged Suna to return to Usoga to fight him. When Suna heard the challenge of the boastful Kura, he only smiled, and said, 'Let him wait a little.' Suna is too great to fight with Rura, for Kasindula, a Mtongoleh of Sekebobo, is sufficient for him. To-night we march to Nakaranga, and to-morrow morning before sunrise Rura shall sleep with his brothers who died before Kitenteh. Warriors, prepare yourselves!"

Though Nakaranga was fully thirty miles from Jinja, Kasindula had reached about midnight the principal village of the chief, and after surrounding it with his people, fired the huts at daybreak, thus expelling the sleeping Wasoga from them, to fall by the spears of the ambushed Waganda. Having made clean work of all Rura's district, Kasindula gathered the spoil, and long before noon was far on his return to Jinja.

The Usoga confederacy, hearing of this raid and of the death of Rura and his sons, hurried to Nakaranga to avenge the slaughter, but they found only black desolation and emptiness in Rura's district, while the raiders had escaped in safety to Jinja, whither they dared not follow them, and accordingly returned, each chief to his own district.

After a few days' rest Kasindula made another raid in a totally different direction with similar results, and again the Wasoga hurried up, only to find the houses all consumed, the warriors all dead, and the women and children and cattle all deported away.

"What manner of man is this," asked the astonished Wasoga of one another, "who comes in the night, like a hyena, and vanishes with the daylight, with his maw gorged with blood?" Consoling themselves, however, with a vow to be revenged on him at a fitting opportunity, they returned again to their own districts.

But hard upon their heels followed the wary and resolute Kasindula; and again he destroyed an entire district, with all its males, and carried the women and children into captivity. This news was too disheartening to the Wasoga, for now they began to dread that they would be utterly destroyed in detail, whereupon, perceiving that their principal chiefs were all dead, they sent an embassy to Suna, with a tribute of the most comely women and a large quantity of maramba, asking his forgiveness.

Kasindula, meanwhile, finding his hands full of spoil, collected all together, and drove his captives and cattle, by forced marches, to Suna, who, warned of his approach, prepared to receive him in state and in a full assembly of the chiefs.

Having arranged the women and children by thousands before him, and parked the cattle in full view of the Emperor, Kasindula, clad in a humble and dingy bark cloth, prostrated himself before him and said: —

"Great Kabaka, I went to Jinja, and built your camp, and housed your women as you commanded me; and hearing how Namujurilwa and Setuba had avenged you on the Wasagara and Wanyoro, I thought myself strong enough to answer the challenge sent by Rura and his friends to you.

"My dear lord, Namujurilwa and Setuba are great chiefs, and stand in your presence daily, but I am only a Mtongoleh under Sekebobo. I have neither farm nor house, wife nor child, and my only wealth consists of my spear and my shield, and my only cloth is this rotten mbugu. Namujurilwa and Setuba brought slaves and cattle by hundreds, but the kopi Kasindula brings his thousands to Suna. Behold where they stand! Kasindula brings them all to Suna." And putting his hands together, he cried aloud, "Twiyanzi, yanzi, yanzi, yanzi!" with all the fervour of one having received a bountiful gift.

The Emperor, upon inquiring the number of the spoil, was told that it amounted to 7000 slaves, 2000 cows and oxen, 3000 goats, and 500 sheep; upon which he said, "Kasindula has spoken truly; he has brought more than either Namujurilwa or Setuba. In return, I make him now a chief of the first rank, with land, cattle, and slaves of his own." And Kasindula was immediately invested with white cloths, and with all the honours, privileges, and greatness of a Mkungu of Uganda.

After this turbulent epoch there were some months of tranquillity, when one day there came a challenge from Kytawa, the mighty king of Uzongora, who had made an alliance with the kings Kyozza, Kamiru, and Rugomero, and with Antari, king of Ihangiro, against Suna.

The Emperor sent the messenger of Kytawa back to him with a bullet and a hoe, saying, "Give these to Kytawa; tell him to choose whether he will take the bullet and have war, or whether he will keep the hoe and cultivate his fields in peace; and bring his answer to me."

Kytawa imagined himself and his allies strong enough to meet Suna in war, and kept the bullet. When the messenger returned with this answer, Suna commanded his Katekiro to make up 300 man-loads of hoes and old iron and to send them to

Kytawa, and to say to him, "Suna sends these hoes and iron to you, for may be that you are short of spears, arrow-heads, and hatchets. Make war weapons for your people in abundance during three months, and prepare for war, for in the fourth month you shall see me and my people in your country, and I shall eat it up clean, and there shall nothing be left alive in it."

This was the last war in which Suna was engaged. After three days' desperate fighting the Wazongora"and their allies were defeated, and Kytawa and the confederate kings were compelled to fly for refuge to the island of Kishakka, where they were besieged, until all the kings implored forgiveness, and swore to become tributary to him.

Falling ill from small-pox, the Emperor accepted their oaths, and, raising the siege, departed for Uganda. When he perceived that he was about to die, he called his chiefs together and commanded them to make Kajumba, his eldest son, his successor.

This Kajumba, the Prince Imperial, however, was no favourite with the Waganda, for he appears to have been a violent, headstrong youth of gigantic size and strength. These qualities recommended him strongly to Suna, who thought that with such a successor Uganda would retain its prestige and supremacy, and apprehended nothing of danger to his own people in a person of such violent passions; and, indeed, it is to be doubted whether, after exercising with the utmost licence his own undisputed authority, he even thought them worthy of consideration.

Kajumba was Suna's favourite, and the war-loving father on his death-bed pointed out with pride to his chiefs the heroic qualities of the prince, reminded them how when a mere boy he had slain a buffalo with a club and an elephant with a single spear, and assured them with his latest breath that Kajumija would become more renowned than either lion-like Kimera or renowned Nakivingi.

After his father's death Prince Kajumba seized his weighty spear and ample shield and proclaimed himself his father's successor and choice, and announced his determination to uphold his dignity to the death. The chiefs, however, fearing Kajumba's violence, laid hands on him, and bound him hand and foot, and selected the mild-spoken, large-eyed boy Mtesa, and made him Emperor of Uganda by acclamation.

Suna was then buried with all the usual pomp attending such ceremonies in Uganda; and the young Emperor, having paid all honour to his father's remains, and feeling himself firmly established in power, began to reveal the true spirit which had been masked by the fair speech and large eyes.

He soon found reasons for slaying all his brothers, and, having disposed of them, turned upon the chiefs, who had elected him Emperor of Uganda, and put them to death, saying that he would have no subject about him to remind, him that he owed his sovereignty to him.

According to his father's custom, he butchered all who gave him offence, and that lion in war, Namujurilwa, as also the Katekiro, he caused to be beheaded. Frequently, when in a passion, he would take his spear in hand and rush to his harem, and spear his women until his thirst for blood was slaked.

It is probable that Mtesa was of this temper when Speke saw him, and that he continued in it until he was converted by the Arab Muley bin Salim into a fervid Muslim. After this, however, he became more humane, abstained from the strong native beer which used to fire his blood, and renounced the blood-shedding custom of his fathers.

Mtesa's reign, like that of his predecessor, has been distinguished by victories over many nations, such as the Wanyankori, Wanyoro, Wasui, Wazongora, and Wasoga, and his Katekiro has carried his victorious Hag to Ruanda and to Usongora on the Muta Nzige. He has likewise sent embassies to the Khedive's pasha of Gondokoro, to Sultans Majid and Barghash of Zanzibar, and, having entertained most hospitably Captains Speke and Grant, Colonel Long of the Egyptian army, myself, and M. Linant de Bellefonds, is now desirous of becoming more intimate with Europe, to introduce specie into his country, and to employ European artisans to teach his people.

For the interesting facts of the preceding pages, the world is indebted to the gossip Sabadu, for until his revelations, as herein recorded, Uganda and a large portion of Equatorial Africa were (to use the words of ancient Pistol) liked a closed oyster, but which now, with his aid, we have partly opened, thus obtaining glimpses, however unsatisfactory, into the origin, custom, and history of the country. An epic poem might be written upon the legend of the search for the lost patriarch, or a prose romance, for there is material enough for a great work in the tale Sabadu told me.

If we begin to speculate as to who this Kintu, the blameless priest, really was, and whether the legend does not bear some dim and vague resemblance to the histories of Adam or Noah, handed down from generation to generation through remote times among an unlettered people, we may easily become lost in a maze of wild theories and conjectures. There is, however, just as much ground for building such suppositions, and to plausibly demonstrate them to be actualities and facts, as there is for many other fables now generally accepted as verities.

It is impossible, while reading the tale of Kintu, the Blameless Priest, not to be reminded at one time of Adam, at another of Noah — for both Adam and Noah found the earth void and uninhabited, as Kintu is said to have found Uganda and the neighbouring lands. In the gigantic Kimera, "the mighty hunter," we remember Nimrod, and in the wicked children of the patriarch can suspect a faint resemblance to the shameless Ham. The prolific wife, and no less prolific cow, goat, sheep, and the wonderful banana-plant, have their counterparts in the traditions of every people under the sun. And do we not ourselves believe

"That all began

In Eden's shade, and one created man'"?

The ingenious mind can also find the prototype of the miraculously flying Kibaga in the angel that destroyed the first-born of Egypt, or that other who smote the host of Assyria; and Nakivingi, or Chabagu and his mighty warrior Wakinguru, might stand for David and his champions, and the final disappearance of Kintu may be taken to represent the end of the age of miracles. But speculation on these points will only lead one into wild and vain theories: and it is enough for the purposes of this book to accept the tale of Kintu as a simple tradition of Central Africa.

There is great reason to believe, however, that Kintu, if not a myth, is a far more ancient personage than Mtesa's list of kings would lead us to suppose. At any rate, from other sources I have collected the names of three kings of Uganda omitted by him. These are Semi-kokiro, Karago, and Kimguvu.

That the reader may be able to estimate the duration of the Uganda monarchy, I append in a tabular form the list of the kings, including the names of the three kings not mentioned by Mtesa: —

1. Kintu.
2. Chwa.
3. Kamiera.
4. Kimera.
5. Almass.
6. Tembo.
7. Kigara.
8. Wanpamba
9. Kaema.
10. Semi-kokiro.
11. Karango.
12. Nakivingi.
13. Morondo.
14 Sekamanya.
15. Kimguvu.
16. Jemba.
17. Suna I.
18. Kimbugwe.
19. Katerega.
20. Ntewi.
21. Juko.
22. Kyemba.
23. Tiwandeke.
24. Mdowra.
25. Kaguru.
26. Kikuruwe.

27. Ma'anda.

28. Msangi.

29. Namugara.

30. Cbabagu.

31. Junju.

32. Waseje.

33. Kamanya.

34. Suna II.

35. Mtesa.

The above forms a very respectable list of kings for a country in Central Africa, and proves Uganda to be a monarchy of no mean antiquity, if the number of names may be taken as any indication. Many names may also have been forgotten — to be resuscitated perhaps by some future traveller with the patience and time at command to rescue them from oblivion.

CHAPTER XV.

Life and manners in Uganda — The Peasant — The Chief — The Emperor — The Land.

To behold the full perfection of African manhood and beauty one must visit the regions of Equatorial Africa, where one can view the people under the cool shade of plantains, and amid the luxuriant plenty which those lands produce. The European traveller, after noting the great length and wondrous greenness of the banana fronds, the vastness of their stalks and the bulk and number of the fruit, the fatness of the soil and its inexhaustible fertility, the perpetual spring-like verdure of the vegetation, and the dazzling sunshine, comes to notice that the inhabitants are in fit accord with these scenes, and as perfect of their kind as the bursting-ripe-mellow bananas hanging above their heads.

Their very features seem to proclaim, "We live in a land of butter and wine and fulness, milk and honey, fat meads and valleys." The vigour of the soil, which knows no Sabbath, appears to be infused into their veins. Their beaming lustrous eyes — restless and quick glancing — seem to have caught rays of the sun. Their bronze-coloured bodies, velvety smooth and unctuous with butter, their swelling sinews, the tuberose muscles of the flanks and arms, reveal the hot lusty life which animates them.

Let me try to sketch one of these robust people, a Kopi or peasant of Uganda, at home.

The " Kopi " or Peasant.

Were it not for one thing, it might be said that the peasant of Uganda realises the ideal happiness all men aspire after and would be glad to enjoy. To see him in the imagination, you must discard from your mind, the inebriated, maudlin, filthy negro surrounded by fat wives and a family of abdominous brats. He may be indolent if you please, but not so indolent as to be unmindful of his own interests. For his gardens are thriving, his plants are budding, and his fields are covered with grain. His house has just been built and needs no repairs, and the fenced courts round it are all in good condition.

Roll the curtain up and regard him and his surroundings!

He steps forth from his hut, a dark-brown -coloured man in the prime and vigour of manhood, a cleanly, decent creature, dressed after the custom of his country in a clay-coloured robe of bark cloth, knotted at the shoulder and depending to his feet — apparently a contented, nay, an extremely happy man, for a streak of sunshine having caught his face, we have a better view of it and are assured it reflects a felicitous contentment.

He saunters — while arranging his robe with due respect to decency — to his usual seat near the gate of the outer court, above which a mighty banana towers, shading it with its far-reaching fronds.

In the foreground, stretched before him, is his garden, which he views with placid satisfaction. It is laid out in several plats, with curving paths between. In it grow large sweet potatoes, yams, green peas, kidney beans, some crawling over the ground, others clinging to supporters, field beans, vetches and tomatoes. The garden is bordered by castor-oil, manioc, coffee, and tobacco plants. On either side are small patches of millets, sesamum, and sugar-cane. Behind the house and courts, and enfolding them, are the more extensive banana and plantain plantations and grain crops, which furnish his principal food, and from one of which he manufactures his wine and from the other his potent pombe. Interspersed among the bananas are the umbrageous fig-trees, from the bark of which he manufactures his cloth. Beyond the plantations is an extensive tract left for grazing, for the common use of his own and his neighbours' cattle and goats.

It is apparent that this man loves privacy and retirement, for he has surrounded his own dwelling and the huts of his family — the cones of which are just visible above — with courts enclosed by tall fences of tough cane. While we leave the owner contemplating his garden, let us step within and judge for ourselves of his mode of life.

Within the outer court we come to a small square hut, sacred to the genius of the family, the household Muzimu. This genius, by the dues paid to him, seems to be no very exacting or avaricious spirit, for the simplest things, such as snail-shells, moulded balls of clay, certain compounds of herbs, small bits of juniper wood, and a hartebeest horn pointed with iron and stuck into the earth, suffice to propitiate him.

Proceeding from the outer court, we enter the inner one by a side entrance, and the tall, conical hut, neatly constructed, with its broad eaves overshadowing the curving doorway, which has a torus consisting of faggots of cane running up and round it, stands revealed.

It is of ample circumference, and cosy. On first entering we find it is rather dark, but as the eye becomes accustomed to the darkness, we begin to distinguish objects. That which first arrests observation is the multitude of poles with which the interior is crammed for the support of the roof, until it resembles a gloomy den in the middle of a dense forest. These poles, however, serve to guide the owner to his cane bunk, but their number would confuse a nocturnal marauder or intruding stranger. The rows of poles form, in fact, avenues by which the inmates can guide themselves to any particular spot or object.

The hut, we observe also, is divided into two apartments, front and rear, by a wall of straight canes, parted in the centre, through which the peasant can survey — himself being unseen — any person entering.

In the rear apartment are bunks arranged round the walls for the use of himself and family. Over the doorway of the hut within may be observed a few charms, into whose care and power the peasant commits the guardianship of his house and effects.

A scarcity of furniture is observable, and the utensils are few in number and of poor quality. Under the former title may be classed a couple of carved stools and a tray for native backgammon; under the latter, some half-dozen earthenware pots and a few wicker and grass basins. Some bark cloth, a few spears, a shield, a drum, a bill-hook or two, a couple of hoes, some knobsticks and pipe stems, and a trough for the manufacture of banana wine, complete the inventory of the household effects.

Behind the peasant's own dwelling are two huts of humbler pretensions, also surrounded by courts, where we may behold the females of the family at work. Some are busy kneading the bananas to extract their juice, which, when fermented, is called maramba — delicious in flavour when well made; others are sorting herbs for broth-food, medicines, or some cunning charm; others, again, are laying out tobacco-leaves to dry, whilst the most elderly are engaged in smoking from long-stemmed pipes, retailing between the leisure -drawn draughts of smoke the experiences of their lives.

Such is the kopi at home.

If the picture is not a faithful one of all his class, it may be attributed to his own indolence, or to some calamity lately befallen him. From it will be seen that the average native of Uganda has an abundance and a variety of good food, that he is comfortably lodged, as far as his wants require, is well and often married, and is secure from enemies so far as a powerful sovereign and warlike multitudes can command security. Still, there is one thing more that is necessary for his happiness — protection from his sovereign.

The "Mkungu " or Chief.

It might be supposed that, if a peasant's lot appears so enviable in that land, a Mkungu's or chief's of the first rank would be happier a thousandfold. That such is not always the case will be seen from the following sketch of the present Premier, or Katekiro, of Uganda, whose name originally, now almost forgotten, was Magassa. It may be proper to state here that all Wagauda, from the Emperor to the peasant, change their names according as they advance in popular estimation.

About the time that Mtesa succeeded his father and beheaded the senior chiefs of Uganda, there was observed at the court a smart, clever, cleanly looking lad, assiduous in his attendance on the monarch, and attentive to his smallest wishes. He was the son of a Mtongoleh or sub-chief, and his name was Magassa. To his other desirable qualities might be added a fine set of white teeth, bright eyes, and general good looks. Mtesa became enamoured of him, and made him guardian over the imperial lavatory, an office of great trust in Uganda.

As Mtesa grew to man's estate, Magassa the boy also became a young man, for he was about the same age as his master, and, retaining and improving those qualities which first attracted the monarch's eyes, was promoted in time to be a Mtongoleh of the body-guard, and a double-barrelled gun was put into his hands, with the power of gunpowder, and a few bullets and percussion caps, which caused the heart of young Magassa to bound with joy. Perhaps he was even prouder in the possession of a gun than he was of his rank, for frequently the Mtongoleh of the body-guard has only the empty name to boast of.

However, being Mtongoleh (or colonel), he was liable to be despatched at a moment's notice to distant parts of the Empire on special service, and the day came finally when Magassa was chosen.

Imagine a young British subaltern despatched by the Queen's command, specially chosen by the Queen for special service. How the young heart palpitates, and the nerves tingle with delight! He spurns the ground, and his head aspires to the stars! If a young British officer feels so joyful at a constitutional sovereign's choice, what must the elect of a despotic autocrat like the Emperor of Uganda, feel?

No sooner has he left the imperial presence with the proud command ringing in his ears than his head seems to swell, and almost burst from delirious vertigo. His back, hitherto bent through long servile dread, has suddenly become rigid and straight as the staff of his spear, and an unusual sternness of face has somehow replaced the bland smiles which hitherto decked it. For is he not "Kabaka" while on the Emperor's errand? Do not his soldiers respond to him when summoned with awful alacrity, saying, "'Kabaka' (Emperor), behold us"?

Woe to the party from whom offence came if young Magassa was sent with his warriors to them! And woe to the warrior who committed any breach of discipline when under Magassa's command, or even to him who crossed his humour when on the march on special service! Magassa's spear was sharp and swift, and his hands were at all times quick to gather spoil, and soon it was observed that the poor Magassa was getting rich in slaves, waxing great in name, and becoming exceedingly influential at court.

Promotions rewarded his adroitness and quick execution of commands, lands of his own and bounties of slaves and cattle were bestowed upon him, until Magassa became a Mkungu, or chief, of the second order.

Such a spirit as Magassa possessed, however, could not longer remain satisfied with this, while many above him could not boast of a tithe of his deftness and ability, and were blind to observe and forestall the humours of the despotic monarch; and a day came when a Mkungu of the first order, named Pokino, offended Mtesa.

Casting his eyes about for a fit man to succeed him, Mtesa's eyes lighted on the sparkling, bright face of Magassa, and his decision was at once made.

"Here, Magassa," cried the Emperor, and the accomplished courtier fell at his feet to the ground, to hear his command. "Haste, Magassa, take men and eat up Pokino's land and name, for old Pokino has forgotten me."

"Twiyanzi, yanzi!" he cried and moaned, "Twiyanzi, yanzi, yanzi!" each time more emphatic, and rubbing his cheeks in the dust; and then, springing to his feet, he seized his spear, and, holding it aloft, as if in the act of launching it, he proclaimed aloud, "By the Emperor's orders, I go to eat up Pokino. I will eat him clean out of land and name, and Magassa shall become Pokino. Emperor behold me!" and again he fell to the ground, screaming his thankful Twiyanzis, and loyally abasing himself in the dust.

After the levee was over, Magassa, eager to change his name for Pokino's, beat his war-drum, unfolded his banner, and mustered his followers, and, like the fell leopard, pounced upon purblind Pokino, whom he quickly deprived of life, land, and name, and in place of their former owner became their master. But with even old Pokino's vast estates and large possessions the young Pokino was apparently discontented. Shortly afterwards the Emperor commanded him to "eat up" Namujurilwa, the Achilles of Uganda, and it is owing to young Pokino's thirst for power and riches that Majwara, an infant son of that great chief, became a slave to Njara of Unyanyemlie, from whom I purchased his freedom in 1871. I afterwards sent him to Livingstone, to whom young Majwara ministered faithful service until that great traveller's death.

With the fall of Namujurilwa, young Pokino became Lord of all Uddu, from the Katonga valley to the Alexandra Nile, a district embracing over 3000 square miles, with twenty sub-chiefs recognizing him as their master, possessing two great capitals, Namujurilwa's at Masaka, and Pokino's, hundreds of women-slaves, and thousands of youthful slaves of both sexes, with cattle also by the thousand, and chief of a population numbering over 100,000. What a change this — from the keeper of the lavatory to the Lord of Uddu!

Pokino's life at his capital of Uddu, Masaka, is almost regal. He has "eaten up" the lands of two great chiefs, old Pokino and the lion-like Namujurilwa, and now out of the eater cometh forth meat, and out of the strong cometh forth sweetness. His sub-regal court is crowded with applicants and claimants for bounties, and slaves requiring to be fed, and good offices are given with a liberal hand, and cattle are slaughtered by hundreds, until Pokino's open hand and large heart is published throughout Uganda. By this politic liberality he secures the affection of the natives of Uddu, the friendship of the great chiefs at the court, and the approbation of the Emperor.

Is Pokino satisfied? Not yet, for there remains one more office which Mtesa can give; but he must wait awhile for this.

The Emperor hears there is a country called Usongora, west of Gambaragara somewhere, rich in vast herds of cattle, and he commands Pokino to go and gather some of them. Immediately the great war-drum of Masaka sounds the call to war, and the natives from the banks of the Alexandra Nile, the slopes of Koki plateau, and all the lake shore from the Alexandra to the Katonga respond to it by thousands, for it is a call to them to gather spoil, and when did a peasant of Uganda linger at such a summons?

When Pokino begins his journey, he discovers he has a vast army at his command, for other chiefs also are represented here by columns. Kitunzi of the Katonga valley has sent Sambuzi, and Mkwenda, Kangau, and Kimbugwe have also sent sub-chiefs with hundreds of warriors. Before Pokino's great army the people of Gambaragara retire up the slopes of their lofty snow mountain, and, pursuing them as far as prudence will permit, Pokino's eyes view from afar the rolling grassy plateau of Usongora, and an immense lake stretching beyond, which he is told is Muta Nzige.

Descending from the slopes of the snow mountain, he marches with incredible speed to Usongora, sweeps in with long sure arms large herds of cattle, despite the frantically brave natives, collects thousands of straight-nosed, thin-lipped, and comely women and children, and drives them towards Uganda.

Several difficulties present themselves in the way. The plain of Usongora is covered with salt and alkali, which, intemperately eaten, causes many deaths; and in the valleys sprout up mud-springs, and from the summits of conical hills strange fire and smoke issue, and now and then the very earth utters a rumbling sound, and appears to shake.

The Wanyoro, also, by thousands, combine with the natives of Gambaragara to dispute his return. They lay ambuscades for him, and obstinately harass him night and day. But Pokino's spirit is up in arms. He defies the supernatural noises of that Land of Wonders, Usongora, and by skill and sagacity avoids the meshes laid to entrap him, and, when opportunity affords, snares his ambushed enemies and annihilates them, and finally appears in Uganda at the imperial capital with a spoil of cattle and slaves fit to gladden even the imperial heart.

The Emperor appoints a day to receive him and his warriors, and, that meed may be given only to the brave, has caused to be brewed immense potfuls of potent pombe, which shall serve as a test to point out the brave and the coward.

The day arrives. The Emperor is seated in unusual state, with his harem behind him, his chiefs on either hand in order of rank, his musketeers on guard, and his drummers and musicians close by, while aloft wave the crimson-and-white-barred standards adopted by the empire. Before the Emperor are arranged the pots of test-beer.

Pokino advances, prostrates himself in the dust, and begins to relate his adventures and his doings in Usongora, while the heroes of the great raid are enmassed in view and within hearing of his words.

After the conclusion of the story, the Emperor says briefly, "Drink, if thou darest."

Pokino rises, advances to the test-pots, receives the ladle, and dips it into the pombe; then taking it up, he holds it aloft, and, turning to the warriors who followed him, cries aloud, "Tekeh?" ("Am I worthy or not?")

"Tekeh!" ("Thou art worthy!") responds the multitude with a shout.

Again he asks "Tekeh?" and again "Tekeh!" is shouted with renewed acclamation, and, being found worthy, he drinks utters his grateful Twiyanzis to the Emperor, and retires to permit others to advance and drink the test-beer. Those found worthy are rewarded, those unworthy are doomed to death by popular condemnation.

Soon after this, Myanja, the Katekiro, was found guilty of the overweening pride of appropriating to himself the most beautiful of the female slaves without regarding his master's right to select his allotment first, and the result of this was that Myanja was disgraced and shortly beheaded.

The Premier's place being now vacant, Pokino was appointed to fill it; and thus was the once humble Magassa elevated to be next in power to the Emperor, with the utmost of his ambition fulfilled.

He is now daily seated on the carpet at the right hand of his sovereign, controls all things, commands all men, and, when leaving the presence of his master, he is escorted by all the chiefs to his own quarters, waylaid by multitudes on the road with profound greeting, has the pick of all females captured in war, the choicest of all cattle, and his shares of all cloths, beads, wine, and other gifts brought to Mtesa; for the Katekiro, alias Pokino, alias Magassa, is now Premier, First Lord, and Secretary of State! But what next?

One day, while on a visit to my quarters, I permitted him to examine my store of medicines. On explaining the various uses of laudanum, he remarked, to my surprise, with a sigh, "Ah I that is the medicine I wish to have. Can you not spare some for me?"

Poor Magassa! poor Pokino! poor Katekiro! He is already watching, while yet young, in the prime and vigour of manhood, for he knoweth not the hour when the Lord of the Cord may beckon to him.

It is left for some future traveller to tell us of his interview with Kasuju, the chief executioner.

The "Kabaka" or Emperor.

The curtain rolls up, and discloses a hill covered with tall conical huts, whose tops peep out above the foliage of plantains and bananas, and lofty fences of cane. Up the hill's gradually ascending slopes run broad smooth avenues, flanked by cane palisades, behind which clusters of huts show grey under a blazing sun, amid the verdure of the leafy groves around them. The avenues are thronged by natives, clad in picturesque costumes. White clothes gleam in the sunshine, in strong contrast to red and brown. The people are wending their way to the imperial quarters on the summit of the hill. While no ingress is permitted, they crowd around the gates in social gossip, exchanging morning greetings.

Suddenly the murmur of voices ceases, and the long rumbling roll of a kettle-drum is heard, announcing that the monarch is seated on the burzah. The gates are at once drawn aside, and a multitude of chiefs, soldiers, peasants, strangers rush up tumultuously, through eight or ten courts, towards the audience-hall, and in their noisy haste we may see the first symptoms of that fawning servility characteristic of those who serve despots.

The next scene we have is a section of a straw house, with a gable-roof — about 25 feet high, 60 feet long, and 18 feet in breadth.

At the farther end, by the light afforded by the wide entrance, we perceive the figure of a man clad in an embroidered scarlet jacket and white skirt seated on a chair, guarded on either side by a couple of spearmen and two men bearing muskets. The chiefs and principal men now hastening through the gates bow profoundly before him; some, after the Muslim's custom, kiss the palms and back of his right hand; others, adhering to the original customs of the country, prostrate themselves to the ground, and, throwing their hands towards him, exclaim, while kneeling, "Twiyanzi, yanzi!" after which they severally betake themselves to their respective seats in order of rank. Two long rows of seated men are thus formed along the caned walls of the hall of audience, facing towards the centre, which is left vacant for the advent of strangers and claimants, and the transaction of business, justice, &c.

Being privileged, we also enter, and take a seat on the right-hand side, near the Katekiro, whence we can scrutinize the monarch at our leisure.

The features, smooth, polished, and without a wrinkle, are of a young man, who might be of any age between twenty-five and thirty-five. His head is clean-shaven and covered with a fez, his feet are bare and rest on a leopard-skin, on the edge of which rests a polished white tusk of ivory, and near this are a pair of crimson Turkish slippers. The long fingers of his right hand grasp a gold-hilted Arab scimitar; the left is extended over his left knee, reminding one of the posture of Rameses at Thebes. The only natural peculiarities of the face, causing it to differ from other faces around me, are the glowing, restless large eyes, which seem to take in everything at a glance. The character of the face, however, is seen to change rapidly; even in repose it lacks neither dignity nor power, but as cross thoughts flash through his mind the corners of the lips are drawn in, the eyes expand, the eyeballs project, his hands twitch nervously, and the native courtier begins to apprehend a volcanic outburst of rage. If pleased, however, the eyes appear to recede and contract, the lips relax their vigour, and soon a hearty laugh rings through the hall.

But hush! here advance some ten or twelve people along the centre, and prostrate themselves before the Emperor, and begin through a spokesman to tell him of something to which, strangely enough, he does not seem to listen.

By means of an interpreter we are informed that it is an embassy from the lawless bandit Mirambo, who, hearing that Mtesa was likely enough to send some 50,000 sharp spears to hunt him up, has sent these men with propitiating gifts, and a humble declaration that he has no cause of quarrel with Uganda. The gifts are unrolled to view and counted.

So many cloths, so much wire, some half-dozen dinner plates of European make, an ample brass coffee tray, an Arab dagger silver-hilted, and a scarlet coat.

Mtesa has been meanwhile carelessly talking to his chiefs while the embassy addressed him, but suddenly he turns on the embassy his large glowing eyes, and speaks quickly and with decision: —

"Tell Mirambo from me that I do not want his gifts, but I must have the head of his man who slew my chief Singiri a year ago, as he was returning from Zanzibar to Uganda, or I will hunt him up with more Waganda than there are trees in his country. Go!"

Another party now comes up. A chief is dead, and they wish to know who shall succeed him, and they have brought his sons along with them, that the Emperor may make his choice.

Mtesa smiles and asks his chiefs to name the successor. One names Bugomba, another Taniziwa, another Kaseje, another Sempa. The chiefs fail to agree, and Mtesa asks playfully, "Which shall be chief?" whereupon the majority name Taniziwa as elected, after which we have to hear the "Twiyanzis" of the favoured one, and his ardent vows of allegiance to the Emperor.

Just at this moment appears a long procession of females, old and young, at the sight of whom the Emperor rises to his feet, and his example is followed by all. Curious to know who they are, we ask, and are told that they are descendants of Kamanya and Suna, wards and members of the imperial family. These ladies, it appears, know when to time their visits, and contrive to enter the levee late, as European ladies, to attract attention, are supposed to enter church late.

As these ladies advance to the carpet, Mtesa greets each with a kind word, and after they are seated proceeds to them, seats himself in their laps, and embraces one after another. In return for these imperial courtesies, they afterwards present him with live fowls, which he is compelled to receive with his own hands, and pass over to a chief to hold, that he may not appear to despise any of them. Surely if such a despotic monarch can condescend to be so affable and kind to females, there must be some good in him.

But the Emperor on this morning has caught a cold, and the watchful chiefs have been observing the little uneasiness, and forthwith half-a-dozen rush forward prone on their knees, and offer their head-cloths, into which the imperial nose may relieve itself.

The Emperor playfully draws back in his chair, and says, "Oh, I don't want all these."

"Well, take mine," says one.

"No, take mine, Kabaka; mine is white, and of fine soft cloth;" and Mtesa, prevailed upon by the whiteness and softness of the texture, takes it, and relieves his afflicted nose, and then hands the cloth back to its owner, who rubs it together hard, as though he wished to punish well the cause of the affliction.

Suddenly from some place in the hall is heard a hawking sound, as from some one likewise afflicted with a cold in the throat, and the eyes of the Emperor are quickly fixed on the person; but the chiefs cry out indignantly, "Out, out with you, quick!" and, peremptorily and sternly, half-a-dozen "lords of the cord" seize upon the unfortunate and eject him in no gentle manner.

After this interruption the tones of the native harp are heard, and the Emperor calls to the minstrel and bids him play on his instrument, which the accomplished musician is nothing loth to do. But while we listen to the monotonous music, all are startled at the loud report of a gun!

A dozen ejaculations are uttered, and as many chiefs rush out to enquire the cause; but they have been forestalled by the adroit and eager lords of the cord, who have thrown their nooses round the man's neck and, half strangling him, drag him into the Presence, whose imperial nerves have been somewhat disturbed by the sudden discharge of gunpowder. The lords of the cord, kneeling, say that the man let his gun fall while on guard, and their eyes seem to ask, "What shall we do to him?" "Give him fifty blows with a stick," cries the angry Emperor, and the unfortunate fellow is hauled away to receive such a punishment as will lame him for a month.

There is now heard a lowing of cattle, of fat beeves and milch-cows, in the court before the audience-hall, and a man advances, and after prostration and "Twiyanzis" says he has brought a present from Mankorongo, king of Usui.

"H'm. See to them, Katekiro, and give one to my steward Ka-uta to dress up, and let each chief have an ox to-day, and give ten to my body-guard." At this liberality all the chiefs rush forward, abase themselves in the dust, and cry aloud their fervid "Twiyanzis."

The chiefs resume their seats after this exhibition of their gratitude, and a messenger arrives from the banks of the Victoria Nile, and relates, to the monarch's surprise, that Namiouju, a petty prince near Unyoro, has cast off his allegiance to him, and opened negotiations with Kabba Rega, king of Unyoro.

On hearing the messenger's news, the Emperor exclaims, his eyes expanding widely, and projecting, "What! are all my people dead at Nakaranga? Have I no chief, no people left, that Namionju treats me so?"

The answer is heard in the voices of the chiefs, who spring to their feet simultaneously and rush out before the entrance of the audience-hall, seize their spears or walking-sticks, and call aloud on the Emperor to behold and number his chiefs, and with wild impressive gestures toss their spears and arms on high until a stranger would fancy that a revolution had suddenly begun. The Emperor, however, calmly answers, "It is well," upon which the chiefs leave their spears without and regain their seats.

Then casting his eyes about him, he selects a fiery-looking young chief — Maoor-ugungu by name — who instantly darts forward from his seat, and prostrating himself exclaims, "Kabaka, I am here."

"Go, Maoor-ugungu, take five Watongoleh and their men, and eat up Namionju and his country."

Maoor-ugungu, prompt as tinder upon receiving such an order, utters many "Twiyanzis," then springs to his feet, and, seizing a couple of spears and a shield, throws himself into a heroic attitude with all the ardour of a true son of Mars, and cries aloud: —

"Emperor, behold me! The Emperor commands, and Namionju shall die, and I will gather the spoil. I will eat the land up clean. Twiyanzi-yanzi-yanzi-yanzi!" and so on ad infinitum.

The Emperor rises. Tori the drummer beats the long roll on his drum, and all the chiefs, courtiers, pages, claimants, messengers and strangers, start to their feet. The Emperor — without a word more — retires by a side door into the inner apartments, and the morning burzah is ended.

Those curious to know further of the Emperor's life must pass through a multitude of sharp-eyed, watchful guards, pages, and executioners, thronging the court of the audience-hall, into the private courts, many of which they will find apparently of no use whatever except to ensure privacy, and to confuse a stranger.

In one they may see Mtesa drilling his Amazons and playing at soldiers with his pets. They are all comely and brown, with fine marginal bosoms. But what strikes us most is the effect of discipline. Those timid and watchful eyes which they cast upon the monarch to discover his least wish prove that, though they may be devoted to him, it is evident that they have witnessed other scenes than those of love.

In another court, perhaps, they may find Mtesa just sitting down to eat a slight noon meal, consisting of ripe bananas and curded milk; or they may find him laughing -and chatting with his favourite wives and female children, who all sit around him, seeming to govern their faces according to the despot's humour; or perhaps he may happen to be found with a favourite page examining the contents of the treasure-house, where the gifts of various travellers, European, Turkish, and Arabic, are stored; or he may be engaged with Tori, his factotum, planning some novelty, in the shape of a waggon, carriage, ship, or boat, or whatever the new fancy may be which has taken possession of his mind.

The Land.

Having learned somewhat through these sketches of the character of the peasant, the chief, and the monarch, it now remains for us to take a view of the land in order to understand its extent, nature, and general aspect.

The form of the Empire governed by Mtesa may be best described as a crescent. Its length is about 300 geographical miles, and its breadth about 60, covering — with the islands of Sesse, Lulaniba, Bufwe, Sadzi, Lulamha, Damba, Lukomeh, Iramba, Irwaji, Kiwa, Wema, Kibibi, Uziri, Wanzi, Uruma, Utamba, Mwama, Ugeyeya, Usamu, and Namungi — an area of 30,000 square miles. If we reckon in also Unyoro, Ukedi, and Ankori, which recognize Mtesa's powder, and pay tribute to him, though somewhat irregularly, we must add a further area of 40,000 square miles, making the total extent of his empire about 70,000 square miles.

Some estimate of the population ought also to be offered. But it is to be understood that it is only a rough estimate, made by a traveller who has had to compile his figures by merely taking into consideration the number of the army assembled at Nakaranga, and enumerating districts and villages along the line of his travels.

Uganda proper (from Ripon Falls) to Katonga river: 750,000
Uddu: 100,000
Bwera: 70,000
Koki: 30,000
Usoga: 500,000
Ukedi: 150,000
Unyoro: 500,000
Usagara or Ankori: 200,000
Karagwe: 150,000
Usui: 80,000
Uzongora: 200,000
Sesse Island: 20,000
Uvuma: 15,000
All other islands: 10,000
Total: 2,775,000

This number gives about thirty-eight persons to the square mile throughout the empire of Uganda.

The productions of the land are of great variety, and, if brought within reach of Europeans, would find a ready market — ivory, coffee, gums, resins, myrrh, lion, leopard, otter, and goat skins, ox-hides, snow-white monkey-skins, and bark cloth, besides fine cattle, sheep, and goats. Among the chief vegetable productions are the papaw, banana, plantain, yams, sweet potatoes, peas, several kinds of beans, melons, cucumbers, vegetable marrow, manioc, and tomatoes. Of grains, there are to be found in the neighbourhood of the capital wheat, rice, maize, sesamum, millets, and vetches.

The soil of the lake coast region from the extremity of Usogo to the Alexandra Nile is of inexhaustible fertility. The forests are tall and dense, and the teak and cottonwood, tamarind, and some of the gum trees grow to an extraordinary height, while many of the lower uninhabited parts near the lake are remarkable for the density, luxuriance, and variety of their vegetation.

The higher land, for the most part devoid of trees and covered with grass, appears better adapted for pasture, though the plantain and fig trees flourish on the summit of the hills with the same vigour as near the lake.

Westward of the smooth, rolling, pastoral country which characterizes the interior of Usoga and Uganda, we observe that the land has lost its surface of pasture grass, and its gently undulating character, and heaves itself upwards into many-headed hills of rugged, abrupt forms, and as we penetrate farther, these hills become mountains of a stupendous type, with summits which, except on a fine clear day, the naked eye cannot define. Deep, deep valleys, from whose depths we hear the roar of resounding cataracts and falls, sunder these lofty mountains. Upon their lengthy slopes great masses of glistening white rock are seen half embedded in debris, where they have remained since they were severed from the parent mountain which raises its head so proudly into the sky above.

Beyond this scene again we come to where the land appears to have concentrated itself, and fused all lesser mountains and hills into one grand enormous mass, the height and size of which dwarfs all hitherto seen, and which, disdaining vulgar observation, shrouds its head with snow and grey clouds.

Indeed, so gradual is the transition and change in the aspect of the land from Lake Victoria to Beatrice Gulf that one may draw this one-hundred-miles-wide belt into five divisions of equal breadth, and class them according to the limits given above. Let us imagine a railway constructed to run from one lake to the other — what scenes unrivalled for soft beauty, luxuriance, fertility, and sublimity would be traversed!

Starting from the sea-like expanse of the Victoria Lake, the traveller would be ushered into the depths of a tall forest, whose meeting tops create eternal night, into leafy abysms, where the gigantic sycamore, towering mvule, and branchy gum strive with one another for room, under whose shade wrestle with equal ardour for mastery the less ambitious trees, bushes, plants, llianes, creepers, and palms. Out of this he would emerge into broad day, with its dazzling sunshine, and view an open rolling country, smooth rounded hills, truncated cones, and bits of square-browed plateaus, intersected by broad grassy meads and valleys thickly dotted with ant-hills overgrown with brushwood. Few trees are visible, and these, most likely, the candelabra or the tamarisk, with a sprinkling of acacia. As some obstructing cone would be passed, he would obtain glimpses of wide prospects of hill, valley, mead, and plain, easy swells and hollows, grassy basins, and grassy eminences, the whole suffused with fervid vapour.

These scenes passed, he would find himself surrounded by savage hills, where he would view the primitive rock in huge, bare, round-backed masses of a greyish-blue colour, imparted to them by moss and lichens, or large fragments flung together as in some Cyclopean cairn, sundered and riven by warring elements. At their base lie, thickly strewn, the debris of quartz-veined gneiss and granite and iron-coloured rock, half choking the passage of some petty stream, which vents its petulance, as it struggles through it to gain the clear, disencumbered valley, and the placid river, guarded by banks of slender cane and papyrus.

And then the traveller would observe that the valleys are gradually deepening, and the hills increasing in height, until suddenly he would be ushered into the presence of that king of mountains. Mount Gordon-Bennett, which towers sheer up to the azure with a white veil about his crown, surrounded by clusters of savage heights and ridges, and before whose indisputable sublimity his soul seems to shrink. Escaping from the vicinity of this mountain monarch, he would be swept over a brown parched plateau for a short hour, and then, all suddenly, come to a pause at the edge of an awful precipice some 1500 feet in depth. At the bottom of this, slumbering serenely, and reflecting the plateau walls on its placid surface, lies the blue Muta Nzige.

General Remarks.

I have still to add some details of interest. Mtesa, in the preceding introduction to the reader, playing the part of Emperor at a public burzah, has still only a vague and indistinct personality, and so, to complete the portrait, I venture to append the following remarks.

On first acquaintance, as I have already said, he strikes the traveller as a most fascinating and a peculiarly amiable man, and should the traveller ever think of saving this pagan continent from the purgatory of heathendom, the Emperor must occur to him as of all men in Africa the most promising to begin with. For his intelligence and natural faculties are of a very high order, his professions of love to white men great, and his hospitality apparently boundless. Had he been educated in Europe, there can be little doubt but that he would have become a worthy member of society; but nursed in the lap of paganism, and graduate only in superstition and ignorance, he is to-day no more than an extraordinary African.

Flattering as it may be to me to have had the honour of converting the pagan Emperor of Uganda to Christianity, I cannot hide from myself the fact that the conversion is only nominal, and that, to continue the good work in earnest, a patient, assiduous, and zealous missionary is required. A few months' talk about Christ and His blessed work on earth, though sufficiently attractive to Mtesa, is not enough to eradicate the evils which thirty-five years of brutal, sensuous, indulgence have stamped on the mind: this only the unflagging zeal, the untiring devotion to duty, and the paternal watchfulness of a sincerely pious pastor can effect. And it is because I am conscious of the insufficiency of my work, and his strong evil propensities, that I have not hesitated to describe the real character of my "convert." The grand redeeming feature of Mtesa, though founded only on self-interest, is his admiration for white men.

When the traveller first enters Uganda, his path seems to be strewn with flowers, greetings with welcome gifts follow one another rapidly, pages and courtiers kneel before him, and the least wish is immediately gratified, for to make a request of the Emperor is to honour him with the power of giving. So long as the stranger is a novelty, and his capacities or worth have not yet been sounded, his life in Uganda seems to be a sunshiny holiday.

Meanwhile, however, the pages, pursuivants, messengers, and courtiers have been measuring him by rules and methods of their own. His faculties have been calculated, his abilities keenly observed and noted, and his general utility and value become accurately gauged, and all the time he has been entertained royally, and courted and favoured beyond all his expectations.

But now approaches the time for him to make return, to fulfil the promise tacitly conveyed by his ready and friendly acceptance of gifts and favours. He is surprised by being asked if he can make gunpowder, manufacture a gun, cast a cannon, build a ship, or construct a stone or a brick house. If a priest ordained, and his garb and meek, quiet behaviour prove it, his work is ready cut for him; he has only to teach and preach. But if a soldier, why should he not know how to make guns, cannon, ships, brick houses, &c.? If he informs the Emperor that he is ignorant of these things, why then he must pay in other coin. He has guns with" him, he must "give"; he has watches, "give"; he has various trifles of value, such as a gold pencil-case, or a ring, "give"; he wears good clothes, "give"; he has. beads, cloth, wire, "Give, give, give"; and so "give "to his utter beggary and poverty. If he does not give with the liberality of a "Speki" or a "Stamlee," who will henceforth be quoted to his confusion and shame, there will be found other ways to rid him of his superfluities. His men will be found unfaithful, and will desert, attracted by the rewards of Mtesa and glowing descriptions of his liberality, and one day, when he is about to congratulate himself that he is more fortunate than others, he will find himself suddenly bereft of half or three-fourths of his entire stock of goods. If the traveller states that he is acquainted with a few arts, he is expected to prove his words to the loss of his time and patience, and the waste of many precious months; even then what little he has been able to do with such lazy knaves as the Waganda will prove insufficient, and he also, by craft, will be relieved of a few guns and bales.

From these exactions only the resident missionary would be exempt, because he will be able to make ample amends for all deficiencies by staying to teach and preach, and he in time would, in reality, be the Emperor. To him Mtesa would bend with all the docility of a submissive child, and look up with reverence and affection. The peculiar wayward, petulant, inconsistent nature would become moulded anew, or be re-born, to be presented henceforth to European travellers in an amiable, nay loveable, aspect. Mtesa is the most interesting man in Africa, and one well worthy of our largest sympathies; and I repeat that through him only can Central Africa be Christianized and civilized.

It will be observed that I have styled Mtesa "Emperor" of Uganda, and not king, like my predecessors Speke and Grant. But my readers may remember that it has been mentioned in the brief sketch of the Premier given above that all the Waganda, from the Emperor to the peasant, change their titles and names according as they are estimated in the popular consideration.

Before Buna's death Mtesa was a Mlangira (prince); when he succeeded his father, being yet young, he received the title of Mukavya or Mkavya (king) of Uganda, but after he had distinguished himself in the conquest of other kings, and won the imperial right, this title was changed for Kabaka or Kawaka (Emperor). For the Empire of Uganda, as already described, embraces several countries besides Uganda proper.

I was not aware of these several distinctions or grades until I had been a long time resident at the court. The title of Mkama, again, such as that of Mkama Rumanika of Karagwe, Mkama Mankorongo of Usui, is synonymous with viceroy or sub-king, though literally translated it means "lord." Polite courtiers prone on the ground, abasing themselves in the dust before Mtesa, will often address him as "Mkama ange" (my own lord).

The children of Mtesa are all styled Ulangira (princes). Below this title there seems to be no other designation of hereditary condition save Kopi (peasant). Wakungu and Watongoleh alike are peasants born, and therefore still peasants, though they may rank as chiefs and sub-chiefs, or governors and lieutenant-governors, or generals and colonels. Thus Mtesa at Nakaranga, when he was pleased to promise to reward him who first landed at Inijira Island with the place of Katekiro, asked the assembled chiefs, "For what is Pokino really? Is he not a peasant?"

The moral character of the people is far below that of the Emperor. Indeed, if it were not for him, no stranger would dare to enter Uganda. They have no respect for human life or human rights. Among themselves they recognise only might, and Mtesa might even be pardoned for exercising greater severity than he does, for this fierce people requires to be governed with the almost unexampled severity of might and power which Suna so cruelly employed. They are crafty, fraudful, deceiving, lying, thievish knaves, taken as a whole, and seem to be born with an uncontrollable love of gaining wealth by robbery, violence, and murder, in which they resemble — except that they have the lawless instinct to a greater degree than most — nearly all African tribes. Owing, however, to their terror of punishment, the stranger is permitted to wander in almost certain safety throughout Uganda, and is hospitably treated as the "Emperor's guest" (Mgeni). One has only to hear the word "Noanya" (spoil) given by a person in authority to be surprised at the greed there and then exhibited.

The adage has long been accepted for true, "Like father like son," and equally true would be the saying, "Like king like people." The conduct of the chiefs proves that in Uganda at least it is true, for, like the Emperor, they adopt a despotic style, and require to be served by their inferiors with abject servility and promptitude. Like him, also, the chiefs are fond of pomp and display, and, as far as their rank and means permit, they exhibit this vanity to the utmost.

Thus, the monarch has always about two score of drummers, a score of fifers, half a score of native guitar-players, several mountebanks, clowns, dwarfs, and albinos, a multitude of errand-boys, pages, messengers, courtiers, claimants, besides a large number of bodyguards and two standard-bearers, either following or preceding him wherever he goes, to declare his state and quality. The chiefs, therefore, have also their followers, standard-bearers, and pages, and so on down to the peasant or cowherd, who makes an infantile slave trot after him to carry his shield and spears.

In person the Waganda are tall and slender. I have seen hundreds of them above 6 feet 2 inches in height, while I saw one who measured 6 feet 6 inches. Of course the native Waganda must be distinguished from strangers and slaves and their descendants imported from conquered lands, and generally they differ from these by their more pleasing looks and more agreeable features. This last, however, may be attributed to a general love of cleanliness, neatness, and modesty, which pervades all, from the highest to the lowest. A naked or immodest person is a downright abomination to a follower of Mtesa's court, and even the poorest peasants frown and sneer at absolute nudity.

It has been mentioned above that the Waganda surpass other African tribes in craft and fraud, but this may, at the same time, be taken as an indication of their superior intelligence. This is borne out by many other proofs. Their cloths are of finer make; their habitations are better and neater; their spears are the most perfect, I should say, in Africa, and they exhibit extraordinary skill and knowledge of that deadly weapon: their shields are such as would attract admiration in any land, while the canoes surpass all canoes in the savage world.

The Waganda frequently have recourse to drawing on the ground to illustrate imperfect oral description, and I have often been surprised by the cleverness and truthfulness of these rough illustrations. When giving reasons firstly, secondly, and thirdly, they have a curious way of taking a stick and breaking it into small pieces. One piece of a stick delivered with emphasis, and gravely received by the listener in his palm, concludes the first reason, another stick announces the conclusion of the second reason, until they come to the "thirdly," when they raise both hands with the palms turned from them, as if to say, "There, I've given you my reasons, and you must perforce understand it all now!"

Nearly all the principal attendants at the court can write the Arabic letters. The Emperor and many of the chiefs both read and write that character with facility, and frequently employ it to send messages to one another, or to strangers at a distance. The materials which they use for this are very thin smooth slabs of cotton-wood. Mtesa possesses several score of these, on which are written his "books of wisdom," as he styles the results of his interview's with European travellers. Some day a curious traveller may think it worth while to give us translations of these proceedings and interviews.

The power of sight of these natives is extraordinary. Frequently a six-guinea field-glass was excelled by them. Their sense of hearing is also very acute.

It is really wonderful into how many uses the ingenious savage of these regions can convert a simple plant. Regard the banana-plant, for instance. At first view in the eyes of the untaught civilized man, it seems to be of no other use than to bear fruit after its kind, for the stalk of it cannot be employed as fuel, and its fronds soon fade and wither and rend, and unless the savage pointed out its various uses, I fear the civilized man would consider it of slight value. It is, however, of exceeding utility to the native of Uganda.

1. Its fruit, green or ripe, forms his principal food. When green, the Waganda peels his bananas, folds them carefully up in the form of a parcel, enclosed in green banana-leaves, and, putting a small quantity of water in his pot, cooks them with the steam alone. This mode of cooking green bananas renders them floury in appearance, and, in taste, most sweet and palatable. When ripe, they form an admirable dessert, and, taken in the morning before coffee, serve with some constitutions as an agreeable laxative.

Of the banana proper, there are several varieties, each distinguished by a special name, just as the European gardener distinguishes his several varieties of potatoes. Some are 3 inches in length, with deep green coats, and seem fat with matter. Others, 6 inches in length, and of a lighter green colour, are considered the best; others are short, plumpy fruit, great favourites also. There is another species, known by a dark point, rather bitter to the taste and unfit for food, but specially reserved for the manufacture of wine, for which it alone is adapted.

2. The fruit of this latter species furnishes the natives with the maramba, a honey-sweet, cider-flavoured wine, and, when mixed with a little millet, sweet beer also. When fermented and perfect, the latter is a potent liquid, and a quart suffices to disturb the equilibrium of many men; but there are old topers, like Prince Kaduma, who would toss off a gallon and be apparently only slightly elated after it. A small draught of maramba taken at dawn I found beneficial to the system.

3. The banana-fronds serve as thatch for houses, fences for enclosures, and as bedding. They are also used to protect milk, water, and flour vessels from dust and impurities, are employed as table-cloths, on which food is spread, and, like newspapers or brown paper, are used as wrappers for gifts of eatables, such as ripe bananas, butter, meat, eggs, fish, &c. while they serve daily and universally as pudding-cloths in the Kiganda households. The cool, thick shade afforded by a banana plantation is well known.

4. The stems are sometimes used for fences and defensive enclosures; they are also frequently employed as rollers, to move heavy logs, or for the transportation of canoes overland from point to point, when the strategies of war demand it. The

pith or heart of the stalk is scraped and made into sponges of a dough-cake pattern, and may be seen in almost all Kiganda lavatories. Frequently the indolent prefer to knead a fresh sponge-cake and make their ablutions with this to going to the river, lake, pond, or well, or troubling themselves to fetch a vessel of water.

The fibres of the stalk are used as cord, and are adapted for almost every purpose for which cord is useful. The poorest peasants make rough but serviceable shields also from the stalk, while the fishermen of the lake make large sun-hats from it. Many other uses might be mentioned, but the above are sufficient to prove that, besides its cool agreeable shade, the banana-plant will supply a peasant of Uganda with bread, potatoes, dessert, wine, beer, medicine, house and fence, bed, cloth, cooking-pot, table-cloth, parcel-wrapper, thread, cord, rope, sponge, bath, shield, sun-hat, even a canoe — in fact almost everything but meat and iron. With the banana-plant, he is happy, fat, and thriving; without it, he is a famished, discontented, woe-begone wretch, hourly expecting death.

CHAPTER XVI
TO MUTA NZIGE AND BACK TO UGANDA.
The ladies of Mtesa's family — Sambuzi ordered to take me to Muta Nzige — My last evening with Mtesa — En route for Muta Nzige — Sambuzi suffers from "the big head" — We come to an understanding — The white people of Gambaragara — War music — Through a deserted country — Sinister auguries — A cowards' council of war — Panic in the camp — Sambuzi announces his intention of deserting me — The flight when none pursued — The "Spoiler" eaten up — Mtesa tries to persuade me to return — At Kafurro.

Oct. 29. — On the 29th of October Mtesa and his grand army arrived at the old capital of Ulagalla. There was but little demonstration made to welcome the monarch from the war, except what was made by the females of the imperial household, who were mustered in strong force under the leadership of Nana Mazuri, the Emperor's mother, a venerable old lady of decidedly masculine mind, and of a revengeful and fierce disposition.

The Emperor honours his mother greatly, and bestowed hearty embraces on her and on the ancient relicts of Suna his father, who were also brought to meet him and to do him honour, and to receive the son of heroic Suna as became their respect for him and their awe of his rank and power. Lu-lu-luing and welcomes and fond smiles were the order of the day; a great drinking of maramba wine and potent beer followed; and musketry salutes, killing of beeves and goats, and interchanging of presents, closed the day of the return to the capital.

After allowing a few days to transpire for rest, I began to recall to the Emperor's mind the original purpose of my visit to him, and of his promise to conform to my request. He consented to my departure, and kindly permitted me to make my own choice out of his chiefs for the leader of the force which was to give its aid to our Expedition for the exploration of the country between Muta Nzige and Lake Victoria. I selected Sambuzi, a young man of thirty years of age or thereabouts, whose gallantry and personal courage had several times been conspicuously displayed during the war with the Wavuma, and whose rank and station guaranteed a force strong enough to withstand, if well managed, a greater power than the king of Unyoro — then at war with Gordon Pasha — could conveniently despatch to oppose us.

Mtesa, admitting that Sambuzi was a wise choice, stated with the usual exaggeration of an African or an Oriental that he should have 5000 warriors, and all the chiefs at the levee concurred with him. On my request to him that he would repeat, clearly and within hearing of all, his commands to Sambuzi, Mtesa called the chief to him, who, while prostrate on the ground, received the following command in a loud and clear voice: —

"Sambuzi, my guest Stamlee is going to Muta Nzige. He has asked that you should lead the Waganda to the lake, and I have consented. Now listen to my words Nearly all the white men who have accepted my people as escort complain that the Waganda gave great trouble to them. Let me not hear this of you. I shall send messengers to Kabba Rega to inform him of your object, and command him to abstain from molesting you. Now go, muster all your men, and I shall send four sub-chiefs with 1000 men each under Watongoleh to assist you. Do whatever Stamlee advises or suggests should be done, and by no means return to Uganda until you have absolutely performed my commands. If you do return without Stamlee's letter authorizing you to abandon the project, you will dare my anger. I have said."

"Thanks, thanks, thanks, oh, thanks, my lord!" Sambuzi replied, rubbing his face in the dust. Then standing up, he seized his spears, and, levelling them, cried out: "I go at the Emperor's command to take Stamlee to the Muta Nzige. I shall take Stamlee through the heart of Unyoro to the lake. We shall build a strong boma, and stay there until Stamlee has finished his work. Who shall withstand me? My drum shall be sounded for the muster to-day, and I shall gather all the young men of the Katonga valley under my flag! When Sambuzi's flag is seen, the Wanyora will fly and leave my road white and free, for it is Kabaka who sends him, and Sambuzi comes in the name of Kabaka! Thanks, thanks, oh, many thanks, my lord, mv own dear lord!"

The eve of my departure was spent in conversation with the Emperor, who seemed really sorry that the time had arrived for a positive and final leave-taking. The chief subject of conversation was the Christian church, which had just begun to be erected, where the rites of the Church were to be performed by Dallington after the style and manner shown to him by the Universities mission at Zanzibar, until one more worthy to take his place should arrive.

We went together over the grounds of the Christian faith, and Mtesa repeated to me at my request as much as he knew of the advantages to be gained by the adoption of the Christian religion, and of its superiority to that of Islam, in which he had first been taught. By his remarks he proved that he had a very retentive memory, and was tolerably well posted in his articles of belief. At night I left him with an earnest adjuration to hold fast to the new faith, and to have recourse to prayer to God to give him strength to withstand all temptations that should tend to violate the commandments written in the Bible.

Early next morning my convert sent me many presents as tokens of his esteem, such as four shields, sixteen spears, twelve knives, ten billhooks, six walking-sticks, twelve finely prepared skins and furs of wild animals, 20 lbs. of myrrh, four white monkey-skins, ten beeves, sixteen goats, bananas and beer and wine, and an escort of one hundred warriors to proceed by the lake to Dumo.

For our mutual friend Lukongeh, king of Ukerewe, he sent at my request five long tusks of ivory, one comely virgin of fifteen as a wife suitable for a king, being of the beautiful race of Gambaragara, also 20 lbs. of fine iron wire, six white monkey-skins, and one large new canoe, capable of carrying fifty men.

For my friend the king of Komeh Island and the lake shore of Uzinja he sent the same, and distributed beeves among the ambassadors from the king, whom I had brought to receive these presents.

From myself I sent to my kind friend Lukongeh one bale of assorted cloth, two coils of brass wire, 60 lbs. of fine beads, and two suits of blue and red flannel, besides a plush velvet rug.

Happy that I had so prospered despite the vexatious delay which was unavoidable, and that I had been able to do even more than I had promised to the kings of Ukerewe and Komeh, I set out from Ntewi with twenty large canoes full of Waganda warriors, five canoes for my own special escort, two to escort the embassy of Ukerewe home, two to escort the embassy of Komeh home, and eleven to open trade by the lake route, with Uuyanyembe via Kagehyi — also a suggestion of mine.

On the same day that I set out from Ntewi, Sambuzi led a thousand men from Ulagalla overland to our rendezvous on the Katonga river, where he was to be joined by the Expedition from Dumo, and the four sub-chiefs Sekajugu, Mkoma, Kurji, and Ngezi.

Our party proceeding by the lake were hospitably entertained at Nakavija by the grand admiral of Mtesa, Gabunga, and by Jumba, vice-admiral at Unjaku, with beeves, milk, wine, beer, bananas, tomatoes, and sweet potatoes.

At Ujaju our india-rubber pontoon was condemned, and a new and light canoe was substituted for it, and named the Livingstone, to take to Muta Nzige to assist the Lady Alice in the exploration of that lake.

After four days' coasting we arrived at Dumo, and greeted the Expedition after an absence of three months and five days. Frank Pocock had enjoyed splendid health, and the soldiers showed by their robust forms that they had lived on the best in Uddu, and that the Emperor's commands respecting them had not been neglected. All this time they had been sustained free of cost to me, and I could not find it in my heart to return the Waganda escort back to the Emperor without some token of my gratitude, and accordingly I made up a present of four bales of cloth, and 140 lbs. of choice beads, besides various other presents.

A few days sufficed to reform the Expedition, repack all loads, and to prepare the boat, which had now seen nearly nine months of rough service on Lake Victoria, for transport overland to Muta Nzige.

The Livingstone canoe was also taken to pieces, and made into portable loads for the journey. This canoe was 23 feet long, 34 inches wide, and 2 feet deep, and was formed of four long planks and one keel-piece sewn together with cane fibre, which, with the thwarts and bow-piece, formed light portable loads for seven men.

On the seventh day after my return to Dumo we began the march towards the general rendezvous of the exploring army on the Katonga river. We journeyed through Uddu in a north-north-westerly direction, until, striking the Kyogia river, we followed the course of that tributary of the Katonga river as far as Kikoma, when we crossed the stream and entered the country of Bwera, which lies parallel to Uddu, and extends from Koki westward of Uddu as far as the Katonga river.

At Kikoma we were compelled to come to a halt until Sambuzi was informed of our arrival, and guides could he obtained from him to lead us to the rendezvous.

Meanwhile I took advantage of the halt to hunt game and to obtain meat-provision for the expedition. During the five days of our halt here I was so fortunate as to shoot fifty-seven hartebeest, two zebra, and one water-buck. The abundance of game in this wild debatable district, and the immunity they enjoy from man — in consequence of the numerous lions and leopards, and also the neighbourhood of raiders from the hostile country of Ankori — was the principal cause of my great success. The first day I set out I bagged five fine animals within a few minutes, which astonished not only the Waganda body-guards of Mtesa, but also myself.

We heard of lions as being abundant in the neighbourhood of Kikoma, but though I roved far into the wilderness west of Kikoma, I never saw the slightest trace of either lions or leopards.

The arrival of guides from "General" Sambuzi broke up our halt, and caused us to resume our march, and the second day brought us to the Katonga river, or rather lagoon, for I could detect no running water. The bed of the Katonga is about half a mile wide, choked with spear grass and papyrus, with stagnant water 3, 4, and even 7 feet deep in some places.

The crossing of the Katonga consumed an entire day, and was effected by means of the Lady Alice, which had to be forced through the dense reeds. At Ruwewa, on the north bank of the Katonga, Sambuzi's delay caused us another halt of five days, which was a sore tax on my patience, and but little in accordance with either my hopes or Mtesa's instructions. However, we were so far entered into the enterprise, and were now so remote from any other possible means of advance, that we had to console ourselves with the reflection that "what cannot be mended must be borne," though mentally I cruelly condemned our dilatory general. The landscape between Dumo and the Katonga river presents smooth, rounded, hilly ridges separated by broad, grassy valleys dotted with ant-hills and scantily clothed with brushwood. It is a fine pastoral country, eminently suited for grazing, but in the absence of a sufficient population it is a famous haunt for noble game, so unsuspicious as to be easily accessible to a tolerable shot. In the uninhabited portions of the country few trees are seen, save the rugged euphorbiae.

The eye here commands many views of extensive prospects of rolling country, of grassy hills and grassy valleys, following one another in regular series.

As we all enjoyed unusual good health during our journey through this country, one could not help fancying that it was to the far-receding prospects opening on every side that we owed much of our healthfulness. It was certain that the blood flowed quicker, that the eye kindled with brighter light, and that we breathed more freely when we stood on one of those high, commanding grassy ridges and somewhat fondly compared the land to others we had seen elsewhere, where fever and ague were not so prevalent.

To describe Uddu and Bwera in detail would be a tedious task, for there is much sameness of outline in hill and valley, swell and hollow, ridge and basin, but viewed as a whole from the summit of any eminence, there is something really noble and grand in the survey.

I observed that the parts inhabited by the Waganda are, as a rule, the ridges and tabular summits of the hills, and that the hollows and basins are left for grazing purposes to the roving Wahuma shepherds.

On the sixth day after our arrival at Kuwewa, in the district of Kahwangau, we marched to Laugurwe, where we met — as courtiers had pre-informed us — General Sambuzi with a thousand men. We camped half a mile off from the general, occupying an entire village, from the plantations of which we were at liberty to help ourselves to our hearts' content. Sambuzi's force occupied the villages north of us.

In the afternoon I called to pay my respects to the general, for common sense informed me that the best way of attaining the objects in view was to pay the utmost possible attention to the failings of this African general, and to observe all ceremony and politeness towards him.

During the war with Uvuma, while I was a constant and honoured attendant at the morning levee of the Emperor, Sambuzi had occupied with his force the ground in rear of our detachment, and this chief had then courted my friendship most assiduously. This in fact was one of the reasons why I had made choice of him, and preferred his name to Mtesa. But when I now saw him, I found his behaviour to be an overacted imitation of the Emperor, without the monarch's courtliness and kindliness of manner.

As I entered the court, which had been constructed with a view to enhance his dignity, if space can be said to increase dignity, I observed that the general stood up from amongst his subordinates and stiffly maintained that position until I grasped him by the hand, when he managed to utter a faint greeting in response to mine.

I was not altogether unprepared for this result of his promotion; still it chilled me, angered me a little, I must confess, and induced me to ask him if anything was wrong. "No," he said, "nothing was wrong."

"Then why are you so stiff with your friend?" I asked. "Do you not like the idea of going to Muta Nzige? If you regret your appointment, I can apply for another man."

"My liking or not liking the journey will not alter the command of Kabaka," he replied. " I have received my commands to take you to Muta Nzige, and I will take you there. I am not a child, I am a man, and my name is known pretty well in Unyoro, for the Wanyoro and Wasongora have felt the sharpness of my spear, and it is not likely that they can turn me back before I bring you to the lake. I stand in the place of Kabaka now, for I represent him here, and the army is under my command. Sambuzi, your friend at Uvuma, is changed now to Sambuzi the general. You understand me?"

"Perfectly," I answered. "I have a few words to say in reply, and you will then understand me as well as I understand you. I wish to go to Muta Nzige lake. So long as you take me there and do exactly as the Emperor has commanded you, you shall have as much honour and respect from me as though you were the Emperor himself, and besides that you shall have so rich a reward that the Katekiro of Uganda himself will envy you. With your mode of marching and camping I have nothing to do so long as we are in Uganda, but when we enter Unyoro, I would advise you as a friend, since we are about to enter the country against the will of the people, that you keep the army together, that one camp be made and good positions occupied, and that when any trouble threatens us, you do not act without the advice of others, able and willing to give advice. That is all."

"It is well," he said, "we understand one another now. We will march by slow degrees as far as the frontier, that the other chiefs may have time to come up, and you shall then judge for yourself whether the Waganda know how to march."

Considered as we would consider of things European, Sambuzi could not be blamed for assuming dignity, and I therefore excused what otherwise might be called gross behaviour on his part. Sambuzi's force would be quite twenty times stronger in numbers than mine, and he was my only means of pushing through Unyoro. Prudence counselled me therefore not to let false pride be an obstacle to the accomplishment and success of the enterprise, and I determined to listen to its counsel.

Our journey to Kawanga, on the frontier of Uganda, was along the north bank of the Katonga, through an open rolling country, cut up frequently by watercourses which feed the Katonga. These watercourses, though called rivers, show no running stream, but only river-like marshes or broad "rush drains," choked with spear-grass and papyrus of the same nature as the Katonga. North or south of the Katonga, at the distance of ten miles or so, the land rises rapidly, and here numerous streams of clear, sweet water take their origin, but in their descent to the Katonga valley they become united and absorbed by great breadths of river-like marshes, the oozy contents of which are drained by the broad lagoon-like Katonga. It maintains this character until near the base of a low hill which separates the feeders of Muta Nzige from those of Lake Victoria. The crest of this hill is not more than 250 feet above the bed of the Katonga, and it is not more than two miles from its eastern to its western base, yet along the eastern base curves the bed of the

Katonga from the north-west, and along the western rushes the Rusango, from the foot of Mount Lawson southward towards the Muta Nzige.

Except in the vicinity of the Katonga there is scarcely one square mile of level ground to be seen. Our eyes dwelt everywhere on grassy hollows, slopes, and ridges, and the prospect each day was bounded by lines of blue hills, which as we progressed westward, assumed mountainous altitudes.

At Kawanga, when Sambuzi's force had been all collected, our army consisted of 2290 fighting-men. Following this little army there were about 500 women and children giving a grand total of nearly 2800 souls.

With Colonel Sekajugu were four men of Gambaragara, who were of a remarkably light complexion, approaching to that of dark-faced Europeans, who differed altogether in habits and manners from the Waganda. They possessed their own milch-cows, and their diet appeared to consist entirely of milk. The features of these people, besides their complexion, were so regular and remarkable that my curiosity was aroused to the highest pitch concerning them. I had seen stray representatives of these people at the court of Mtesa, but I had not the opportunity then that I had now to enquire definitely about them. I here set down, as I was told, what I gathered respecting them, both from their own lips and those of Colonel Sekajugu, who was the best informed of the Waganda.

These light-complexioned, regular-featured people are natives of Gambaragara — a country situated between Usongora and Unyoro. Gamliaragara embraces all the immediate districts neighbouring the base of the lofty Mount Gordon-Bennett, upon the summit of which snow is often seen. We caught a view, as we travelled through Unyoro, of this lofty mountain, which lay north-westerly from Western Benga, in Unyoro; but the distance was too great for me to describe it exactly. It appeared to be an enormous and blunted cone about 14,000 or 15,000 feet high.

According to Sekajugu, the mountain springs up in a series of terraces from a level plain; numerous waterfalls plunge down its steep slopes, and two days are usually occupied in the ascent to the highest summit. The king, Ny-ika, with his principal chiefs and their families, live during war-time on the highest part of the mountain, which appears to be, from report, something like an extinct crater. They described it to me as a hollow surrounded by high walls of rock, which contains a small round lake, from the centre of which rises a lofty columnar rock. It is very cold there, and snow frequently falls. The slopes, base, and summit are thickly populated, but though powerful in numbers, the courage and skill of the people in war are much derided by the Waganda, who speak of them as preferring to take refuge in caves, and on the summits of almost inaccessible rocks, to venturing into the open for a fair fight.

Though probably inferior in courage to the Waganda, they must have distinguished themselves in war at one time, otherwise I cannot account for the brave and warlike people of Usongora being the subjects of Ny-ika, king of Gambaragara.

This king possesses several villages in different parts of the mountain, and appears to move from one to another, as his numerous herds of cattle become stinted in their pasture. Milk being the principal diet of these people, it may be supposed that cattle are abundant in Gambaragara and Usonoora. The Katekiro of Uganda in his great raid on this region is said to have collected "50,000" head of cattle. General Sambuzi accompanied him during that famous time, and has often amused my leisure hours with lively descriptions of his adventures.

The people are a peculiarly formed race. At one time they are said to have been all white, and to have emigrated from Northern Unyoro, but at the present time the black and light-complexioned are about equal in numbers. The blacks are the result of successive wars during ancient times and intermarriages between the captors and captives, the result being a singularly long-limbed and slender-bodied people. The royal family and the chiefs' families continue to preserve their exclusiveness, and hence it is that the original colour of the founders of the state has been preserved. The women are said to be singularly beautiful; I have seen several of them, and though I will not call them beautiful, as we understand the term in Europe and America, they are superior to any women I have seen in Africa, and have nothing in common with negroes except the hair. They are said also to be entrusted with the keeping of the charms of Kabba Rega, and to be endowed by hereditary right with the privilege of priests of the Muzimu of Unyoro.

To my disappointment I heard of nothing that would lead me to suppose they were superior to their less favoured neighbours in manners or customs or their ways and means of life.

Jan. 1. — On New Year's Day, 1876, the exploring army, nearly 2800 strong, filed out from under the plantain shades of Kawanga, each detachment under the flag of its respective leader, and each known by the particular style of music adopted by the great chief to whom it owed martial service. Thus Sambuzi's own force could be distinguished at a great distance by a peculiar strain, which, as the Waganda explained, announced, "Mta-usa, Mta-usa is coming!" or, "The Spoiler, the Spoiler is coming!" Lukoma's bands of music in the same way rang out, "Mkoma, Lukoma is near!" "Look out for Lukoma!" Sekajugu's name, on the other hand, appeared after the style of ding-dong-bell, or drawn out into "Se-ka-ju-gu, Sekajugu!"

On emerging from under the shelter of our plantain-embowered camp, we were drawn up in a long line along the narrow road. Sekajugu was appointed to take the advance, Lukoma the rear, Sambuzi and the Anglo-American Expedition the centre, while the smaller detachments, under Colonel Ngezi, Mrowla, and Kurji, took positions on the right and left, to keep the main column undisturbed by ambuscades. There was no time lost in these arrangements, and at sunrise the great drum of Sambuzi gave the signal for the march. At noon we occupied a deserted camp, known as the Salt Bunder, on the Nabutari river, which separated Unyoro from Uganda. The heights on the opposite side were observed to be manned by many Wanyoro.

With the eastern bank of the Nabutari, or Nabwari, river terminated the soft pastoral scenes among which our route had lain ever since leaving Dumo, on Lake Victoria, for from the western bank began a more rugged country, which, as we proceeded westward, daily assumed a more mountainous character. The country resolved itself into mountain masses of great altitude — bare and serrated hilly ridges, isolated craggy hills, separated by a rolling country, whose surface often presented great sheets of ironstone rock, mixed with fragments of granite. Each day's march presented two or three mountains of unusual height, which, dwarfing all others, became of great service to us in taking bearings and laying down a correct route.

Jan. 2. — On the 2nd of January we crossed the Nabutari, or Nabwari, river, and entered hostile Unyoro, and, undisturbed, made a march of ten miles, occupying at the end of it several villages in Southern Ruoko, Unyoro. Had we not been informed of the change, we should have recognised at once the fact that we had entered into a new country, by the difference in the construction of the huts, and in the vegetables which formed the principal subsistence of the natives. While in Uganda bananas formed our principal food — and very good, wholesome, and digestible they proved — throughout Unyoro our diet consisted of sweet potatoes and salt, varied with such other vegetables as foraging could obtain.

It was an amusing scene to see the haste with which the several detachments rushed about to dig up their rations. It appeared at first glance as if we had brought the exploring army to recultivate Unyoro, so thickly strewn and so busy were the diggers over the village fields. The digging was continued until sunset, and such quantities of potatoes came to camp that I fancied something like a desire to plunder the Wanyoro animated our people.

In the meantime our advance was unchecked, and our occupation of Southern Ruoko unmolested; Sambuzi and Sekajugu drew from this sinister auguries. "The Wanyoro," said they, "must be mustering elsewhere to oppose us; for usually, when we make a raid on this country, the natives hail us from the hill-tops, to learn the motive of our coming; but now the country is all silent and deserted; not one native can be seen." They therefore determined to send out spies in all directions, to ascertain the feeling of the natives respecting our strange invasion of their country; and in order to give time to obtain correct information, a halt was ordered for the next day.

Jan. 5. — On the 5th January the various musical bands and war-drums announced another march. The Waganda being unencumbered with baggage, except such bedding mats, and superfluous robes as their women carried, marched quickly, and tasked the heavily loaded expedition greatly; but my people did not fail me; they had long ago been thoroughly drilled for such occasions as the present, and they kept step and pace with the lightly equipped Waganda. The men who carried the boat-sections and canoe raced like horses, and arrived soon after the advanced-guard at camp. Traversing the district of South Ruoko, we plunged into an uninhabited tract of mountain country, and, after a march of eleven miles, camped at Kazinga, in Eastern Benga.

Jan. 6. — The next day we crossed the Katonga, for our course was now westerly, and occupied Western Benga, from the summit of a tall hill in which we obtained a faint view of an enormous blue mass afar off, which we were told was the Great Mountain in the country of Gambaragara, I named it Gordon-Bennett, in honour of my American chief.

Our foragers here obtained for the first time a sight and hearing of some natives, who shouted out that we might proceed without fear, though they doubted our ability to return, unless we took wings like birds and flew aloft. Some hiding-places of the natives were also discovered by accident amongst the tall grass beyond the fields. A little way from the village we found many deep pits, with small circular mouths, which proved, on examination, to lead by several passages from the mouth of the pit to more roomy excavations, like so many apartments. These underground dwellings are numerous in Southern Unyoro.

Jan. 8. — After a march of sixteen miles through a wild country we camped, on the 8th of January, on the east bank of tlhe Mpanga river. This stream takes its rise near the base of Mount Gordon-Bennett, and, flowing a few miles to the east of the lofty hump of Mount Edwin Arnold, is met by the Kusango river, flowing north-west from Mount Lawson, in the district of Kibanga, in Ankori; the two streams then, united, rush with impetuous force a little north of west, and, after several falls, plunge into Beatrice Gulf. Mount Edwin Arnold, of an altitude of some 9000 feet above the sea, stood west of our camp, on the Mpanga, at the distance of six miles.

We had now left Unyoro proper and entered Ankori, or Usagara. An old dilapidated wooden enclosure denoted that this extreme corner of Ankori was sometimes visited by Wasagara herdsmen for the sake of pasture.

The average altitude of our several camps since leaving the Victoria Lake did not exceed 4600 feet; but as we drew west, the nights were bitterly cold. On the night of the 7th the thermometer fell to 53° Fahr., and on the night of the 8th to 55° Fahr., this cold temperature being, no doubt, caused by night winds from Gordon -Bennett Mountain. Fogs, rivalling the famed November fogs in London, prevailed as a rule every morning, rendering the earlier part of each day damp, disagreeable, and cheerless. It was so thick that a man's form could not be seen at the distance of fifty yards, and horn and drums alone guided us on our march. During the afternoons the atmosphere slightly cleared, and the sun, struggling in the western skies from behind deep banks of sullen clouds, endeavoured to announce to us that the day was far spent.

Jan. 9. — On the 9th of January, 1876, the drums sounded for the march two hours before sunrise, for we had a long journey before us, and Uzimba, the country of chief Ruigi, was to be entered on this day.

Until daylight we journeyed along, or not far from, the Rusango, its many falls, rapids, and cascades telling of the rapid rush and furious plunge of the river towards Muta Nzige. Dawn found us in a singularly wild and beautifully picturesque country, the Switzerland of Africa.

Peaks, cones, mountain humps, and dome-like hills shot up in every direction, while ice-cold streams rolled between riven and dismantled rocks or escaped beneath natural bridges of rock, with furious roar. These gritty sandstone obstructions to the Rusango's waters presented most distorted and eccentric forms, appearing often like masses of scoriae. The traces of some agency, which long ago had convulsed this region, were visible in what appeared to be the wreck of mountains. The strata were perpendicular, seams of white quartz travelled along the lay of the strata in some places, and in others it appeared to have been encased in round moulds, which the impetuous waters, with their ceaseless wear and tear, had worn through, sweeping away the quartz, and leaving large hollows, cavities, and fissures in the sandstone. A small tributary of the Rusango from the south ran over a bed of polished basalt, which likewise contained large veins of quartz.

Soon after noon the main column arrived at the centre of a dip in the Uzimba ridge, 5600 feet above the sea, whence, far below us, we viewed the fields, gardens, and villages of the populous country of King Ruigi. But the sudden advance of the vanguard amongst the surprised natives, with banners flying and drums beating, had depopulated for the time the fair, smiling country, and left a clear, open road for the main body. Had the natives known of our approach, they might have reaped a rich harvest of revenge amongst the laggards in the rear, for the long; march of nineteen miles had irremediably dissolved the hitherto compact Expedition into small knots of dispirited and tired stragglers. One fellow, named Andrew, of the British Mission at Zanzibar, had thrown his load down, and plunged into the bushes to sleep his weariness off, and a rescue party of twenty men had to be sent back five miles from camp to hunt up news of him, and they, fortunately, saved him, though menaced by a band of natives. Some sick Waganda fell victims in the evening to the wrath of a roving party of the natives, who had been disturbed in mind by our presence.

Our descent into the fields of Uzimba was so unexpected that the inhabitants were utterly ignorant of our character and country. As they ran away, they asked the advance guard why the king of Ankori had sent his people to their country, and warned them that the next day they would come to fight. At night, however, the great war-drum of General Sambuzi revealed far and wide the character of the force, and announced that the Waganda were amongst them.

A council of all the chiefs and leaders of our Expedition was held next day, at which it was resolved to send out that night 200 men to capture a few prisoners, through whom we could communicate our intentions to Ruigi of Uzimba, and Kasheshe, king of Unyampaka, which country bordered the lake west of Uzimba. As the lake was only four miles distant, it became necessary to know how we were regarded by the natives, and whether we might expect peaceful possession of a camp for a month or so.

Some ten prisoners were captured, and, after receiving gifts of cloth and beads, were released, to convey the news to their respective chiefs that the Waganda had brought a white man, who wished to see the lake, and who asked permission to reside in peace in the country a few days; that the white man intended to pay for all food consumed by the strangers; that he would occupy no village, and injure no property, but would build his camp separate from the villages, into which the natives, having food to sell, were requested to bring it, and to receive payment in cloth, beads, brass, or copper, assured that, so long as they offered no cause, and kept the peace, they should receive no annoyance. An answer, we said, was expected within two days.

Jan. 11. — On the 11th of January we left the villages of Uzimba, and marched to within a mile of the edge of the plateau, at the base of which, about 1500 feet below, lay the lake. True to our promise, we occupied no village, but built our camp on the broad summit of a low ridge, whence we commanded a clear, open view of our neighbourhood. The Expedition occupied the lake end of the ridge, while the Waganda occupied the centre and eastern end. On the southern and northern sides the hill sloped down to open grassy hollows. No trees or other obstructions impeded our command of the approaches. The Waganda camps were surrounded by huts, the doors of which turned outwards, whence night and day the inmates could observe, without being observed.

Jan. 12. — The next day an answer was brought that the inhabitants were not accustomed to strangers, and did not like our coming into their country; that Uzimba and Unyampaka belonged to Unyoro; that as the king of Unyoro was fighting with white men, how could the white man come behind him and expect peace? that our words were good, but our purposes, they were assured, were none the less wicked; and that we must, therefore, expect war on the morrow.

This answer was brought by about three hundred natives, who, while they delivered their message, were observed to have taken precautions not to be caught at a disadvantage. Having announced their object, they withdrew in the direction of Mount Uzimba.

This declaration of war unsettled the nerves of the Waganda chiefs, principally the inferior chiefs and the bodyguards of Mtesa, and a stormy meeting was the result. Sabadu and Bugomba, the brother of the Premier, used their utmost eloquence to persuade Sambuzi to return; while Sekajugu and Lukoma cunningly held out strong reasons why they should, return immediately. At the same time they said they were quite willing to stay by Sambuzi to the death.

The danger of a panic was imminent, when I begged that Sambuzi would listen to a few words from me. I explained to him that, though we were only a bullet's flight from the Nyanza, we had not yet seen the lake, and that Mtesa had ordered him to take me to the Nyanza; that, before we had even looked for a strong camp, we were talking of returning; that, if they were all resolved to return, I required them to give me two days only, at the end of which I would give them a letter to Mtesa, which would absolve them from all blame; that, in the meantime, five hundred of the Waganda and fifty of my people should be sent out to select a path to the lake by which the boat, canoe, and loads could be let down the plateau wall without injury, and to endeavour to discover, on their arrival at the lake, whether canoes were procurable, to embark the expedition. This advice pleased the chiefs; and, as no time was to be lost, at 8 A.M. five hundred Waganda and fifty of our Expedition were sent, under Lukoma and Manwa Sera, my captain, to the lake, with instructions to proceed cautiously, and by no means to alarm the natives of the lake shore. I also led a party of fifty men to explore the plateau edge for a feasible and safe descent to the lake. The lake lay below us like a vast mirror, tranquil and blue, except along the shore, which was marked with a thin line of spluttering surf. The opposite coast was the high ridge of Usongora, which I should judge to be about fifteen miles distant, though the atmosphere was not very clear. Usongora bounds Beatrice Gulf westward.

At noon Lukoma and Manwa Sera returned from the lake and reported that it would be a difficult job to lower the boat down the precipice of 50 feet, which marked the first descent to the lake, without long and strong ropes; that the natives in passing up from the salt market on the lake hoisted their salt-bags, well wrapped in bull-hides, up the precipice; that no man could either descend or ascend with load on his back, as he required the use of both his hands for the climbing. They also reported that they could only find five small fishing canoes, which would be perfectly useless for the transport of men or goods on the lake. Great stores of salt had been seen, which had come from Usongora, and abundance of Indian corn, millet, sweet potatoes, bananas, and sugarcane had also been seen on the lake shore.

This unwelcome news infused a fever in the minds of the Waganda to be gone on the instant. Large numbers of natives, posted on the summit of every hill around us, added to the fear which took possession of the minds of the Waganda, and rumours were spread about by malicious men of an enormous force advancing from the south for the next day's fight. This urged the Waganda to pack up large stores of sweet potatoes for their return journey through the wilderness of Ankori. The members of the Expedition even caught the panic, and prepared in silence to follow the Waganda, as common-sense informed them, that, if a force of over 2000 fighting men did not consider itself strong enough to maintain its position, our Expedition consisting of 180 men could by no means do so. They were observed openly preparing for flight, before any commands had been issued to that effect, or even the alternative had been discussed. Others wandered off to mix with gadding crowds of Waganda, well disposed in mind to participate in their fears.

The Wangwana captains of the Expedition, extremely depressed in spirit, came to me in the afternoon, and requested to know what I had determined upon. I informed them that I hoped to be able to bribe Sambuzi with one-fourth of the entire property of the Expedition to stay by us two days, during which time I hoped to be able to lower the boat and canoe down the cliffs, and launch them on the Nyanza, by which I could free sixty soldiers from encumbrances, to act as guard for the land party. The boat and canoe would follow the coast line, to act as auxiliaries to the land party, in case of attack, or to transport them across rivers, until we should arrive in the neighbourhood of some uninhabited island, to which place of safety the Expedition might be conveyed, until exploration should discover more peaceable lands or other means of prosecuting our journey. The captains approved this method of meeting the danger which threatened us.

At 5 P.M. a messenger from Sambuzi called me to a council, at which all of his chief men were present, to discuss what advantages we possessed for offence and defence, for meeting the danger or for flight. Sabadu the captain of the detachment of Mtesa's bodyguard with us, was called upon to speak, which he did with all the cowardly malice of a Thersites. Every hint that could damp a virtuous resolution to obey Mtesa's commands was thrown out with all the effect that his position as chief of the bodyguard and his supposed influence with the Emperor lent his opinions, and he confidently assumed the power to charm away the anger of his dread master, and turn it upon the head of Kabba Rega, the king of Unyoro. Bugomba, the brother of the Premier of Uganda, though only a lad of sixteen, having far more influence in this council, and far more ability than would possibly be believed by Europeans, seconded Sababu in an assumed humble voice, and what Sabadu had neglected to urge, youthful Bugomba, the Emperor's page, adroitly threw in, and thus clenched the argument for absolute and immediate flight.

The council heard him with great approval, and many were of the opinion that it would be best to fly at once, without waiting for night or for morning. Lukoma and Sekajugu, the colonels under Sambuzi, gravely besought Sambuzi to think well of the numbers that would certainly oppose us in the battle next day; to remember that we were far from assistance, if overcome; that all the advantages of war were on the side of the enemy. The enemy would fight on his own soil, and mindful that he was fighting for his own home. If repulsed the first day the enemy would come again in greater numbers than ever, and each day, as the bruit of war should spread and time gained, the whole strength of Unyoro, a country as large as Uganda, would be drawn to dislodge and massacre us. However, Sambuzi, was their general and chief, and if he thought it best to stand by "Standee," they would stand by their chief to the death.

Sambuzi then asked me to speak. Wrath almost choked my speech, for I felt bitterly angry that I should be asked to speak when they were all so resolved to act contrary to the object and purpose of the journey that even fear of the Emperor was not sufficient to induce them to stay, and that a chief like Sambuzi, of such experience and acknowledged bravery, should stoop to listen to boys like Bugomba and such men as Sabadu. However, I summoned up my patience, and said: "I do not see much use in my saying anything, because I know you will act against all advice I can give; but, that you may not blame me for not giving the advice, and pointing out the danger you run into in returning, I will speak. You, Sambuzi, at Laugurwe, told me you were not a child, but a man. If you are a man how comes it that you allow a boy like Bugomba, whose fears have run away with his wits, to speak in a council of tried warriors such as I see here? Do you think that Bugomba can save your head when the Emperor hears of your cowardly flight? No; that boy's love which he professes to have for you, will fly when he sees the frown on Mtesa's face. Will the Katekiro stand by you because you love his brother Bugomba? No; the Premier will scourge Bugomba, and be the first to slay you. If you are a man and a chief, why is it that you listen to this slave Sabadu, who no more dares approach the footstool of Mtesa than he would dare meet the Wanyoro to-morrow in battle? Is Sabadu the chief and general of the Waganda, or is it Sambuzi, the chief who fought so well at Uvuma? If your chiefs, Lukoma and Sekajugu, advise you to run away, you do wrong to listen to them, for it is not they whom Mtesa will punish, but you. I therefore, as your friend, advise you to stay here two days, while I fix the boat and canoe. At the end of two days I will write a letter to Mtesa, which will absolve you from all blame; and if you so far concede to me two days, I will give one-fourth of my moneys — nay, I will give one-half of all beads, wire, and cloth I have to you, with which you may reward yourself and your friends. Be not afraid of the Wanyoro; to-night we can build a palisade so strong that, were Kabba Rega himself here, he could do nothing against us. There is no great danger in staying a couple of days, but in returning to Uganda without my letter you go to certain death. I have spoken."

After a little pause, during which he interchanged some remarks with his people, Sambuzi said: "Stamlee, you are my friend, the Emperor's friend, and a son of Uganda, and I want to do my duty towards you as well as I am able to; but you must hear the truth. We cannot do what you want us to do. We cannot wait here two days, nor one day. We shall fight to-morrow, that is certain; and if you think I speak from fear, you shall see me handle the spear. These people know me from past times, and they are well aware that my spear is sharp and fatal. We shall fight to-morrow at sunrise, and we must cut our way through the Wanyoro to Uganda. We cannot fight and continue in camp; for once the war is begun, it is war which will last as long as we are alive — for these people take no slaves as the Waganda do. Then the only chance for our lives that I see is to pack up to-night, and to-morrow morning at sunrise to march and fight our way through them. Now tell me as your friend what you will do. Will you stop here, or go with us, and try another road. For I must tell you, if you do not know it and see it for yourself, that you will never put your boat and the canoe on the Nyanza at this place. How can you get your boat down the cliff's while you are fighting, and thousands pressing round you? Even if you reach the water's edge, how can you work on her two days, and fight?"

To his questions I replied: — "I knew what your decision would be from what the Waganda have done on former occasions. When Magassa was sent with me to Usukuma by the lake, he ran away and left me to fight Bumbireh alone. When the Waganda were sent with Abdul Assiz Bey (M. Linant de Bellefonds) to Gondokoro, they followed him as far as Unyoro, and when they saw the Wanyoro coming, they deserted him, and stole nearly all his boxes, and Abdul Assiz Bey had to fight his way to Gondokoro alone. We white men will soon learn that there is no man so cowardly as a native of Uganda. For your advice I thank you; to-night I will give you my answer."

As soon as I left the council, Sambuzi caused the great war-drum to be sounded for the morrow's march and expected battle. It also announced to the anxious members of the Expedition that the Waganda had resolved to return. On arriving at camp, I saw looks of dismay on each face. I called Pocock and the captains of the Expedition, and proceeded to unfold our position and Sambuzi's intention to return, described to them what dangers environed us, and what hopes were left, and then asked them to give their own opinion of the matter freely.

After a long hesitation and silence the gallant and ever faithful Kacheche spoke and said: — "Master, I do not know what my brothers here think of the matter, but I see plainly that we have been brought to the edge of a deep pit, and that the Waganda will push us into it if we do not follow them. For my part, I have nothing further to say, except that I will do exactly as you command. Live or die, all is one to me. If you say, let us go on, and leave the Waganda to return without us, I say so also; if you say, return, I also say, return. That is my opinion. But I would like to ask you, if we determine to go on by ourselves, have we any chance at all of being able to start from this camp, because I see we are surrounded by natives bent on war? If all these Waganda with our help are not able to make our position good, how can such a small party as we are hope to do so? This is what is in my heart, and what I believe is the cause of the panic in the Expedition. And I will tell you one thing; when Sambuzi beats the drum to-morrow to march, more than half of this Expedition will follow him, and you cannot prevent it."

"Well," I replied, "this is my decision. I was sent to explore this lake. When I started from Usukuma, I doubted if I could do it unaided by Waganda, because there are no people on this lake friendly to strangers; it was for this reason I requested Mtesa to lend me so large a body of men. As no friendly port could be found where you might rest while I navigated the lake in my boat, I thought of taking possession of a port for a month or two and holding it. The force I relied on now fails me, and the people are hostile; it therefore only remains for me to return with Sambuzi, and to try the lake by another road. If no other road can be found, we must even be content with what we have done."

The Wangwana outside heard the decision with joy, and shouted, "Please God, we shall find another road, and the next time we go on work of this kind we shall do it without Waganda."

Sambuzi was made acquainted with our resolution, and requested to send twenty men to assist our wearied men to carry the goods back to Uganda. At dawn we mustered our forces, and with more form and in better order than we had entered Unyampaka, prepared to quit our camp on the cliffs of Muta Nzige. A thousand spearmen with shields formed the aclvauced guard, and a thousund spearmen and thirty picked Wangwana with shields composed the rear-guard. The goods and Expedition occupied the centre. The drums and fifes and musical bands announced the signal for the march.

The natives, whom we expected would have attacked us, contented themselves with following us at a respectful distance until we were clear of Uzimba, when, perceiving that our form of march was too compact for attack, they permitted us to depart in peace.

Our return route was to the southward of that by which we had entered the lake-land of Uzimba. It penetrated Ankori, and our camp that day was made at 4 P.M. on the banks of the Rusango river.

Jan. 15. — On the morning of the 15th, after crossing a low ridge, two miles in width, we crossed the Katonga coming from the north-west, and entered Unyoro once more. Our Expedition was the rear-guard this day, and when within a few miles of Kazinga, in Benga, a furious attack was made on our rear from an ambuscade, which was in a short time repulsed without loss to us.

Jan. 27. — On the 27th we were encamped at Kisossi, in Uganda, a little east of where Sambuzi had joined us with his force. At this camp we parted; Sambuzi, or Mta-usa, the Spoiler, to his own land close by, I to what fortune, or misfortune, had still reserved in store for me and mine. The "Spoiler" made his cognomen good, for on the road from the lake he despoiled me of 180 lbs. of variously assorted beads, by failing to return three loads of beads given him for carriage to Uganda, thus adding another reason to my dissatisfaction with him.

I halted at Kisossi three days to give the Expedition a little of that rest they so well deserved. During this time I despatched Kacheche and two others with a letter to Mtesa, wherein I did not fail to report to him of the failure of Sambuzi to perform what he had promised me, of his theft of three bags of beads, and of the strange conduct of Sabadu and Bugomba.

The effect of my letter on Mtesa and his court, Kacheche informed me a few days later, when he overtook us at Charugawa, was one of shame, surprise, and rage. Kacheche was called to the Durzah, and told to repeat in a loud voice all that had happened between Sambuzi and myself since we had met at Laugurwe, while

Mtesa and his chiefs listened intently, the recital broken by violent exclamations and ominous ejaculations from the Emperor.

When Kacheche had ended, Mtesa said, "Do you see now how I am shamed by my people? This is the third time I have been made to break my word to white men. But, by the grave of Suna" (a strong oath in Uganda), "my father, I will teach Sambuzi, and all of you, that you cannot mock Kabaka! Stamlee went to this lake for my good as well as for his own, but you see how I am thwarted by a base slave like Sambuzi, who undertakes to be more than I myself before my guest. When was it I dared to be so uncivil to my guest as this fellow has been to Stamlee? You, Saruti," he said suddenly to the chief of his bodyguard, "take warriors, and eat up Sambuzi's country clean, and bring him chained to me."

Saruti prostrated himself, and swore he would eat the "Spoiler's" land clean, and become the "Spoiler" himself, and that Sambuzi should be brought to him chained like a slave. Yet let it be noted here that Saruti and Sambuzi were as loving at the Nakaranga camp as two sworn brothers.

"And you, Katekiro," said Mtesa, turning his glowing eyes on him, "how is it that your brother Bugomba — a mere little boy — plays the great man on duty? Tell me whence he obtained this 'big head' of his?"

"My lord" ("Mkama ange"), "Bugomba is a child, and deserves a rod for this conduct, and I myself will see that he suffers for it."

"Very well, send for Bugomba, and that long-tongued Sabadu, and bring them to me at once, and I will see that they never use their tongues against a guest of mine again."

"Now, Kacheche," said Mtesa, "what is Stamlee going to do now. Do you suppose that, if I give him 100,000 men, under Sekebobo and Mkwenda, that he will be induced to try the lake Muta Nzioe again?"

"He may, Kabaka, but I do not think he will believe the Waganda again, for this is twice they have deceived him. Magassa ran away, and Sambuzi ran away, and he, perhaps, will say Sekebobo will do the same. The Waganda are very good before you, Kabaka, but when away from you they forget your commands, and steal people, cattle, and goats," said plain-spoken Kacheche.

Sekebobo and Mkwenda sprang to their feet before the Emperor, and said loudly, "Nay, let us go, Kabaka, and we will cut through the heart of Kabba Rega of Unyoro, or through Mtambuko, king of Ankori, to the Muta Nzige, and all the nations round about shall not drive us back!"

"It is well," said the Emperor. "Now you, Dallington," said he to the English mission pupil left at his court, "write a letter to Stamlee. Tell him to come to the Katonga once again, and Sekebobo and Mkwenda with 60,000, even 100,000, shall take him to Muta Nzige, and stay there until he has finished his work. Tell him that if these fail him he shall execute his own pleasure on every chief that returns to Uganda."

At Charugawa, near the Alexandra Nile, I received Dallington's letter, asking me to return and attempt the lake once more. This letter plunged me into perplexity, but after long and calm deliberation I decided that it was not safe to trifle away time in this manner; besides, such an undisciplined force would be uncontrollable, and would no doubt entail misery on the people. I was also too far from Muta Nzige now, and to return for an uncertainty, such as the character of the Waganda caused me to believe it to be. despite the protestation and promises of the Emperor, was in my opinion well deserving a fool's cap. I accordingly wrote to this effect to Mtesa, and closed the letter with thanks for his kindness, and a friendly farewell.

Kacheche, on returning from the capital with the Emperor's letter met the unfortunate Sambuzi loaded with chains, and the blunt, plain-spoken soldier, far from pitying him, could not refrain from taunting him with, "Ah, ha, Sambuzi, you are not so fine as you were a while ago. You are going to Mtesa to play Kabaka before him; fare you well, Sambuzi."

Saruti, the "eater," obtained great spoil, for he was now lord over 200 wives and 300 milch-cows, besides a large, fat district in the Katonga valley, well populated with lusty, industrious peasants and warriors, all of whom were from henceforth subject to him.

The final farewell letter to Mtesa terminated our intercourse with the powerful monarch of Uganda, and concluded our sojourn in that land of bananas and free entertainment. Henceforth the Expedition should be governed by one will only, and guided by a single man, who was resolved not to subject himself or his time to any other man's caprice, power, or favour any more.

As we neared the Alexandra Nile, at a place called Ndongo, this virtuous resolution came near being put to the test, for the unquiet immigrants settled here proclaimed that we should not pass through until we had paid something to the chief to obtain his good-will. But, after receiving a firm refusal they permitted us to cross the Alexandra Nile without molestation.

Reports and rumours of the breadth and powerful current of the river called the "Kagera," the "Kitangule," and the "Ingezi," received from representatives of Uganda, Kiziwa, and Karagwe, some of whom were very intelligent natives, and professed a perfect knowledge of its course, had created in me a constant desire to examine the river more carefully than I had previously done at its exit into Lake Victoria. At the crossing between bank and bank it was about 450 yards in width; but about 350 yards of this breadth flowed or oozed, with little current, amongst sedge, water-cane, and papyrus. The remaining 100 yards was a powerful and deep body of water, with a current of three knots and a half an hour. The water had a dull iron colour, yet extremely pure for a large river, and such as might proceed from some lake at no great distance off.

The Waganda and Wanyambu of Rumanika's court style this river the "Mother of the River at Jinga" (Victoria Nile), but the former have very wild ideas about its source. They say it issues from Muta Nzige in Mpororo, and, flowing south, cuts Ruanda in halves, and, rounding Kishakka, runs north, dividing Karagwe from Ruanda.

Rumanika, king of Karagwe, is no less singular in his theory of the source of the Alexandra Nile, for he says it issues from Lake Tanganika, through Urundi. However, these and sundry other reports only roused my interest in the noble river, and created a greater inclination to pursue the subject to its ultimate end. For a very few soundings of it enabled me, after my circumnavigation of Lake Victoria, and on examination of the several streams emptying into it, to judge this to be the principal affluent and feeder of the lake.

A journey of fourteen miles southerly across the valley of the Alexandra from its southern bank brought us to the base of the lofty ranges of Karagwe. This country comprises all the mountainous ridges between Usongora on the east and the Alexandra Nile to the west. It appears as if at a distant epoch these ridges had been connected with the uplands of Koki and Ankori north, and Ruanda west, but that, as Lake Victoria had channelled a way for its outlet through the clays and shale of Usoga and Uganda, and its altitude above the sea had subsided, the furious current of the Kagera or Alexandra had channelled a deeper course through the heart of what was formerly a lofty plateau, and that its thousands of petty tributaries then rushed down into the deep depression formed by it.

On the 24th of February we were camped at Nakahanga, a village situated twelve miles west of south of Kiyanga, and the next day, after a march of thirteen miles, we entered the Arab depot of Kafurro, in Karagwe.

CHAPTER XVII.

Kafurro and its magnates — Lake Windermere — Rumanika, the gentle king of Karagwe — His country — The Ingezi — Among the mosquitoes — Ihema Island — The triple cone of Ufumbiro — Double-horned rhinoceros — The hot springs of Mtagata — The Geographical Society of Karagwe — The philosophy of noses — Rumanika's thesauron — Some new facts about the rhinoceros and elephant — Uhimba — Paganus, var. esuriens — Retrospect.

Feb. 25. — Kafurro owes its importance to being a settlement of two or three rich Arab traders, Hamed Ibrahim, Sayid bin Sayf, and Sayid the Muscati. It is situated within a deep hollow or valley fully 1200 feet below the tops of the surrounding mountains, and at the spring source of a stream flowing east and afterwards north to the Alexandra Nile.

Hamed Ibrahim is rich in cattle, slaves, and ivory. Assuming his own figures to be correct, he possesses 150 cattle, bullocks, and milch cows, forty goats, 100 slaves, and 450 tusks of ivory, the greater part of which last is reported to be safely housed in the safe keeping of his friend the chief of Urangwa in Unyamwezi.

Hamed has a spacious and comfortable gable-roofed house. He has a number of concubines, and several children. He is a fine, gentlemanly-looking Arab, of a light complexion, generous and hospitable to friends, liberal to his slaves, and kind to his women. He has lived eighteen years in Africa, twelve of which have been spent in Karagwe. He knew Suna, the warlike Emperor of Uganda, and father of Mtesa. He has travelled to Uganda frequently, and several times made the journey between Unyanyembe and Kafurro. Having lived so long in Karagwe, he is friendly with Rumanika, who, like Mtesa, loves to attract strangers to his court.

Hamed has endeavoured several times to open trade with the powerful Empress of Ruanda, but has each time failed. Though some of his slaves succeeded in reaching the imperial court, only one or two managed to effect their escape from the treachery and extraordinary guile practised there. Nearly all perished by poison.

He informed me that the Empress was a tall woman of middle age, of an almost light Arab complexion, with very large brilliant eyes. Her son, the prince, a boy of about eighteen, had some years ago committed suicide by drinking a poisonous potion, because his mother had cast some sharp cutting reproaches upon him, which had so wounded his sensitive spirit that, he said, "nothing but death would relieve him."

Hamed is of the belief that these members of the imperial family are descendants of some light-coloured people to the north, possibly Arabs; "for how," asked he, "could the king of Kishakka possess an Arab scimitar, which is a venerated heir-loom of the royal family, and the sword of the founder of that kingdom?"

"All these people," said he, "about here are as different from the ordinary Washensi — pagans — as I am different from them. I would as soon marry a woman of Ruanda as I would a female of Muscat. When you go to see Rumanika, you will see some Wanya-Ruanda, and you may then judge for yourself. The people of that country are not cowards. Mashallah! they have taken Kishakka, Muvari, and have lately conquered Mpororo. The Waganda measured their strength with them, and were obliged to retreat. The Wanya-Ruanda are a great people, but they are covetous, malignant, treacherous, and utterly untrustworthy. They have never yet allowed an Arab to trade in their country, which proves them to be a bad lot. There is plenty of ivory there, and during the last eight years Khamis bin Abdullah, Tippu-Tib, Sayid bin Habib, and I myself have attempted frequently to enter there, but none of us has ever succeeded. Even Rumanika's people are not allowed to penetrate far, though he permits everybody to come into his country, and he is a man of their own blood and their own race, and speaks with little difference their own language."

Hamed Ibrahim was not opening out very brilliant prospects before me, nevertheless I resolved to search out in person some known road to this strange country that I might make a direct course to Nyangwe.

Feb. 28. — On the third day after arrival, the king having been informed of my intended visit, Hamed Ibrahim and Sayid bin Sayf accompanied me on an official visit to Rumanika, king of Karagwe, and a tributary of Mtesa, Emperor of Uganda.

Kafurro, according to aneroid, is 3950 feet above the ocean. Ascending the steep slope of the mountain west of Kafurro, we gained an altitude of 5150 feet, and half an hour afterwards stood upon a ridge 5350 feet above the sea, whence we obtained a most grand and imposing view. Some 600 feet below us was a grassy terrace overlooking the small Windermere Lake, 1000 feet below, its placid surface rivalling in colour the azure of the cloudless heaven. Across a narrow ridge we looked upon the broad and papyrus-covered valley of the Alexandra, whilst many fair, blue lakelets north and south, connected by the winding silver line of the Alexandra Nile, suggested that here exploring work of a most interesting character was needed to understand the complete relations of lake, river, and valley to one another.

Beyond the broad valley rose ridge after ridge, separated from each other by deep parallel basins, or valleys, and behind these, receding into dim and vague outlines, towered loftier ridges. About sixty miles off, to the north-west, rose a colossal sugar-loaf clump of enormous altitude, which I was told was the Ufumbiro mountains. From their northern base extended Mpororo country and to the south, Ruanda.

At the northern end of the Windermere Lake, an irregular range, which extends north to Ugoi, terminates in the dome-like Mount Isossi. South of where I stood, and about a mile distant, was the bold mount of Kazwiro, and about thirty miles beyond it I could see the irregular and confused masses of the Kishakka mountains.

On the grassy terrace below us was situated Rumanika's village, fenced round by a strong and circular stockade, to which we now descended after having enjoyed a noble and inspiriting prospect.

Our procession was not long in attracting hundreds of persons, principally youths, all those who might be considered in their boyhood being perfectly nude.

"Who are these?" I inquired of Sheikh Hamed.

"Some of the youngest are sons of Rumanika, others are young Wanya-Ruanda," he replied.

The sons of Rumanika, nourished on a milk diet, were in remarkably good condition. Their unctuous skins shone as though the tissues of fat beneath were dissolving in the heat, and their rounded bodies were as taut as a drum-head. Their eyes were large, and beaming and lustrous with life, yet softened by an extreme gentleness of expression. The sculptor might have obtained from any of these royal boys a dark model for another statue to rival the classic Antinous.

As we were followed by the youths, who welcomed us with a graceful curtesy, the appropriate couplet came to my mind —

"Thrice happy race! that innocent of blood,
From milk innoxious, seek their simple food."

We were soon ushered into the hut wherein Rumanika sat expectant, with one of the kindliest, most paternal smiles it would be possible to conceive.

I confess to have been as affected by the first glance at this venerable and gentle pagan as though I gazed on the serene and placid face of some Christian patriarch or saint of old, whose memory the Church still holds in reverence. His face reminded me of a deep still well; the tones of his voice were so calm that unconsciously they compelled me to imitate him, while the quick, nervous gestures and the bold voice of Sheikh Hamed, seeming entirely out of place, jarred upon me.

It was no wonder that the peremptory and imperious, vivid-eyed Mtesa respected and loved this sweet-tempered pagan. Though they had never met, Mtesa's pages had described him, and with their powers of mimicry had brought the soft modulated tones of Rumanika to his ears as truly as they had borne his amicable messages to him.

What greater contrasts can be imagined than the natures of the Emperor Mtesa and the King Rumanika? In some of his volcanic passions Mtesa seemed to be Fury personified, and if he were represented on the stage in one of his furious moods, I fear that the actor would rupture a blood-vessel, destroy his eyes, and be ever afterwards afflicted with madness. The Waganda always had recourse to action and gesture to supplement their verbal description of his raging fits. His eyes, they said, were "balls of fire and large as fists," while his words were "like gunpowder."

Nature, which had endowed Mtesa with a nervous and intense temperament, had given Rumanika the placid temper, the soft voice, the mild benignity, and pleasing character of a gentle father.

The king appeared to me, clad as he was in red blanket cloth, when seated, a man of middle size, but when he afterwards stood up, he rose to the gigantic stature of 6 feet 6 inches or thereabouts, for the top of my head, as we walked side by side, only reached near his shoulders. His face was long, and his nose somewhat Roman in shape; the profile showed a decidedly refined type.

Our interview was very pleasing, and he took excessive interest in every question I addressed to him. When I spoke, he imposed silence on his friends, and leaned forward with eager attention. If I wished to know anything about the geography of the country, he immediately sent for some particular person who was acquainted with that portion, and inquired searchingly of him as to his knowledge. He chuckled when he saw me use my note-book, as though he had some large personal interest in the number of notes I took. He appeared to be more and more delighted as their bulk increased, and triumphantly pointed out to the Arabs the immense superiority of the whites to them.

He expressed himself as only too glad that I should explore his country. It was a land, he said, that white men ought to know. It possessed many lakes and rivers, and mountains and hot springs, and many other things, which no other country could boast of.

"Which do you think best, Stamlee — Karagwe or Uganda?"

"Karagwe is grand, its mountains are high, and its valleys deep. The Kagera is a grand river, and the lakes are very pretty. There are more cattle in Karagwe than in Uganda, except Uddu and Koki; and game is abundant. But Uganda is beautiful and rich; its banana plantations are forests, and no man need to fear starvation, and Mtesa is good — and so is Father Rumanika," I replied smiling to him.

"Do you hear him, Arabs? Does he not speak well? Yes, Karagwe is beautiful," he sighed contentedly. "But bring your boat up and place it on the Rweru (lake), and you can go up the river as far as Kishakka, and down to Morongo (the falls), where the water is thrown against a big rock and leaps over it, and then goes down to the Nianja of Uganda. Verily, my river is a great one; it is the mother of the river at Jinga (Ripon Falls). You shall see all my land; and when you have finished the river, I will give you more to see — Mtagata's hot springs!"

March 6. — By the 6th of March, Frank had launched the boat from the landing at Kazinga village on the waters of the Windermere Lake, or the Rweru of Rumanika, and the next day Rumanika accompanied me in state to the water. Half-a-dozen heavy anklets of bright copper adorned his legs, bangles of the same metal encircled his wrists, a robe of crimson flannel was suspended from his shoulders. His walking-staff was 7 feet in length, and his stride was a yard long. Drummers and fifers discoursing a wild music, and fifty spearmen, besides his sons and relatives, Wanya-Ruanda, Waganda, Wasui, Wanyamwezi, Arabs, and Wangwana, followed us in a mixed multitude.

Four canoes manned by Wanyambu were at hand to race with our boat, while we took our seats on the grassy slopes of Kazinga to view the scene. I enjoined Frank and the gallant boat's crew to exert themselves for the honour of us Children of the Ocean, and not to permit the Children of the Lakes to excel us.

A boat and canoe race on the Windermere of Karagwe, with 1200 gentle-mannered natives gazing on! An African international affair! Rumanika was in his element; every fibre of him tingled with joy at the prospective fun. His sons, seated around him, looked up into their father's face, their own reflecting his delight. The curious natives shared in the general gratification.

The boat-race was soon over; it was only for about 800 yards, to Kankorogo Point. There was not much difference in the speed, but it gave immense satisfaction. The native canoemen, standing up with their long paddles, strained themselves with all their energy, stimulated on the shouts of their countrymen, while the Wangwana on the shore urged the boat's crew to their utmost power.

March 8. — The next day we began the circumnavigation of the Windermere. The extreme length of the lake during the rainy season is about eight miles, and its extreme breadth two and a half. It lies north and south, surrounded by grass-covered mountains which rise from 1200 to 1500 feet above it. There is one island called Kankorogo, situated midway between Mount Isossi and the extreme southern end. I sounded three times, and obtained depths of 48, 44, and 45 feet respectively at different points. The soil of the shores is highly ferruginous in colour, and, except in the vicinity of the villages, produces only euphorbia, thorny gum, acacia, and aloetic plants.

March 9. — On the 9th we pulled abreast of Kankorogo Island; and, through a channel from 500 to 800 yards wide, directed our course to the Kagera, up which we had to contend against a current of two knots and a half an hour.

The breadth of the river varied from 50 to 100 yards. The average depth of all the ten soundings we made on this day was 52 feet along the middle; close to the papyrus walls, which grew like a forest above us, was a depth of 9 feet. Sometimes we caught a view of hippopotamus creeks running up for hundreds of yards on either side through the papyrus. At Kagayyo, on the left bank, we landed for a short time to take a view of the scene around, as, while in the river, we could see nothing except the papyrus, the tops of the mountain ridge of Karagwe, and the sky.

We then learned for the first time the true character of what we had imagined to be a valley when we gazed upon it from the summit of the mountain between Kafurro and Rumanika's capital.

The Ingezi, as the natives called it, embraces the whole space from the base of the mountains of Muvari to that of the Karagwe ridges with the river called

Kagera, the Funzo or the papyrus, and the Rwerus or lakes, of which there are seventeen, inclusive of Windermere. Its extreme width between the bases of the opposing mountains is nine miles; the narrowest part is about a mile, while the entire acreage covered by it from Morongo or the falls in Iwanda, north to Uhimba, south, is about 350 square miles. The Funzo or papyrus covers a depth of from 9 feet to 14 feet of water. Each of the several lakes has a depth of from 20 to 65 feet, and they are all connected, as also is the river, underneath the papyrus.

When about three miles north of Kizinga, at 5 P.M., we drew our boat close to the papyrus, and prepared for a night's rest, and the Wanyambu did the same.

The boat's crew crushed down some of the nearest papyrus, and, cutting off the broom-like tops, spread their mats upon the heap thus made, flattering themselves that they were going to have a cozy night of it. Their fires they kindled between three stalks, which sustained their cooking-pots. It was not a very successful method, as the stalks had to be replaced frequently; but finally their bananas were done to a turn. At night, however, mosquitoes of a most voracious species attacked them in dense multitudes, and nothing but the constant flip-flap of the papyrus tops mingled with complaints that they were unable to sleep were heard for an hour or two. They then began to feel damp, and finally wet, for their beds were sinking into the depths below the papyrus, and they were compelled at last to come into the boat, where they passed a most miserable night, for the mosquitoes swarmed and attacked them until morning with all the pertinacity characteristic of these hungry bloodsuckers.

March 10. — The next day, about noon, we discovered a narrow, winding creek, which led us to a river-like lake, five miles in length, out of which, through another creek, we punted our boats and canoes to the grazing island of Unyamubi.

From a ridge which was about 50 feet above the Ingezi we found that we were about four miles from Kishakka and a similar distance due east from a point of land projecting from Muvari.

March 11. — The next day we ascended the Kagera about ten miles, and returning fourteen miles entered Ihema Lake, a body of water about 50 square miles, and camped on Ihema Island, about a mile from Muvari.

The natives of Ihema Island stated to me that Lake Muta Nzige was only eleven days' journey from the Muvari shores, and that the Wanya-Ruanda frequently visited them to obtain fish in exchange for milk and vegetables. They also stated that the Mworongo — or, as others called it, Nawarongo — river flows through the heart of Ruanda from the Ufumbiro mountains, and enters the Kagera in a south-west by west direction from Ihema: that the Akanyaru was quite a large lake, a three days' journey round in canoes, and separated Ruanda, Uhha, and Urundi from each other; that there was an island in the midst, where canoes leaving Uhha were accustomed to rest at night, arriving in Ruanda at noon.

They were a genial people those islanders of Ihema, but they were subject to two painful diseases, leprosy and elephantiasis. The island was of a shaly substructure, covered with a scant depth of alluvium. The water of the Lake Ihema was good and sweet to the taste, though, like all the waters of the Alexandra Nile, distinguished for its dull brown iron colour.

We began from the extreme south end of the lake the next day to coast along the Muvari or Ruanda coast, and near a small village attempted to land, but the natives snarled like so many spiteful dogs, and drew their bows, which compelled us — being guests of Rumanika — to sheer off and leave them in their ferocious exclusiveness.

Arriving at the Kagera again, we descended it, and at 7 P.M. were in our little camp of Kasinga, at the south end of Windermere.

On the 11th we rowed into the Kagera, and descended the river as far as Ugoi, and on the evening of the 12th returned once more to our camp on Windermere.

March 13. — The next day, having instructed Frank to convey the boat to Kafurro, I requested Rumanika to furnish me with guides for the Mtagata hot springs, and faithful to his promise, thirty Wanyambu were detailed for the service.

Our route lay north along the crest of a lofty ridge between Kafurro and Windermere. Wherever we looked, we beheld grassy ridges, grassy slopes, grassy mountain summits, and grassy valleys — an eminently pastoral country. In a few gorges or ravines the dark tops of trees are seen.

When Windermere Lake and Isossi, its northern mount, were south of us, we descended into a winding grassy valley, and in our march of ten miles from Isossi to Kasya I counted thirty-two separate herds of cattle, which in the aggregate probably amounted to 900 head. We also saw seven rhinoceroses, three of which were white, and four a black brown. The guides wished me to shoot one, but I was scarce of ammunition, and as I could not get a certain shot, I was loath to wound unnecessarily, or throw away a cartridge.

March 14. — The next day, at 8 A.M., near the end of the valley, we came to Merure Lake, which is about two miles long, and thence, crossing three different mountains, arrived at Kiwandare mountain, and from its summit, 5600 feet above the sea, obtained a tolerably distinct view of the triple cone of Ufumbiro, in a west-north-west direction, Mag. I should estimate the distance from Kiwandare to Ufumbiro to be about forty-five miles, and about sixty miles from the mountain height above Rumanika's capital. Several lines of mountains, with lateral valleys between, rose between the valley of the Alexandra Nile and Ufumbiro.

From Kiwandare we descended gradually along its crest to a lower terrace. About 5 P.M. one of our party sighted a dark brown double-horned rhinoceros, and as we had no meat, and the nature of the ground permitted easy approach, I crept up to within fifty yards of it unperceived and sent in a zinc bullet close to the ear, which bowled it over dead.

The quantity of meat obtained from the animal was more than would supply the eighteen men, Wangwana, of my party; therefore, acceding to their wish, we camped on the spot, exposed to the chilly mountain winds, which visited us during the night. The men, however, continued to pick up abundance of fuel from a wooded gorge close by, and, engaged in the interesting and absorbing task of roasting meat before many blazing fires, did not suffer greatly.

March 15. — At 9 A.M. the next day we descended to the wooded gorge of Mtagata, having travelled thirty-five miles, almost due north from Kafurro.

This gorge is formed by an angle where the extreme-northern end of Kiwandare mountain meets a transverse ridge. It is filled with tall trees which have been nourished to a gigantic size and density of foliage by the warm vapours from the springs and the heated earth. A thick undergrowth of plants, llianes, and creepers of all sizes has sprung up under the shade of the aspiring trees, and the gloom thus caused within the gorge is very striking, I imagine a person would find it a most eerie place at night alone. Great baboons and long-tailed monkeys roared and chattered in the branches, causing the branches to sway and rustle as they chased one another from tree to tree.

At the time of our visit the springs were frequented by invalids from Iwanda, Ngoi, Kiziwa, Usongora, and Usui, for, as may be believed, they have obtained a great repute throughout the districts of Karagwe and neighbouring countries.

The springs are six in number, and at their extreme source they had, when I tested them, a temperature of 129° Fahr. The bathing pools, which are about 12 feet in diameter, and from 2 to 5 feet deep, showed a temperature of 110° Fahr., except one on the extreme north, which was. only 107° Fahr.

I bottled eight ounces of water from one of these springs and on arriving in London sent it to Messrs. Savory and Moore, the well-known chemists, 148 Bond Street, who in a few days kindly returned me the following analysis: —

"The fluid was clear, colourless, and odourless; on standing at rest, a small quantity of red granular matter was deposited.

"Examined chemically, it was found to have a faint alkaline reaction, and its specific gravity, corrected to 60° F., was 1004, water being considered 1000.

"One hundred grammes evaporated left a white crystalline residue, weighing 37 of a gramme, and it was composed of sodium carbonate, calcium carbonate, calcium sulphate and sodium chlorine; this order represents their proportions, sodium carbonate being the chief constituent, and the other salts existing in more minute quantities.

"The deposit was removed and examined microchemically: it was thus found to consist of ferruginous sand, and two minute pieces of vegetable cellulose.

"It was therefore a faintly alkaline water, and its alkalinity depended on the presence of sodium carbonate possibly existing in solution as bicarbonate, as the water held in solution carbonic acid gas, and this gas was evolved by heating the water."

The natives praised the water of these springs so highly that I resolved to stay three days to test in my own person what virtues it possessed. I drank an enormous quantity of the water with a zealous desire to be benefited, but I experienced no good — on the contrary, much ill, for a few days afterwards I suffered from a violent attack of intermittent fever, occasioned, I fancy, by the malaria inhaled from the tepid atmosphere. It is true I luxuriated morning and evening in the bath which was reserved for me by Luajumba, son of Rumanika, but that was all the advantage that accrued to me.

Patients suffering from cutaneous diseases profit rapidly from, I believe, the unusual cleanliness; and during the few days we camped here numbers of natives came and went, and merriment and cleansing, bathing and lounging, music and barbarous chanting, kept awake the echoes of the gorge.

Our stay at the springs was cheered also by the presence of Luajumba, who, following the example of his father Rumanika, was hospitable and bland in his manners. An ox, two goats, ten fowls, besides bananas, sweet potatoes and flour, and fourteen large gourdfuls of maramba were received with thanks and paid for.

March 18. — On the 18th of March we set out on our return to Kafurro from the hot springs, and on the road I shot a white rhinoceros, which the people soon cut up to convey to their comrades. On the 19th we arrived at Kafurro, each of the Wangwana being loaded with over twenty Ibs. of meat.

March 21. — After two days' rest I paid another visit to Rumanika, where we had a great geographical discussion. It is unnecessary to describe the information I had to give Rumanika respecting the geographical distribution of tribes and races over the Dark Continent, but conscious that the geographical world will take an interest in what Rumanika and the native travellers at his court imparted, I here append, verbatim, the notes I took upon the spot.

Hamed Ibrahim spoke and said: —

"My slaves have travelled far, and they say that the Ni-Nawarongo River rises on the west side of Ufumbiro mountains, takes a wide sweep through Ruanda, and enters Akanvaru, in which Lake it meets the Kagera from the south. United they then empty from the lake between Uhha and Kishakka, and flowing between Karagwe and Ruanda, go into the Nianza (Nyanza).

"The Rwizi River, also rising at the northern base of the Ufumbiro cones, in Mpororo, flows through Igara, then Shema, then Ankori, into the king of Koki's (Luampula) lake, and becoming the Chibarre or Kiware River, joins the Kagera below Kitangule.

"If you proceed toward sunset from Mpororo, you will see Muta Nzige, the Nianza of Unyoro. There are many large islands in it. Utumbi is a country of islands, and the natives are very good, but you cannot proceed through Mpororo, as the people are Shaitans — devils — and the Wanya-Ruanda are wicked; and because something happened when Wangwana first tried to go there, they never tolerate strangers. A strange people, and full of guile verily.

" West of Ruanda is a country called Mkinyaga, and there is a large lake there, so I have heard — no Arabs have ever been there."

Then a native of Western Usui, at the request of Rumanika, said: —

"Mkinyaga is west of Kivu Lake or Nianja Cha Ngoma, from which the Rusizi River flows into the lake of Uzige (Tanganika). To reach Mkinyaga, you must pass through Unyambungu first, then you will see the great Lake of Mkinyaga. Lake Kivu has a connection with the lake Akanyaru, though there is much grass; as in the Ingezi, below here. A canoe could almost reach Kivu from Kishakka, but it would be hard work.

"Akanyaru, which the Wahha call Nianja Cha-Ngoma, is very wide. It will take a day and a half to cross, and is about two or three days' canoe journey in length. It lies between Ruanda, Uhha, and Urundi. The Kagera coming from between Uhha and Urundi flows into it. The Nawarongo empties into the Ruvuvu between Ugufu and Kishakka. The Ruvuvu between Kishakka and Karagwe enters the Kagera; the Kagera comes into the Ingezi, and flows by Kitangule into the Nianja of Uganda; Kivu lake is west-south-west from Kibogora's capital, in West Usui. Kivu has no connection with Muta Nzige, the lake of Unyoro."

Then a native of Zanzibar who had accompanied Khamis bin Abdallah to North-Western Uhha said: —

"I have been west of King Khanza's Uhha, and I saw a large lake. Truly there is much water there. Urundi was to my left. Ruanda fronted me across, and I stood on Uhha."

Rumanika followed, and imparted at length all his information, of which I append only the pith: —

"Leaving Mpororo, you may reach by canoes Makinda's, in Utumbi, in half a day. The island is called Kabuzzi. Three hours will take a canoe thence to Karara Island, and from Karara Island another half-day will take you to Ukonju, where there is a tribe of cannibals.

"Mkinyaga is at the end of Ruanda, and its lake is Muta Nzige, on which you can go to Unyoro. There is a race of dwarfs somewhere west of Mkinyaga called the Mpundu, and another called the Batwa or Watwa, who are only two feet high. In Uriambwa is a race of small people with tails.

"Uitwa, or Batwa — Watwa, is at the extreme south end of Uzongora.

"From Butwa, at the end of a point of land in Ruanda, you can see Uitwa, Usongora.

" From Butwa, Mkinyaga is to the left of you about three days' journey.

"Some of the Waziwa saw a strange people in one of those far-off lands who had long ears descending to their feet; one ear formed a mat to sleep on, the other served to cover him from the cold like a dressed hide! They tried to coax one of them to come and see me, but the journey was long, and he died on the way."

Dear old Rumanika, how he enjoyed presiding over the Geographical Society of Karagwe, and how he smiled when he delivered this last extraordinary piece of Munchhausenism! He was determined that he should be considered as the best informed of all present, and anticipated with delight the pleasure old and jaded

Europe would feel upon hearing of these marvellous fables of Equatorial Africa. He was also ambitious to witness my note-book filled with his garrulity, and I fear he was a little disposed to impose upon the credulity of sober Christians. However, with this remark of caution to the reader, his fables may be rendered harmless, and we can accord him thanks for his interesting information. Since I am publishing these geographical items, I may as well append here, also in brief, some other information obtained elsewhere relating to Muta Nzige from a native of Usongora, whom we found at Kawanga with Sekajugu, one of the Watongoleh who accompanied us to Beatrice Gulf.

"When you leave Ruoko in Unyoro, you will have Gambaragara to your right, and Usagara or Ankori will be on your left. Uzimba, Ruigi's country, will be four days' journey west of you.

"On reaching Uzimba, if you turn to the left you will reach Luhola. Usongora will be on your right hand.

"On your left will also be Unyampaka, Kasita, Kishakka, Chakiomi, Nytere, Buhuju, Makara, Uuyamururu, Munya Chambiro, and the Bwambu, who are cannibals.

"If you go to your right from Ruigi's, you reach Usongora, Mata, two days after Nabweru, then Butwa. Standing at Butwa, you will see Ruanda on the left hand.

"The country of Ruigi is called Uzimba.

"Kitagwenda is the name of the neighbouring country.

"Unyanuruguru lies between Ruanda and Usongora.

"All the Wasongora emigrated from Unyoro."

The following is information from a native of Unyampaka upon Muta Nzige; —

"My king's name is Bulema. Kasheshe is the great king of Uzimba. Ruigi is dead. Usongora, as you look towards sunset, will lie before you as you stand at Kasheshe's. To go to Usongora from Kasheshe's, you go to Nkoni Island, then to Ihundi Island, and then to Usongora.

"Far to your left, as you face the sunset, you have Utumbi, the Mahinda, Karara, and Kabuzzi Islands.

"There is abundance of salt in Usongora, and we go from Unyampaka (my country) to get salt, and sell it to all the country round. Ankori country does not extend to Muta Nzige. Buhuju and Unyanuruguru lie between Ankori and the lake.

"Nyika is king of Gambaragara and Usongora. North of Gambaragara is Toru, or Tori, country, a part of Unyoro. Kabba Rega is the great king of all those lands. The medicines (charms) of Unyoro are kept by Nyika on the top of his high mountain. There are as many white people there as there are black. On the top there is a little Nianja, and a straight rock rises high out from the middle. There is plenty of water falling from the sides of the mountain, sometimes straight down, with a loud noise. Herds upon herds of cattle, hundreds of them are in Gambaragara and Usongora. The people of Usongora are great fighters, they carry three spears and a shield each, and they live on nothing but milk and potatoes."

I now proceerd to give some "reflections" of a young philosopher of Uganda, one of the pages of Sambuzi, who had accompanied his master in the Katekiro's great raid upon Usongora three years before.

This young lad startled me out of the idea that philosophizing was not a common gift, or that only members of the white race were remarkable for their powers of observation, by the following question: —

"Stamlee, how is it, will you tell me, that all white men have long noses, while all their dogs have very short noses, while almost all black men have short noses, but their dogs have very long noses?"

A youth of Uganda, thought I, who can propound such a proposition as that, deserves attention.

"Speak," I said, "all you know about Muta Nzige and the Kagera."

"Good; you see the Kagera, it is broad and deep and swift, and its water though dark is clear. Where can it come from? There is an enormous quantity of water in that river. It is the mother of the river at Jinja, because were it not for this river our Niyanza would dry up!

"Tell me where it can come from? There is no country large enough to feed it, because when you reach Rumanika's it is still a large river. If you go to Kishakka, farther south, it is still large, and at Kibogora's it is still a large river. Urundi is not far, and beyond that is the Tanganika.

"Tell me, where does the water of the Muta Nzige go to? It goes into the Kagera, of course; the Kagera goes into our Niyanza, and the river at Jinja (Victoria Nile) goes to Kaniespa (Gondokoro). I tell you truly that this must be the way of it. You saw the Kusango and Mpauga, did you not, go to Muta Nzige? Well, there must be many rivers like that going to Muta Nzige also. And what river drinks all those rivers but the Kagera?" he asked triumphantly.

"Usongora is a wonderful land! Its people are brave, and when the Kateldro, who was accompanied by Mkwenda and Sekebobo's chiefs, and some of Kitunzi's, met them, they were different people from Gambaragara. They are very tall, long-legged people, and are armed with spears and shields. They tried every dodge with us. When we stood on the banks of a river going north, through the Tinka-tinka, like that in the Katonga, the Wasongora stood on the opposite side and shouted out to us that they were ready. Sambuzi came near being killed next day, and we lost many men, but the Katekiro, he does not fight like other chiefs, he is exceedingly brave, and he wanted to please Mtesa. We fought six days.

"The Wasongora had a number of large dogs also which they set upon us; as we drove their cattle towards Gambaragara, the earth shook, springs of mud leaped up, and the water in the plain was very bitter, and killed many Waganda; it left a white thing around its borders like salt.

"We first saw Muta Nzige as we followed Nyika to the top of his big mountain in Gambaragara. We could not quite get to the top, it was too high." (This is Mount Gordon-Bennett.) "But we could see Usongora, and a great lake spreading all round it. "When we came back with our spoil to Mtesu, he sent us back a short time afterwards to Ankori, and from the top of a high mountain near Kibanga (Mount Lawson) we saw Muta Nzige again spreading west of us. Oh, it is a grand lake, not so wide as our Niyanza, but very long. We get all our salt from Usongora, as Nyika pays tribute to us with so many bags, collected from the plains, but it is unfit to cat, unless you wash it and clean it."

This young lad accompanied me to Karagwe, and by his intelligence and his restless curiosity extracted from the Wanyambu courtiers at King Rumanika's information which he delivered to me in the following manner: —

"Master, I have been asking questions from many Wanyambu, and they say that you can take a canoe from here to Ujiji, only a certain distance you will have to drag your canoes by land. They say also that Ndagara, Rumanika's father, wishing to trade with the Wajiji, tried to cut a canal or a ditch for his canoes to pass through. They say also that Kivu is connected with Akanyaru, and that the Rusizi leaves Kivu and goes to Tanganika through Uzige, but the Kigera comes through Karagwe towards Uganda. Do you believe it?"

To close the interesting day, Rumanika requested Hamed Ibrahim to exhibit the treasure, trophies and curiosities in the king's museum or armoury, which Hamed was most anxious to do, as he had frequently extolled the rare things there.

The armoury was a circular hut, resembling externally a dome thatched neatly with straw. It was about 30 feet in diameter.

The weapons and articles, of brass and copper and iron, were in perfect order, and showed that Rumanika did not neglect his treasures.

There were about sixteen rude brass figures of ducks with copper wings, ten curious things of the same metal which were meant to represent elands, and ten headless cows of copper. Billhooks of iron, of really admirable make, double-bladed spears, several gigantic blades of exceedingly keen edge, 8 inches across and 18 inches in length, exquisite spears, some with blades and staves of linked iron; others with chained-shaped staves, and several with a cluster of small rigid ring's massed at the bottom of the blade and the end of the staff; others, copper-bladed, had curious intertwisted iron rods for the staff. There were also great fly-flaps set in iron, the handles of which were admirable specimens of native art; massive cleaver-looking knives with polished blades and a kedge-anchor-shaped article with four hooked iron prongs, projecting out of a brass body. Some exquisite native cloths, manufactured of delicate grass, were indeed so fine as to vie with cotton sheeting, and were coloured black and red, in patterns and stripes. The royal stool was a masterpiece of native turnery, being carved out of a solid log of cotton-wood. Besides these specimens of native art were drinking-cups, goblets, trenchers and milk dishes of wood, all beautifully clean. The fireplace was a circular hearth in the centre of the building, very tastefully constructed. Ranged round the wall along the floor were other gifts from Arab friends, massive copper trays, with a few tureen lids of Britannia ware, evidently from Birmingham. Nor must the revolving rifle given to him by Captain Speke be forgotten, for it had an honoured place, and Rumanika loves to look at it, for it recalls to his memory the figures of his genial white friends Speke and Grant.

The enormous drums, fifty-two in number, ranged outside, enabled us, from their very appearance, to guess at the deafening sounds which celebrate the new moon or deliver the signals for war.

My parting with the genial old man, who must be about sixty years old now, was very affecting. He shook my hands many times, saying each time that he was sorry that my visit must be so short. He strictly charged his sons to pay me every attention until I should arrive at Kibogora's, the king of Western Usui, who, he was satisfied, would be glad to see me as a friend of Rumanika.

March 26. — On the 26th of March the Expedition, after its month's rest at Kafurro, the whole of which period I had spent in exploration of Western Karagwe, resumed its journey, and after a march of five miles camped at Nakawanga, near the southern base of Kibonga mountain.

The next day a march of thirteen miles brought us to the northern extremity of Uhimba lake, a broad river-like body of water supplied by the Alexandra Nile.

March 27. — On the 27th I had the good fortune to shoot three rhinoceroses, from the bodies of which we obtained ample supplies of meat for our journey through the wilderness of Uhimba. One of these enormous brutes possessed a horn 2 feet long, with a sharp dagger-like point below, a stunted horn, 9 inches in length. He appeared to have had a tussle with some wild beast, for a hand's breadth of hide was torn from his rump.

The Wangwana and Wanyambu informed me with the utmost gravity that the elephant maltreats the rhinoceros frequently, because of a jealousy that the former entertains of his fiery cousin. It is said that if the elephant observes the excrement of the rhinoceros unscattered, he waxes furious, and proceeds instantly in search of the criminal, when woe befall him if he is sulky, and disposed to battle for the proud privilege of leaving his droppings as they fall! The elephant in that case breaks off a heavy branch of a tree, or uproots a stout sapling like a boat's mast, and belabours the unfortunate beast until he is glad to save himself by hurried flight. For this reason, the natives say, the rhinoceros always turns round and thoroughly scatters what he has dropped.

Should a rhinoceros meet an elephant, he must observe the rule of the road and walk away, for the latter brooks no rivalry; but the former is sometimes headstrong, and the elephant then despatches him with his tusks by forcing him against a tree and goring him, or by upsetting him, and leisurely crushing him.

At the distance of twenty-six miles from Kafurro we made our third camp near some wave-worn sheets and protruding humps of brown-veined porphyry, and close to an arm of the Uhimba lake, which swarmed with hippopotami.

There were traces of water or wave action on this hard porphyry visible at about fifty feet above the present level. Some of these humps were exposed in the water also, and showed similar effects to those observed behind our camp.

March 27. — During the next two days we travelled twenty-seven miles south through a depression, or a longitudinal valley, parallel to Uhimba lake and the course of the Alexandra, with only an intervening ridge excluding the latter from our view. Tall truncated hill-cones rise every now and then with a singular resemblance to each other, to the same altitude as the grassy ridges which flank them. Their summits are flat, but the iron-stone faithfully indicates by its erosions the element which separated them from the ridges, and first furrowed the valley.

Uhimba, placed by Rumanika in the charge of his sons Kakoko, Kananga, and Ruhinda, is sixty-eight miles south of his capital, and consists of a few settlements of herdsmen. It was, a few years ago, a debatable land between Usui and Karagwe, but upon the conquest of Kishakki by Ruanda, Rumanika occupied it lest his jealous and ill-conditioned rival, Mankorongo of Usui, should do so.

At this place I met messengers from Mankorongo despatched by him to invite me to go and see him, and who, with all the impudence characteristic of their behaviour to the Arabs, declared that if I attempted to traverse any country in his neighbourhood without paying him the compliment of a visit, it would be my utter ruin.

They were sent back with a peaceful message, and told to say that I was bound for Kibogora's capital, to try and search out a road across Urundi to the west, and that if I did not succeed I would think of Mankorongo's words; at the same time, Mankorongo was to be sure that if I was waylaid in the forest by any large armed party with a view to intimidation, that party would be sorry for it.

I had heard of Mankorongo's extortions from Arabs and Waganda, and how he had proved himself a worthy successor to the rapacious Swarora, who caused so much trouble to Speke and Grant.

During the second day of our courteous intercourse with Kakoko, I ascended a mount some 600 feet high about three miles from camp, to take bearings of the several features which Kananga was requested to show me. Five countries were exposed to view, Karagwe, Kishakka, Ruanda beyond, Ugufu, and Usui. Parallel with Usui was pointed out King Khanza's Uhha; beyond Uhha we were told was Urundi, beyond Urundi, west, the Tanganika and Uzige, and then nobody knew what lands lay beyond Uzige. Akanyaru stretched south of west, between Ruanda, Uhha, and Urundi; in a south-west direction was said to be Kivu; in a west by north Mkinyaga, and in the west Unyambungu. Ugufu was separated from Kishakka by the Nawarongo or Ruvuvu, and from Uhha and Usui by the Alexandra Nile which came from, between Uhha and Urundi. A river of some size was also said to flow from the direction of Unyambungu into the Akanyaru.

March 30. — The next day we entered Western Usui, and camped at Kafurra's. In Usui there was a famine, and it required thirty-two doti of cloth to purchase four days' rations. Kibogora demanded and obtained thirty doti, one coil of wire, and forty necklaces of beads as tribute; Kafurra, his principal chief, demanded ten doti and a quantity of beads; another chief required five doti; the queen required a supply of cloth to wear; the princes put in a claim; the guides were loud for their reward. Thus, in four days, we were compelled to disburse two bales out of twenty-two, all that were left of the immense store we had departed with from Zanzibar. Under such circumstances, what prospect of exploration had we, were we to continue our journey through Uhha, that land which in 1871 had consumed at the rate of two bales of cloth per diem? Twenty days of such experience in Uhha would reduce us to beggary. Its "esurient" Mutwares and rapacious Mkamas and other extortionate people can only be quieted with cloth and beads disbursed with a princely hand. One hundred bales of cloth would only suffice to sustain a hundred men in Uhha about six weeks. Beyond Uhha lay the impenetrable countries of Urundi and Ruanda, the inhabitants of which were hostile to strangers.

Kibogora and Kufurra were sufficiently explicit and amiably communicative, for my arrival in their country had been under the very best auspices, viz. an introduction from the gentle and beloved Rumanika.

I turned away with a sigh from the interesting land, but with a resolution gradually being intensified, that the third time I sought a road west nothing should deter me.

April 7. — On the 7th of April we reluctantly resumed our journey in a southerly direction, and travelled five miles along a ravine, at the bottom of which murmured the infant stream Lohugati. On coming to its source we ascended a steep slope until we stood upon the summit of a grassy ridge at the height of 5600 feet by aneroid.

Not until we had descended about a mile to the valley of Uyagoma did I recognize the importance of this ridge as the water-parting between one of the feeders of Lake Victoria and the source of the Malagarazi, the principal affluent of Lake Tanganika.

Though by striking across Uhha due west or to the south-west we should again have reached the Alexandra Nile and the affluents of the Alexandra Lake, our future course was destined never to cross another stream or rivulet that supplied the great river which flows through the land of Egypt into the Mediterranean Sea.

From the 17th of January, 1875, up to the 7th of April, 1876, we had been engaged in tracing the extreme southern sources of the Nile, from the marshy plains and cultivated uplands where they are born, down to the mighty reservoir called the Victoria Nyanza. We had circumnavigated the entire expanse; penetrated to every bay, inlet, and creek; become acquainted with almost every variety of wild human nature — the mild and placable, the ferocious and impracticably savage, the hospitable and the inhospitable, the generous-souled as well as the ungenerous; we had viewed their methods of war, and had witnessed them imbruing their hands in each other's blood with savage triumph and glee; we had been five times sufferers by their lust for war and murder, and had lost many men through their lawlessness and ferocity; we had travelled hundreds of miles to and fro on foot along the northern coast of the Victorian Sea, and, finally, had explored with a large force the strange countries lying between the two lakes Muta Nzige and the Victoria, and had been permitted to gaze upon the arm of the lake named by me "Beatrice Gulf," and to drink of its sweet waters. We had then returned from farther quest in that direction, unable to find a peaceful resting-place on the lake shores, and had struck south from the Katonga lagoon down to the Alexandra Nile, the principal affluent of the Victoria Lake, which drains nearly all the waters from the west and south-west. We had made a patient survey of over one-half of its course, and then, owing to want of the means to feed the rapacity of the churlish tribes which dwell in the vicinity of the Alexandra Nyanza, and to our reluctance to force our way against the will of the natives, opposing unnecessarily our rifles to their spears and arrows, we had been compelled, on the 7th of April, to bid adieu to the lands which supply the Nile, and to turn our faces towards the Tanganika.

I have endeavoured to give a faithful portrayal of nature, animate and inanimate, in all its strange peculiar phases, as they were unfolded to us. I am conscious that I have not penetrated to the depths; but then I have not ventured beyond the limits assigned to me, viz. the Exploration of the Southern Sources of the Nile, and the solution of the problem left unsolved by Speke and Grant — Is the Victoria Nyanza one lake, or does it consist of five lakes, as reported by Livingstone, Burton, and others? This problem has been satisfactorily solved, and Speke has now the full glory of having discovered the largest inland sea on the continent of Africa, also its principal affluent, as well as the outlet. I must also give him credit for having understood the geography of the countries he travelled through better than any of those who so persistently assailed his hypothesis, and I here record my admiration of the geographical genius that from mere native report first sketched with such a masterly hand the bold outlines of the Victoria Nyanza.

CHAPTER XVIII.

The twin rivers — Mankorongo baulked of his loot — Poor Bull! True to the death — Msenna breaks out again — The Terror of Africa appears on the scene — Mars at peace — "Dig potatoes, potatoes, potatoes" — Mirambo, the bandit chief, and I make blood-brotherhood — Little kings with "big heads" — Practical conversion of the chief of Ubagwe — The Watuta, the Ishmaels of Africa — Their history — African nomenclature — From Msene across the Malagarazi to Ujiji — Sad memories.

April 7. — Along the valley of Uyagoma, in Western Usui, stretches east and west a grass-covered ridge, beautiful in places with rock-strewn dingles, tapestried with ferns and moss, and Insight with vivid foliage. From two such fair nooks, halfway down either slope, the northern and the southern, drip in great rich drops the sources of two impetuous rivers — on the southern the Malagarazi, on the other the Lohugati. Though nurtured in the same cradle, and issuing within 2000 yards of one another, the twin streams are strangers throughout their lives. Through the thick ferns and foliage, the rivulets trickle each down his appointed slope, murmuring as they gather strength to run their destined course — the Lohugati to the Victoria Lake, the Malagarazi to distant Tanganika.

While the latter river is in its infancy, collecting its first tribute of waters from the rills that meander down from the mountain folds round the basin of Uyagoma, and is so shallow that tiny children can paddle through it, the people of Usui call it the Meruzi. When we begin our journey from Uyagoma, we follow its broadening course for a couple of hours, through the basin, and by that time it has become a river nomine dignum, and, plunging across it, we begin to breast the mountains, which, rising in diagonal lines of ridges from north-east to south-west across Usui, run in broken series into Northern Uhha, and there lose themselves in a confusion of complicated masses and clumps.

The Meruzi wanders round and through these mountain masses in mazy curves, tumbles from height to height, from terrace to terrace, receiving as it goes the alliance or myriads of petty rivulets and threads of clear water, until, arriving at the grand forest lands of Unyamwezi, it has assumed the name of Lukoke, and serves as a boundary between Unyamwezi and Uhha.

Meanwhile we have to cross a series of mountain ridges clothed with woods; and at a road leading from Kibogora's land to the territory of the turbulent and vindictive Mankorongo, successor of Swarora, we meet an embassy, which demands in a most insolent tone that we should pass by his village. This means, of course, that we must permit ourselves to be defrauded of two or three bales of cloth, half-a-dozen guns, a sack or two of beads, and such other property as he may choose to exact, for the privilege of lengthening our journey some forty miles, and a delay of two or three weeks.

The insolent demand is therefore not to be entertained, and we return a decided refusal. They are not satisfied with the answer, and resort to threats. Threats in the free, uninhabited forest constitute a casus belli. So the chiefs are compelled to depart without a yard of cloth on the instant, and after their departure we urge our pace until night, and from dawn next morning to 3 P.M. we continue the journey with unabated speed, until we find ourselves in Nyambarri, Usambiro, rejoiced to find that we have foiled the dangerous king.

April 13. — On the 13th of April we halted to refresh the people. Usambiro, like all Unyamwezi, produces sufficient grain, sesamum, millet, Indian corn, and vetches, besides beans and peas, to supply all caravans and expeditions. I have observed that lands producing grain are more easy of access than pastoral countries, or those which only supply milk, bananas, and potatoes to their inhabitants.

At Nyambarri we met two Arab caravans fresh from Mankorongo, of whom they gave fearful accounts, from which I inferred that the extortionate chief would be by no means pleased when he came to understand how he had been baffled in his idea of spoliating our Expedition.

Here the notorious Msenna for the third time ruptured the peace. He was reported to be inciting a large number of Wangwana and Wanyamwezi to desert in a body, offering himself as guide to conduct them to Unyanyembe; and several young fellows, awed by his ungovernable temper and brutal disposition, had yielded to his persuasions. Msenna was therefore reduced to the ranks, and instead of being entrusted with the captaincy of ten men, was sentenced to carry a box, under the watchful eye of Kacheche, for a period of six months,

April 14. — During the march from Nyambarri to Gambawagao, the chief village of Usambiro, ancient "Bull," the last of all the canine companions which left England with me, borne down by weight of years and a land journey of about 1500 miles, succumbed. With bulldog tenacity he persisted in following the receding figures of the gun-bearers, who were accustomed to precede him in the narrow way. Though he often staggered and moaned, he made strenuous efforts to keep up, but at last, lying down in the path, he plaintively bemoaned the weakness of body that had conquered his will, and soon after died — his eyes to the last looking forward along the track he had so bravely tried to follow.

Poor dog! Good and faithful service had he done me! Who more rejoiced than he to hear the rifle-shot ringing through the deep woods! Who more loudly applauded success than he with his deep, mellow bark! What long forest tracts of tawny plains and series of mountain ranges had he not traversed! How he plunged through jungle and fen, morass and stream! In the sable blackness of the night his voice warned off marauders and prowling beasts from the sleeping camp. His growl responded to the hideous jabber of the greedy hyaena, and the snarling leopard did not dismay him. He amazed the wondering savages with his bold eyes and bearing, and by his courageous front caused them to retreat before him; and right bravely did he help us to repel the Wanyaturu from our camp in Ituru. Farewell, thou glory of thy race! Rest from thy labours in the silent forest! Thy feet shall no more hurry up the hill or cross mead and plain; thy form shall rustle no more through the grasses, or be plunging to explore the brake; thou shalt no longer dash after me across the savannahs, for thou art gone to the grave, like the rest of thy companions!

The king of Usambiro exchanged gifts with us, and appeared to be a clever, agreeable young man. His people, though professing to be Wanyamwezi, are a mixture of Wahha and Wazinja. He has constructed a strong village, and surrounded it with a fosse 4 feet deep and 6 feet wide, with a stockade and "marksmen's nests" at intervals round it. The population of the capital is about 2000.

Boma Kiengo, or Msera, lies five miles south-south-east from the capital, and its chief, seeing that we had arrived at such a good understanding with the king, also exerted himself to create a favourable impression.

April 18. — Musonga lies twelve miles south-south-east of Boma Kiengo, and is the most northerly village of the country of Urangwa. On the 18th of April, a march of fifteen miles enabled us to reach the capital, Ndeverva, another large stockaded village, also provided with "marksmen's nests," and surrounded by a fosse.

We were making capital marches. The petty kings, though they exacted a small interchange of gifts, which compelled me to disburse cloth a little more frequently than was absolutely necessary, were not insolent, nor so extortionate as to prevent our intercourse being of the most friendly character.

But on the day we arrived at Urangwa, lo! there came up in haste, while we were sociably chatting together, a messenger to tell us that the phantom, the bugbear, the terror whose name silences the children of Unyamwezi and Usukuma, and makes women's hearts bound with fear; that Mirambo himself was coming — that he was only two camps, or about twenty miles, away — that he had an immense army of Ruga-Ruga (bandits) with him!

The consternation at this news, the dismay and excitement, the discussion and rapid interchange of ideas suggested by terror throughout the capital, may be conceived. Barricades were prepared, sharp-shooters' platforms, with thick bulwarks of logs, were erected. The women hastened to prepare their charms, the Waganga consulted their spirits, each warrior and elder examined his guns and loaded them, ramming the powder down the barrels of their Brummagem muskets with desperately vengeful intentions, while the king hastened backwards and forwards with streaming robes of cotton behind him, animated by a hysterical energy.

I had 175 men under my command, and forty of the Arabs' people were with me, and we had many boxes of ammunition. The king recollected these facts, and said, "You will stop to fight Mirambo, will you not?"

"Not I, my friend; I have no quarrel with Mirambo, and we cannot join every native to fight his neighbour. If Mirambo attacks the village while I am here, and will not go away when I ask him, we will fight; but we cannot stop here to wait for him."

The poor king was very much distressed when we left the next morning. We despatched our scouts ahead, as we usually did when traversing troublous countries, and omitted no precaution to guard against surprise.

April 19. — On the 19th we arrived at one of the largest villages or towns in Unyamwezi, called Serombo or Sorombo. It was two miles and a half in circumference, and probably contained over a thousand large and small huts, and a population of about 5000.

The present king's name is Ndega, a boy of sixteen, the son of Makaka, who died about two years ago. Too young himself to govern the large settlement and the country round, two elders, or Manyapara, act as regents during his minority.

We were shown to a peculiar-shaped hut, extremely like an Abyssinian dwelling. The height of the doorway was 7 feet, and from the floor to the top of the conical roof it was 20 feet. The walls were of interwoven sticks, plastered over neatly with brown clay. The king's house was 30 feet high from the ground to the tip of the cone, and 40 feet in diameter within; but the total diameter including the circular fence or palisade that supported the broad eaves, and enclosed a gallery which ran round the house, was 54 feet.

Owing to this peculiar construction a desperate body of 150 men might from the circular gallery sustain a protracted attack from a vastly superior foe, and probably repel it.

Ndega is a relative of Mirambo by marriage, and he soon quieted all uneasy minds by announcing that the famous man who was now advancing upon Serombo had just concluded a peace with the Arabs, and that therefore no trouble was to be apprehended from his visit, it being solely a friendly visit to his young relative.

Naturally we were all anxious to behold the "Mars of Africa," who since 1871 has made his name feared by both native and foreigner from Usui to Urori, and from Uvinza to Ugogo, a country embracing 90,000 square miles, who, from the village chieftainship over Uyoweh, has made for himself a name as well known as that of Mtesa throughout the eastern half of Equatorial Africa, a household word from Nyangwe to Zanzibar, and the theme of many a song of the bards of Unyamwezi, Ukimbu, Ukonongo, Uzinja, and Uvinza.

On the evening of our arrival at Serombo's we heard his Brown Besses — called by the natives Gumeh-Gumeh — announcing to all that the man with the dread name lay not far from our vicinity.

At dusk the huge drums of Serombo signalled silence for the town-criers, whose voices, preceded by the sound of iron bells, were presently heard crying out: —

"Listen, O men of Serombo. Mirambo, the brother of Ndega, cometh in the morning. Be ye prepared, therefore, for his young men are hungry. Send your women to dig potatoes, dig potatoes. Mirambo cometh. Dig potatoes, potatoes, dig potatoes, to-morrow!"

April 20. — At 10 A.M. the Brown Besses, heavily charged and fired off by hundreds, loudly heralded Mirambo's approach, and nearly all my Wangwana followed the inhabitants of Serombo outside to see the famous chieftain. Great war-drums and the shouts of admiring thousands proclaimed that he had entered the town, and soon little Mabruki, the chief of the tent-boys, and Kacheche, the detective, on whose intelligence I could rely, brought an interesting budget to me.

Mabruki said: "We have seen Mirambo. He has arrived. We have beheld the Ruga-Ruga, and there are many of them, and all are armed with Gumeh-Gumeh. About a hundred are clothed in crimson cloth and white shirts, like our Wangwana. Mirambo is not an old man."

Kacheche said: "Mirambo is not old, he is young: I must be older than he is. He is a very nice man, well dressed, quite like an Arab. He wears the turban, fez, and cloth coat of an Arab, and carries a scimitar. He also wears slippers, and his clothes under his coat are very white. I should say he has about a thousand and a half men with him, and they are all armed with muskets or double-barrelled guns. Mirambo has three young men carrying his guns for him. Truly, Mirambo is a great man!"

The shrill Lu-lu-lu's, prolonged and loud, were still maintained by the women, who entertained a great respect for the greatest king in Unyamwezi.

Presently Manwa Sera, the chief captain of the Wangwana, came to my hut, to introduce three young men — Ruga-Ruga (bandits), as we called them, but must do so no more lest we give offence — handsomely dressed in fine red and blue cloth coats, and snowy white shirts, with ample turbans; around their heads. They were confidential captains of Mirambo's bodyguard.

"Mirambo sends his salaams to the white man," said the principal of them. "He hopes the white man is friendly to him, and that he does not share the prejudices of the Arabs, and believe Mirambo a bad man. If it is agreeable to the white man, will he send words of peace to Mirambo?"

"Tell Mirambo," I replied, "that I am eager to see him, and would be glad to shake hands with so great a man, and as I have made strong friendship with Mtesa, Rumanika, and all the kings along the road from Usoga to Unyamwezi, I shall be rejoiced to make strong friendship with Mirambo also. Tell him I hope he will come and see me as soon as he can."

April 22. — The next day Mirambo, having despatched a Ruga-Ruga — no, a patriot, I should have said — to announce his coming, appeared with about twenty of his principal men.

I shook hands with him with fervour, which drew a smile from him as he said, "The white man shakes hands like a strong friend."

His person quite captivated me, for he was a thorough African gentleman in appearance, very different from my conception of the terrible bandit who had struck his telling blows at native chiefs and Arabs with all the rapidity of a Frederick the Great environed by foes.

I entered the following notes in my journal on April 22, 1876: —

"This day will be memorable to me for the visit of the famous Mirambo. He was the reverse of all my conceptions of the redoubtable chieftain, and the man I had styled the 'terrible bandit.'

"He is a man about 5 feet 11 inches in height, and about thirty-five years old, with not an ounce of superfluous flesh about him. A handsome, regular-featured, mild-voiced, soft-spoken man, with what one might call a 'meek' demeanour, very generous and open-handed. The character was so different from that which I had attributed to him that for some time a suspicion clung to my mind that I was being imposed upon, but Arabs came forward who testified that this quiet-looking man was indeed Mirambo. I had expected to see something of the Mtesa type, a man whose exterior would proclaim his life and rank; but this unpresuming, mild-eyed man, of inoffensive, meek exterior, whose action was so calm, without a gesture, presented to the eye nothing of the Napoleonic genius which he has for five years displayed in the heart of Unyamwezi, to the injury of Arabs and commerce, and the doubling of the price of ivory. I said there was nothing; but I must except the eyes, which had the steady, calm gaze of a master.

"During the conversation I had with him, he said he preferred boys or young men to accompany him to war; he never took middle-aged or old men, as they were sure to be troubled with wives or children, and did not fight half so well as young fellows who listened to his words. Said he, 'They have sharper eyes, and their young limbs enable them to move with the ease of serpents or the rapidity of zebras, and a few words will give them the hearts of lions. In all my wars with the Arabs, it was an army of youths that gave me victory, boys without beards. Fifteen of my young men died one day because I said I must have a certain red cloth that was thrown down as a challenge. No, no, give me youths for war in the open field, and men for the stockaded village.'

"'What was the cause of your war, Mirambo, with the Arabs?' I asked.

"'There was a good deal of cause. The Arabs got the big head' (proud), 'and there was no talking with them. Mkasiwa of Unyanyembo lost his head too, and thought I was his vassal, whereas I was not. My father was king of Ilyoweh, and I was his son. What right had Mkasiwa or the Arabs to say what I ought to do? But the war is now over — the Arabs know what I can do, and Mkasiwa knows it. We will not fight any more, but we will see who can do the best trade, and who is the smartest man. Any Arab or white man who would like to pass through my country is welcome. I will give him meat and drink, and a house, and no man shall hurt him.'"

Mirambo retired, and in the evening I returned his visit with ten of the principal Wangwana. I found him in a bell-tent, 20 feet high and 25 feet in diameter, with his chiefs around him.

Manwa Sera was requested to seal our friendship by performing the ceremony of blood-brotherhood between Miramba and myself. Having caused us to sit fronting each other on a straw-carpet, he made an incision in each of our right legs, from which he extracted blood, and, inter-changing it, he exclaimed aloud: —

"If either of you break this brotherhood now established between you, may the lion devour him, the serpent poison him, bitterness be in his food, his friends desert him, his gun burst in his hands and wound him, and everything that is bad do wrong to him until death."

My new brother then gave me fifteen cloths to be distributed among my chiefs, while he would accept only three from me. But not desirous of appearing illiberal, I presented him with a revolver and 200 rounds of ammunition,, and some small curiosities from England. Still ambitious to excel me in liberality, he charged five of his young men to proceed to Urambo — which name he has now given Uyoweh, after himself — and to select three milch-cows with their calves, and three bullocks, to be driven to Ubagwe to meet me. He also gave me three guides to take me along the frontier of the predatory Watuta.

April 23. — On the morning of the 23rd he accompanied me outside Serombo, where we parted on the very best terms with each other. An Arab in his company, named Sayid bin Mohammed, also presented me with a bar of Castile soap, a bag of pepper and some saffron. A fine riding-ass, purchased from Sayid, was named Mirambo by me, because the Wangwana, who were also captivated by Mirambo's agreeable manners, insisted on it.

We halted on the 23rd at Mayangira, seven miles and a half from Serombo, and on the 24th, after a protracted march of eleven miles south-south-east over flooded plains, arrived at Ukombeh.

April 24. — At Masumbwa, ten miles from Ukombeh, we encountered a very arrogant young chief, who called himself Mtemi, or king, and whose majesty claimed to be honoured with a donation of fifteen cloths — a claim which was peremptorily refused, despite all he could urge in satisfaction of it.

Through similar flooded plains, with the water hip-deep in most places, and after crossing an important stream flowing west-south-west towards the Malagarazi, we arrived at Myonga's village, the capital of southern Masumbwa.

This Myonga is the same valorous chief who robbed Colonel Grant as he was hurrying with an undisciplined caravan after Speke. (See Speke's Journal, page 159, for the following graphic letter: —

"In the Jungles, near M'yonga's,

"16th Sept. 1861.

"My dear Speke, — The caravan was attacked, plundered, and the men driven to the winds, while marching this morning into M'yonga's country.

"Awaking at cock-crow, I roused the camp, all anxious to rejoin you; and while the loads were being packed, my attention was drawn to an angry discussion between the head men and seven or eight armed fellows sent by Sultan M'yonga to insist on my putting up for the day in his village. They were summarily told that as you had already made him a present, he need not expect a visit from me. Adhering, I doubt not, to their master's instructions, they officiously constituted themselves our guides till we chose to strike off their path, when, quickly heading our party, they stopped the way, planted their spears, and dared our advance!

"This menace made us firmer in our determination, and we swept past the spears. After we had marched unmolested for some seven miles, a loud yelping from the woods excited our attention, and a sudden rush was made upon us by, say, two hundred men, who came down seemingly in great glee. In an instant, at the caravan's centre, they fastened upon the poor porters. The struggle was short; and with the threat of an arrow or spear at their breasts, men were robbed of their cloths and ornaments, loads were yielded and run away with before resistance could be organised; only three men of a hundred stood by me; the others, whose only thought was their lives, fled into the woods, where I went shouting for them. One man, little Rahan — rip as he is — stood with cocked gun, defending his load against five savages with uplifted spears. No one else could be seen. Two or three were reported killed, some were wounded. Beads, boxes, cloths, &c., lay strewed about the woods. In fact, I felt wrecked. My attempt to go and demand redress from the sultan was resisted, and, in utter despair, I seated myself among a mass of rascals jeering round me, and insolent after the success of the day. Several were dressed in the very cloths, &c., they had stolen from my men.

"In the afternoon about fifteen men and loads were brought me, with a message from the sultan, that the attack had been a mistake of his subjects — that one man had had a hand cut off for it, and that all the property would be restored!

"Yours sincerely,

"J. A. Grant")

Age had not lessened the conceit of Myonga, increased his modesty, or moderated his cupidity. He asserted the rights and privileges of his royalty with a presumptuous voice and a stern brow. He demanded tribute! Twenty-five cloths! A gun and five fundo of beads! The Arabs, my friends, were requested to do the same!

"Impossible, Myonga!" I replied, yet struck with admiration at the unparalleled audacity of the man.

"People have been obliged to pay what I ask," the old man said, with a cunning twinkle in his eyes.

"Perhaps," I answered; "but whether they have or not, I cannot pay you so much, and, what is more, I will not. As a sign that we pass through your country, I give you one cloth, and the Arabs shall only give you one cloth."

Myonga blustered and stormed, begged and threatened, and some of his young men appeared to be getting vicious, when rising I informed him that to talk loudly was to act like a scolding woman, and, that, when his elder should arrive at our camp, he would receive two cloths, one from me and one from the Arabs, as acknowledgment of his right to the country.

The drum of Myonga's village at once beat to arms, but the aft air went no further, and the elder received the reasonable and just tribute of two cloths, with a gentle hint that it would be dangerous to intercept the Expedition on the road when on the march, as the guns were loaded.

Phunze, chief of Mkumbiro, a village ten miles south by east from Myonga, and the chief of Ureweh, fourteen miles and a half from Phunze's, were equally bold in their demands, but they did not receive an inch of cloth; but neither of these three chiefs were half so extortionate as Ungomirwa, king of Ubagwe, a large town of 3000 people.

April 27. — We met at Ubagwe an Arab trader en route to Uganda, and he gave us a dismal tale of robbery and extortion practised on him by Ungomirwa. He had been compelled to pay 150 cloths, five kegs or 50 lbs. of gunpowder, five guns double-barrelled, and 35 lbs. of beads, the whole being of the value of 625 dollars, or £125, for the privilege of passing unmolested through the district of Ubagwe.

When the chief came to see me, I said to him: —

"Why is it, my friend, that your name goes about the country as being that of a bad man? How is it that this poor Arab has had to pay so much for going through Ubagwe? Is Ubagwe Unyamwezi, that Ungomirwa demands so much from the Arabs? The Arab brings cloths, powder, guns into Unyamwezi. If you rob him of his property, I must send letters to stop people coming here, then Ungomirwa will become poor, and have neither powder, guns, nor cloths to wear. What has Ungomirwa to say to his friend?"

"Ungomirwa," replied he, "does no more than Ureweh, Phunze, Myonga, Nclega, Urangwa, and Mankorongo: he takes what he can. If the white man thinks it is wrong, and will be my friend, I will return it all to the Arab."

"Ungomirwa is good. Nay, do not return it all; retain one gun, five cloths, two fundo of beads, and one keg of powder; that will be plenty, and nothing but right. I have many Wanyamwezi with me, whom I have made, good men. I have two from Ubagwe, and one man who was born at Phunze's. Let Ungomirwa call the Wanyamwezi, and ask them how the white man treats Wanyamwezi, and let him try to make them run away, and see what they will say. They will tell him that all white men are very good to those who are good."

Ungomirwa called the Wanyamwezi to him, and asked them why they followed the white man to wander about the world, leaving their brothers and sisters. The question elicited the following reply: —

"The white people know everything. They are better than the black people in heart. We have abundance to eat, plenty to wear, and silver for ourselves. All we give to the white man is our strength. We carry his goods for him, and he bestows a father's care on his black children. Let Ungomirwa make friends with the white man, and do as he says, and it will be good for the land of Unyamwezi."

To whatever cause it was owing, Ungomirwa returned the Arab nearly all his property, and presented me with three bullocks; and during all the time that I was his guest at Ubagwe, he exhibited great friendship for me, and boasted of me to several Watuta visitors who came to see him during that time; indeed, I can hardly remember a more agreeable stay at any village in Africa than that which I made in Ubagwe.

Unyamwezi is troubled with a vast number of petty kings, whose paltriness and poverty have so augmented their pride, that each of them employ more threats, and makes more demands, than Mtesa, Emperor of Uganda.

The adage that "Small things make base men proud" holds true in Africa as in other parts of the world. Sayid bin Sayf, one of the Arabs at Kafurro, begged me as I valued my property and peace of mind not to march through Unyamwezi to Ujiji, but to travel through Uhha. I attribute these words of Sayid's to a desire on his part to hear of my being mulcted by kings Khanza, Iwanda, and Kiti in the same proportion that he was. He confessed that he had paid to Kiti sixty cloths, to Iwanda sixty cloths, and to King Khanza 138, which amounted in value to 516 dollars, and this grieved the gentle merchant's soul greatly.

On my former journey in search of Livingstone, I tested sufficiently the capacity of the chiefs of Uhha to absorb property, and I vowed then to give them a wide berth for all future time. Sayid's relation of his experiences, confirmed by Hamed Ibrahim, and my own reverses, indicated but too well the custom in vogue among the Wahha. So far, between Kibogora's capital and Ubagwe, I had only disbursed thirty cloths as gifts to nine kings of Unyamwezi, without greater annoyance than the trouble of having to reduce their demands by negotiation.

No traveller has yet become acquainted with a wilder race in Equatorial Africa than are the Mafitte or Watuta. They are the only true African Bedawi; and surely some African Ishmael must have fathered them, for their hands are against every man, and every man's hand appears to be raised against them.

To slay a solitary Mtuta is considered by an Arab as meritorious, and far more necessary, than killing a snake. To guard against these sable freebooters, the traveller, while passing near their haunts, has need of all his skill, coolness, and prudence. The settler in their neighbourhood has need to defend his village with impregnable fences, and to have look-outs night and day: his women and children require to be guarded, and fuel can only be procured by strong parties, while the ground has to be cultivated spear in hand, so constant is the fear of the restless and daring tribe of bandits.

The Watuta, by whose lands we are now about to travel, are a lost tribe of the Mafitte, and became separated from the latter by an advance towards the north in search of plunder and cattle. This event occurred some thirty years ago. On their incursion they encountered the Warori, who possessed countless herds of cattle. They fought with them for two months at one place, and three months at another; and at last, perceiving that the Warori were too strong for them — many of them having been slain in the war and a large number of them (now known as the Wahehe, and settled near Ugogo) having been cut off from the main body — the Watuta skirted Urori, and advanced north-west through Ukonongo and Kawendi to Ujiji. It is in the memory of the old Arab residents at Ujiji how the Watuta suddenly appeared and drove them and the Wajiji to take refuge upon Bangwe Island.

Not glutted with conquest by their triumph at Ujiji, they attacked Urundi; but here they met different foes altogether from the negroes of the south. They next invaded Uhha, but the races which occupy the intra-lake regions had competent and worthy champions in the Wahha. Baffled at Uhha and Urundi, they fought their devastating path across Uvinza, and entered Unyamwezi, penetrated Usumbwa, Utambara, Urangwa, Uyofu, and so through Uzinja to the Victoria Nyanza, where they rested for some years after their daring exploit. But the lands about the lake were not suited to their tastes, and they retraced their steps as far as Utambara. Kututwa, king of Utambara, from policy, wooed the daughter of the chief of the Watuta, and as a dower his land was returned to him, while the Watuta moving south occupied the neighbouring country of Ugomba, situate between Uhha and Unyamwezi. It is a well-watered and a rich grazing country, therefore well adapted to their habits and modes of life. The Kinyamwezi kings of Serombo, Ubagwe, Ureweh, Renzeweh, and kings Mirambo and Phunze have contracted alliances with influential chiefs, and are on tolerably good terms with them; but stubborn old Myonga still holds aloof from the Watuta.

It will be remembered by readers of 'How I Found Livingstone' how Mirambo appeared at Tabora with thousands of the Watuta free-lances, slaughtered Khamis bin Abdullah and five other Arabs, and ravaged that populous settlement. From the above sketch of these terrible marauders, they will now be able to understand how it was that he was able to obtain their aid, while the following paragraph explains how I obtained the facts of this predatory migration.

The wife of Wadi Safeni — one of the Wangwana captains, and coxswain of the Lady Alice during her cruise round the Victoria Nyanza — when proceeding one day outside the stockade of Ubagwe to obtain water, accidentally heard our Watuta visitors gossiping together. The dialect and accent sounding familiar to her, she listened, and a few moments afterwards she was herself volubly discussing with them the geography of the locality inhabited by the Mafitte between Lake Nyassa and Tanganika. It was mainly from this little circumstance — confirmed by other informants, Arab, Wangwana, and Wanyamwezi — that the above brief sketch of the wanderings of the Watuta has been obtained.

"Mono-Matapa," that great African word, which, from its antiquity and its persistent appearance on our maps — occupying various positions to suit the vagaries of various cartographers and the hypotheses of various learned travellers — has now become almost classic, bears a distant relation to the tribe of the Watuta.

The industrious traveller, Salt, in his book on Abyssinia, dated 1814, says:

"This country is commonly called Monomatapa, in the accounts of which a perplexing obscurity has been introduced, by different authors having confounded the names of the districts with the titles of the sovereigns, indiscriminately styling them Quiteve, Monomatapa, Benemotapa, Bene-motasha, Chikanga, Manika, Bokaranga and Mokaranga. The fact appears to be that the sovereign's title was Quiteve, and the name of the country Motapa, to which Mono has been prefixed, as in Monomugi, and many other names on the coast, that beyond this lay a district called Chikanga, which contained the mines of Manica, and that the other names were applicable solely to petty districts at that time under the rule of the Quiteve."

Zimbaoa, the capital of this interesting land, was said to be fifteen days' travel west from Sofala, and forty days' travel from Sena.

Indefatigable and patient exploration by various intelligent travellers has now enabled us to understand exactly the meaning of the various names with which early geographers confused us. The ancient land of the Mono-Matapa occupied that part of South-East Africa now held by the Matabeles, and the empire embraced nearly all the various tribes and clans now known by the popular terms of Kaffirs and Zulus.

The reputation which Chaka obtained throughout that upland, extending from the lands of the Hottentots to the Zambezi, roused, after his death, various ambitious spirits. His great captains, leading warlike hosts after them, spread terror and dismay among the tribes north, south, and west. Mosele-katze overran the Transvaal, and conquered the Bechuanas, but was subsequently compelled by the Boers to migrate north, where his people, now known as the Matabeles, have established themselves under Lo Bengwella, his successor.

Sebituane, another warlike spirit after the style of Chaka, put himself at the head of a tribe of the Basutos, and, after numerous conquests over small tribes, established his authority and people along the Zambezi, under the name of Makololo. Sebituane was succeeded by Sekeletu, Livingstone's friend, and he by Impororo — the last of the Makololo kings.

One of Chaka's generals was called Mani-Koos. It ought to be mentioned here that Mani, Maua, Mono, Moeni, Muini, Muinyi, are all prefixes, synonymous with lord, prince, and sometimes son: for example, Mana-Koos, Mani-Ema, now called Man-yema and Mana-Mputu, lord of the sea; Mono-Matapa, Mana-Ndenga,

Mana-Butti, Mana-Kirembu, Mana-Mamba, and so forth. In Uregga the prefix becomes Wana, or Wane, as in Wane-Mbesa, Wane-Kirmnbu, Wane Kamankua, Wana-Kipangu, Wana-Mukwa, and Wana-Rukura; while in the Bateke and the Babwende lands it is changed into Mwana, as Mwana-Ibaka, or Mwana-Kilungu, which title was given to the Livingstone river by the Babwende, meaning "lord of the sea." To return. This Mani-Koos, a general of Chaka's, attacked the Portuguese at Delagoa Bay, Sofala, and Inhambane, and compelled them to pay tribute. The party then crossed the Zambezi river above Tete, the capital of the Portuguese territory, and, after ravaging the lands along the Nyassa, finally established itself north-west of the Nyassa, between that lake and the Tanganika. To-day they are known as the Manitu, Mafitte, or Ma-viti; and three offshoots of this tribe are — the Watuta in the neighbourhood of Zombe, south-east end of Lake Tanganika; the Wahehe, who cause such dire trouble to the Wagogo; and the Watuta, the allies of Mirambo, and called by the Wanyamwezi the Mwangoni.

May 4. — On the 4th of May, having received the milch cows, calves, and bullocks from my new brother Mirambo, we marched in a south-south-west direction, skirting the territory of the Watuta, to Puwinga, a village occupying a patch of cleared land, and ruled by a small chief who is a tributary to his dreaded neighbours.

May 5. — The next day, in good order, we marched across a portion of the territory of "the Watuta." No precaution was omitted to ensure our being warned in time of the presence of the enemy, nor did we make any delay on the road, as a knowledge of their tactics of attack assured us that this was our only chance of avoiding a conflict with them. Msene, after a journey of twenty miles, was reached about 2 P.M., and the king, Mulagwa, received us with open arms.

The population of the three villages under Mulagwa probably numbers about 3500. The king of the Wacuta frequently visits Mulagwa's district; but his strongly fenced villages and large number of muskets have been sufficient to check the intentions of the robbers, though atrocious acts are often committed upon the unwary.

Maganga, the dilatory chief of one of my caravans during the first Expedition, was discovered here, and, on the strength of a long acquaintance with my merits, induced Mulagwa to exert himself for my comfort.

I saw a poor woman, a victim of a raid by the Watuta, who, having been accidentally waylaid by them in the fields, had had her left foot barbarously cut off.

Ten miles south-west of Msene is Kawangira, a district about ten miles square, governed by the chief Nyambu, a rival of Mulagwa. Relics of the ruthlessness and devastating attacks of the Watuta are visible between the two districts, and the once populous land is rapidly resuming its original appearance of a tenantless waste.

May 9. — The next village, Nganda, ten miles south-west from Kawangira, was reached on the 9th of May. From this place, as far as Usenda (distant fourteen miles south-south-west), extended a plain, inundated with from 2 to 5 feet of water from the flooded Gombe which rises about forty miles south-east of Unyanyembe. Where the Gombe meets with the Malagarazi, there is a spacious plain, which during each rainy season is converted into a lake.

We journeyed to the important village of Usagusi on the 12th, in a south-south-west direction. Like Serombo, Myonga's, Urangwa, Ubagwe, and Msene, it is strongly stockaded, and the chief, conscious that the safety of his principal village depends upon the care he bestows upon its defences, exacts heavy fines upon those of his people who manifest any reluctance to repair the stockade; and this vigilant prudence has hitherto baffled the wolf-like marauders of Ugomba.

I met another old friend of mine at the next village, Ugara. He was a visitor to my camp at Kuziri, in Ukimbu, in 1871. Ugara is seventeen miles west-south-west. I found it troubled with a "war," or two wars, one between Kazavula and Uvinza, the other between Ibaugo of Usenye and Mkasiwa of Unyanyembe.

Twenty-five miles in a westerly direction, through a depopulated land, brought us to Zegi, in Uvinza, where we found a large caravan, under an Arab in the employ of Sayid bin Habib. Amongst these natives of Zanzibar was a man who had accompanied Cameron and Tippu-Tib to Utotera. Like other Munchhausens of his race, he informed me upon oath that he had seen a ship upon a lake west of Utotera, manned by black Wazungu, or black Europeans!

Before reaching Zegi, we saw Sivue lake, a body of water fed by the Sagala river: it is about seven miles wide by fourteen miles long. Through a broad bed, choked by reeds and grass and tropical plants, it empties into the Malagarazi river near Kiala.

Zegi village also swarmed with Rusunzu's warriors. Rusunzu has succeeded his father, Nzogera, as king of Uvinza, and, being energetic, is disposed to combat Mirambo's ambitious projects of annexation. I took care not to disclose our relationship with Mirambo, lest the warriors might have supposed we countenanced his designs against their beloved land.

These warriors, perceiving that the word Ruga-Ruga, or bandits, influences weak minds, call themselves by that name, and endeavour to distinguish themselves by arresting all native travellers suspected of hostility or property. One of these unfortunates just captured was about to have his weasand cut, when I suggested that he had better be sold, as his corpse would be useless.

"You buy him, then," said the excited fellows; "give us ten cloths for him."

"White men don't buy slaves; but rather than you should murder an innocent man, I will give you two for him."

After considerable discussion, it was agreed that he should be transferred to me for two cloths; but the poor old fellow was so injured from the brutal treatment he had undergone that he died a few days afterwards.

Zegi, swarming with a reckless number of lawless men, was not a comfortable place to dwell in. The conduct of these men was another curious illustration of how "small things make base men proud." Here were a number of youths suffering under that strange disease peculiar to vain youth in all lands which Mirambo had called "big head." The manner in which they strutted about, their big looks and bold staring, their enormous feathered head-dresses and martial stride, were most offensive. Having adopted, from bravado, the name of Ruga-Ruga, they were compelled in honour to imitate the bandits' custom of smoking banghi (wild hemp), and my memory fails to remind me of any similar experience to the wild screaming and stormy sneezing, accompanied day and night by the monotonous droning of the one-string guitar (another accomplishment de rigueur with the complete bandit) and the hiccupping, snorting, and vocal extravagances which we had to bear in the village of Zegi.

May 18. — We paid a decent tribute of fifteen cloths to Rusunzu, out of the infamous "sixty" he had demanded through his Mutware or chief; and the Mutware received only four out of the twenty he had said should be paid to himself; and after the termination of the bargaining we marched to Ugaga, on the Malagarazi, on the 18th.

May 20. — The Mutware of Ugaga the next day made a claim of forty doti or cloths before giving us permission to cross the Malagarazi. I sent Frank with twenty men to a point three miles below Ugaga to prepare our boat; and meanwhile we delayed negotiations until a messenger came from Frank informing us that the boat was ready, and then after making a tentative offer of two cloths, which was rejected with every ludicrous expression of contempt, we gave four. The Mutware then said that Rusunzu the king had commanded that we should return to Zegi to fight his enemies, otherwise he withheld his permission to cross the river. At this piece of despotism we smiled, and marched towards the boat, where we camped. At 4 A.M. of the 20th of May I had eighty guns across the mile-wide Malagarazi, and by 3 P.M. the entire Expedition, and our Arab friends whom we had met at Zegi, were in Northern Uvinza.

May 21. — The next day, avoiding the scorched plains of Uhha, of bitter memory to me, we journeyed to Ruvvhera, eleven miles; thence to Mansumba, due west, nine miles and a half through a thin jungle; whence we despatched some Wanyamwezi across the frontier to Uhha to purchase corn for the support of the Expedition in the wilderness between Uvinza and Ujiji.

Strange to say, the Wahha, who are the most extortionate tribute-takers in Africa, will not interfere with a caravan when once over the frontier, but will readily sell them food. About fifty Wahha even brought grain and fowls for sale to our camp at Mansumba. Though truth compels me to say that we should have fared very badly had we travelled through Uhha, I must do its people the justice to say that they are not churlish to strangers beyond their own limits.

It is a great pity that the Malagarazi is not navigable. There is a difference of nearly 900 feet between the altitude of Ugaga and that of Ujiji. One series of falls are south-south-west from Ruwhera, about twenty-five miles below Ugaga. There is another series of falls about twenty miles, from the Tanganika.

May 24. — At noon on the 24th we camped on the western bank of the Rusugi river. A small village, called Kasanga, is situated two miles above the ford. Near the crossing on either side are the salt-pans of Uvinza, which furnish a respectable revenue to its king. A square mile of ground is strewn with broken pots, embers of fires, the refuse of the salt, lumps of burnt clay, and ruined huts. As Rusunzu now owns all the land to within fifteen miles of Ujiji, there is no one to war with for the undisputed possession of the salt-pans.

Through a forest jungle separated at intervals by narrow strips of plain, and crossing six small tributaries of the Malagarazi by the way, we journeyed twenty-three miles, to a camp near the frontier of the district of Uguru, or the hill country of Western Uhha.

The northern slopes of these mountain masses of Uguru, about fifteen miles north of the sources of the Liuche, are drained by the southern feeders of the Alexandra Nile; the western, by the Mshala; the southern by the Liuche; and the eastern, by the Uhha tributaries of the Malagarazi. The boundaries of Uhha, Urundi, and Ujiji meet at these mountains, which are probably 6500 feet above the sea.

We greeted our friend of Niamtaga, whom we had met in November in 1871, but, alas for him! two weeks later he was taken by surprise by Rusunzu, and massacred with nearly three-fourths of his people.

May 27. — At noon of the 27th of May the bright waters of the Tanganika broke upon the view, and compelled me to linger admiringly for a while, as I did on the day I first beheld them. By 3 P.M. we were in Ujiji. Muini Kheri, Mohammed bin Gharib, Sultan bin Kassim, and Khamis the Baluch greeted me kindly. Mohammed bin Sali was dead. Nothing was changed much, except the ever-changing mud tembes of the Arabs. The square or plaza where I met David Livingstone in November 1871 is now occupied by large tembes. The house where he and I lived has long ago been burnt down, and in its place there remain only a few embers and a hideous void. The lake expands with the same grand beauty before the eyes as we stand in the market-place. The opposite mountains of Goma have the same blue-black colour, for they are everlasting, and the Liuche river continues its course as brown as ever just east and south of Ujiji. The surf is still as restless, and the sun as bright; the sky retains its glorious azure, and the palms all their beauty: but the grand old hero, whose presence once filled Ujiji with such absorbing interest for me, was gone!